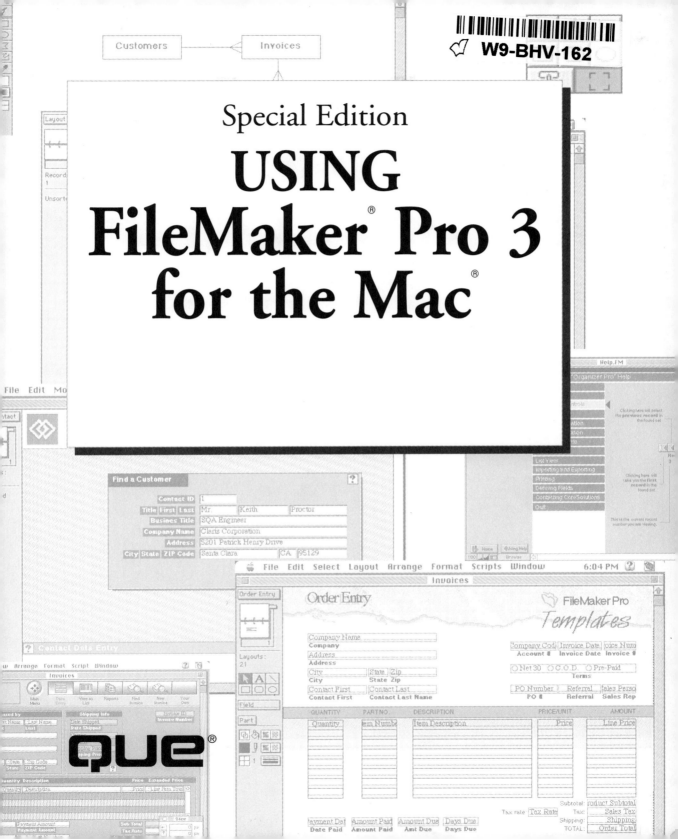

Special Edition
USING
FileMaker® Pro 3
for the Mac®

Special Edition
USING
FileMaker® Pro 3
for the Mac®

Written by Chris Moyer

with

Shelly Brisbin
Barney Lawn

Eoin Mac an Aircinnigh
Ron Wilder

que®

Special Edition Using FileMaker Pro 3 for the Mac

Library of Congress Catalog No.: 95-72576

ISBN: 0-7897-0662-8

98 97   6   5   4   3

Interpretation of the printing code: the rightmost double-digit number is the year of the book's printing; the rightmost single-digit number, the number of the book's printing. For example, a printing code of 96-1 shows that the first printing of the book occurred in 1996.

Screen reproductions in this book were created using Capture from Mainstay, Camarillo, CA.

Composed in *Stone Serif* and *MCPdigital* by Que Corporation.

Credits

President
Roland Elgey

Vice President and Publisher
Marie Butler-Knight

Editorial Services Director
Elizabeth Keaffaber

Managing Editor
Michael Cunningham

Director of Marketing
Lynn E. Zingraf

Senior Series Editor
Chris Nelson

Acquisitions Editor and Product Director
Stephanie Gould

Production Editors
Theresa Mathias
Lori Lyons

Assistant Product Marketing Manager
Kim Margolius

Technical Editor
Eoin Mac an Aircinnigh

Technical Specialist
Carl Skaggs

Acquisitions Coordinator
Tracy M. Willams

Operations Coordinator
Patty Brroks

Editorial Assistant
Carmen Phelps

Book Designer
Ruth Harvey

Cover Designer
Dan Armstrong

Production Team
Stephen Adams, Brian Buschkill, Claudia Bell, Anne Dickerson, Chad Dressler, Jenny Earhart, Joan Evan, DiMonique Ford, Bryan Flores, Trey Frank, Amy Gornik, Jason Hand, Damon Jordan, Daryl Kessler, Clint Lahnen, Kevin Laseau, Stephanie Layton, Michelle Lee, Vic Peterson, Nancy Price, Julie Quinn, Laura Robbins, Michael Thomas, Kelly Warner, Jody York

Indexer
Carol Sheehan

For Rosemary

About the Author

Chris Moyer worked as a Sales Engineer for Claris Corporation from 1991 through 1994. He now does FileMaker consulting from Chicago and Atlanta. He also works as a contract trainer for Claris, teaching FileMaker Pro 3.0 to people around the United States and in Switzerland.

Barney Lawn started his computer career as a programmer in Dublin, Ireland in 1978 and moved to Toronto, Canada three years later. In 1989, he moved to London, Ontario to start his own business. Today, CoreSolutions Inc. has evolved to become a very successful computer consulting company whose major focus is the development of custom database solutions using FileMaker Pro. CoreSolution's own office management software package, "Organizer Pro," has just been upgraded to take advantage of the new feature set of FileMaker Pro 3.0. This package was designed to help manage the day-to-day tasks for small businesses, individuals, and corporate work groups who sell services and/or bill their time. Barney lives in London, Ontario, with his wife Cathy and his two children, Christopher, age 15, and Shannon, age 10.

Acknowledgments

I always wondered why authors profusely thank their editors in their books. Now I know. My life has been completely chaotic this year, with two deaths in the family, a move from Chicago to Atlanta, and a killer training and consulting schedule. Because of this, I dropped out of sight for long periods of time. This caused great anxiety for my long-suffering product director, Stephanie Gould, at Que. She never knew if I'd been hit by a bus or if I just hadn't gotten my chapter finished yet. She tells me they have a list of all the excuses that authors give to explain their absent chapters, and that I've gone through most of them. Sorry to put you through it all, Stephanie. Thanks for everything.

I also want to thank everyone who contributed to this book. Although my name is on the cover, several people had their hands in this effort in ways large and small. I'd like to thank Barney Lawn, a great FileMaker developer in Canada for his chapter on the SDK, Shelly Brisbin, for her chapter on networking, and my father Duane Moyer (hey, if you can't go to your dad for help, who can you go to?) for the section on trial and error database design in Chapter 13. I also want to thank Eric Culver and Rich Coulombre, my fellow FileMaker Pro 3.0 Sneak Preview trainers, for all the great ideas they gave me as we went around giving FileMaker Pro 3.0 training sessions. They're both exceptional FileMaker developers.

Thanks also to everyone at Claris who made this book a lot easier to write. Linda Waldon in the training department got me involved in the Sneak Preview training and put the whole course together. John Phelan and Michael DeNardi, product managers for FileMaker Pro and FileMaker Pro Server, got the latest versions of the software to me.

We'd Like to Hear from You!

As part of our continuing effort to produce books of the highest possible quality, Que would like to hear your comments. To stay competitive, we *really* want you, as a computer book reader and user, to let us know what you like or dislike most about this book or other Que products.

You can mail comments, ideas, or suggestions for improving future editions to the address below, or send us a fax at (317) 581-4663. For the online inclined, Macmillan Computer Publishing has a forum on CompuServe (type **GO QUEBOOKS** at any prompt) through which our staff and authors are available for questions and comments. The address of our Internet site is **http://www.mcp.com** (World Wide Web).

In addition to exploring our forum, please feel free to contact me personally to discuss your opinions of this book: I'm **73602,2077** on CompuServe, and I'm **sgould@que.mcp.com** on the Internet.

Thanks in advance—your comments will help us to continue publishing the best books available on computer topics in today's market.

Stephanie Gould
Product Development Specialist
Que Corporation
201 W. 103rd Street
Indianapolis, Indiana 46290
USA

Contents at a Glance

Integrating FileMaker Pro

Appendixes

Contents

II Enhancing FileMaker Pro Databases   77

4 Using Lookups and Relationships   79

5 Working with Calculation Fields   103

VII Integrating FileMaker Pro   401

17 Networking Issues   403

18 Using FileMaker Pro Server   413

19 Using the Solutions Development Kit   429

Introduction

FileMaker Pro 3 provides users with an easy approach to creating and displaying relationships between multiple files; it also includes hundreds of new features, such as enhanced file conversion, greater scripting capabilities, improved word processing, and much more. This book is targeted to users in small businesses, corporate workgroups, and education who want to take maximum advantage of all the new features in FileMaker Pro 3.

Why You Should Use this Book

This book isn't just another version of the manual—it provides information that will help you customize your databases so you can get the information you need to make important business decisions. This book is a comprehensive reference and guide to using FileMaker Pro 3 to manage data effectively. You learn how to plan and build databases from the ground up; you can get correct information in the format you need when you need it.

For readers who are upgrading from earlier versions of FileMaker Pro, this book clearly explains the problems and issues, and provides solutions. It also has topics that will benefit experienced FileMaker Pro developers, such as the chapter on the Solutions Development Kit and a section on how to time-bomb your demos.

How this Book Is Organized

Special Edition Using FileMaker Pro 3 for the Mac is organized in seven parts to help you find the information you need quickly and easily.

- Part I, "FileMaker Pro Fundamentals," is for the new user of FileMaker Pro. Chapter 1, "Creating Your First Database," takes you step-by-step through the basics of how to create that first database. Chapter 2,

"Designing Simple Layouts," shows you how to create data entry screens. Chapter 3, "Creating and Printing Reports," explains how to create reports using subtotals and totals, and how to print those reports.

■ Part II, "Enhancing FileMaker Pro Databases," introduces relational concepts and explains how to work with calculation fields and value lists. Chapter 4, "Using Lookups and Relationships," deals with the nuts and bolts of creating relationships, working with related fields and portals, and using lookup fields and how they've changed. Chapter 5, "Working with Calculation Fields," discusses how to set up calculations in your database to get subtotals, averages, and so on. Chapter 6, "Using Value Lists," explains how to create pop-up menus, check boxes, and radio buttons to speed up data entry and to reduce the potential for error. Finally, Chapter 7, "Scripting—The Basics," provides an introduction to automating simple tasks.

■ Part III, "FileMaker Pro 3.0 Conversion Issues," is for the experienced FileMaker Pro user. In Chapter 8, "What's Different in FileMaker Pro 3," the benefits of the new features are discussed. Chapter 9, "Converting Existing FileMaker Pro Databases to 3," provides expert advice on how to upgrade old databases to the latest version and take advantage of the new relational capabilities. Chapter 10, "More on Conversion Issues," looks at some of the workarounds that might have been implemented in your 2.x databases and that might need special treatment when you convert to FileMaker Pro 3.

■ Part IV, "Interface Design," looks at two distinct issues. Chapter 11, "Designing Layouts that Work," provides guidelines for creating layouts and covers tabbed interfaces, color schemes, 3D layout tricks, and cross-platform issues. Chapter 12, "Controlling File Access," explains how to set up access privileges, build password systems, and, for developers, how to create time bombs to protect demo versions of your databases.

■ Part V, "Relational Design Issues," uses a detailed example in Chapter 13, "Applying Relational Concepts," to clearly explain the mistakes you can make as you create a relational database. Chapter 14, "Refining Your Database Design," provides a plan for you to follow so you can avoid these errors.

■ Part VI, "Automating FileMaker Pro," discusses in greater depth how to automate routine tasks. Chapter 15, "Scripting with ScriptMaker," covers how to create dialog boxes with ScriptMaker and how to set up conditional scripts. Chapter 16, "Using AppleScript," covers using AppleScript to control applications, create custom FileMaker menus, and more.

■ Part VII, "Integrating FileMaker Pro," looks at issues not directly related to how FileMaker Pro works but are nevertheless important to FileMaker Pro users. Chapter 17, "Networking Issues," looks at problems associated with using FileMaker on a network. Chapter 18, "Using FileMaker Pro Server," discusses how to use this program to improve performance in multi-user situations. Chapter 19, "Using the Solutions Development Kit," describes how to create commercial quality runtime solutions using the Solutions Development Kit from Claris. Using FileMaker with Excel is discussed in Chapter 20, "Using FileMaker Pro with Excel." There is even a chapter on the World Wide Web: Chapter 21, "FileMaker Pro and the World Wide Web," explains how to use FileMaker Pro to update Web pages.

■ Part VIII includes three appendixes. Appendix A, "Glossary of Relational Terms," defines the new terms in this book. Appendix B, "Installing FileMaker Pro," gives you in-depth coverage on installing this new version. Appendix C, "Functions Reference," is a list of functions grouped by category.

Conventions Used in this Book

Conventions used in this book have been established to help you learn how to use the program quickly and easily.

At the beginning of each chapter is a bulleted list of chapter contents. This list serves as a road map to the chapter so you can tell at a glance what is covered.

An icon is used throughout this book to mark new features in FileMaker Pro 3.

In the text are elements designed to help you identify important sections of text. These are notes, tips, cautions, troubleshooting, and cross-references.

> **Note**
>
> This element is used to provide additional information that might help you avoid problems or that you should consider when using the described features.

> **Tip**
>
> This element suggests alternative methods for performing some tasks, maybe a shortcut or simply another option you might like to try.

Caution

Cautions warn the reader of hazardous procedures (for example, activities that might corrupt your data).

Troubleshooting

What's troubleshooting?

The purpose of these sections is to provide solutions for common problems. A typical user question is followed by one or more possible solutions.

Special Edition Using FileMaker Pro 3 for the Mac uses margin cross-references to help you access related information in other parts of the book. Right-facing triangles point you to related information in later chapters. Left-facing triangles point you to information in previous chapters.

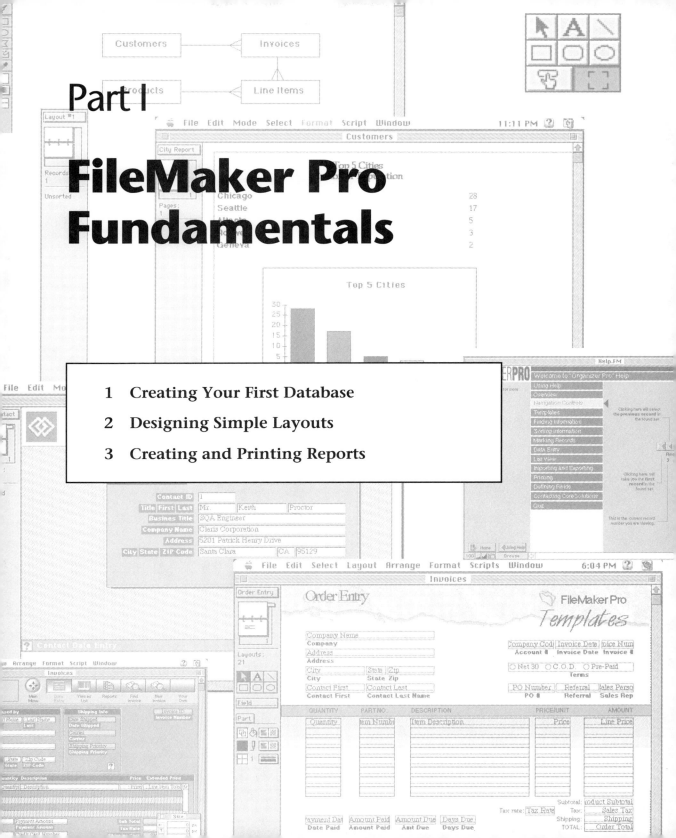

Part I

FileMaker Pro Fundamentals

CHAPTER 1

Creating Your First Database

If you're a first-time database designer and are apprehensive about getting started, fear not; FileMaker Pro is one of the easiest database programs to learn. If you've worked with other database packages before and this is your first exposure to FileMaker Pro, you're going to be amazed at how easy it is to do everything. You'll find that in terms of time spent in building a database system, FileMaker Pro is one of the fastest environments to build in. Even if a project might ultimately end up on a different database platform, FileMaker's speed of development makes it an ideal prototyping tool. I've seen many situations where a customer was so satisfied with the functionality of the FileMaker prototype, they decided they didn't even need to move the database to a different platform. With FileMaker's graphical interface and point-and-click scriptability, you can go from nothing to a finished database in no time at all. This chapter will be the proof of that.

Two databases will be created in this chapter. One will be created using one of the templates that ships with FileMaker Pro and another will be built from the ground up. It will be designed to track Customer information.

This chapter covers the following topics:

- Creating a new database from templates
- Creating a new database from scratch
- Changing existing layouts
- Adding new fields and layouts
- Scripting FileMaker Pro

Creating a New Database Using the FileMaker Templates

Before you can get started, you need to launch FileMaker Pro. After you install FileMaker on your computer, you can find a folder called FileMaker Pro 3.0 Folder on your hard drive. Open that folder, and you should see something like figure 1.1. Double-click the FileMaker Pro icon to launch the program. If you're running FileMaker for the first time, you need to enter your registration information. If you need help with installing FileMaker Pro, refer to Appendix B, "Installing FileMaker Pro."

Fig. 1.1
Launch FileMaker by double-clicking the icon or selecting it and choosing File, Open.

 When you launch the program, FileMaker gives you some options in the New Database dialog box (see fig. 1.2). FileMaker ships with several database templates already created. If you click the Create a New File Using a Template radio button, you can use the pop-up menu on the right to toggle between templates designed for business, education, and home use.

Fig. 1.2
FileMaker ships with over 40 templates you can use to create your own databases.

To create a Names and Addresses database using a template, follow these steps:

1. From the pop-up menu, choose Business.

2. Select the Names and Addresses template and click OK to open the Save dialog box.

3. In the Save dialog box, FileMaker is asking you to pick a location for your new database. Don't put the new file in the same folder as the template unless you change the database name. If you don't change the name, your new database will overwrite the template. If you want, you can use the new folder button to create a dedicated folder for your projects. Choose the folder where you want to store your new database and click Save to have FileMaker create the new database (see fig. 1.3).

Current
Book record

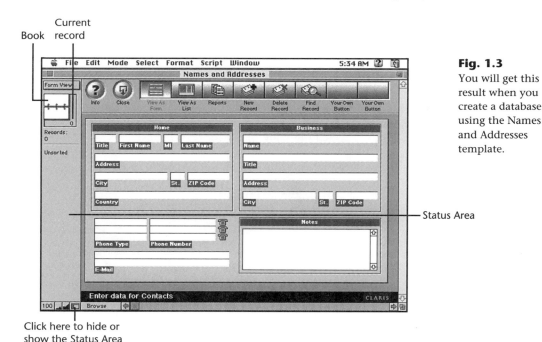

Click here to hide or
show the Status Area

Fig. 1.3
You will get this result when you create a database using the Names and Addresses template.

Status Area

The Status Area

On the left side of your screen is a gray area. This area is called the Status Area and it's part of every FileMaker database. The Status Area shows how many records there are, whether the records are sorted, what the results of the last search were, and what the current layout is. More about layouts in a minute.

Before you go on, you need to know some basic database anatomy. This database keeps track of information about people. For a given person, you need to keep track of their name, address, and so on. This detailed information gets stored in separate fields. This database has a field for the person's city, state, zip code, and so on. Together, these fields make up a record. A record in this case is the collection of information you have about one person. Because you want to keep track of more than one person, you will eventually have multiple records in your database. A database is a collection of records that are described by information in fields.

You can hide the Status Area by clicking the button to the left of Browse at the bottom of your screen. Click the button again to show the Status Area. Sometimes, if you need to show a lot of information on a layout or if you have an extra wide report, it can be useful to hide the Status Area and use the extra space for your layout.

The Status Area should show that there are zero records in the database. When you create a new database from a template, you start out with an empty database.

Creating a New Record

Right now, the Status Area shows that there are zero records (refer to fig. 1.3). To create a new record follow these steps:

1. Choose Mode, New Record or press ⌘-N (see fig. 1.4).

Fig. 1.4
You need to create a new record before you can enter any information.

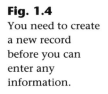
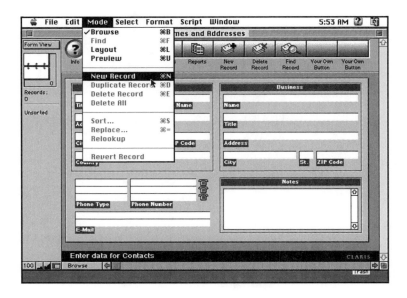

2. Click a title to enter it. The cursor will automatically advance to the First Name field.

3. In the First Name field, type your first name.

4. Tab to the Last Name field and type your last name.

5. Continue until you fill out the record.

As you can see, the Tab key moves the cursor through the fields in your database. You use the Tab key—not the Return key—to navigate from field to field. FileMaker fields can contain several lines of data—up to 64,000 characters—the Return key adds a new line in a field. You can actually have several paragraphs of information in a single text field if you want.

Tip

Press Shift-Tab to tab through the fields backwards.

When you have a large field like the Notes field, try using the Return key to create a new line or paragraph. If you enter enough text, you can use the scroll bar on the right side of the field. You can use all of the standard text-editing features. Choose Edit, Select All to select all of the text in the Notes field. You can also choose Edit, Copy to copy text to the Clipboard, and choose Edit, Paste to paste copied text.

Notice that once you click in a field, if you drag the mouse to slightly above the top edge of the field or slightly below the bottom edge of the field, you can scroll the field very slowly up or down. I call this teleprompter mode. If you drag farther above or below the field, the text flies by in what I call turbo mode. FileMaker Pro has a very fast text engine.

Try creating a few more records so you can practice navigating between records in the next section.

The Book

There are many items in the Status Area. There is the Book, and under the Book is the number of the current record. If you're on the first record, there will be lines on the bottom page of the book but not on the top page. This means that if you click the bottom page, you can go to the next record. If you click the top page, you can't go to the previous record because you're already at the beginning of the database. Try navigating between records by clicking the pages of the Book.

> **Tip**
>
> There are shortcut keys for navigating through the Book. Press ⌘-Tab to go forward through the database one record at a time. ⌘-Shift-Tab takes you backward through the database one record at a time.

Sticking out of the side of the Book is the Bookmark. Click and drag the Bookmark up or down to move forward or backward several records at a time.

If you click the record number directly beneath the Book, you can type the number of a specific record and then press Enter to go to that record.

> **Tip**
>
> If you're the type of person who prefers using the keyboard instead of the mouse, you can select the record number in the Status Area by pressing the Escape key.

The Layout Pop-Up Menu

A *layout* is a formatted view of the database. To see the different layouts in Personnel Records, click and hold the layout pop-up menu at the top of the Status Area (see fig. 1.5). Try switching between layouts by using this menu. Come back to the Form View - Job layout when you're done looking around.

Fig. 1.5

The layout pop-up menu is directly above the Book.

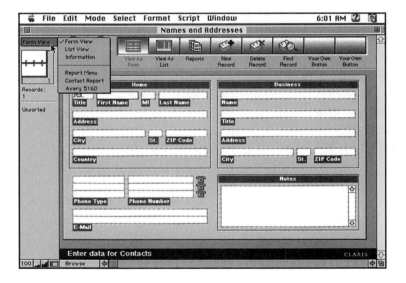

This particular database has been set up with buttons. Click the View As List button. Now try using the Book to navigate through the records. In List view, you can see more than one record at a time. Choose Select, View as Form. Try navigating through the records with the Book again. In Form view, you can only view one record at a time. Click the View As Form button to go back to the Form View - Job layout.

About Modes in FileMaker

If you click and hold the Mode menu, it shows that you're in Browse mode. It also says this at the bottom of the window. The mode display at the bottom of the window is actually a pop-up menu, as shown in figure 1.6.

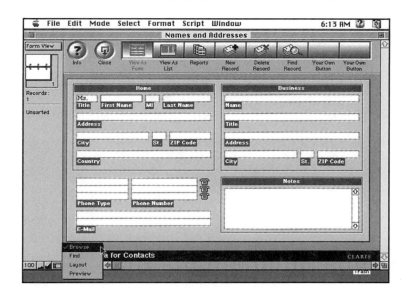

Fig. 1.6
You can switch modes with the mode pop-up menu at the bottom of the window.

There are four modes in FileMaker: Browse, Find, Layout, and Preview. Browse mode is for viewing and entering data. In fact, it's the only mode where you can enter data. Think of it as the data entry mode.

Find mode is for running searches on the data. In FileMaker, you can search on a single field or all fields at once. When you're in Find mode, you're not actually working with a single record, so while it looks like you can do data entry, all you can really do is enter search criteria. Ad-hoc searches are a snap in FileMaker. You'll find out more about searches in the next section.

Layout mode is literally a page layout mode. You can draw layout elements, import graphics, and move, edit, or resize fields and labels. Layout mode is where you actually control the look of your database. While you can type text in Layout mode, anything you type is on the layout background for every record. You can't enter data in fields in Layout mode.

Preview mode is exactly what it sounds like, a print preview. Certain types of reports can only be viewed in Preview mode. When you're in Preview mode, you can't type anything or click on any buttons.

Basic Searching

When you have a lot of information in your database, you'll need to be able to find specific records. To search for something in a FileMaker database, follow these steps:

1. Choose Mode, Find to go to Find mode. The screen changes so that it looks as if all of your information has disappeared.

2. Tab to the First Name field and type your name.

3. Click the Find button in the Status Area, as shown in figure 1.7.

Fig. 1.7
When you're in Find mode, the Status Area changes.

Omit check box
Symbols pop-up
Find button

Click here to hide or show the Status Area

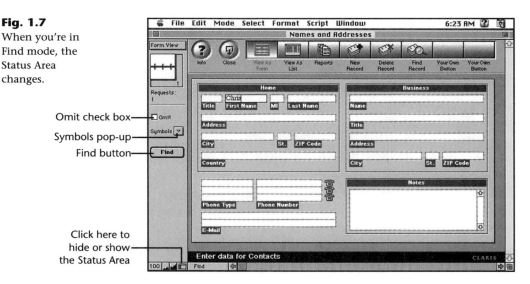

If you have the Status Area hidden (which means you can't see the Find button), you can show it by clicking the button at the bottom of the window, or you can just press the Return key—they trigger the find when you're in Find mode.

4. FileMaker gives you the results of a find, and puts you back in Browse mode.

The Status Area now shows not only how many records there are in the database, but also how many there are in the found set (see fig. 1.8).

The found set is an important concept in FileMaker. It is a subset of the database.

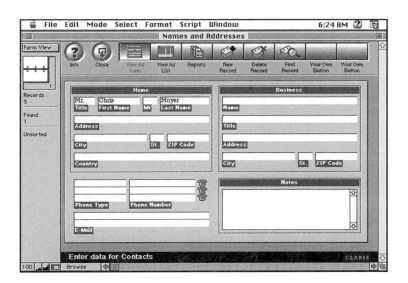

Fig. 1.8
After a find has been performed, the Status Area shows how many records were found.

You can navigate through the found set using the Book. If you have a found set of one, there are no other records to navigate to. Records that are not in the found set are hidden. Found sets are extremely useful for making reports. If you only want to know statistics about customers who are in Chicago, for example, you can do a find with the City field and create a found set that only contains Chicago customers. With that found set, you can then find out how many Chicago customers there are, how many different zip codes they might be in, or whatever you want to know.

To see all of the records in the database and discard a found set, choose Select, Find All. This, in effect, gives you a found set of all the records in the database. The shortcut key for Find All is ⌘-J.

If you want to find information in your database but are unsure of the exact spelling of what you're looking for, you can try this:

1. Choose Mode, Find.

2. Tab to the field you want to search and type in your search criteria. You don't have to be exact. For example, if you're not sure if a person's name is Jeanne or Jenny, you can perform a search on part of the name. In this case, you could just type **Je**.

3. Click the Find button in the Status Area. FileMaker gives you a found set of any records that match, which will include all records with a first name that starts with "Je."

If you type "**nne**" (as in Jeanne), however, you won't get a match. That's because the search criteria wasn't at the beginning of the word. You can make this kind of search work, though.

There are symbols that allow you to customize your finds. You can search for dates that are greater than a certain date, invoices with a subtotal less than some number, and you can also do what are called wildcard text searches. If you want to search using the last part of a word, you can force FileMaker to check all words by inserting the * character at the front of the search. This means that FileMaker will look at as many characters in a word as it needs to.

To find Jeanne's record using "*nne," follow these steps:

1. Choose Mode, Find.

2. Tab to the First Name field.

3. In the Status Area, click the Symbols pop-up menu (see fig. 1.9).

4. Type ***nne** and click Find.

The found set of records includes any with a first name that ends in *nne*, including all records with a first name of Jeanne.

If you're just unsure about one character, maybe you can't remember if the name is Jill or Julie, you can try a different character, @, which is a single character wildcard. The search criteria for Jill or Julie would be "J@l*."

Enough searching for now. Searching is covered in detail in Chapter 3, "Creating and Printing Reports." At this point, you know the basics of how a FileMaker database works. You know how to navigate between fields, how to create a new record and enter information in it, how to navigate between records, run searches, and even how to switch layouts and modes. Now that you know how a FileMaker database works, you can build one of your own.

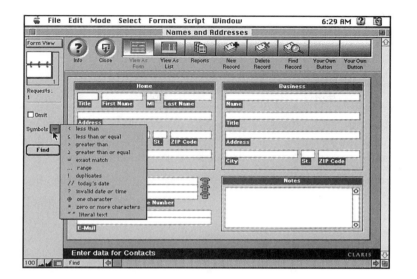

Fig 1.9
Click the Symbols button to display the Find symbols.

Creating a New Database from Scratch

Before you start building a database, you should have the design thought out ahead of time. Because FileMaker is so easy to change on the fly, even when it's full of information, a lot of FileMaker users get into the bad habit of designing-as-you-go. Designing before building in FileMaker is kind of like flossing your teeth: You don't have to do it, but you'll probably wish you had when you get farther down the road.

Because this is an introductory chapter, I did the design work for you. This database is going to store information about customers, so its name is Customers and it will have the following fields:

Customer ID

Customer Name

Address1

Address2

City

State

Zip Code

Phone

Creation Date

Last Modified

Modified By

The Zip Code field is a text field for two reasons. If you need to enter customers with addresses in Canada, zip codes there have letters and numbers. The other reason is that text fields enable you to search on part of a number, while number fields require you to search on the entire number.

The Customer ID, Creation Date, Last Modified, and Modified By fields are known as auto entry fields. Every time you create a new record, data automatically gets put into these fields. The Last Modified and Modified By fields will continue to have information automatically entered every time you update the record.

If you don't have FileMaker open, launch the program again by double-clicking the FileMaker icon.

Note

It can be confusing trying to figure out whether your program is running. When you close a window in your word processor, or spreadsheet, or database, that doesn't mean you closed the program as well. It's possible to have the program running without having any documents open. The problem is that you can see all of your files on your desktop (what you see when you don't have any programs running) even when you're still in your program.

The key is to look at the Application menu in the upper-right corner of your screen. Click the icon at the far right of the menu and hold the mouse button down. The bottom part of the menu shows what programs you have running (see fig. 1.10). The Finder is your operating system. It starts when you start your computer and it runs the entire time your computer is on. You can't shut down the Finder without shutting down your computer.

You can tell what program you're currently in by checking to see which program has a check mark beside it. Try switching between the different programs and notice how your menus change. The Application menu is an easy way for you to switch between programs, especially when you have a program running without any documents open.

Fig. 1.10
You can check to see if FileMaker is running by looking in the Application menu.

If FileMaker is already open, make sure you're in FileMaker by selecting it from the Application menu.

To begin creating your customer database, follow these steps:

1. Choose File, New to open the New Database dialog box.

2. Select the Create a New Empty File radio button (see fig. 1.11). Click OK to open the Save dialog box.

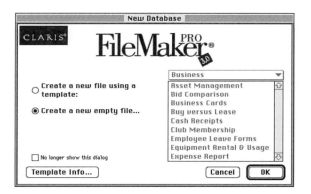

Fig. 1.11
Select the Create a New Empty File radio button if you want to create a database from scratch.

3. The first step in creating a new database is to give it a name. Names in FileMaker Pro 3.0 for the Macintosh can be up to 31 characters long and can include spaces. Because this database is going to store information about customers, type **Customers** in the Create a New File Named text box (see fig. 1.12). Click Save to open the Define Fields dialog box.

Fig. 1.12
You always have to name a database before you can work on it.

Defining the Fields

The Define Fields dialog box is where you tell FileMaker what kinds of information you want to keep track of (see fig. 1.13). Again, because this is a customer database, set up fields to hold customer information.

Fig. 1.13

The Define Fields
dialog box is
where you actually
construct your
database.

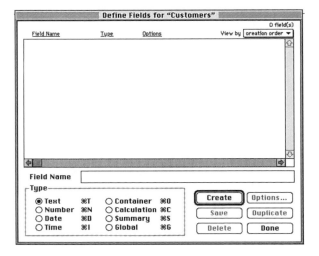

> ### Note
>
> It's always a good idea to design your database so you have one field that's unique to
> each record. To see why, think of a database that keeps track of products a manufac-
> turing company might make.
>
> If you manufacture widgets, they all look the same. To tell one widget from another
> for warranty purposes, you put a serial number on each widget. You do the same for
> records in a database. While the different records might not look the same when you
> start putting information in the database, that can change down the road.
>
> As your database grows, the likelihood that two records contain similar or the same
> information increases. For example, there are a lot of John Smiths in the world. If you
> have more than one of them in your database, you need to have a quick way to tell
> one from the other. A field that's unique to each record, like a serial number field, is
> the easiest way to do this.

It's important to be able to uniquely identify a record in your database; an excellent habit for you to get into is to have the first field you create in any database be an identification field. If you're making an invoice database, it will
be an Invoice ID. Because you will be making a Customer database, the first

field is a Customer ID. In the Field Name text box in the Define Fields dialog box, type **Customer ID**.

Resist the urge to type a return (for now) after you type in field names. In FileMaker Pro, when you type a return after a new field name, that automatically creates the field. This enables you to create several fields very quickly without having to use the mouse. That's all fine and good, but you want to make sure you have the right field type selected before you create the field. For those of you who charged ahead and hit the Return key (I know you're out there), don't worry. FileMaker is very forgiving. In fact, you should probably hit the Return key just to see how easy it is to reformat a field.

Say you just created the Customer ID field and, due to excess enthusiasm, hit the Return key. The field was formatted with the default format type: Text. In addition, the design calls for this field to be formatted as a Number field. To change a Text field to a Number field, follow these steps:

1. Select the field in the list by clicking it once (see fig. 1.14).

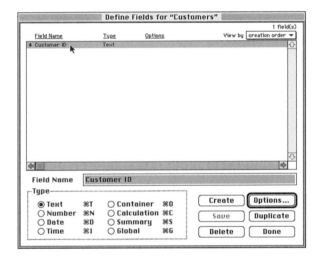

Fig. 1.14
Select the Customer ID field by clicking it once.

2. Click the Number radio button. The Save button becomes available.

3. Click Save. A message warns you that Number fields can only contain 255 characters and, because Text fields can hold up to 64,000 characters, any information after the first 255 characters will be lost. This field doesn't have any information in it yet, so you don't need to worry.

4. Click OK. Look at the Customer ID field in the field list. It should now say Number under the Type heading.

That's all you have to do to change a field's type in FileMaker Pro. By the way, you can even change a field's type after the database is full of data. This is radically different from how most databases work.

> **Tip**
>
> You can also select field types using the shortcut key combinations to the right of the field types. For example, if you want to select the Date type for a field, press ⌘-D. Each field type has its own shortcut key combination.

Because the real design calls for the Customer ID field type to be Text, change the field back to a Text field. Select the Customer ID field and click the Text radio button. Click Save.

The design also calls for the Customer ID field to have a serial number assigned to it. A serial number is one of several options you can attach to a field. To add a serial number option:

1. Click the Options button to open the Entry Options dialog box (see fig. 1.15).

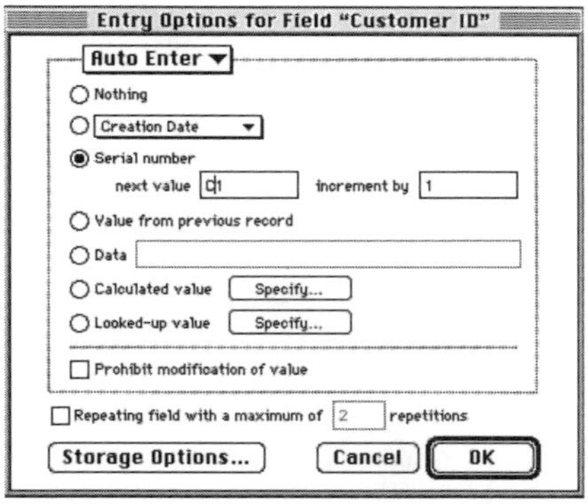

Fig. 1.15
The Auto Enter options execute whenever a new record is created.

2. To create a serial number for the Customer ID field, click the Serial Number radio button.

3. Click in the Next Value box.

4. Type **C1** in the Next Value textbox and leave the Increment By value at 1.

5. Select the Prohibit Modification of Value check box. Because you want to make sure this serial number is always unique, you can't allow people to change the serial numbers and possibly duplicate a value.

> ### Note
>
> The serial number will work as is, but as you build more database files and link them together, it's likely that you'll have more than one serial number showing on-screen at one time. To make it easier to tell one database's serial number from another, you can assign leading characters to the different numbers. For example, a vendor serial number might start at V1000 and go up in increments of 1: V1001, V1002, and so on. The Customer serial number can start with C, Products with P, and so on. Having distinctive serial numbers makes viewing a screen full of serial numbers less confusing, although at the small cost of storing an extra character for each record.

6. At the top of the Entry Options dialog box, it says Auto Enter. Click the pop-up menu and drag down to Validation (see fig. 1.16). The Entry Options dialog box now displays the Validation options (see fig. 1.17).

Validation options allow you to force the user to enter data in a certain way. For example, if you don't want to use a serial number and want users to create their own Customer ID codes, you could ensure that no two codes would be the same by selecting the Unique check box. With this option checked, FileMaker will warn a user if they try to create a duplicate value. For now, leave validation alone. Click OK to close the Entry Options dialog box and return to the Define Fields dialog box.

Fig. 1.16
Switch between Auto Enter and Validation options by using the pop-up menu.

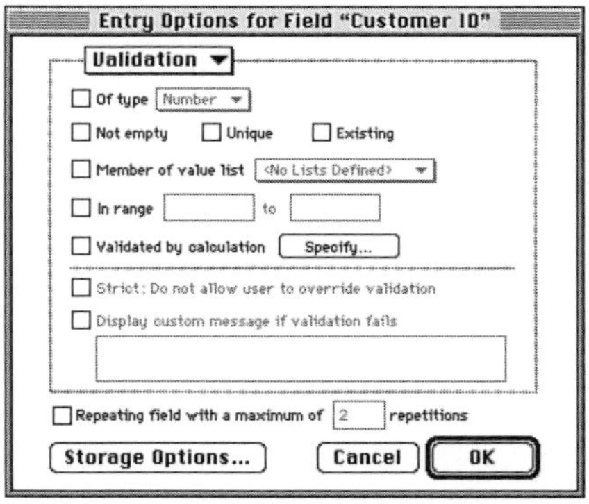

Fig. 1.17
Validation options
are triggered as
soon as a user tries
to exit a field.

So that's the basic process for creating a serial number field. The next fields are all Text fields. To add several fields quickly, follow these steps:

1. If you're not in the Define Fields dialog box already, choose File, Define Fields to open the Define Fields dialog box.

2. In the Field Name text box, type the name of your first field. In this example, it's Customer Name. Click Create or press Return.

3. Type the next name over the last field name, and press Return again. In the current example, you would repeat this process for Address 1, Address 2, City, State, Zip Code, and Phone. A lot of people want to format the phone number as a number, but if you format it as Text, you can search for a number based on part of the number. If it was formatted as a Number field, you would have to know the entire number to find it.

The last three fields in this example are special cases. Creation Date, Last Modified, and Modified By are fields that aren't filled out by the database user. Just like the serial number field, FileMaker will enter values in these fields automatically. To set up these auto enter fields, follow these steps:

1. If you're not in the Define Fields dialog box already, choose File, Define Fields to open the Define Fields dialog box.

2. In the Field Name text box, type the name of your first auto entry field. In this example, it's Creation Date. Format it as a Date field by selecting the Date radio button in the Type area. Click Create or press Return.

3. Click Options to open the Entry Options dialog box. If you're not in Auto Enter options, select it from the pop-up at the top of the dialog box.

4. Select the Creation Date radio button. Click OK to close the Entry Options dialog box and return to the Define Fields dialog box.

5. In the Field Name text box, type **Last Modified** and click Create. Because the last field created was a Date field, Last Modified should automatically be a Date field.

6. Click Options to open the Entry Options dialog box. Select the Creation Date radio button. Click on the Creation Date pop-up menu and choose Modification Date. Click OK to close the Entry Options dialog box and return to the Define Fields dialog box.

7. In the Field Name text box, type **Modified By**. Format it as a Text field by selecting the Text radio button in the Type area. Click Create.

8. Click Options to open the Entry Options dialog box. Select the Creation Date radio button. Click on the Creation Date pop-up menu and choose Modifier Name. Click OK to close the Entry Options dialog box and return to the Define Fields dialog box.

9. When you finish typing all the fields, the Define Fields dialog box should look like figure 1.18. That finishes all the fields for this example, so you can click Done to start working with the database.

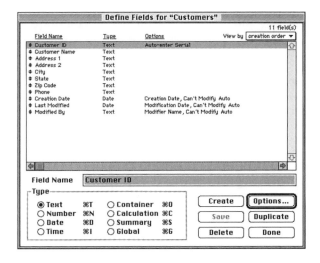

Fig. 1.18
The Define Fields dialog box displays any options attached to fields.

Congratulations! You have just built your first database. It should look like figure 1.19.

Fig. 1.19
FileMaker
automatically
created the first
record of the
Customers
database.

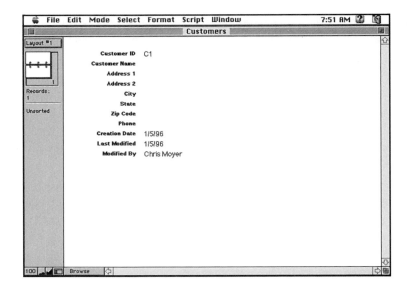

Entering Data

You enter data in Browse mode. The layout you can see when you first create your database is the Standard layout. Click and hold the Layout pop-up. Currently, you only have one layout, but ultimately you can have several layouts containing such things as mailing labels, form letters, or reports.

Notice that the first record was created for you, and that Customer ID is showing the first serial number, C1. Every time you create a new record, this number will increment by 1 (or whatever you set the increment to be in the Entry Options dialog box). Creation Date shows the current date.

To enter your data, follow these steps:

1. Tab to the Customer Name field and enter your name.

2. Tab to the Address1 field and type your address. Continue like this until you fill out the record.

   You now have a database containing data.

Changing the Layout

This standard layout is okay, but it could have a better look. Try changing the layout to make it a little more appealing. To view the database in Layout mode, choose Mode, Layout (see fig. 1.20).

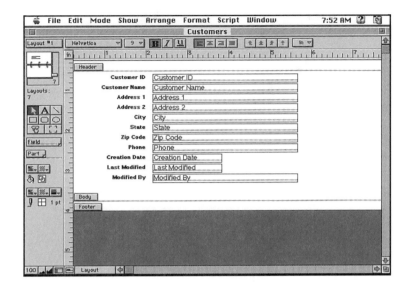

Fig. 1.20
This is how the
Customers
database looks in
Layout mode.

FileMaker Fundamentals

Take a look at the layout in figure 1.20. Notice that different areas of the layout are labeled. These areas are called parts, and the three parts here are the Header, Body, and Footer.

If you print this database, anything in the Header part prints at the top of every page. Anything in the Footer prints at the bottom of every page. The Body part fills in on what's left of the page. If you have a very tall Header and Footer, you can only fit one record on a page. If you have a short Header and Footer and a short Body, you can fit several records on each page. You can figure out how many records will fit on a page by adding up the heights.

If you choose Show, Graphic Rulers, you can see how tall each layout part is.

Setting Page Margins

New in FileMaker 3.0 is the capability to manipulate page margins on your database layouts. To set your page margins:

1. Choose Mode, Layout Setup to bring up the Layout Setup dialog box, as shown in figure 1.21.

2. Select the Fixed Page Margins check box.

3. Set the margins to the measurements you want, then click OK to exit the Layout Setup dialog box.

4. Choose Show, Page Margins to see the affect of your margin settings.

Fig. 1.21
The Layout Setup dialog box allows you to set page margins and keep layouts from appearing in the layouts menu.

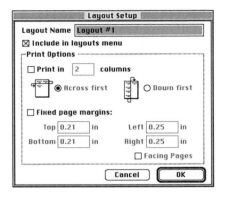

Now you can use the rulers to figure out how many records will fit on a page. Take the height of the top and bottom page margins, plus the Header and Footer. If that comes out to about two inches, that means on an 8 1/2 by 11 sheet of paper, you have nine inches for the Body. If you size the Body to be three inches tall, you can get three records per page. If you make it larger, but less than 4 1/2 inches, you can get two records per page.

Titling the Layout

If other people will use this database, give them an idea of what the database is for. An easy way to do this is to put a title on each layout. One layout might be for data entry while another might be for printing invoices.

To add a title to a layout, follow these steps:

1. In Layout mode, select the Text tool in the Layout Tools palette (see fig. 1.22). Don't drag it, just click it once.

2. Move your cursor to the center of the Header and type **Customer Database - Data Entry**.

3. Press the Enter key or click outside of the text. The text should be selected and have handles, as shown in figure 1.23.

4. With the text selected, choose Format, Style, Bold. To make it larger, you can either choose Format, Size, 18 point, or you can press ⌘-> a few times. Either will work. If you make the text too big, press ⌘-<. You might have to resize the Header so the new title is entirely in the Header.

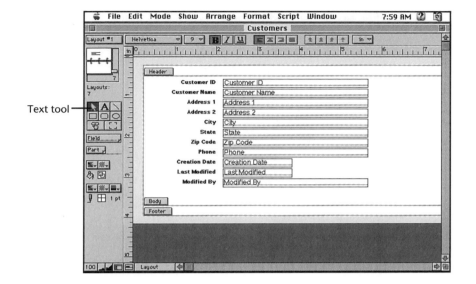

Fig. 1.22
Select the Text tool by clicking it once—don't click and drag.

Text tool

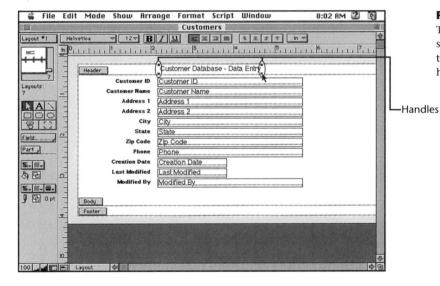

Fig. 1.23
The four black squares around the text are selection handles.

Handles

Rearranging and Resizing Fields

To rearrange fields, all you have to do is click and drag them. To resize a field, click it once to select it, then position the tip of the mouse arrow over one of the handles and drag. You can make fields larger, smaller, taller, shorter—whatever you want. Try arranging your fields so they look like figure 1.24.

Fig. 1.24
It's easy to
customize the look
of any database.

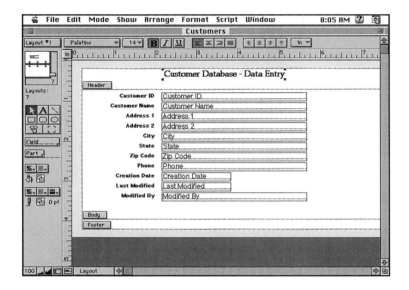

As you can see, customizing layouts in FileMaker Pro is a piece of cake. To make the database even easier to use, it's worth adding one more item to this layout.

Creating Buttons

It's not too much trouble for you to choose Mode, New Record to create a record, but if you need to hire someone to do a lot of data entry for you—who might not be familiar with databases—it would be nice if you made it possible to create a new record by simply pushing a button.

One way of automating FileMaker is by creating scripts. Scripts are a little like macros. FileMaker has its own scripting capability through a program called ScriptMaker. You access it from the Script menu. ScriptMaker by itself is a huge subject. See Chapter 7, "Scripting—The Basics," for more information about making FileMaker scripts. A simpler way to automate FileMaker Pro is to create buttons.

You can add some nice functionality to a layout by creating a button that creates a new record every time you click it.

To create a new record button, follow these steps:

1. Choose Mode, Layout to switch to Layout mode.
2. Click the Button tool, as shown in figure 1.25.
3. Move your mouse onto your layout and drag a rectangle (see fig. 1.26).

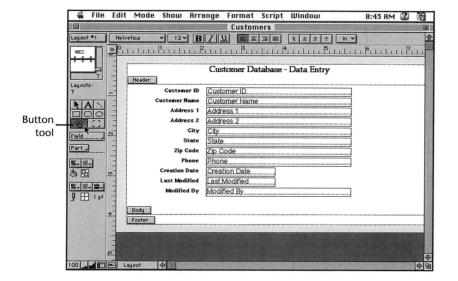

Fig. 1.25
Select the Button tool by clicking on it once.

Button tool

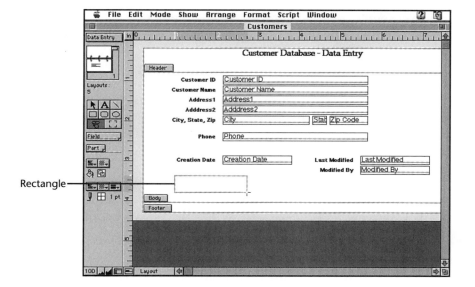

Fig. 1.26
Drag out a button the same way you would drag to create a rectangle.

Rectangle

4. Release the button and the Specify Button dialog box appears (see fig. 1.27).

Fig. 1.27
The Specify Button
dialog box allows
you to assign a
function to the
button.

This dialog box contains a list of commands that the button can execute. You might want to scroll through the list to get a feel for what you can set a button to do.

5. Select New Record/Request and click OK to close the Specify Button dialog box. Notice that you automatically have a text cursor in the middle of your button.

6. Type **New Record** for your button label so people will know what it's for.

7. Choose Mode, Browse to return to Browse mode.

Try out your new button. Watch the record count in the Status Area to see if the button is creating new records. If you feel like it, try creating a button that deletes records using basically this same process.

From Here...

So now you know how to create new databases, define fields, modify layouts, create buttons, and enter and find data. Try reading the following chapters:

- Chapter 2, "Designing Simple Layouts," covers how to create mailing labels, envelopes, form letters, and basic reporting.

- Chapter 3, "Creating and Printing Reports," looks in more depth at how to create reports. It also goes into detail about how to find and sort information in a FileMaker database.

- Chapter 4, "Using Lookups and Relationships," describes the fundamentals of setting up relationships between databases and how to use relationships to look up information from one file to another.

CHAPTER 2

Designing Simple Layouts

The standard layout FileMaker creates when you first create a database is serviceable enough for creating new records and entering data, but that's about the extent of its usefulness. If you want to create mailing labels, form letters, or reports, you need to create new layouts.

This chapter uses examples of common layouts to give you an overview of FileMaker's layout features. In this chapter, you learn about the following:

- Making layouts for mailing labels
- Creating form letters and envelopes
- Using List view for reports

Creating Mailing Labels

FileMaker Pro makes it easy to create and print labels for mailing, shipping, media labeling, and more. Label layouts contain only those fields that should appear on a label. You can create layouts that print correctly on standard Avery or CoStar label stock, or you can create labels with dimensions you specify. In this section, you learn how to create labels with dimensions you customize.

To create a new layout for mailing labels, follow these steps:

1. Open your database.
2. Choose Mode, Layout.

   A set of layout tools appears in the Status area (see fig. 2.1).

Fig. 2.1
The Layout mode shows tools you can use to manipulate fields, text, and objects in a database file.

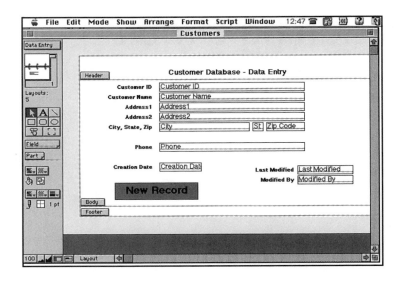

3. Choose Mode, New Layout to open the New Layout dialog box (see fig. 2.2).

   The New Layout dialog box gives you a variety of options for database layouts. You can use one of the formats provided as is or modify it to suit your particular need.

   - The Standard layout lists all database fields, vertically. Layout #1, the layout you got automatically after defining your fields, is a Standard layout. The Standard layout is the only layout that does not allow you to choose fields to show on the layout; you automatically get every field in the database. All other layout options allow you to specify some subset of the total number of fields you want on the layout.

Fig. 2.2
You can name and choose the type of layout you want in the New Layout dialog box.

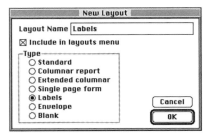

- The Columnar Report and Extended Columnar layouts create list views. When you create a Columnar Report layout, the fields are displayed horizontally across the screen. When you view multiple records, the information appears in columns, with each record being a line item in a list. The effect is similar to a spreadsheet view.

  When you add more fields to a Columnar layout than can fit on a single line, the fields wrap onto a second line. Fields added to an extended Columnar layout do not wrap onto a second line.

- The Single Page Form layout does not have a header or footer. It is one page in size. Like the Standard layout, it's a good choice for data entry, or for browsing records with large numbers of fields.

- The Labels layout allows you to create many kinds of labels, including mailing and shipping labels, badges, tent cards, and more. All Avery and CoStar label formats are built into FileMaker Pro, so you can choose a label layout that will match your chosen label stock.

- The Envelope layout allows you to create layouts for printing envelopes. FileMaker includes built-in support for a number of popular envelope sizes.

- The Blank layout just gives you a blank page to use for creating menu screens or form letters.

4. Because you are creating a layout for mailing labels, select the Labels radio button.

5. Click OK. The Label Setup dialog box appears (see fig 2.3).

If you want to use a specific Avery or CoStar label stock to print your labels, you can choose the label format to match your stock.

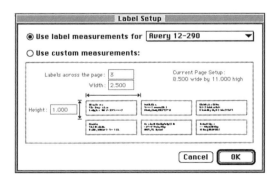

Fig. 2.3
The Label Setup dialog box lets you pick a label format and see a sample of how the Avery- or CoStar-based labels will appear when printed.

> **Note**
>
> You can use standard Avery and CoStar label formats by selecting the Use Label Measurements For radio button, and choosing your label from the pop-up menu.

6. To create a custom label format, select the Use Custom Measurements radio button.

7. Enter the dimensions of your custom label in the Height and Width text boxes, and enter the number you want to print across a page in the Labels Across the Page text box.

> **Note**
>
> The number of labels that can fit across the page is constrained by the dimensions of the stock you're using and by the width of the paper. If you create a custom label five inches wide, you can only print a single column of those labels if the sheet of paper is 8 1/2 inches wide. However, if you set up your page to print labels designed for landscape format, you can print two labels across the 11-inch page.

> **Caution**
>
> When you set the measurements for custom labels, remember that the measurements are not from one edge of the label to the other edge of the label. The measurements are from the leading edge of the first label to the leading edge of the next label. The measurements need to include any spaces between labels. It's a subtle difference, but important—especially when you're measuring the distances on label stock you already have.

8. After you choose your measurements, click OK. The Specify Layout Contents dialog box appears (see fig. 2.4).

This dialog box is very different from the way it looked in previous versions of FileMaker Pro. There are two key differences in the functionality:

- You can use fields from other FileMaker databases on your label format. You access these fields through *relationships*, also a new feature of FileMaker Pro 3.0. For more information on how relationships work, see Chapter 4, "Lookups and Relationships."

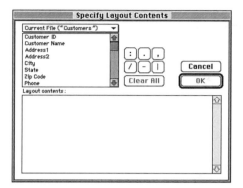

Fig. 2.4
The Specify Layout
Contents dialog
box allows you to
choose the fields
that will appear in
your labels.

FileMaker Fundamentals

- You're no longer placing fields on the layout. FileMaker Pro 3.0 has a merge field capability, similar to doing a mail merge in a word processor. The Label layout type takes advantage of this new feature—what actually goes on the layout is a text block containing field merge codes.

9. For mailing labels, you only want the address-related fields. Double-click the Name field to create a merge code for that field in the Layout Contents list box. If you have ever performed a mail merge in a word processor, this type of coding should look familiar to you.

10. Press Return to move the cursor to the next line. You'll want the Address1 information to be on the next line, so use your Return key to move the cursor to the next line.

11. Double-click the Address1 field to create a merge code for it. Again, press Return to move the cursor to the next line. Repeat the process until you have added all of the fields you want to appear on your mailing label.

12. If you want several fields to appear on a single line, don't press Return when you've finished adding the first one. You can type commas, spaces, or other characters to separate your fields, or use the buttons in the dialog box to add common characters.

13. To add another field to this line, double-click the field you want. If you are making mailing labels, you should now have something that looks like figure 2.5.

14. If you have all of your merge codes in the right places, click OK. This will bring you to your new label layout, similar to the one shown in figure 2.6.

Fig. 2.5
This dialog box shows a mailing label with fields and merge codes.

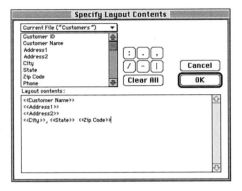

Fig. 2.6
The finished label layout looks like this.

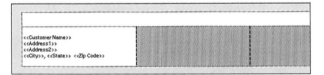

Formatting Text

If you're unhappy with the type style, size, or other text attributes of your labels, you can use FileMaker's text formatting tools to make labels look just the way you want them to.

Although you used multiple fields to create this layout, you can't view or manipulate fields in this label layout. What you created is a block of text containing merge codes. This is unique to the label layout. In other cases, you can move fields around in Layout mode. When you've created a merge-based label layout, you can move or edit the text block as a whole.

> **Note**
>
> If fields in some records in your database are empty, the text block will collapse so no gaps appear in your labels.

One advantage to this text-based label is that controlling the format is simpler than it is with fields. You can just set the text format for the text block, as opposed to having to select and format individual fields.

To format the text, follow these steps:

1. Make sure you are in Layout mode.

2. Click the text block once to select it.

3. Choose Format, Text to open the Text Format dialog box (see fig. 2.7).

In the Text Format dialog box, you can make basic text formatting changes.

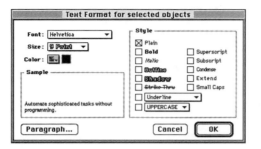

Fig. 2.7
You can change the font, style, size, and other attributes in this dialog box.

4. If you want, you can also make paragraph style changes. Click the Paragraph button. The Paragraph dialog box appears.

5. Try a left indent of .25 inches (see fig. 2.8).

You can use a number of paragraph formatting options, including tabs. While tabs aren't used much in making labels, they can be quite useful in other instances where you use text blocks, such as generating form letters. Click the Tabs button to open the Tabs dialog box (see fig. 2.9). Here you can add tabs and align them if you want.

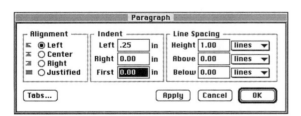

Fig. 2.8
In the Paragraph dialog box, you have full control over your line spacing, indents, and alignment.

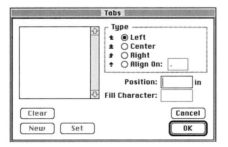

Fig. 2.9
Like most word processors, FileMaker lets you choose from a variety of tab options.

You can get to FileMaker's text formatting tools in several ways. For example, choose Show, Text Ruler. A word processing style text ruler appears at the top of your document (see fig. 2.10).

Fig. 2.10
Here is the Label layout showing the text ruler.

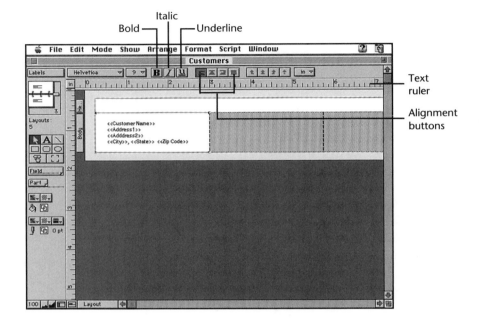

With the text block selected, click the alignment buttons on the text ruler. Notice how the text in the text block behaves (see fig. 2.11). You can also apply the style buttons. The style buttons will bold, italicize, or underline the selected text.

Fig. 2.11
Clicking the Center Alignment button in the text ruler centers the label text.

You can also change the vertical alignment. You change it from center to, say, top alignment by selecting the text, then choosing Format, Align Text, Top (see fig. 2.12).

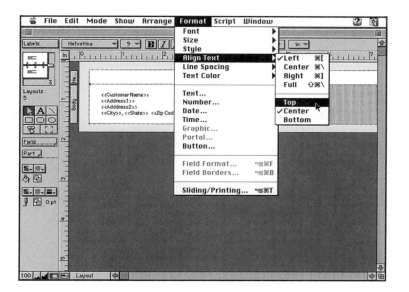

Fig. 2.12
You can set the
text to vertically
align along the
top.

Another way to manipulate the text block is to double-click it. When you do, a small text ruler for just that text block appears at the top of the window. The tabs in the larger text ruler become selectable as well. If you want to set tabs without having to go through the Format menu, just click one of the tab styles (left, center, right, or decimal tabs), then click the spot on the ruler where you want the tab to be (see fig. 2.13).

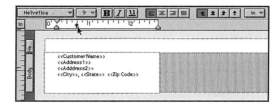

Fig. 2.13
You can set a left-justified tab from the text ruler.

Notice that any indents you might have set are reflected in the ruler as well. You can click and drag the indent marker to any position you want.

Fine-Tuning Your Labels for Printing

Now you've formatted the text block to within an inch of its life. Choose Mode, Browse to see what this label actually looks like. You can duplicate your first record a few times by choosing Mode, Duplicate Record. To see multiple labels displayed vertically, choose Select, View as List. Don't worry that you see only one column of labels when in Browse mode. The instructions you gave FileMaker about printing multiple columns of labels per page will become apparent when you print. To verify the look of your printed labels, choose Mode, Preview.

By default, the labels will print down the page before they print across. If you want the labels to print across first, choose Mode, Layout, then choose Mode, Layout Setup. This opens the Layout Setup dialog box (see fig. 2.14).

Fig. 2.14
This dialog box lets you set printing attributes.

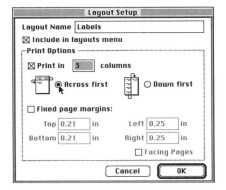

In the Layout Setup dialog box, you can specify how many columns you want printed per page, although you're limited by the width of your labels and the width of the paper. You can't print 15 four-inch wide labels across an 8 1/2 inch piece of paper.

To print your labels across the page instead of down the page, click the Across First radio button.

Now that you know how to do mailing labels, creating a layout for envelopes will be a snap.

Creating An Envelope Layout

If you have a printer that can print on envelopes, you'll get a nicer appearance by printing directly to the envelope instead of printing to a mailing label.

At this point, you probably understand that every time you want to print in a specialized format, you need to create a new layout. You literally have to lay out the look of your printed output.

To print on envelopes, you need to create an envelope layout:

1. Choose Mode, Layout, then choose Mode, New Layout to open the New Layout dialog box.

2. In the Layout Name text box, type **Envelope**.

3. Select the Envelope radio button and click OK.

   The Specify Layout Contents dialog box opens.

4. As you did when you created labels, double-click all of the fields you want to print on the envelope, in the Layout Contents box. Press Return after each line. To place several fields on one line, add spaces or punctuation, instead of pressing Return. Click OK.

This should give you a layout that looks like figure 2.15.

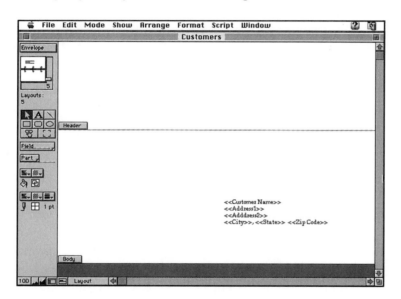

Fig. 2.15
Here's the finished envelope layout.

This looks pretty good. If the envelopes do not already have a return address on them, you might want to add one to this layout. To add a return address, follow these steps:

1. Select the Text tool and click in the upper-left corner of the envelope, just below the Header.

2. Type in your return address information (see fig. 2.16).

   FileMaker "remembers" your last text settings, so if the last thing you worked on was large header text, your text might be big and bold.

Don't worry about the text format—just finish typing what you want to type, then click outside of the text block. The text will then show handles.

Fig. 2.16
It's easy to add return address information to the Envelope layout.

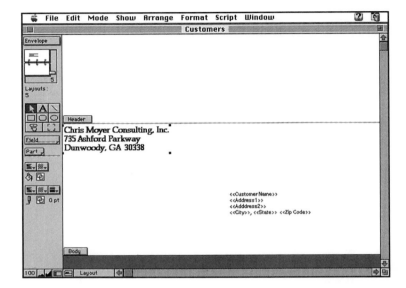

3. With the text block selected, press ⌘-Shift-< a few times to shrink the text.

4. To change the text style to or from bold, press ⌘-Shift-B.

5. Choose Format, Font and note what font is used by your return address. Don't change the font.

6. Now select your addressee information and choose Format, Font again.

Are the fonts the same? If not, change either the addressee font or the return address font to make them the same. Stylistically, the envelope might look odd if you use different fonts. Also, make sure the type size is the same, or at least close, for the two text blocks. Your finished envelope should look similar to figure 2.17.

7. Choose Mode, Preview to view an actual envelope.

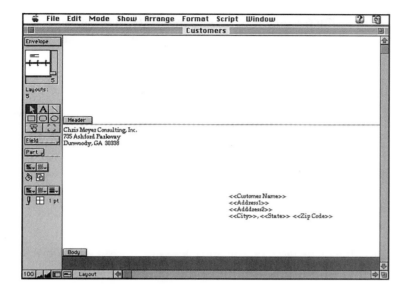

Fig. 2.17
Here is the
finished Envelope
layout.

Tip

Will the layout actually print properly on your envelope? Try this: print one record to
a regular sheet of paper. Choose File, Page Setup, and set the orientation to landscape before you do. Take the printed page and one of the envelopes you're going
to use and put the envelope behind the paper. Make sure it's centered. Hold the
papers toward the light and see if all of the text on the page will fit on the envelope
properly. Do you like the text positioning? You might want to move the addressee
information up or to the left. Or, if you have narrow envelopes, you might want to
move the return address information down.

That's how you make your envelope layout. In the next section, you find out
how to create something to put in the envelope, a form letter.

Designing Form Letters

In previous versions of FileMaker Pro, it wasn't impossible, but it was pretty
inconvenient to create form letter layouts. There wasn't anything like a
merge field. (Hmm. This is beginning to sound like one of those "When I was
your age, I had to walk 16 miles..." kind of stories.) If you wanted to have

some field value in the middle of a paragraph, you had to create separate fields for the beginning of the paragraph, the end of the paragraph, and the value you wanted in the middle. Then, you had to put the three pieces together with a text calculation. It was less than elegant. I just wanted to tell you so you'll know how good you have it with FileMaker Pro 3.0.

You have almost unlimited applications for form letters. You can send welcome letters, thanks for the order letters, past due notices, or any kind of communication you can think of.

To create a form letter layout:

1. Choose Mode, Layout, then choose Mode, New Layout to open the New Layout dialog box.

2. In the Layout Name text box, type **Letter**.

3. Select the Blank radio button and click OK. This will give you an empty layout.

4. Because you're not going to have any header information on this letter, you can delete the Header part. Just click the Header part label and press Delete.

5. You might need lots of space for this letter, so click the Body part label and drag it down. If you drag it past the bottom of the window, the window will begin to scroll down. Do that, and drag down to the 11 inch mark on the ruler at the side, then let go of the Body part label.

> **Note**
>
> At about the 10 1/2 inch mark, you should see a dashed line going across the page. This is your page boundary. Everything above the line will print on the first page, everything below it and down to the next page boundary will print on the second page.

6. Choose Show, and deselect Page Margins.

   If Page Margins are on, there is a check mark in front of the Page Margins command. To turn Page Margins off, just select the Page Margins command (see fig. 2.18). Do the same to turn them back on if you want them on later.

FileMaker Fundamentals

Fig. 2.18
Page Margins are off, Text Ruler and Graphic Rulers are on.

7. Scroll to the right side of the window. At about the 8 1/4 inch mark, you'll see a vertical dashed line. This is the right side page boundary. If you want the letter to print on a single page, the letter text needs to be completely enclosed by this right side page boundary and the bottom edge page boundary.

8. Scroll to the top of the page and select the Text tool. Click to place the insertion point in the upper-left corner.

9. Probably the first thing you'll want on the form letter will be the date, so choose Edit, Paste Special, Date Symbol (see fig. 2.19).

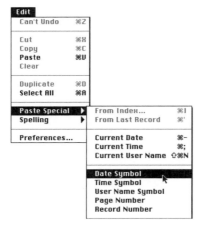

Fig. 2.19
You can choose the date symbol, among other things, from the Paste Special menu.

10. Press Return twice.

11. Choose Edit, Paste Special, Merge Field. The Specify Field dialog box appears (see fig. 2.20).

Fig. 2.20
Choose a field
from the Specify
Field dialog box.

12. Select a field and click OK. The field name appears in brackets, indicating that it is a merge field.

13. Press Return, then repeat the process until you have added all of the fields you want to appear on your letter. If you want multiple fields to appear on one line, don't press Return before you add the next fields.

14. When you've added all of your fields, press Return twice, then type **Dear Customer,** (with a comma at the end).

15. Press Return twice, then type the letter. If your letter exceeds the space available within the body of the layout, extend the Body part by dragging it downward.

If you choose Mode, Browse and view your form letter, you can see actual customer information in it. Because you now have merge fields, you can merge information right into the middle of your letter. If you have a field with a contact name in it, you can have the salutation be more personal. And not only can you thank a customer for their order, you can mention the date they ordered it. Past due notices can include the amount past due and the date of the invoice. The text automatically wraps around merge fields, so the page will always look right.

Now you have a form letter. It would be nice if you had a report so you could figure out who you want to send your letters to. The next section shows you how to create that report.

Building Simple Reports

You can view and use the information in a FileMaker database in many ways. To get a sense of the entire database, you might want to create reports that show some or all of your records in a columnar format. To do this, use the Columnar layout and choose the fields you want to display or print in your report.

1. Choose Mode, Layout to get to Layout mode, then choose Mode, New Layout. The New Layout dialog box appears.

2. In the Layout Name text box, type **List View**.

3. Click the Columnar Report radio button and click OK. The Specify Field Order dialog box appears (see fig. 2.21).

Fig. 2.21
The Specify Field Order dialog box lets you choose fields that will appear in a report.

This dialog box works in a similar fashion to the Specify Layout Contents dialog box you used with the Label and Envelope layouts. In this case, though, you're not specifying merge fields, you're specifying actual fields. To use a field in the layout, you can double-click it or you can select a field, then click Move. If you want every field on your layout, just click Move All.

4. Select the fields you want to include, and click Move. Then click OK. Your screen should look similar to figure 2.22.

   If you select more fields than will display on-screen, they wrap to a second row. Choose Mode, Browse to look at the report. If you have a second row, it makes it confusing and difficult to read, so you need to do some work to the layout and get all of the fields on one line.

Fig. 2.22
When you bring fields into a Columnar layout, they might initially wrap from one line to the next.

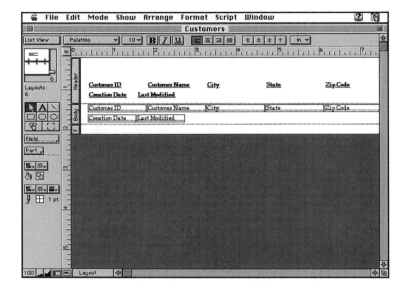

5. Choose Mode, Layout.

6. Move the fields on the second row, along with their labels, by pressing the Shift key while you select each item (see fig. 2.23). Release the Shift key and the mouse button when you've selected all the items you want to move.

Fig. 2.23
Select the fields and labels on the second row so you can move them.

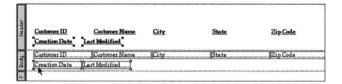

7. Click and drag the fields to the right of the first line.

When you drag past the right edge of the screen, it begins to scroll, so you can see the area to the right (see fig. 2.24). After you move the fields and labels, you can't view all the fields at one time. You need to resize some of the fields.

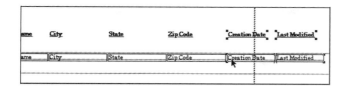

FileMaker Fundamentals

Fig. 2.24
When you move fields to the right, they might appear beyond the dotted margin.

8. If you have a field that has more space than it needs, such as the State field in the example, click once to select it. Then click the lower-right handle and drag it to the left, resizing the field (see fig. 2.25). You can resize all your fields so you can see more, if not all, of your information (see fig. 2.26).

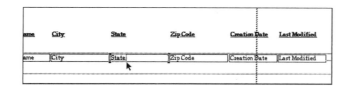

Fig. 2.25
You can resize fields by dragging their handles.

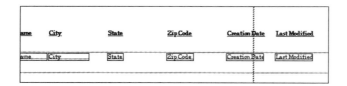

Fig. 2.26
I resized all of the fields in the List View layout.

9. Slide all the fields over so they sit right next to each other. When you do this, it's helpful to select both the field and its label before dragging. When you have all of the fields and labels arranged, drag the bottom of the Body layout part up so it touches the bottom of the fields. Your final result should look similar to figure 2.27.

Fig. 2.27
The final List View layout displays all of the fields on a single line.

Now choose Mode, Browse to view all your records in this basic report.

From Here...

Now you know how to create new layouts, and you've even worked with different kinds of layouts. The Label and Envelope layouts use merge fields, while the Columnar Report layout uses actual fields you can drag around. For more information, try reading the following chapters:

- In Chapter 3, "Creating and Printing Reports," you learn more about creating elaborate reports.
- Chapter 4, "Using Lookups and Relationships," teaches you the fundamentals of setting up relationships between databases. This chapter also describes how to use relationships to look up information in other files.

Creating and Printing Reports

FileMaker Pro is a good place to store data; more importantly, it can help you analyze and understand the significance of your data. It accomplishes this by making it easy for you to design reports.

Reports structure information in a way that's useful to you. If you want to track your monthly expenses, you can create a simple report in FileMaker to do that for you. You can also use the program to generate invoices and print summaries of your income broken down by customers, dates, and other categories. You could even track your golf scores and print reports that track your average score over time.

In this chapter, you learn how to do the following:

- Design a basic list screen report
- Find information you need for a report
- Sort the data
- Create a layout for a more sophisticated, printed report
- Print a report

Types of Reports

You can display reports on-screen and print them on paper; however, it is wise to design separate layouts for each kind of report. A report designed to be viewed on-screen should be designed quite differently than a printed report. For example, you can use colors very effectively to define different areas for an on-screen report. For a printed report, however, colors might be irrelevant. Especially if you use a black and white printer!

> **Tip**
>
> Try to ensure that screen reports don't extend beyond the edge of the screen. That forces users to use the scroll bar to see "off-screen" data.

A report is more than just data displayed on-screen or printed. A report consists of information you have selected and sorted so the information is presented in a meaningful pattern. Consider your city's Yellow Pages. It's actually a printed database report. It displays thousands of business names, addresses, and telephone numbers that are displayed meaningfully by means of hierarchical alphabetical sorting.

The Yellow Pages work by presenting you with an easy way to find the goods or services you need. Want insurance? Turn to the I's and search until insurance shows up in the natural (alphabetical) order of things. Under that heading, you'll find the businesses listed that sell insurance. And, hey, they're also listed alphabetically. So what you have here is hierarchical alphabetical sorting. Think of it as first-level and second-level sorting. The types of goods and services are at the first level of the sort and the companies that provide those services are at the second level.

You can create lots of valuable reports in FileMaker using first-level and second-level sorts. For example, if you're a consultant with a number of clients, you could create a monthly income report that sorted your financial records first by client and then by the date of the invoices you sent out. It all depends on what information you need and how you want to display that information.

Creating a List Report

Chapter 2 deals with how to create custom forms and how to design new layouts. Much of that information applies to your work in this chapter as you design the layouts necessary to generate reports. List reports display some or all of the records in your database, usually sorted in a meaningful way.

To create a list report, follow these steps:

1. Choose Mode, Layout.
2. Choose Mode, New Layout. The New Layout dialog box appears (see fig. 3.1).

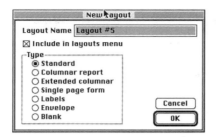

Fig. 3.1
The New Layout
dialog box allows
you to choose
from a number of
layout options.

3. Select the Columnar Report radio button.

4. In the Layout Name text box, type a name for the layout and click OK.

    The Specify Field Order dialog box appears (see fig. 3.2).

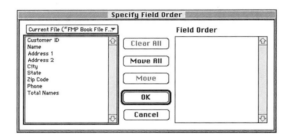

Fig. 3.2
Choose the fields
you want to
display on a
columnar table
and where you
want to place
them.

5. To select a field from the box on the left, click the field once and
    choose Move or double-click the field. The fields appear in the Field
    Order list.

    In figure 3.3, Customer ID, Name, City, State, and Phone were selected
    in that order so they appear in that order in the Field Order list.

6. Click OK.

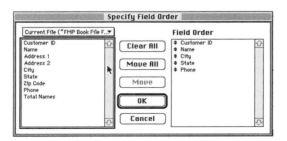

Fig. 3.3
The fields listed in
the window on the
right will appear in
your report.

After you choose all the fields you require for your report, the Field Order list shows you the order your fields will appear on a horizontal layout. The fields will be placed from left to right on the layout, depending on their vertical position in this list (see fig. 3.4). The field at the top of this box will appear on the left of the layout and each field lower will be placed, in sequence, from left to right across the layout.

Fig. 3.4
This is the layout that FileMaker automatically created based on the choices made in the Specify Field Order dialog box.

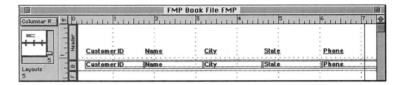

Viewing the Report

Notice the Header, Body, and Footer parts in figure 3.5. These define important characteristics of a layout and how information will be presented.

Fig. 3.5
The Header, Body, and Footer labels appear vertically by default.

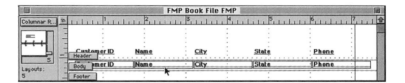

To view the report you created, choose Mode, Browse (see fig. 3.6). If your database contains only one record, choose Edit, Duplicate to make enough records to fill the screen.

Tip

If you can only see one record in your database and you have more, FileMaker has been set by default to show only one record at a time. Choose Select and you'll probably see that View as Form has a check mark next to it. To see more than one record on-screen at the same time, choose Select, View as List. Now, you should see several rows of records marching down your screen at the same time.

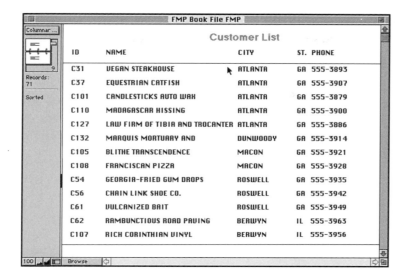

Fig. 3.6
This screen report allows you to see and scroll through a number of records on-screen at the same time.

FileMaker Fundamentals

- Press Page Up or Page Down. You scroll up or down the page one screen at a time.

- Use the cursor to move the scroll box up or down.

- Click the pages of the FileMaker Book in the upper-left of the Status area. This function works exactly as it does when you select View as Form.

Also, notice that there is a very narrow column on the left of the screen, between the status area on the left and the layout area. Inside that column, you'll see a black bar. As you click the pages of the Book, you'll notice the black bar going up or down, depending on whether you're paging backwards or forwards.

You probably noticed that, as you flipped through your records, the labels for the fields remained stationary at the top of the screen. The reason is that the labels are in the Header section of your layout. Check this out, if you like, by switching to Layout and noting the position of the field labels in the Header section of the page. On screen, just as in a printed report, Headers do not change—with the exception of varying page numbers.

The most important thing to note about the layout that FileMaker creates is that it is *fully* functional. It might be a little rough, but it does the job. You can see every field across the page, the data is clearly visible beneath a well defined label, and the records scroll when you click the book or use keyboard commands.

However, you might want to make some improvements to the layout. You can change the font used for displaying the field data, change the font size, or create an attractive Header for your screen report.

Modifying the Report

The first thing you might have noticed was that all of the fields FileMaker creates are exactly the same width. This is the "best guess" FileMaker can make, but it's not necessarily the best choice for your layout. For example, if you have a State field, you only really need room for two characters. Other fields might need to be bigger to display all the information.

To check the size of your fields:

1. Choose Mode, Layout or press ⌘-L to move back into Layout mode.

2. Choose Show, Size. The Size dialog box appears (see fig. 3.7). In the Size dialog box, you can place fields, text, and objects on-screen with mathematical precision.

Fig. 3.7
The Size dialog box is a valuable tool for creating layouts.

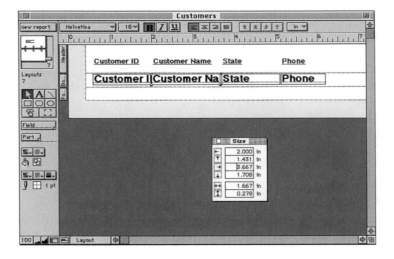

3. Select a field and note the width measurement in the Width field in the Size dialog box. It's identified by a horizontal line with two arrows.

You can now change the size of the fields to more appropriately meet the needs of your layout. If you have a State field, you might want to make that much narrower to provide space for other fields.

Another way to change the size of fields is as follows:

1. Select a field. Selection boxes appear at each corner.

2. Drag one of the four selection points until the field is as wide as you want.

To make sure your fields align correctly on the page, use the T-squares or the Alignment and Set Alignment commands on the Arrange menu.

T-squares provide a horizontal and vertical line against which you can align fields of objects in FileMaker. To use T-squares, follow these steps:

1. In Layout mode, choose Show, T-squares.

Notice that horizontal and vertical cross-hairs appear on the layout.

2. Drag the horizontal T-square up, so it aligns with the top of the fields in your Columnar layout.

If you add or move a field, you can align it with the T-square and thus, with the other fields on the same horizontal line. Similarly, you can use the vertical T-square to align fields and objects along a vertical line. T-squares move independently of one another.

You can automate the alignment process with the Align and Set Alignment commands. To align fields or object in FileMaker:

1. Make sure you are in Layout mode.

2. Select two objects (either fields or labels) by clicking an object, holding down the Shift key, and clicking a second object.

3. Choose Arrange, Set Alignment (see fig. 3.8).

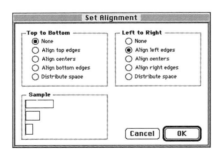

Fig. 3.8
The Set Alignment dialog box lets you choose horizontal and vertical alignments, and displays the result of the choices you make.

4. Select the Align Left Edges radio button. Notice how the rectangles in the lower-left corner of the dialog box change.

5. Select the None radio button in the Top to Bottom area.

You have told FileMaker to align the two items you selected along a vertical line.

FileMaker has one more alignment aid: AutoGrid. By default, AutoGrid is active. If you move fields or objects around a layout, AutoGrid aligns them to an invisible grid. If this constrains you, choose Show, AutoGrid. Now, when you move items around the layout, they will not snap to a grid.

Work with your fields until you achieve the look you want on-screen by flipping back and forth between Layout and Browse modes.

You can also improve the look of the text. Follow these steps:

1. Choose Mode, Layout.

2. Select a field.

3. Choose Format, Font.

   You can select a new font or change the size, style, alignment, spacing, or color of the text. You can also change the background color of the field by clicking the fill palette in the Status area of the screen and dragging to select a new color.

When the fields look the way you want them, you can improve the look of the Header. Try a different font or a different size of font for the labels. You can use all the same options that are available for fields.

Tip

For better on-screen results, you might try the classic Chicago font (at 12 points, plain) for layout text and field text. This font was originally designed for the Mac as an optimum screen font—it always shows up clear and crisp. It's probably the most readable on-screen font ever designed.

Finding Records

After you have a report layout, you need to select and sort the data you want to display on-screen. Fortunately, with FileMaker, both of those functions are a breeze.

You can find records from any FileMaker screen. It's as simple as choosing Mode, Find or pressing ⌘-F. Notice that there is now a Find button in the Status area (see fig. 3.9).

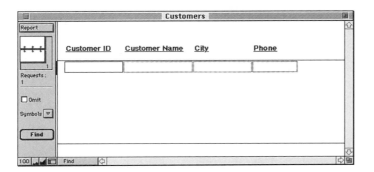

Fig. 3.9
Find mode gives you tools for finding records, and displays an empty request in which you can enter the information you want to search for.

Notice the other two objects in the Status area: the Omit check box and the Symbols drop-down arrow. If you click the Symbols drop-down arrow, you activate a pop-up menu displaying a number of mathematical symbols. These two apparently simple features actually create astonishingly complex options for finding particular records.

To search for specific records:

1. Choose Mode, Find.
2. Select the field where you want to find a match and type in what you want to search for. In this example, the field selected is State and the search is for any records for the state WA.
3. Click the Find button or press Enter. FileMaker automatically returns you to Browse mode.

Now, scroll through your records. All the records should match the search specified. Check out the FileMaker Book in the Status area (see fig. 3.10). Beneath the Book you will notice the text Records with a number under it. This number shows the total number of records contained in your database. Beneath that it says Found and a number next to it. That number indicates the number of records in the found set; in this case, the number of customers located in the state of Washington.

Fig. 3.10
When FileMaker finds records, it switches to Browse mode and displays them.

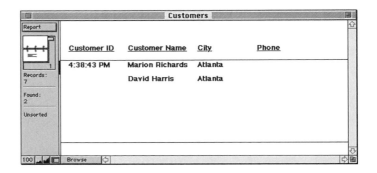

If you want to see all of your records again, Choose Select, Find All or press ⌘-J. Now the number beneath Records and Found is the same. In this case, the found set is the same as the total number of records in the database.

Sorting Records

When you select a field to sort, you are also selecting what is technically known as a *Break* field. When you select a Break field, all of the information in a database is sorted according to that field. Using the Yellow Pages example, the first Break field is type of business, so Automobiles are listed ahead of Computers, Retail Stores, and so on.

Before sorting your database, always check that all of your records are included in the found set by choosing Select, Find All. Then follow these steps to sort your database:

1. Choose Mode, Browse.
2. Choose Mode, Sort. The Sort Records dialog box appears (see fig. 3.11).

Fig. 3.11
You can choose how to sort your records using the fields in your database.

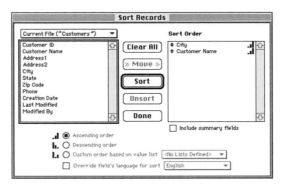

This dialog box looks very similar to the Specify Field Order dialog box. It also works in much the same way. You select a field in the list on the left to move it to the Sort Order list on the right.

3. Select a field for your first level sort by double-clicking the field name or by selecting the name and choosing Move.

> **Note**
>
> Not much has changed in the Sort Records dialog box from FileMaker 2.x to 3.0. The only significant new feature is the Override Field's Language for Sort check box. This new option allows you to sort your records using a language other than English. If you select a field and then select this check box, FileMaker displays a pop-up list of several languages. This can be a very handy feature when data has been entered into a field in a language other than English.

4. Select a field for your second level sort.

5. Choose the Sort button or press Return.

FileMaker immediately returns to Browse mode but notice the difference in your records!

Layout Parts

Here's the full list of layout parts used in FileMaker. It's important to note that you can only place these parts on your layout in the following order. You cannot place a Title Footer part above a Header part. Nor can you place a Trailing Grand Summary above a Body part.

- Title Header
- Header
- Leading Grand Summary
- Body
- Sub-summary when sorted by:
  - Trailing Grand Summary
  - Footer
  - Title Footer

Header and Footer Parts

The terms Headers and Footers are pretty much self-explanatory. You've probably run across them in the word processing world. By now you might have a pretty good handle on the way they work. Good. Because the way they work is pretty much the same in FileMaker. If you want the same text or the same design to appear at the top of every page, you create a Header. If you want the same text or design to appear at the bottom of every page, you create a Footer. In either location, you can place page numbers, dates, user names, and other special symbols. You can also place these symbols in other parts of the layout but they usually go in Headers and Footers.

FileMaker even approaches the complexity of options available in high-end word processors by including the option of creating differently designed Title Headers and Title Footers for the first page of every report.

Body Parts

Header and Footer are intuitive names. But a Body part? What is that? The Body part displays information from only one record. No matter what fields you choose to place in your Body part, the Body section of your layout can only display information for one record.

This is a key concept. All of the reports you produce from FileMaker are based on how information from various records is displayed in the Body part of the layout. You don't have to include all of the information for any record in the Body; just the information you want to appear on that layout, for that record.

Sub-Summary Parts

When you create a Sub-summary part, you create an area on your layout where you can place a Summary field.

Use Break fields to define the areas on your layout where totals and sub-totals appear. Totals and sub-totals are calculated by Summary fields. These are special fields in FileMaker that perform calculations across a group of records. In addition to totals and sub-totals, Summary fields can also calculate averages, standard deviations, and, for a sub-set of records, the ratio of those records divided by the total. What is the percentage of your sales in Kalamazoo, for example, compared with the entire country?

You might, for example, create an invoice system in FileMaker with Clients as a Break field. You can automatically generate income summaries that include all invoices for each client. You can create an even more sophisticated report by setting Invoice Date as another Break field. That way you can track the amount of money you made per client in a given time period.

Grand Summary Parts

When you create a Grand Summary part, you create another area on your layout where you can place a Summary field. However, in a Grand Summary field, the value of all of your selected records is calculated, including Sub-summaries. In a Grand Summary part, a Summary field can perform the same kind of calculations as it does in a sub-summary, but the calculations are carried out across all records.

Like sub-summaries, a Grand Summary part can be either a Leading Grand Summary or a Trailing Grand Summary. Which one you choose depends on your needs for any given report. That means that the summary fields can appear above or below the records they summarize. You must decide whether your summary parts will be leading or trailing before you design the report.

Summary Fields

As previously explained, a Summary field is a special FileMaker field that calculates values across a group of records and is usually placed in a Sub-summary or Grand Summary part.

Follow these steps to create a Summary field:

1. Choose File, Define Fields.
2. In the Define Fields dialog box, select the Summary radio button or press ⌘-S (see fig. 3.12).
3. Name your summary field by typing in the Field Name box.

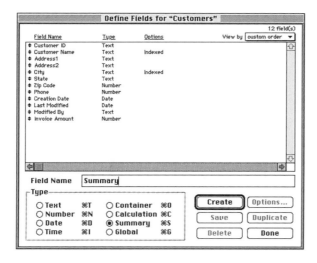

Fig. 3.12
Use the Define Fields dialog box to add new fields to a layout.

You will be presented with the Options for Summary Field dialog box show in figure 3.13.

Fig. 3.13

FileMaker can perform a range of mathematical operations across a group of records.

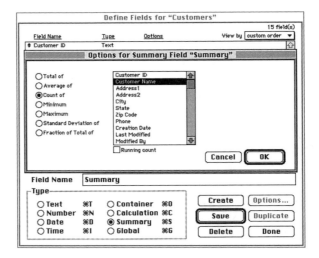

In this dialog box, you choose the mathematical operations you want the Summary field to perform across a sorted group of records. You can choose from:

- Total of
- Average of
- Count of
- Minimum
- Maximum
- Standard Deviation of
- Fraction of Total of

4. Select the field on which you want to perform calculations.

The calculated value displayed by a Summary field depends on whether you placed it in the boundaries of a Sub-summary part or a Grand Summary part, and on how the database is sorted. In figure 3.14, you can see that an identical Summary field, Total Customers, has been placed in two Sub-summary parts (one for Customers by State and one for Customers by City) and a Grand Summary part on the layout. However, the value that the field will display depends on the part that encloses it. To use Sub-summary fields and parts, you must sort your database by the fields in the summary. If you use multiple summaries, your sort order must mirror the order of your Summary parts. In Print Preview mode, you can see the different values displayed.

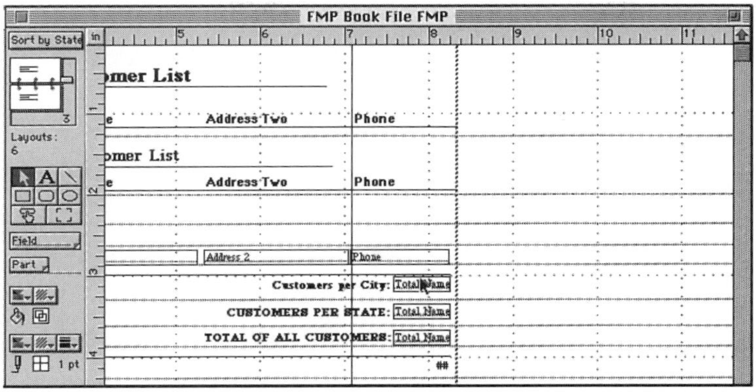

Fig. 3.14
In Layout view, a Summary field looks exactly the same placed in a Sub-summary and Grand Summary part.

Note

If you're using FileMaker for invoicing, you might create an income summary report in which Client is the first Break field, Date Of Invoice is the second Break field, and Invoice Total is the third Break field. That way you can generate subtotals (Sub-summaries) of income for each client, sorted by date, and a grand total (Grand Summary) of all your income from all of your clients.

Troubleshooting

I printed my report, but it doesn't look like I planned it. What happened?

When you design reports, make sure any objects or fields you place in any FileMaker parts do not overlap beyond that Body part into another part of the layout. If this happens, your report will not print or preview as you intend. For example, if the edge of a field or object in the Body overlaps into a Sub-summary part, your records will not properly sort for the display you want. Be very careful about this point. Many users have been baffled to find that reports would not print out properly not knowing that the reason was that they had been sloppy in positioning fields and objects in a layout.

Creating a Printed Report

The following section shows how to create a layout that uses all the parts available in FileMaker Pro, beginning with the Title Header.

Adding a Title Header

Title Headers give your report a heading. As the name implies, they are usually used to title a report.

To add a Title Header part to your layout, follow these steps:

1. Select the Part control button and drag it onto the layout, just above the Header part. When you let the Part button go, the Part Definition dialog box appears (see fig. 3.15).

Fig. 3.15
The Part Defini-
tion dialog box
lets you choose a
Part.

Part control button —

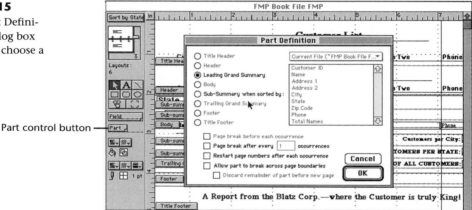

In this case, because you dragged the Part button above the horizontal header bar, FileMaker provides you only one alternative when it comes to defining what part goes on the page—Title Header. The reason is simple: the Title Header and only the Title Header can go above a Header.

2. Choose OK.

3. Choose the Text tool on the tool palette (the big A) and click in the Title Header area.

4. Type **Customer List** at the top of the page.

5. Format the text by choosing a suitable font, font size, and font style from the Format menu (see fig. 3.16).

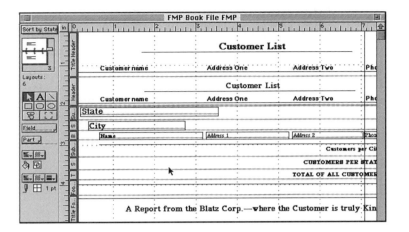

Fig. 3.16
This is how your layout should look when you are finished.

Adding a Header

To get double value for the layout work you've already done, you can copy the text in the Title Header and place it in the Header. While the Title Header appears at the top of the report, the Header text appears at the top of each page in the report. You can then reduce the size of the font used for the title of the report. It's standard practice to have a title on the title page that is bigger that the title on subsequent pages of a report.

To use the Title Header for the Header:

1. Click in the Title Header area.
2. Click the header text you created earlier. You will see object boundaries on all four corners.
3. Choose Edit, Copy or press ⌘-C.
4. Click inside the area bounded by the Header part and choose Edit, Paste or press ⌘-V.
5. Format the Header text by choosing a suitable font, font size, and font style from the Format menu.

If you think you might not have enough space in the area defined by the horizontal Header bar, move the Header part down a little to make room for the labels. To move the horizontal Header bar, simply click it and drag it down. All FileMaker parts work this way. To change the area enclosed by a part, you need only click one of the part bars and pull it up or down.

It's important to note, though, that if you place objects, text, or fields in a part, FileMaker will not let you drag the part bar through them. For example, if you place a field on the layout in the Body part, you cannot drag the Body bar up and through the field. However, if you press Option while you drag, you can drag the Body bar through the field. FileMaker assumes that no one would want to drag a part through objects on the layout. But the program is wise enough to realize that you need the freedom to be a little crazy now and then.

Adding Break Fields

Your next task is to define the Break fields: the primary and secondary sort fields. This example creates a report that does the following:

- Sorts all records first by State and counts how many records there are in each state.
- Performs a second sort by City and counts how many records there are in each city.

State and City are, therefore, the Break fields in this report.

Follow these steps to define the Break fields:

1. Click the Part control button and drag it across to the layout, until the bar is in the Body part. When you release the mouse button, the Part Definition dialog box appears. This time, however, you have two choices: Leading Grand Summary or Sub-Summary When Sorted By.

2. Select the Sub-Summary When Sorted By radio button.

3. Choose the field you want to use as the first Break field on your layout—the primary sort. In this example, this field is State.

   Your layout appears, and you see another horizontal part bar, this time the Sub-Summary By State (Leading).

4. Drag the Sub-summary bar down until you have enough space to place the State field in the Sub-summary part.

5. Choose Format and select suitable font, size, style, and alignment options.

6. To choose the field for the secondary sort (the next Break field on your layout), drag the Part control button onto the layout and select the Sub-Summary When Sorted By radio button. Choose the field for the secondary sort, City in the example.

Adding Fields for the Body

The next part to set up is the Body. You can place the following fields on the layout in the following order: Name, Address One, Address Two, and Phone Number.

To place the fields, follow these steps:

1. Choose Mode, Layout.

2. Click and drag the Field tool. As you drag the tool onto the layout, you will see a rectangle, representing the field.

3. Let go of the mouse button when the field is located approximately where you want it in the Body part of the Layout. When you do, the Specify Field dialog box appears.

4. Choose a field from the list and select the Create Field Label check box. Your field appears in the layout.

5. To make sure the new field looks right when printed, line it up with the other fields along a horizontal line.

    If you need to, use T-squares or the Set Alignment command to put the field in its proper place. These features were discussed earlier in this chapter.

6. Drag the field label you created and the new field into the Header part of the layout. Line it up with other labels, just as you did with the field.

7. Repeat this procedure for all fields you want to appear on your printed report.

After you place them, you can format the fields.

When the Body part is complete, drag the bar right up against the fields until FileMaker won't let you go any further. By doing so, and by minimizing the space above the fields in the Body part, you create a very narrow space for the body, which saves space when printing.

Creating Sub-Summary and Grand Summary Fields

The next step is to create a Summary field that counts the number of customers by City and State. Follow these steps:

1. Choose File, Define Fields. The Define Fields dialog box appears.

2. Click the Summary Field radio button or press ⌘-S.

3. In the Field Name text box, type a name.

4. Choose Options or press Return. The Options for Summary Field dialog box appears (see fig. 3.17).

Fig. 3.17
You can choose
which fields to
summarize and
how to summarize
them in this
dialog box.

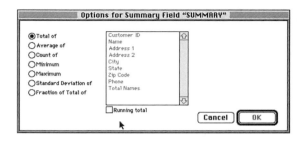

5. Select the Count Of radio button.

6. Select Name by highlighting this field in the list box and choosing OK.

7. In Layout mode, drag the Part button beneath the Body part. FileMaker gives you the option of creating another Sub-Summary When Sorted By or a Trailing Grand Summary.

8. Choose Sub-Summary When Sorted By and choose City from the list on the right. When you return to your layout, the horizontal Sub-summary bar says Sub-summary by City (Trailing).

9. In this Sub-summary part, place the layout text Customers per City on the right of the layout. You might want to format the field so the text is a different size or bold to stand out.

10. Immediately to the right of this text, place the Total Names summary field. Format this field appropriately.

11. Drag the Part button below the last Sub-summary.

12. In the Options for Summary Field dialog box, choose Sub-Summary When Sorted By and State. This creates another sub-summary part identified by a part bar that says Sub-summary by State (Trailing).

13. Drag this bar until you have enough space in this part to type in the text Customers by State and format the field.

14. Immediately to the right of this text, place the Total Names Summary field and format this field.

15. Drag the Part button below the Sub-Summary By State bar. This time, from the options presented to you, choose the Trailing Grand Summary radio button.

16. Finally, place the layout text Total Of All Customers and the Total Names Summary field in the Trailing Grand Summary part of the layout, on the right. Again, you can format the field.

Adding Title Footers and Page Specification

You can also add a Title Footer or place a page number on the page. Follow these steps to add a Title Footer:

1. In Layout mode, click and drag the Part box to the bottom of the layout, below all other parts. When you let go of the mouse button, a dialog box appears.

2. Click the Title Footer radio button.

When you specify parts in the Part Setup dialog box, you can tell FileMaker how to handle multi-page reports.

With the following options, you have control over whether page breaks split up groups of records, which are tied to the parts you select:

- Page Break Before Each Occurrence begins a new page before printing the contents of the selected layout part.

- Page Break After Every *x* Occurrences begins a new page after a specified number of occurrences. This is most useful for determining how many records (usually found in Body parts) to print before beginning a new part, such as a Summary.

- Restart Page Numbers After Each Occurrence begins a new page after each part in the layout.

- Allow Part to Break Across Page Boundaries does not alter the pagination of the file.

- Discard Remainder of Part Before New Page is only available when you allow parts to break across page boundaries. This option prints as much of a given part as can be printed on a page, and does not print the remainder on subsequent pages.

You probably want to put a page number in the Footer area. That way, your pagination will continue past the title page on every page of your report. To do this:

1. Choose Edit, Paste Special, Page Number.

   You can also use the Paste Special command to add today's date, the current time, or other information to your layout.

2. Click inside the Title Footer and paste in the page number. Two number signs (#) will appear.

   You can move the page number to any location in the Title Header, and format the text, just as you did when you created header text.

3. Choose File, Print Preview to see what your report looks like. If everything has worked properly, your records should look similar to figure 3.18.

Fig. 3.18
This is a sample report preview.

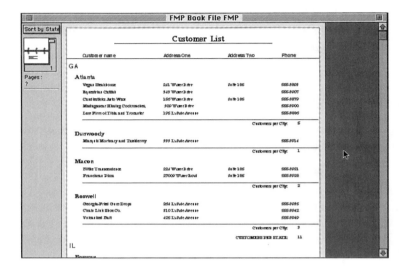

Printing Your Report

Printing is the real test of your report design. You can check it out in Print Preview and get a pretty good idea, but you need to print the report to find whether it meets your needs.

Page Setup

When you are printing, of course, you must make sure your Page Setup is correctly set for the kind of page you designed. Choose File, Page Setup. In this case, you designed a vertical 8.5 by 11 inch page layout. In the Page Setup dialog box, choose Portrait (the default position). If you designed a wide report page, 11 by 8.5, choose Landscape in the Page Setup dialog box.

FileMaker Printing Options

FileMaker presents you with a much greater variety of printing options than most other programs. As you can see in figure 3.19, beyond the usual options for number of copies, pages, and destination, there are a number of other selections you can make.

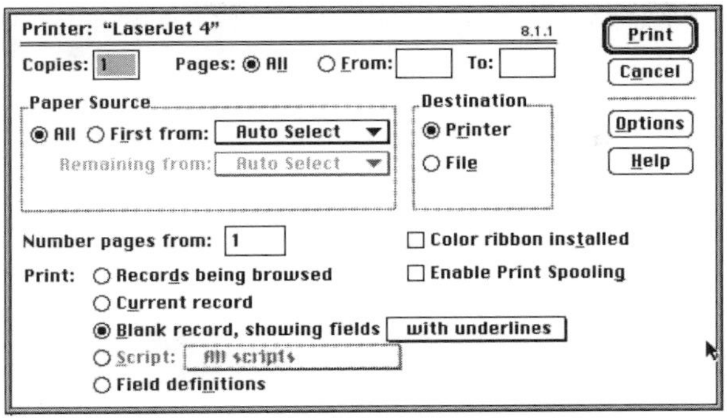

FileMaker Fundamentals

Fig. 3.19
There's more than one way to print in FileMaker.

Here are some of the most important printing options available from the FileMaker Print dialog box. Choose File, Print to get there.

- *Records Being Browsed.* Select this radio button if you want to print a series of records you have found, for example, if you are printing envelopes for a particular zip code.

- *Current Record.* Prints a report of one record only. This option is suitable if, for example, you are printing an envelope with a single address.

- *Blank Record, Showing Fields.* Allows you to choose from further options in a pop-up list. You can print a layout with the fields printed as you formatted them—as outlined boxes or as underlines. This is a useful way of printing your layout to check the design. But you probably won't choose it very often, because it prints no records.

The last two options allow you to print script or field definitions used in the current file. In this example, you cannot print your script definitions because you haven't defined any scripts for the file. You might want to print your field definitions, though. As your database designs become more complex, you'll find that printouts of your field and script definitions can be very useful in analyzing the operations of your files and in troubleshooting problems.

Borders

Every printer is different in how it handles printing to the edge of the paper. Some printers are capable of printing closer to the edge than others. Because every printer is different, you need to tweak your layout a few times to achieve the borders you want and the overall look you want when you print out your report.

Tip

Be patient. Each report you design might serve you for years, so it's worth spending a little time on it to make it work properly. Remember also that FileMaker provides you the option of duplicating entire layouts—you can duplicate this layout and use it as the basis for a new layout.

Troubleshooting

Why am I not getting what I want in my layout?

There are two possibilities you should check:

- Make sure none of the objects, text, or fields you have placed in any of the parts of your layout overlap onto another part.

- Make sure you sorted all of your records by State and then by City. If you change the sort order and attempt to print or preview this report, it will not work properly. The sort order must be in place for this report to print correctly.

From Here...

In this chapter, you learned in-depth how to create reports using subtotals and totals, and how to print those reports. You also learned a great amount about finding and sorting information in a FileMaker database.

From here, you might want to read the following chapters:

- Chapter 2, "Designing Simple Layouts," teaches you how to create mailing labels, envelopes, and form letters. Read this chapter if you need more information on basic reporting.

- Chapter 4, "Using Lookups and Relationships," describes the fundamentals of setting up relationships between databases and how to use relationships to look up information from one file to another.

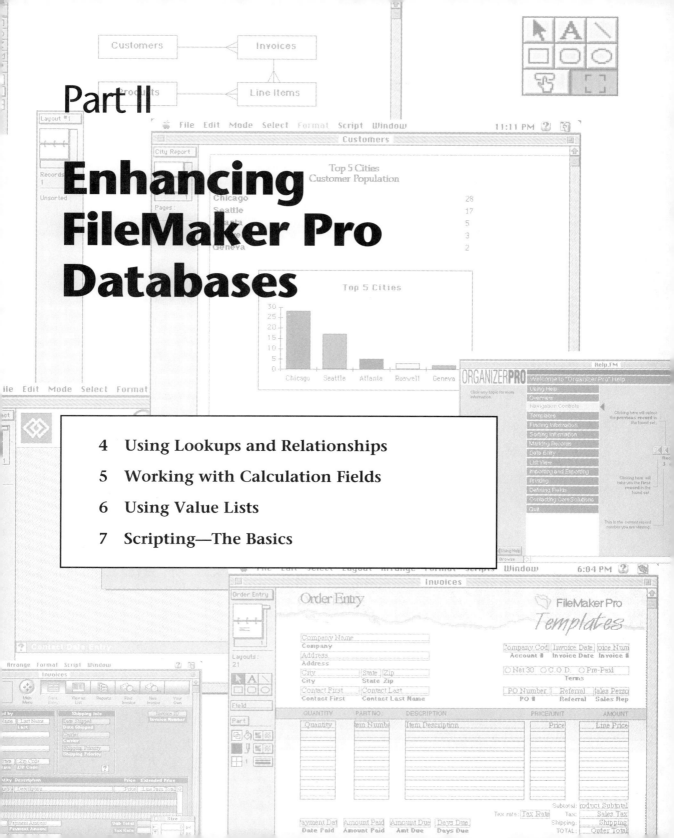

Part II

Enhancing FileMaker Pro Databases

Using Lookups and Relationships

Although it might seem premature to talk about relationships at this point in the book, they are so fundamental to everything that follows that you need to know about them now. Relational design issues are covered beginning with Chapter 13, "Applying Relational Concepts."

Lookups have been part of FileMaker's feature set for several revisions now, but with the advent of FileMaker 3.0 and relationships, lookups have changed slightly. In version 3.0, lookups require a relationship; without a relationship, there can be no lookup.

In this chapter, you learn about:

- The nuts and bolts of creating relationships
- Working with related fields and portals
- Using lookup fields and how they've changed

Creating a Relationship

A *relationship* is a link between two databases that allows information from one database to be displayed and changed in another database. Suppose you have two databases, Database1 and Database2. In Database1, you create a relationship to Database2. Because of this relationship, you can now view information from Database2 in Database1. It's almost as if you cut a hole in Database1 and you're viewing information from Database2 through that hole.

For those of you familiar with FileMaker Pro 2.1, this is radically different from a *lookup*, where information would actually be copied into Database1.

The easiest way to understand how this works is to do it. The following example creates two new databases to demonstrate how to create a relationship.

1. Launch FileMaker and click the Create a New Empty File radio button. Name the new database Invoices and click Save.

2. In the Define Fields dialog box, create a new text field called Invoice ID. Click the Options button to open the Entry Options dialog box.

Troubleshooting

I can't find the serial number options. It's not under Options.

You're probably in Validation Entry Options. Choose Auto Enter from the pop-up at the top of the Entry Options dialog box.

---

3. Click the Serial Number radio button and set the Next Value to 100 (see fig. 4.1). Click OK to exit the Entry Options dialog box and return to the Define Fields dialog box.

Fig. 4.1
You add serial numbering to a field in the Entry Options dialog box.

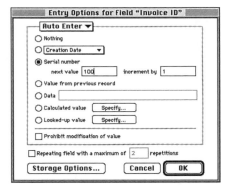

4. Create a new text field called Customer ID. Similar to the Invoice ID field, the Customer ID field will contain a serial number, but the serial number will be generated in another database—the Clients database. Because a particular client can have more than one invoice, the serial number won't be unique in the Invoices database.

   You're formatting both of these serial number fields as text fields because text fields allow you to search on part of the total value. For example, if you try to find invoice 950110, you could search for *110 and get a match. If the field were a number field, you would have to know the full number to successfully find the invoice.

5. Click Done to close the Define Fields dialog box.

You should see one record with the Invoice ID field showing a first serial number of 100. You now have one database.

Troubleshooting

I got my first record but didn't get a serial number. What went wrong?

You probably accidentally clicked Cancel instead of OK when you set up your entry options. Choose File, Define Fields to open the Define Fields dialog box. Select the Invoice ID field and click Options. Set up the serial number and make sure you click OK when you exit the Entry Options dialog box. Click Done to close the Define Fields dialog box. Choose Mode, New Record (Entry Options only work when a record is created) and you should see a serial number in Invoice ID.

To create the second database to link to:

1. Choose File, New to open the New Database dialog box. Click the Create a New Empty File radio button. Name the file Clients and click Save.

2. In the Define Fields dialog box, create a new text field called CustID then click Options.

3. In the Entry Options dialog box, click the Serial Number radio button. Make the Next Value C1000 and click OK to close the Entry Options dialog box.

4. Create the following text fields:

    Customer Name

    Address

    City

    State

    Zip Code

    Your Define Fields dialog box should now look similar to figure 4.2.

5. Click Done to exit the Define Fields dialog box. Your first record should already have a Customer ID of C1000.

6. Tab to the Customer Name field and enter a customer name. Tab to the rest of the fields to complete the address information.

7. When you finish the first customer, choose Mode, New Record to create a new record.

Fig. 4.2
You would probably have more fields than this for a real database, but for the purposes of this example, these fields will do for the Clients database.

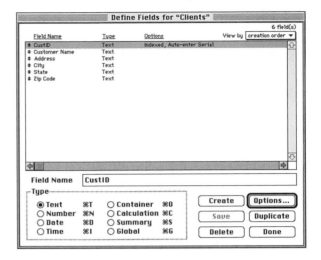

8. Create one more complete customer record.

   You should now have two customers, one with the Customer ID of C1000, the other with C1001.

9. Choose Window, Invoices to switch back to the Invoices database.

It's time to create your first relationship. Follow these steps:

1. Choose File, Define Relationships to open the Define Relationships dialog box. Click New. The Open dialog box appears.

2. Select the database you want to link to or establish a relationship with—in this case, the Clients database you just created—and click Open.

   The Edit Relationship dialog box opens (see fig. 4.3). The Invoices list shows all the fields in the current database file. The Clients list shows all the fields in the database you're linking to.

   Note that the text in the dialog box says A relationship defines a set of matching related records for each record in the current file. What does that mean? If you want to have a relationship between two databases, you need to have a field in each database that can have matching information. In this case, you defined both databases to have a Customer ID field. This doesn't mean the fields have to be named exactly the same.

> **Tip**
>
> While the match fields in a relationship don't have to be named exactly the same, the fields should be the same type—number fields match with number fields, text with text, and so on.

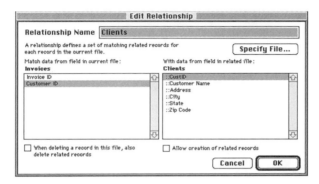

Fig. 4.3
You create links between databases in the Edit Relationships dialog box.

3. Select the Customer ID field in the Invoices list. In the Clients list, select the ::CustID field.

Notice that all the fields in the Clients list have a double colon appended to the beginning of their names. This designates these fields as *related fields*. They are related to the database you're viewing them in, but the data doesn't actually reside there.

4. Click OK to close the Edit Relationship dialog box then click Done to close the Define Relationships dialog box.

You just created a relationship. Although the database looks the same as it did before, it is now capable of new behavior.

Working with Related Fields

A database that has a relationship to another database is capable of displaying fields from that other database. When a field on a layout exists in another database, it's called a *related field*. To add a related field to a database layout, follow these steps:

1. Choose Mode, Layout to put the database in Layout mode.

II

Enhancing Databases

2. Click and drag the Field tool onto your layout, placing it directly below the Customer ID field (see fig. 4.4).

This opens the Specify Field dialog box.

Fig. 4.4
Drag the Field tool into position.

The Field tool —

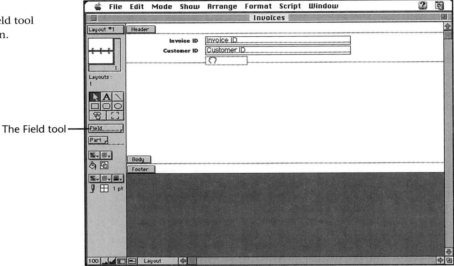

3. Here's the new behavior: click and hold the Current File pop-up menu (see fig. 4.5).

Fig. 4.5
New in FileMaker Pro 3.0, the Specify Field dialog box is now capable of specifying fields from other databases via a relationship.

4. Drag down to the new related file, Clients.

Now the dialog box displays fields from the Clients database (see fig. 4.6). This is a radical departure from how FileMaker worked in the past. Using relationships, you can now place related fields on a layout. Notice that the field names are all still preceded by a double colon. Again, this means the data does not exist in the current database. You're only displaying it.

Fig. 4.6
When you select a relationship from the pop-up menu, you can see all of the related fields associated with that relationship.

5. Select the ::Customer Name field and click OK.

   Notice that even when the field is placed on the layout, it still displays the double colon to denote its special status as a related field.

6. Repeat this process for the rest of the related fields in the Clients relationship. Lay the fields out so they are similar to figure 4.7.

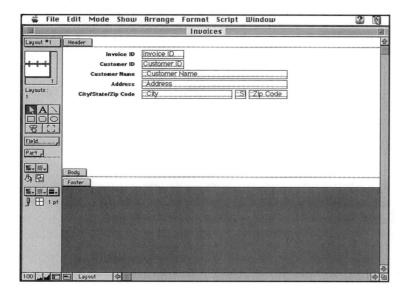

Fig. 4.7
This Invoices layout displays local and related fields.

7. Choose Mode, Browse to return to Browse mode. Tab to the Customer ID field and enter **C1000**. Tab out of the field or type the Enter key (not the Return key).

II

Enhancing Databases

All of the related fields should display the information from the corresponding record in your Clients database. If you change the Customer ID to C1001 and tab out of the field, the related fields should now show the information from your second Clients record.

Troubleshooting

I can't see any information in my related fields. Where do I look to solve this problem?

If you don't have any information showing in your related fields after you type in the Customer ID code, switch over to the Clients database and make sure you have information in the record that has Customer ID C1001. If you do, you might have created a relationship to the wrong file. FileMaker opens related databases in the background when you show a layout containing related fields. In the Window menu, see if you have a database other than Clients and Invoices listed. If you do, close it. If it's related, it will continue to reopen in the background and appear in that list. If that's the case, you need to redo the create relationship steps, taking care to select the Clients file when you set up the relationship.

Tip

Although related fields display information from another database, you can still format and use them like regular fields. You can even enter data information from local value lists. The field's validation settings, however, are in effect wherever the field is used.

It's hard to appreciate how related fields work unless you can see both databases at the same time. It's helpful to resize your database windows so you can see what's happening to the same field in both places.

You can resize the Invoices window so it only takes up the top half of your computer screen. Choose Window, Clients to bring the Clients database to the foreground. Resize the Clients window so it only takes up the top half of your computer screen, then drag the window so that it sits on the bottom half of your computer screen. You should now be able to see both the Invoices window and the Clients window at the same time, as shown in figure 4.8.

It's important that you're looking at the same information in both databases. Make sure your Clients database shows the CustID being used in the Invoices record. If Invoices is showing customer C1001, then make sure Clients is also. Tab to the Customer Name field in Clients and change the name. As you tab out of the field, note that the Customer Name related field in Invoices shows the new change.

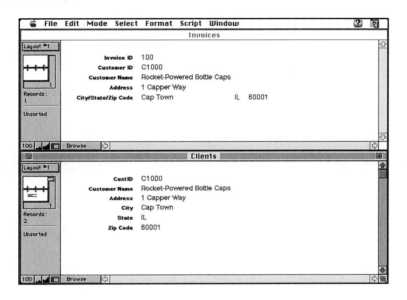

Fig. 4.8
Setting up a split view like this enables you to see how related fields can actually update information in the related databases.

Now try it the other way. Click anywhere on the Invoices database to make it active. Tab to the Address field and change the address. As you tab out of the field, notice that the Address information in Clients reflects the change.

When you enter information in a related field, you actually change information in the related database. This is fundamentally different from how FileMaker worked in past versions.

Working with Portals

Now you know how related fields works—almost. There is a special circumstance when a related field by itself doesn't work correctly. This is when you have more than one corresponding record. If you have two records in your Clients database that have CustID C1001, you only see the first occurrence— the record created first in a related field in Invoices.

There are times, however, when you do have more than one matching record. Look at the current example, an invoice database. You don't have any line items on this invoice. FileMaker 2.1 veterans will immediately think of adding repeating fields to contain the quantity, description, price, and so on.

In a relational database, however, line items are best stored in a related file. Why? If you need to report on how many widgets you sold in the month of May, you can't do it when all of your line items are in repeating fields. You need to break the repeating information into separate records to report the information properly. For more information on how to do this and what all of the issues are, see Chapter 10, "More on Conversion Issues."

Anyway, if line items are stored in a separate database file, you typically have more than one line item per invoice. This means you have more than one record that corresponds to your match field (it would be Invoice ID), and that means related fields by themselves aren't a workable solution.

> **Tip**
>
> When you have more than one matching related record, you need to use a portal to accurately display your data.

The following database example demonstrates the issues:

1. Choose File, New to open the New Database dialog box. Click the Create a New Empty File radio button and click OK.

2. Name the file Line Items and click Save.

3. In the Define Fields dialog box, define the following fields:

Field Name	Type	Options
Invoice ID	Text	
Quantity	Number	
Description	Text	
Price	Number	
Line Price	Calculation	= Quantity * Price

When you create Line Price as a calculation field, you'll automatically bring up the Specify Calculation dialog box. Double-click the Quantity field in the field list, type an asterisk, then double-click the Price field. Click OK to exit the Specify Calculation dialog box.

4. Click Done to close the Define Fields dialog box.

5. Choose Mode, Layout, then choose Mode, New Layout to create a new layout.

6. Name the layout List View and select the Columnar Report radio button. Click OK.

7. In the Specify Field Order dialog box, click Move All (see fig. 4.9).

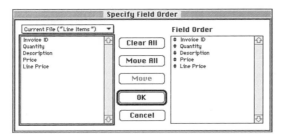

Fig. 4.9
The Specify Field Order dialog box allows you to choose which fields are going to be on a new layout, and in what order.

8. Click OK to close the Specify Field Order dialog box.

If you set the new layout to be a columnar report, your layout should look similar to figure 4.10.

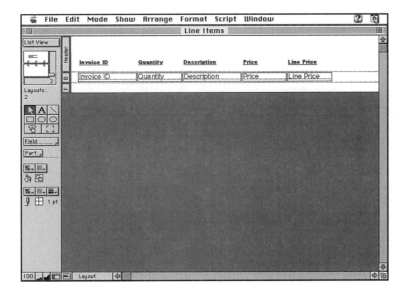

Fig. 4.10
This is how a columnar report layout displays in Layout mode.

9. Choose Mode, Browse.

10. Tab to the Invoice ID field and type **100**. Tab to the next field and type the quantity of your choice. Tab to the Description field and type **Large Widget**. Tab to the Price field and type a price. Because the Line Price field is a calculation field, as soon as you tab out of the Price field, the Line Price calculates.

11. Choose Mode, Duplicate Record twice so you have three records. Change the description, quantity, and price in the second and third records so you can tell the three records apart.

12. Choose Window, Invoices to bring the Invoices database to the foreground. Resize the Invoices database so it fills the screen.

13. In Invoices, choose File, Define Relationships to open the Define Relationships dialog box. Click New.

14. In the Open dialog box, select the Line Items database and click Open.

15. The Edit Relationship dialog box appears (see fig. 4.11). On the left side of the dialog box, select the Invoice ID field. On the right side of the dialog box, select the ::Invoice ID field.

Fig. 4.11
The Edit Relationship dialog box is the only place where you can create a relationship to another database.

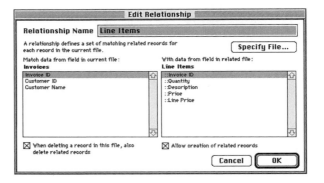

At the bottom of the dialog box are two check boxes. The one below the Invoices fields says, `When deleting a record in this file, also delete related records`. The real question is, if you delete an invoice, do you also want to delete any line items on the invoice? Because line items not attached to an invoice don't have any meaning, the answer is yes. You don't want any line items to exist without being attached to an invoice. This kind of dependency is called a parent-child relationship. You can't have a line item without first having an invoice. The Invoices database is the parent database, while the Line Items database is the child database.

If the Invoices database is the parent, then it needs to be able to create "child" records in the Line Items database.

16. To allow this to happen, select the Allow Creation of Related Records check box. Click OK then click Done.

17. Choose Mode, Layout to put the database in Layout mode. Click and drag the Field tool onto your layout, placing it directly below the City/State/Zip Code label.

18. The Specify Field dialog box opens. Click and hold the pop-up menu at the top of the dialog box and drag down to the Line Items relationship. The dialog box should now display fields from the Line Items database.

19. Select the ::Quantity field and click OK. Repeat this process for the rest of the related fields in the Line Items relationship. Lay the fields out so they look similar to figure 4.12.

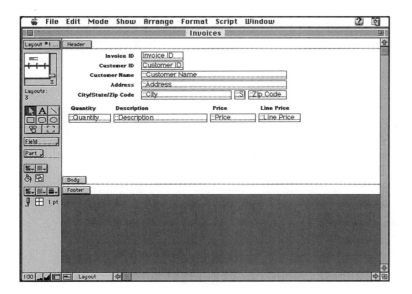

Fig. 4.12
Now the Invoices layout has related fields from both Clients and Line Items.

20. Select the ::Price field. Hold down the Shift key and also select the ::Line Price field. Choose Format, Number to open the Number Format dialog box. Click the Format as Decimal radio button. Select the Fixed Number of Decimal Digits check box. Leave the number set at 2. Select the Use Notation check box (see fig. 4.13). Click OK.

21. Choose Mode, Browse.

You should see the information from the first Line Items record on your screen. You should also see a problem: even though you have three line items that belong to invoice 100, you can only display the first matching record when you use related fields.

Fig. 4.13
The Number
Format dialog box
allows you to
properly format
currency.

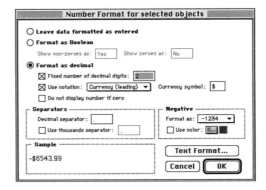

The solution to this problem is to use a combination of related fields and a portal. A *portal* is a layout object that allows you to show multiple rows of matching data. Each row in a portal corresponds to a related record in another database. To add a portal to the Invoices layout, follow these steps:

1. Choose Mode, Layout to return to Layout mode.
2. Click the Portal tool once to make it active (see fig. 4.14). Then (without dragging the Portal tool) move your mouse onto the layout. Notice that the cursor has changed to a cross-hair.

Fig. 4.14
Select the Portal
tool by clicking
it once, then
releasing the
mouse button.

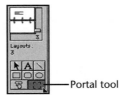

Portal tool

3. Starting from the top left of the ::Quantity field, drag a portal down and to the right, so the size is similar to the portal shown in figure 4.15.
4. When you have the right size, release the mouse button. This opens the Portal Setup dialog box.
5. Click the Show Records From pop-up menu and select Line Items.
6. Because you need to be able to delete line items from an invoice if you make a mistake or if a customer changes their mind, select the Allow Deletion of Portal Records check box. Make sure the number of rows is at least 3, but don't make the number too large or the portal will be larger than the layout. Select the Show Vertical Scroll Bar and Alternate Background With check boxes (see fig. 4.16). Choose a color from the color palette. Click OK.

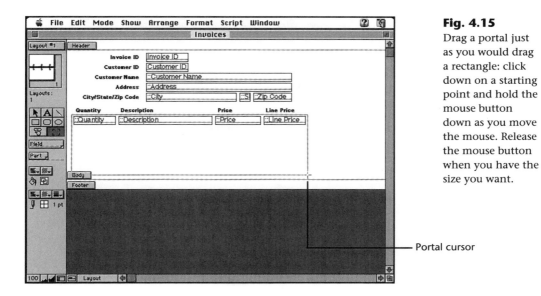

Fig. 4.15
Drag a portal just
as you would drag
a rectangle: click
down on a starting
point and hold the
mouse button
down as you move
the mouse. Release
the mouse button
when you have the
size you want.

Portal cursor

II

Enhancing Databases

Fig. 4.16
The Portal Setup
dialog box is the
only place where
you can specify the
number of rows in
a portal.

You might need to resize the portal or move the related Line Items fields around so the first line of the portal entirely contains them (see fig. 4.17).

Choose Mode, Browse to view the three related records in the portal. Because you specified this relationship to allow the creation of related records, you can create new Line Items records using the portal. To do so, just click in the first empty row. As soon as you enter data in one field and either tab out of the field, press Enter, or click the mouse outside of the field, a new record gets created in Line Items. Also, a new blank entry gets created in the next row of the portal.

Fig. 4.17
If you don't have
the related fields
completely in the
first row of the
portal, they won't
display properly.

Line Items field

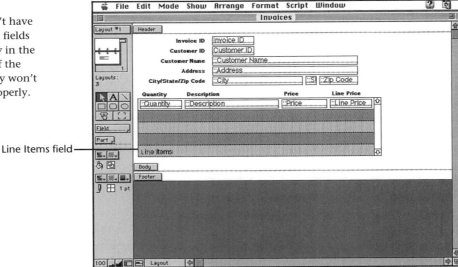

Troubleshooting

*I have multiple portal rows and one of my fields is only working in the first row of the
portal.*

That means the field is touching the edge of the first portal row. Choose Mode,
Layout to switch to Layout mode. Move the offending field so that it's entirely contained in the first row of the portal. When you're through, choose Mode, Browse to
return to Browse mode.

If you type a quantity in the Quantity field then choose Window, Line Items,
you see a new record in your List View layout. Notice that the Invoice ID is
automatically entered for you. Because you created the line item while you
were on a specific invoice, the relationship specifies the Invoice ID.

Choose Window, Invoices to return to the Invoice database. To delete a line
item from the portal, click inside the portal row—but not in any field. If you
click in a field, you just get a flashing cursor in that field; if you click outside
of a field, the entire portal row is highlighted. Choose Mode, Delete Record to
delete the related record.

Pay close attention to the message you get when you delete a portal record. If
you're in a field in a portal row and you choose Mode, Delete Record, you get
a message that looks like figure 4.18. This means you're about to delete the
entire parent record, not the single record in the portal row.

Fig. 4.18
Although you were
in a field in a por-
tal row, you still
get this delete
entire record
warning.

To make sure you're only deleting the single related record, click inside the portal row, but not in any field in that row. When you do, the entire portal row is highlighted. When the entire row is selected, then you can delete that row only. The message you get looks like figure 4.19.

Fig. 4.19
You have to have
the entire portal
row selected to get
the delete related
record warning.

Now you know how to create a relationship, how to place related fields on a layout, how to create and delete related records using a portal, and how to display multiple related records using a portal. It's time to look at lookup fields.

Using Lookup Fields

Lookup fields are fields that copy information from another database. These are very different from related fields, where the information stays in the other database and is only displayed in the current database. Using lookups means you will have multiple copies of specific information. This can be good or bad.

The lookup feature has been in FileMaker Pro for several revisions now, but has changed a little in the 3.0 release. Now a lookup requires the use of a relationship. If there are no relationships in a database, there can be no lookups.

You already know how to create relationships. Look at how you create a lookup after you have established a relationship.

1. In the Invoices database, choose File, Define Fields to open the Define Fields dialog box.

2. Create a new text field called Customer Name. Click Options and, in the Entry Options dialog box, click the Looked-up Value radio button. The Lookup dialog box appears (see fig. 4.20).

3. Click the pop-up menu in the upper-right corner and choose the Clients relationship.

Fig. 4.20

You can't create a new lookup without using a relationship.

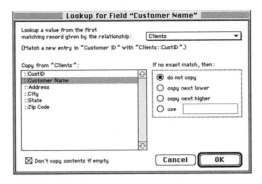

Because this field is going to display customer name information, select the related field ::Customer Name.

If you don't get a match on the relationship, you have some options from the radio buttons on the right of the Lookup dialog box. In this case, if you don't get a match, you don't want to copy any information over. If you do get a match and the related field is empty, performing the lookup has the effect of erasing your current information. You have the option to choose not to copy that empty information into the lookup field with the check box at the bottom.

4. Make sure the Don't Copy Contents If Empty check box is selected and click OK. Click OK again and click Done.

This might seem like a pointless option, but it isn't. You can refresh a lookup; you can recheck the match and copy information over again any time you want. If you already have information in a lookup field and you copy over empty information, your original information is lost.

The field should have been added to the bottom of your Invoices layout. If it wasn't, that means that one of your preference settings has been set so that newly created fields don't get added to your layout. To fix this, follow these steps:

1. Choose Edit, Preferences. Click the pop-up menu at the top of the Preferences dialog box and choose Layout.

2. Select the Add Newly Defined Fields to Current Layout check box. Click Done.

3. The new preference setting will take effect for any new fields you create in the future, but for the field you just created, you'll have to place it manually. Add the Customer Name field to the layout using the Field tool.

Lookup fields are not dynamic like related fields. For a lookup field to work, you need to change the value in your lookup trigger field. This is the field the relationship uses to match records. To trigger the Customer Name lookup field, follow these steps:

1. Tab into the Customer ID field.

2. Choose Edit, Select All to select the entire ID code, then choose Edit, Copy.

3. Choose Edit, Paste and tab out of the field to trigger the lookup. Notice that the new customer name field now shows the same information as the related ::Customer Name field. You had to refresh the Customer ID field to trigger the lookup, while the related field always showed the current information.

You should now be in the related ::Customer Name field. Change the customer name and tab out of the field. The Customer Name lookup field still displays the now outmoded information, although the information has changed in the related database. You have to trigger the lookup again to make it show the right information.

Another way to refresh a lookup field is to perform a *relookup*. This database only has one lookup field, but it's possible to have different lookup fields that utilize different relationships. A relookup triggers any lookup fields that use the field your cursor is in. For example, if your lookup trigger field is Customer ID, you need to put the cursor in that field before you run the relookup. A relookup affects all records in your found set. If you have 20 records in a found set, a relookup will refresh the lookup fields in all 20 records.

This is much simpler to do than it is to explain. Click in the related ::Customer ID field. Choose Mode, Relookup. You should see a message similar to the one shown in figure 4.21.

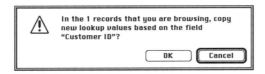

Fig. 4.21
The relookup warning gives you one last chance to change your mind before updating your lookup fields.

Click OK, and the Customer Name field will now have the current information. Now click in the lookup field Customer Name and change the data. Choose Window, Clients to bring the Clients database to the foreground. Check to see whether your change was reflected in the Clients database.

You'll find that it wasn't. That's because lookup fields only contain copies of the original information. Changing the copied information has no effect on the original information. This can lead to problems when you have several versions of the same information. How do you know which version is the right one?

Lookup fields behave in a similar fashion to related fields, but they have some disadvantages. Related fields make for smaller databases and consistent data because the information only exists in one place. With lookups, the information can be copied into several records, making data redundant and making database file sizes unnecessarily large.

By now, it probably seems that a lookup field is a poor substitute for a related field. In many cases, that's true. However, the same characteristics that make lookup fields undesirable for some applications make them very desirable for others.

One desirable feature is that lookups are relatively static. After you perform a lookup and copy the information, the data remains the same until either the match field is changed or you perform a relookup. This is good when you need to preserve a moment in time. Think of product pricing on an invoice. If you had a related price field, every time the price changed, you would have all of your old invoices showing current prices. That would be bad. A lookup field, on the other hand, would not be updated as the price for a product changed over time.

The other desirable feature is that lookups don't require an exact match to do their work. This doesn't sound that significant, but take a look at the following example.

A classic example is a table of shipping rates. All weights that fall in a certain range get a single rate. Weights in the next higher range get a higher rate. The same thing goes for telethon premiums, if you donate 20 dollars, you get a coffee mug. If you donate 25 dollars, you still get a mug; but if you donate 50 dollars, you get a videotape. The shipping rate example is a little more common. To create a shipping rate system, follow these steps:

1. Create a new file called Rates.

2. Create two number fields: Weight and Rate. Click Done to close the Define Fields dialog box.

3. Choose Mode, Layout, then choose Mode, New Layout. Name the new layout List View and select the Columnar Report radio button. Click OK to open the Specify Field Order dialog box.

4. Click Move All, then click OK to exit the Specify Field Order dialog box.

5. Choose Mode, Browse. Tab to the Weight field and enter **1**, then tab to the Rate field and enter **3.50**. Add new records until you have the following data set:

Weight	Rate
1	3.50
2	4.50
3	6.00
5	7.25
7.5	9.00
10	12.00
25	18.00
50	28.00
9999999999	ERROR

6. Create a second file called Shipments.

7. Create two number fields: Weight and Shipping Charges. Select the Shipping Charges field and click Options.

8. Click the Looked-Up Value radio button to open the Lookup dialog box.

9. Click the pop-up menu at the top of the dialog box. Because you don't have any relationships defined, your only option is Define Relationships. Choose Define Relationships to open the Define Relationships dialog box.

10. Click New to open the Open dialog box. Select the Rates database and click Open.

11. In the Edit Relationship dialog box, match the databases on the Weight and ::Weight fields. Click OK to close the Edit Relationship dialog box. Click Done to close the Define Relationships dialog box and return to the Lookup dialog box.

12. Select the ::Rate field. On the right side, select the Copy Next Higher radio button and click OK to close the Lookup dialog box. Click OK to close the Entry Options dialog box. Click Done to close the Define Fields dialog box.

Resize both databases so you can view them side by side (see fig. 4.22).

Fig. 4.22
With the Rates and Shipments databases side by side, you can see how the lookup copies the next highest value.

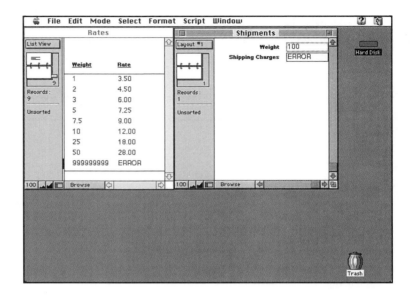

Note

A nice thing about FileMaker Pro 3.0 is that when you're in a dialog box that might require another operation to be done, such as create a relationship, you have access to that function without having to close the dialog box. You can define relationships from the Lookup dialog box, from the Specify Field dialog box, or from the Portal Setup dialog box.

In the Shipments database, tab to the Weight field and enter **.5**. Click out of the field and notice that the rate for a one pound shipment gets copied. Try a 1.5 pound shipment. You get the rate for two pounds. Try a 100 pound shipment. You get the ERROR message because it's beyond the maximum weight.

This is something that a straight relationship can't do. Relationships require an exact match to work properly—or do anything at all. Lookups can act with a sort of fuzzy logic. If you don't get an exact match, you can settle for the next higher match or the next lower match, or even some standard data that you can enter yourself. When exact matches aren't guaranteed, lookups are far preferable to related fields. Lookups are flexible.

To summarize, relationships are the fundamental way to link two databases. They are required if you want to view information from another database via related fields. Related fields by themselves work best if there is only one corresponding record in the related database. If there are multiple corresponding records in the related database, then you need to use related fields in a portal. A portal is a layout object that is capable of showing multiple related records in a list format.

Relationships are required to create lookup fields. Lookup fields copy information from a related database, while related fields only display the information. Changing information in a related field actually changes the information in the related database, while changing the information in a lookup field has no effect on the information in the related database.

Related fields require less space in the database than lookup fields, and there are no concerns about the legitimacy of different versions of the same piece of information. Lookups, on the other hand, are relatively static—only changing when the match field is changed or a relookup is performed. Because of this characteristic, they are ideal for capturing information in a specific time. Lookups also are more flexible than related fields in terms of the match fields. A lookup field does not require an exact match to work properly, while a related field does.

From Here...

In this chapter, you learned how to use related fields by themselves and with portals. You also learned the differences between related fields and lookup fields. This information is pretty fundamental to building databases in FileMaker Pro 3.0.

From here, you might want to read the following chapters:

- Chapter 3, "Creating and Printing Reports," teaches you how to use related fields in reports and as sort criteria.

- Chapter 5, "Working with Calculation Fields," describes how to perform calculations across multiple related records. This is useful in totaling line items on an invoice.

- In Chapter 9, "Converting Existing FileMaker Pro Databases to 3," now that you know how relationships work, you can apply this knowledge to converting some of your existing databases. This chapter is useful if you need to convert older FileMaker files to 3.0 files.

CHAPTER 5

Working with Calculation Fields

This chapter deals with calculation fields. With the advent of FileMaker Pro 3.0, there are more than 45 new functions, nearly doubling the number of powerful functions already in FileMaker Pro 2.1. Needless to say, this is a huge subject. Instead of painstakingly going through everything function by function, this chapter focuses on real-world examples, often using a combination of functions.

In this chapter, you learn about:

- Creating a calculation
- Text, Date, and Time calculations
- Using aggregate functions, including subtotaling a portal, and finding an average
- Incorporating logical functions into your database
- Creating summary calculations
- Using status functions to monitor your database

Creating a Calculation

A Calculation field is a field type that uses a function to manipulate variables and field values in a record or set of records. Because your field data can include text, dates, times, or numbers, FileMaker has various functions or predefined formulas to help make manipulating the data easy. Included in these functions are formulas that help you summarize values, work with repeating fields, and perform financial, trigonometric, or logical operations. Furthermore, FileMaker Pro 3.0 includes Status functions, which are new functions that help you customize a database.

When you first create a Calculation field, FileMaker displays the Specify Calculation dialog box shown in figure 5.1. The dialog box is divided into several areas. The upper-left area displays a list of the database fields, and a pop-up menu that lets you switch to related databases. The top middle part shows a list of operators you can use to tie the functions together. The upper-right area shows a list of the functions. Notice that the function list box also includes a pop-up menu that lets you display the list box by name or by function.

Fig. 5.1
You define a calculation in the Specify Calculation dialog box by entering the formula into the formula box.

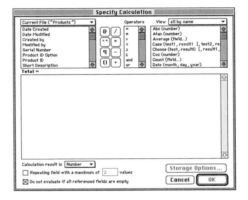

Note

If you view the function list box by its default, View All By Name, you'll never find the Status functions. To use the Status functions, display the list by type, or choose Status Functions from the View pop-up menu.

The bottom part of the dialog box is the formula area. This is where you store the calculation's formula. To create a formula, you can type it in, select the fields, operators, and functions by the point-and-click method, or use a combination of both. Now look at the first type of calculation functions: Text functions.

Note

For the most part, you don't have to worry about creating an invalid Calculation field. When you click the OK button to close the Specify Calculation dialog box, FileMaker checks the formula to make sure it's valid. When you make a mistake, FileMaker tells you there's an error, and often tells you where the problem lies.

While this validity check is great, it only checks the syntax of the formula. So, if you meant for a Calculation field to total the subtotal and tax in a database and instead it defines the field to add the tax to the commission rate, FileMaker won't alert you to a problem.

Using Text Calculations

Perhaps the most confusing types of calculations are the Text calculations; they don't deal with the conventional math you learned in grade school. The arguments and results are text, not numbers, so the whole concept is different.

There are several "classic" reasons to use Text calculations. Often, you don't have control over the kind of data imported into a FileMaker database. A tab-delimited file might have come from a mainframe, a spreadsheet, or even a word processing document. At any rate, you often get data that needs to be manipulated. Text calculations are the massaging implement of choice.

Perhaps the most common text problem is the need to extract first and last names from a full name. Sometimes you have a salutation like Mr. or Ms.; and sometimes you don't have a salutation. It gets sticky really fast. Extracting this kind of information also uses the same techniques you would use to parse out something like an e-mail message as well, so the name extraction is a good sample problem for text calculations. While it used to be labor intensive to do all this in FileMaker 2.1, it has actually gotten easier with the new 3.0 version of FileMaker.

Extracting the First, Last, or Middle Name from a Full Name

This example creates a database to show you how you can extract a first name from a full name:

1. Choose File, New to open the New Database dialog box.
2. Type **Text Calculations** in the Create a New File text box and click Save.
3. The Define Fields dialog box opens. Create a new text field called Name and click Done.
4. Create a new record and type your own first and last name in the Name field.

5. Choose File, Define Fields and create a new calculation field called First Name.

   This opens the Specify Calculation dialog box.

6. Click the View pop-up menu and choose Text Functions. The third function down is LeftWords (text, number of words). Double-click it to move it into the calculation box.

   The LeftWords function returns any number of words you want from a field or a string of text, starting from the left side. For example:

   LeftWords ("The cow jumped over the moon", 2)

   This would return "The cow." You can use a field name in place of the text string if you want. That's how it's usually used.

   The LeftWords function has two arguments. The text argument is the text you want to pull words from. In this case, pull the first name from the Name field. Highlight the word `text`, then double-click the Name field to move it to the function.

   The second argument of the LeftWords function is the number of words you want to pull from the text. Because you only want the first name, highlight the phrase `number of words` (you can also double-click to select it) and type the number **1**.

7. The last thing you need to do is make sure your calculation result is formatted properly. At the bottom of the Specify Calculation dialog box, click the Calculation Result Is pop-up menu and choose Text, because your calculation is returning a text result. If you forget to do this and leave it formatted as a number, you can get some strange results (see the following note).

   After you format your text properly and enter your equation, the Specify Calculation dialog box should look similar to figure 5.2.

8. Click OK, then click Done. The First Name field should display your first name.

Note

When you enter text in a number field, FileMaker disregards the text information and reads only the number values. For example, "1 for all and all for 1" would evaluate to 11. This gets a little more complicated when a calculation field returns text information but is formatted to have a numeric result. If there is a number anywhere in the text string, FileMaker returns the number value.

Multiple numbers work the same. If there are no numbers in the text string, FileMaker tries to evaluate the text result as Boolean. A Boolean calculation returns either True or False. A Yes or No works out to the same thing, as does a 1 or 0, the digital equivalent of true or false. FileMaker doesn't even need the whole word. T, F, Y, or N are just as good.

Therefore, if you have a calculation that returns a text result and you leave the result format set to number, FileMaker checks the first letter to see if it's a T or Y. If it is (and there are no numbers in the text), the calculation evaluates to 1 (true). If it's anything else, the calculation evaluates to 0.

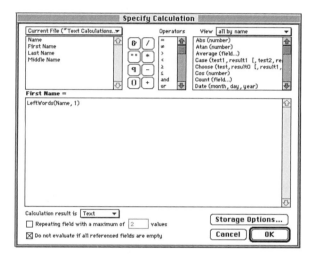

Fig. 5.2
This calculation will return the first word in the Name field.

To extract the last name rather than the first, repeat the previous steps but choose RightWords instead of LeftWords. The RightWords function returns any number of words you want from a field or a string of text, starting from the right side. Using the previous example:

> RightWords ("The cow jumped over the moon", 2)

This would return "the moon." Just like the LeftWords function, you usually use a field name instead of a text string.

The MiddleWords function is slightly different from the LeftWords and RightWords functions. It has an extra argument, starting word. The starting word is a number that tells FileMaker where to begin extracting words. Using the previous example again:

> MiddleWords ("The cow jumped over the moon", 3, 2)

This would return "jumped over."

So, you've set up formulas to extract first name, last name, and middle name and everything is working great, right? Well, probably not. The problem is that there are many ways to enter a name. Here are some of the possibilities:

Chris Moyer

Mr. Chris Moyer

Christopher James Moyer

Mr. Christopher James Moyer

Chris Moyer, Sr.

Mr. Chris Moyer, Jr.

C. J. Moyer

As you can see, there are lots of possible name formats. Each set of data is different. You need to look at your own data to see what kind of hoops you'll have to jump through.

In the next example, I'm going to go for the worst possible situation and say that all of the above name formats will be possible in the data.

Extracting the First Name—A Better Way

If you have a salutation such as Ms. or Mr., you need to extract the first name from the second word. As you can see from the previous list, you can't just test for a period at the end of the first word—some people use their first initial. Think of F. Scott Fitzgerald. You will actually have to test for Ms., Mr., Miss, Mrs., and Dr. Thus, the logic for detecting salutations is:

If the first word of the Name field is Ms., Mr., Miss, or Mrs., then the first name is the second word of the Name field.

If the first word of the Name field is not Ms., Mr., Miss, or Mrs., then the first name is the first word of the Name field.

The If function is most efficient if you just need to test for one condition, although you can nest If functions or combine tests to test for several conditions. (For more information on nest If functions, see the section "Working with Logical Functions," later in this chapter.) An example of a simple If statement might be:

```
If (Today's Date - Invoice Date > 30, "Past Due", "")
```

This calculation checks the age of an invoice to see if it's past due. If it is, it returns "Past Due." If it isn't, it returns nothing. (Because there isn't anything between the quotes in the false argument, it literally returns no text.)

The first argument, the test, needs to be a true or false (Boolean) statement. In the previous example, an invoice is past due or it isn't. Result one is what gets returned when the test is true. Result two is what gets returned when the result is false.

The salutation test checks whether the first word equals one of several possible salutations. If you think of any others you might run into, maybe "Sir," you can add as many as you like.

To implement the test in the First Name calculation:

1. Choose File, Define Fields and then double-click the First Name field to open the Specify Calculation dialog box.

2. Press Return at the end of the calculation to move the cursor to the next line.

3. In the View pop-up menu, choose Logical functions. Double-click the If function into the Calculation area (see fig. 5.3).

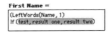

First Name =
(LeftWords(Name, 1)
If (test, result one, result two)

Fig. 5.3
The If function evaluates a test and returns a value based on the results of that test.

4. The first line of the calculation already contains the function to extract the first word of the Name field, so select the entire first line of the calculation and choose Edit, Copy or press ⌘-C to copy the selected text.

5. Highlight the `test` portion of the If function and choose Edit, Paste or press ⌘-V to paste the calculation on top of `test`.

6. In the Operators list box, double-click the = symbol. You can also just type = on your keyboard.

7. Click the quotes button or type two quotation marks to the right of the equal sign. Type **Ms** between the quotes, making sure you don't have any spaces on either side.

> **Note**
>
> You'll notice in the formula that you don't include periods after the salutation in the If statements. The LeftWords function returns just the word—no punctuation. Therefore, if you included the period after the salutation, the If test would compare Ms to Ms. and never give you a true result.

II

Enhancing Databases

So far, all you're testing for is whether the first word in the Name field is Ms. To test for other possibilities, you need to string several tests together using the OR operator.

8. Because you have five nearly identical tests, the fast way to set them up is to copy the first test, including the OR and the space following it, and then paste it four times. Now all you have to do is change the Ms to Mr, Miss, Mrs, and Dr.

When you finish, the test area of your calculation should look similar to figure 5.4.

Fig. 5.4

The If statements in this formula determine whether the first value in the Name field is Ms, Mr, Miss, Mrs, or Dr.

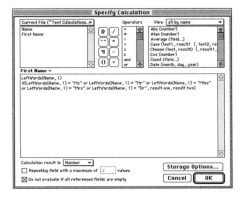

Now you have a test that determines if the first word of the Name field is a salutation. If it is, meaning if the test is true, then result one needs to be a formula for extracting the second word. To set this up, follow these steps:

1. Highlight the argument `result one`.

2. Choose Text Functions from the View pop-up menu and double-click the MiddleWords function.

3. Replace the text argument with the Name field. Type **2** for the starting word, and **1** for the number of words.

   If the test is false, meaning there is no salutation, then you can just use the formula on the first line of the calculation. Copy the first line and paste it in for `result two`. Delete the first line and your finished calculation should look like figure 5.5.

4. Click OK, then click Done.

Try changing your name field so you have a salutation in front of your name. Does the first name field still work properly? It should. If not, check the calculation again.

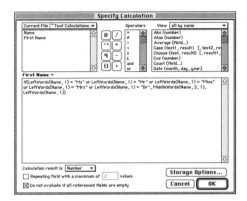

Fig. 5.5
This calculation returns the second word in the Name field if the first word is a saluta-tion.

The Ultra Bulletproof First Name Extraction for the Paranoid

When I do presentations, I always run into that one "glass-is-half empty" per-son who says, "Yeah, but what if THIS happens?" This section is for that per-son. If you are a little more relaxed about things, you might want to skip to the next section.

Here's a possibility: what if the people entering the data, that you will ulti-mately import, sometimes put a period after Ms., Mr., and so on, but some-times forget? If the actual first word is Ms or Mr, then the previous test will fail—Ms and Mr will become the first name.

You often cannot control the data you receive. In such an environment, it's not uncommon to get what I call "dirty" data—data that needs some clean-ing up. Sometimes this means you have to load it into a word processor and do search and replace operations on it before it will even import properly.

Say that you need to allow for the possibility of salutations that may or may not end with a period. The logic for this test would go like this:

> If the first word of the Name contains the text string "Ms" or "Mr" or "Miss" or "Mrs" or "Dr," then the first word is a salutation and the first name is the second word.

There is one small problem, however. If you look through the functions list, there is no Contains function. You can kind of cheat that functionality by relying on the Position function. Here's the Position function:

```
Position (text, search string, start, occurrence)
```

The Position function tells you at what character you can find a given string. Here are two examples:

Given: field Name contains "Dr. Laura Stahl"

```
Position (Name, "Dr", 1, 1)
```

This returns 1, because "Dr" starts at character 1.

```
Position (Name, "r", 1, 2)
```

This returns 8, because the second occurrence of "r" is at character 8.

This is all fine and good, but how does this work as a Contains function? Here's how: FileMaker will evaluate the test argument as Boolean; it's either true or false. If it's zero, it's false. If it's *anything other than zero*, FileMaker considers it to be true. Therefore, if you use a position statement in place of the test and the position statement finds the text string, it will return a number greater than zero, and will therefore evaluate to true.

The new fault-tolerant First Name field would now have a calculation that looks like the one in figure 5.6.

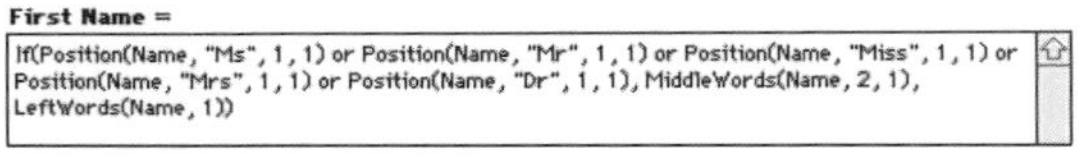

Fig. 5.6
This calculation can handle just about any combination of name you throw at it.

First Name =
```
If(Position(Name, "Ms", 1, 1) or Position(Name, "Mr", 1, 1) or Position(Name, "Miss", 1, 1) or
Position(Name, "Mrs", 1, 1) or Position(Name, "Dr", 1, 1), MiddleWords(Name, 2, 1),
LeftWords(Name, 1))
```

Extracting the Middle Name—A Better Way

So now you have the first name working, but what about middle names? To find out if there is a middle name, you not only have to find out if there's a salutation, but also a suffix. You then have to check the number of remaining words. Look at these examples:

Mr. Chris Moyer, Sr.

Mr. Christopher James Moyer

There are three words after the salutation for both of these names, but in one case that means there is a middle name, in the other that means there is a suffix. The logic for middle names might run as follows:

If the Name field contains five words and there is a salutation and a suffix, there is a middle name.

If the Name field contains four words and there is a salutation but no suffix, there is a middle name.

If the Name field contains four words and there is no salutation but there is a suffix, there is a middle name.

If the Name field contains three words and there is no salutation and no suffix, there is a middle name.

To test for a suffix, you can either check for a period at the end of the last word in the Name field, or you can check for a comma at the end of the next-to-last word in the Name field. I prefer the comma test, because someone could conceivably spell out Esquire instead of Esq. In either case, the next-to-last word would have a comma at the end of it:

Mr. Chris Moyer, Esq.

Mr. Chris Moyer, Esquire

So regarding suffixes, the logic would be:

If the next-to-last word ends with a comma, the last name is the next-to-last word in the Name field.

If the next-to-last word doesn't end with a comma, the last name is the last word in the Name field.

Because it's unlikely that there would be a comma anywhere else in the name, you could probably just test to see if a comma is anywhere in the name. To make sure you're looking at the last name, you need see if the last letter of the next-to-last word is a comma. This is much more convoluted than it sounds.

To find the next-to-last word, you first need to find the last two words:

```
RightWords (Name, 2)
```

To get the next-to-last word, you need the first word of the last two words:

```
LeftWords (RightWords (Name, 2), 1)
```

To get the last character of the next-to-last word and to check to see if it's a comma:

```
Right (LeftWords (RightWords (Name, 2), 1), 1) = ","
```

Now that you can do that, you need to combine the test for salutations with the test for a suffix and check the number of words actually composing the name. If you have three words, not counting salutation and suffix, then you have a middle name. The test would look like this:

```
If (WordCount (Name) -
If (Right (LeftWords (RightWords (Name, 2), 1), 1) = ",", 1, 0) -
If (Position (Name, "Ms", 1, 1) or Position (Name, "Mr", 1, 1) or
Position (Name, "Miss", 1, 1) or Position (Name, "Mrs", 1, 1) or
Position (Name, "Dr", 1, 1), 1, 0)
=3
```

Pretty frightening, huh? It gets worse. Now that you know there's a middle name, you need to figure out where it is. If there's a salutation, it's the third word. If there isn't a salutation, it's the second word. Figure 5.7 shows how the final formula would look.

Fig. 5.7
This calculation returns the middle name of the value entered in the Name field.

```
Middle Name =
If(WordCount(Name) -
If(Right(LeftWords(RightWords(Name, 2), 1), 1) = ",", 1, 0) -
If(Position(Name, "Ms", 1, 1) or Position(Name, "Mr", 1, 1) or Position(Name, "Miss", 1, 1) or
Position(Name, "Mrs", 1, 1) or Position(Name, "Dr", 1, 1), 1, 0)
= 3,
If(Position(Name, "Ms", 1, 1) or Position(Name, "Mr", 1, 1) or Position(Name, "Miss", 1, 1) or
Position(Name, "Mrs", 1, 1) or Position(Name, "Dr", 1, 1), MiddleWords(Name, 3, 1),
MiddleWords(Name, 2, 1))
, "")
```

Extracting the Last Name—A Better Way

Just to save your sanity, assume there will always be a last name, although that's not always the case in the real world. Even if you know that a last name is missing from a particular incoming record, that doesn't really help you. You cannot sort meaningfully or send mail without a last name, so you should probably reject that record from your database. If your data is much more uniform than you are assuming for these worst-case scenario examples, you can probably just use a WordCount function to check for a missing last name. With the current examples, though, it's almost impossible to determine whether a last name is present.

Because you've now allowed the possibility of having a suffix, all you really need to do to locate the last name is to find out whether there is a suffix. The logic is:

> If there is a suffix, the last name is the next-to-last word in the Name field.

> If there is no suffix, the last name is the last word in the Name field.

Figure 5.8 shows the calculation.

Fig. 5.8
This calculation removes only the last name from the Name field; it ignores any suffix that the field might contain.

```
Last Name =
If(Right(LeftWords(RightWords(Name, 2), 1), 1) = ",", LeftWords (RightWords (Name, 2), 1),
RightWords(Name, 1))
```

To create the calculation, follow the steps outlined below:

1. Change your last name formula so it reads like the formula in figure 5.8.

2. Click OK and click Done.

Try typing every possible combination of names with salutations and suffixes and make sure your First Name, Middle Name, and Last Name fields work.

By the way, if you want to break out the salutations or suffixes as well, those are easy adaptations from the calculations you already performed. Figures 5.9 and 5.10 show the formulas.

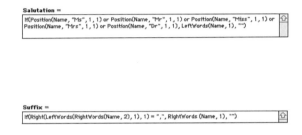

Fig. 5.9

This calculation extracts the salutation from the Name field.

Fig. 5.10

This calculation extracts the suffix from the Name field.

Using Date Calculations

After those text calculations, you're going to think Date calculation functions are a snap. Date calculation functions let you calculate dates or manipulate date information.

The following example takes you step-by-step through how to use Date calculations:

1. Choose File, New to open the New Database dialog box.

2. Type **Date Calculations** in the Create a New File text box and click Save.

3. In the Define Fields dialog box, create a new Date field called Start Date. Create another date field called End Date. Create a calculation field called Date Number, which equals the Start Date field. Make sure the calculation result is formatted as a number (see fig. 5.11).

Fig. 5.11
This calculation
will convert the
Start Date value
into a number.

Formatted as a number ——

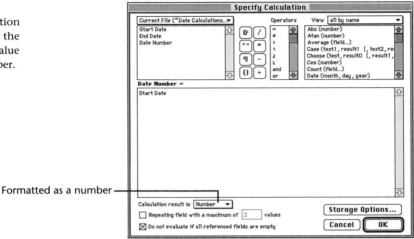

4. Click OK and click Done.

5. Choose Mode, New Record to create a new record and type your own birth date in the Start Date field.

Look at the Date Number field. My birth date, 9/29/63, has a Date Number value of 716877. This is a big number. What does it mean?

When you formatted the Date Number field as a number, you forced FileMaker to show the date as it's formatted for internal storage. 716877 is how FileMaker stores 9/29/63. It's a serial number of sorts. It's actually the number of days that have elapsed since the date 1/1/0001. Type that date into Start Date and you'll get a 1 in Date Number.

By the way, this is a very unconventional start date. Most database system use January 3, 1904 as their serial number start date. Why is FileMaker 1/1/0001? I have no idea.

Anyway, the upshot of this is that when you subtract one date from another, the number you get back will be the number of days between the two dates. If you want the number of weeks, you'll need to divide that number by seven. In a similar fashion, if you want to add a week to a date, you need to add seven days to it.

To find the number of days that have elapsed since your birth date:

1. Change the value in Start Date back to your birth date.

2. Click in End Date and press ⌘- - (a hyphen). You can also choose Edit, Paste Special, Current Date.

3. Choose File, Define Fields and create a new calculation field called Elapsed Days.

4. In the Specify Calculation dialog box, make the Elapsed Days equal to:

   ```
   End Date - Start Date
   ```

5. Make sure the Calculation result is Number, click OK, and click Done. The Elapsed Days field now shows the number of days that have gone by since you were born.

You can also add dates to other fields or values. For example, you could use this technique to determine a future billing date for an invoice or to calculate when a library book is due to return. To add days to a date:

1. Choose File, Define Fields and create a new calculation field called Week Later.

2. In the Specify Calculation dialog box, make the following calculation:

   ```
   End Date + 7
   ```

3. Format the Calculation result as a date and click OK. Click Done, and you'll see that Week Later shows a date one week after the End Date.

What if you want a date exactly one month into the future? That's a little different, because different months have different lengths. It's not a matter of adding 30 days or 31 days or 28 days for February (except in Leap Year).

Before you get into adding a month, you need to learn some other date functions. First, take a look at the Month function by working through the following example:

1. Choose File, Define Fields and create a new calculation field called End Date Month.

2. In the Specify Calculation dialog box, choose View, Date Functions. Double-click the Month function to move it to the calculation area. Highlight the date argument and double-click the End Date field. The formula should read like this:

   ```
   Month (End Date)
   ```

3. Format the result as a number, because you're returning the number of the month. Click OK.

4. Create another calculation field called Month Name. Again, choose View, Date Functions. Double-click the MonthName function to move it to the calculation area. Highlight the date argument and double-click the End Date field.

II

Enhancing Databases

The formula should read like this:

```
MonthName (End Date)
```

5. Format the result as text, because you're returning a name. Click OK.

FileMaker also includes several calculation functions to determine the day of the month or the name of the day. These functions can be helpful when you need to know what day a specific date falls on. To calculate the day of the month follow these three simple steps:

1. Create a Calculation field called Day.

2. Choose View, Date Functions and move the Day function to the calculation area. Highlight the date argument and double-click the End Date field. The formula should read like this:

```
Day (End Date)
```

3. Format the result as a number, because you're returning the day of the month. Click OK.

To find out the name of the day a particular date falls on, you use the DayName function. To test this function, create a Calculation field called Day Name.

1. Choose View, Date Functions.

2. Double-click the DayName function to move it to the calculation area. Highlight the date argument and double-click the End Date field. The formula should read like this:

```
DayName (End Date)
```

3. Format the result as text, because you're returning a name. Click OK.

You can also use calculation functions to isolate the year from a Date field. This comes in handy when you want to add years to a Date field. Create one more calculation field called Year.

1. Choose View, Date Functions.

2. Double-click the Year function to move it to the calculation area. Highlight the date argument and double-click the End Date field. The formula should read like this:

```
Year (End Date)
```

3. Format the result as a number, because you're returning the year. Click OK and Done and survey the results of your handiwork.

You should now see the month, month name, day, day name, and year of the End Date. Now that you know how to pull out the month, day, and year as separate pieces of data, you can easily add months, days, or years to any date. At this point, you can now create the calculation to return a value exactly one month after the End Date. To do so, work through the following steps:

1. Choose File, Define Fields and create a new calculation field called Month Later.

2. Choose View, Date Functions. Double-click the Date function to move it to the calculation area.

3. Highlight the month argument and double-click the Month function.

4. Highlight the date argument of the Month function and double-click the End Date field.

5. Click an insertion point right after Month (End Date).

6. Click the "+" button and type a **1**.

7. Highlight the day argument and double-click the Day function.

8. Highlight the date argument of the Day function and double-click the End Date field.

9. Highlight the year argument and double-click the Year function.

10. Highlight the date argument of the Year function and double-click the End Date field. The formula should read like this:

    Date (Month(End Date) + 1, Day (End Date), Year (End Date))

11. Format the Calculation result as a date and click OK. Click Done and check to see that Month Later contains a date one month later than End Date.

Now, regardless of whether a month has 28, 30, or 31 days, this calculation will always return a date on the same day of the month one month after End Date. By adding or subtracting values to month, day, and year arguments, you can calculate dates that are a year and a day in the past, six months into the future, or on the last day of the month.

Actually, that's a little tricky. To do the last day of whatever month you're in, you add one to the month argument, set the day argument to one, then subtract one from the entire function, like so:

```
Date (Month(End Date) + 1, 1, Year (End Date))-1
```

Make sure you format the result as text.

Okay, here's a nasty one. What if you want to find the number of working days between two dates? If you subtract Start Date from End Date, you get a number of days. If you divide that number by seven, you get some number, but it's unlikely that the number of days would divide by seven evenly. There will probably be a remainder. Say it's six with a remainder of two days. Take the number of whole weeks, in this case six, and multiply by five, the number of working days in a week.

Next, you add the remaining two days that are in that fraction of a week. There's a special case you need to watch out for, though. What if the Start Date is a Friday and the End Date is the following Monday? The total elapsed time would be three days, but you need to subtract two days for the weekend whenever the End Date is earlier in the week than the Start Date.

So, to find the number of whole weeks, use the Int function, which disregards any decimals:

```
Int ((End Date - Start Date)/7)
```

To get actual working days, multiply that by five, and then add the leftover days. To find leftover days, you need to find the modulus of the days/7 result, also known as the remainder. The formula would be:

```
Int ((End Date - Start Date)/7)*5 + Mod (End Date - Start Date, 7)
```

To determine whether you wrapped around a weekend during the remainder days, take into account FileMaker's day numbering system. Sunday is the first day of the week for FileMaker. If you wrapped around the weekend, then the Start Date day of the week will be greater than the End Date day of the week. For example, Friday, day six, will be greater than Tuesday, day three. If the day of the week for Start Date is greater than the day of the week for End Date, then you did include a weekend, and you need to subtract those two weekend days. By the way, if the days of the week are equal, then there will be no remainder because it works out to a whole week.

The whole calculation would read like this:

```
Int ((End Date - Start Date)/7)*5 + Mod (End Date - Start Date, 7)
➥- If (DayofWeek (End Date) < DayofWeek (Start Date), 2, 0)
```

Tip

Claris' TechInfo database, used by their Technical Support people, has a cool way to extend this formula so it also takes into account any holidays that may have reduced the number of actual working days. It uses lookups, and even though FileMaker Pro 3.0 has relationships, straight relationships still can't match the functionality of a lookup when it comes to using data when there's no exact match on the trigger fields. If you're interested in accounting for holidays when you calculate working days, see Appendix A, because this solution has more to do with lookups and relationships than with calculations. The TechInfo Database is available on most online services or at the Claris Web site at **http://www.claris.com**.

Including Time Calculations

FileMaker stores time data in a similar way to the method it uses for date data. It stores time as a number value, that number being the number of seconds that have elapsed since midnight. Stay in the Date Calculations database to work with the time fields because there are some interesting calculations involving elapsed hours between two dates.

1. Choose File, Define Fields to display the Define Fields dialog box and create a Time field called Start Time. Create a second Time field called End Time.

2. Create a calculation field called Elapsed Time and in the Specify Calculation dialog box that appears, create the following formula:

   End Time – Start Time

   Make sure you format the result as time.

3. Click OK and click Done.

4. Tab to the Start Time field and enter **1:30 AM**.

5. Tab to the End Time field and choose Edit, Paste Special, Current Time. Look at the Elapsed Time field and note the result. It will be formatted in hours:minutes:seconds.

This is fine for finding the elapsed time between two times on the same day, but what if the times are on different days? This sounds easy, but it requires a lot of planning. Take a look at the logic that the formula would require. You quickly see that such a formula would be very difficult to create. The logic is as follows:

> Each full day is 24 hours. For the sake of this example, each day will equal a working day—eight hours, from 8:00 AM to 5:00 PM.
>
> If the Start Time is later in the day than End Time, then subtract one day (eight hours) from the total amount of elapsed hours. If you have a Start Time at 4:45 PM on a Tuesday, and an End Time at 8:15 AM on a Thursday, two days have elapsed. That makes 16 hours. However, you really only have one full day: Wednesday. Tuesday only has 15 minutes and Thursday only has 15 minutes. If the Start Time were earlier in the day than the End Time, that would mean there was at least a full day between the two times and you could rely on the date math being right. Because the Start Time is later in the day than the End Time, you're over by one day and should subtract eight hours.
>
> Accounting for lunch breaks, the working hours in an eight hour day are from 8:00 AM to 12:00 PM, and 1:00 PM to 5:00 PM. If the End

Time is after 1:00 PM, nine hours will be subtracted from the time: one hour for 12:00 PM to 1:00 PM and eight hours for 12:00 midnight to 8:00 AM. If the End Time is between 8:00 AM and 12:00 PM, only eight hours are subtracted from it.

For Start Times between 8:00 AM and 12:00 PM, the working hours for that day are calculated by taking the time it takes to get to 12:00 PM and adding four hours for the afternoon time. This is only for when Start and End Times are on different dates.

If you're not accounting for lunch breaks, then each day is actually nine hours.

Okay, so this can get pretty convoluted in a hurry.

Working with Aggregate Functions

Aggregate functions are functions that work across multiple records or multiple repeats in a repeating field. If you're using relationships, for example, to show line items in a portal on an invoice, Aggregate functions are the way you can subtotal several individual line items, or find an average number of items sold per invoice, or anything that has to do with pulling information from more than one record. See Chapter 4, "Using Lookups and Relationships," for more information. By the way, you don't have to have a portal to use Aggregate functions—you just need a relationship.

Subtotaling a portal

To illustrate how to subtotal values in a portal, use a simple database that contains related Number fields. As you can see in figure 5.12, the portal contains a total of individual invoices. While it's nice to know the separate totals, it would be even better to include a customer total. Luckily, this is very easy to do. To follow along with this example, open or create a database that contains related Number fields then complete the following steps.

Note

If you need more information on working with related fields and set up data relationships, see Chapter 4, "Using Lookups and Relationships."

---

1. Choose File, Define Fields and enter **Customer Total** in the Define Fields text box. Then select the Calculation radio button and click Create.

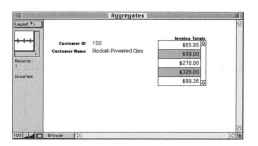

Fig. 5.12
You can create a total of the Invoice Totals field, even though the values reside in a separate database.

2. Choose View, Aggregate Functions. Double-click the Sum (field) function to move it to the calculation area.

3. Choose the relationship for the related Number field (in this case Invoices) from the Relationships pop-up menu in the Specify Calculation dialog box.

4. Highlight the `field` argument and double-click the Number field you want to subtotal. The formula should read

   `Sum(Related Database::Subtotal Number field)`

   or, as in this example,

   `Sum(Invoices::Invoice Totals)`

5. Make sure the Calculation result is a number, click OK, and click Done. Figure 5.13 shows that the Customer Total Calculation field adds the values in the Invoice Totals field together.

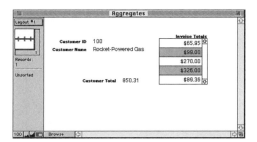

Fig. 5.13
The Customer Total Calculation field totals the Invoice Totals for each record.

> **Note**
>
> Notice that when you use a related field in a calculation, FileMaker actually displays both the field name and the relationship the field is accessed through. This is good, because you can have more than one relationship to the same database. It's important to be able to see what match field is controlling the access to the field.

Finding an Average Invoice

You can have a database create a relationship with itself. When you do this, you can have Aggregate functions give you values that in prior versions of FileMaker Pro, you could only get with summary fields.

You still need to have a match field, and if you want to do math with all records, which is what you need to do if you want to find out, for example, what your average invoice subtotal is, you need to create a field that is guaranteed to have the same value for each record. The best way to do this is to create a constant value field, a calculation that just equals a number. To do this, follow these steps:

1. Choose File, New and create a database called Averages.

2. In the Define Fields dialog box that appears, enter **Salary** in the Name text box and create the field as a Number field.

3. Create another field named Constant as a Calculation field and make sure it's formatted as a Number field.

4. Create a final Calculation field called Average Salary. FileMaker then displays the Specify Calculation dialog box.

5. Choose the Aggregate functions from the View pop-up menu.

6. Double-click the Average (field) function to move it to the formula area.

7. From the Current File pop-up menu, select the Define Relationships option.

8. Click New in the Define Relationships dialog box and double-click the Averages file in the Open dialog box to select it as the related field.

9. The Edit Relationship dialog box appears. Select the Constant field in both of the field boxes (see fig. 5.14). Click OK to close the dialog box. Click Done to close the Define Relationships dialog box.

Fig. 5.14
Create a self-relationship, relating the Constant field to itself.

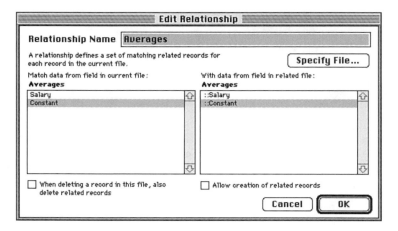

10. Double-click the ::Salary field to replace the `field` argument in the Average Salary formula (see fig. 5.15). Click OK to close the Specify Calculations dialog box.

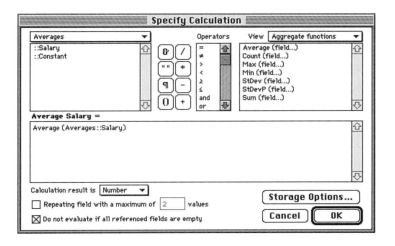

Fig. 5.15
The Average Salary field relies on the related Constant field to work correctly.

11. Click Done to close the Define Fields dialog box.

12. Press the Tab key to enter the Salary field and type **43000**.

13. Choose Mode, New Record and enter **76000** in the Salary field.

14. As you continue entering new values in the Salary field, the Average Salary calculate the average of Salary field values.

Caution

I don't know how many times I've created a calculation of this nature and had it not work right—I forgot to select the field through the relationship instead of choosing it from the Current File field list. If you're doing Aggregate calculations with a self-relationship and you're not getting the right values, you probably forgot to select the field through the relationship. It's a very easy mistake to make.

Finding the Number of Prior Invoices

Say you want to give a customer a discount, but you don't know how good of a customer they are. It would be helpful if you had a quick way of finding out how many orders this customer had placed with you before. What you need is a calculation that, given a particular customer number, will tell you how many invoices the customer has in the database.

First, you need to create a self-relationship based on Customer ID. Do this because you only want to count the invoices for a specific customer, so you need to match on the one field that uniquely identifies a customer—Customer ID.

1. Choose File, New and create a database called Customers.

2. In the Define Fields dialog box that appears, enter **Customer ID** in the Name text box and create the field as a Number field.

3. Create another Number field named Invoice.

4. Create a final Calculation field called Past Invoices. FileMaker then displays the Specify Calculation dialog box.

5. Choose the Aggregate functions from the View pop-up menu.

6. Double-click the Count (field) function to move it to the formula area.

7. From the Current File pop-up menu, select the Define Relationships option.

8. Click New in the Define Relationships dialog box and double-click the Customers file in the Open dialog box to select it as the related field.

9. The Edit Relationship dialog box appears. Select the Customer ID field in both of the field boxes and click OK to close the dialog box. Click Done to close the Define Relationships dialog box.

10. Double-click the ::Customer ID field to replace the `field` argument in the Average Salary formula. Click OK to close the Specify Calculations dialog box.

11. Click Done to close the Define Fields dialog box.

Because you're only counting fields, you can choose almost any field from this relationship. For example, if you use ::Customer ID, your calculation should now look like this:

```
Count (Customers::Customer ID)
```

This calculation will work fine, but there's one minor glitch. When you create a new invoice for a customer, that new invoice is included in the count. If a customer had never ordered from you before, because you just created an invoice for their first order, this Prior Invoices field will show one, which is wrong. This isn't a terrible thing, but strictly speaking, the current invoice should not be reflected in a *prior* invoices calculation. To fix this, just subtract one from the whole calculation. The final calculation should look like this:

```
Count (Invoices Cust ID::Customer ID) - 1
```

Make sure the result is formatted as a number and click OK. Try duplicating the current invoice a few times and watch the Prior Invoices field increase as you do.

Aggregate Functions—Working in a Single Database

Now that you know to use Aggregate functions with related fields, take a quick look at using them for fields in a single database. Earlier versions of FileMaker Pro let you use the Aggregate functions only with repeating Number fields. However, with FileMaker Pro 3.0 you can use these functions with multiple Number fields. For example, add the Number fields Item Cost 1, Item Cost 2, Item Cost 3, and Item Cost 4 to the Customer database. Now, take a look at how to create a field that uses Aggregate functions to average these fields. To do so, follow these steps:

1. Choose File, Define Field.

2. Enter **Average Cost** in the Field Name text box. Then select the Calculation Type option and click Create.

3. Choose Aggregate Functions from the View pop-up menu and double-click the Average function to add it to the formula box.

4. Double-click the Item Cost 1 field to add it to the formula box and enter a comma after the field. Repeat this process until you've included all four fields. When you finish, your formula should look like this:

   Average (Item Cost 1, Item Cost 2, Item Cost 3, Item Cost 4)

5. Click OK to accept the script then click Done to close the Define Fields dialog box.

As you enter values in the four Number fields, you'll see that the Average Cost field correctly averages these values. Using the same format for the calculation, you can also determine the count, the maximum value, the minimum value, the standard deviation of the sample or population, and the sum of the fields. In fact, if you want to experiment with the functions, you can just replace the Average function in the formula with any of the other function names.

Using Aggregate Functions with Multiple Repeating Fields

Going a step further, you can use the Aggregate functions to add multiple repeating fields or a mixture of repeating fields and non-repeating fields in a single calculation. You'll find these types of calculations helpful when your database includes both types of fields.

Working with Logical Functions

In prior releases of FileMaker Pro, the only logical function was the If function. The use of the If function is covered earlier in this chapter in the section "Text, Date, and Time Calculations." FileMaker Pro 3.0 has several new logical functions, so the If function now has company. These new functions are:

```
Case (test1, result1 [, test2, result2, default result]…)
Choose (test, Result 0 [, result1, result2]…)
IsEmpty (field)
IsValid (field)
```

The Case and Choose functions work in a similar fashion to the If function. You have a test or tests, and you get a result back based on the test. Use the Case function for situations where you need to test for several possible situations. For example, suppose you have an employee database and each employee can work for one of several different departments in a company. Suddenly, a new organizational scheme gets implemented, and you now need to assign a department number to each department. Worse, these numbers might change again, so if you spend hours running searches on each department and adding in the number for that department, you might have to do it again in a few months.

If you were to implement this with an If function, you would have to nest several If statements, because you can really only have one test per If function. It would look something like this:

```
If (Department = "Sales", 100, If (Department = "Accounting", 200,
If (Department = "Marketing", 300, If (Department = "Manufactur-
ing", 400, "No Department"))))
```

If there is no department for an employee, this calculation would return No Department. Otherwise, it would return the department number. This same calculation done with a Case function would look like this:

```
Case (Department = "Sales", 100, Department = "Accounting", 200,
Department = "Marketing", 300, Department = "Manufacturing", 400,
"No Department")
```

Only one function is called, and figuring out the commas and parentheses is much less confusing. The Case function can make nested If functions a thing of the past. Another problem with nested If functions is that there's a limit to how many nested If functions FileMaker will evaluate. If you have If functions nested more than 128 levels deep, FileMaker will not evaluate the If functions beyond the 128th level. With a Case function, there isn't any nesting, because all tests are specified in the first level of the function. Case functions have a limit of a total text size of 64,000 characters.

The Choose function is different. It only has one test, but it has multiple test results. This function is very useful in finding out which button was pushed in a dialog box by incorporating the Status(CurrentMessageChoice) function, as illustrated in the following steps.

1. Go to any database that contains a Text field. For this example, use a database that contains the Text field Choice.

2. Choose Script, ScriptMaker and in the Script Name text box enter **Display Message**. Then click the Create button to display the Script Definition dialog box.

3. Click Clear All to remove the standard script from the script list box.

4. Locate the Show Message command in the Available Steps list box and double-click it to add it to the script.

5. Click Specify to display the Specify Message dialog box and fill in the text boxes as shown in figure 5.16. When you finish, click OK to close the dialog box.

Fig. 5.16
The resulting dialog box will display a short message and three buttons from which to choose.

6. Locate the Set Field command in the Available Steps list box and double-click it to add it to the script.

7. Click the Specify Field button and double-click the Choice field (or the field you're using to store the results of the example) to add it to the script.

8. Click the Specify button to open the Specify Calculation dialog box.

9. Double-click the Choose function to add it to the script. Then, double-click the test expression in the formula.

10. Select the Status functions from the View pop-up menu.

11. Locate the Status(CurrentMessageChoice) function to add it as the test case for the Choose function.

II

Enhancing Databases

12. Double-click the text `result 1` in the formula and replace it with "Button 1". Use the same technique to replace the `result 2` with "Button 2", and the `result 3` expression with "Button 3". Also, remove the extraneous brackets and ellipses.

13. Insert the cursor after the Status(CurrentMessageChoice) function and type –**1**. You must do this because the Choose function's default results returns 0, while the Status(CurrentMessageChoice) returns the default results of 1. This equalizes the two expressions. Figure 5.17 shows how your calculation should look when you finish.

Fig. 5.17
This calculation will store your button selection in the Choice field.

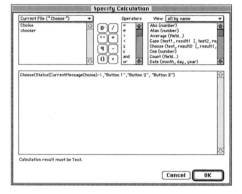

14. Click OK to close the Specify Calculation dialog box, click OK to close the Script Definition dialog box, and click Done to close the Define Scripts dialog box.

Now, choose Script, Display Message. FileMaker opens the dialog box you created in the script. Click any of the three buttons and the Choose function will store your selection in the Choice field.

The IsEmpty function is used to detect when a field has not had anything entered in it. In previous versions of FileMaker, a field would not evaluate as empty unless something had been entered then deleted. The IsEmpty function means that some of the workarounds from old FileMaker databases will no longer be necessary.

While this function is not particularly useful by itself, it's quite handy when you include it with other calculation functions. For example, say you want to ensure that a user enters the Zip Code in a field if they've already entered an address in the record. To do this, you could use the following calculation that returns a text value. You'll notice that I use the IsEmpty function as the test for the If statements.

```
If(IsEmpty(Zip Code) = 1 and IsEmpty(Address) = 0, "Please enter a
corresponding Zip Code for this address.", "")
```

Tip

When you're testing for a true value only, you can omit the numeric expression altogether. Therefore, you could also express the `IsEmpty(Zip Code)` = 1 calculation with simply `IsEmpty(Zip Code)`.

IsValid (field) allows you to check a field to see whether its data matches the data type of the field. For example, you could make sure the Number field Customer ID contained only numeric data by using the formula IsValid(Customer ID). If the field contained only numbers, the IsValid function would return a 1. Otherwise, the function returns 0. This calculation function is good to build into other calculations to ensure that the data types are correct.

To determine if the Customer ID is valid, and to display a warning if it isn't, you could use the following calculation:

```
If(IsValid(Customer ID),"","The Customer ID must be a number.")
```

Tip

You can also check that the field entry is valid with the Validation options available in the Define Fields dialog box.

A New Way to Look at Summaries

You can use Summary field total field values in a database. To add even more power to these fields, you can break these summary values into smaller similar groups using the GetSummary function. While this function operates like subsummaries and grand summaries, the Summary function isn't dependent on the layout parts. In fact, unlike subsummaries and grand summaries, you can include the GetSummary function in other calculations.

For an example of the GetSummary function, imagine you have a database that tracks manufacturing costs of Products A, B, and C. You enter the cost of each production lot into the database. Now, you want to create fields that display the total and the average production costs by product. Here's how to do it.

II

Enhancing Databases

1. Choose File, New and create a database named Summaries.

2. In the Name text box, enter **Product** and click Create. Then, enter **Cost of Production** in the Name text box and choose Number from the Type list box.

3. Now you want to create a field that will create a total of the Cost of Production values. Therefore, enter **Total Production Cost** in the Name text box, choose the Summary option, and click Create. FileMaker opens the Options for Summary dialog box. The default setting, which is to total the Production Cost field, is what you want so click OK.

4. Create another Summary field named Average Production Cost in the same manner, but this time select the Average option in the Options for Summary dialog box.

   At this point, you have the total and average production costs but those values are for all products, not by product type. This is where the GetSummary functions come in.

5. Enter **Total Production by Product** in the Name text box, choose the Calculation option and click Create.

6. Choose Summary Functions from the View pop-up menu.

7. Double-click the GetSummary function to add it to the formula box.

8. Now, replace the summary field expression with Total Production Cost and the break field expression with Product. When you finish, the Specify Calculation dialog box should look like the one in figure 5.18.

Fig. 5.19
This GetSummary calculation will return the total production costs per product.

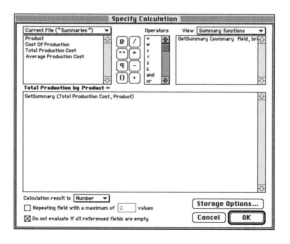

9. Create a Calculation field named Average Production by Product and insert the GetSummary function into the formula text box.

10. Replace the summary field expression with Average Production Cost and the break field expression with Product. Click OK to close the dialog box.

11. Click Done to close the Define Fields dialog box.

12. Choosing Mode, New Record to create records, enter the following seven records into the database:

Product	Cost of Production
Product A	12.59
Product B	378.78
Product C	2323.93
Product C	3299.01
Product A	21.76
Product A	17.89
Product B	423.97

Just by glancing at the values, you'll notice that the total and average production costs won't be too representative for Product A because its costs are so much less than the other two products. However, if you break down these two costs by Product, the values become more legitimate. To display the Total Production by Product and the Average Production by Product, choose Mode, Sort and double-click the Product item in the Sort Records list box that appears. Next, click Sort.

After you sort the database, the Total Production by Product and the Average Production by Product display correct and believable values. For example, the Average Production by Product is $17.41—a much more representative average than the $925.42 value that the Total Production Cost field returned.

Tip

Remember that for Summary functions to display the correct total, the database must be sorted by the appropriate break field or summary field. Remember to sort the database if you use the GetSummary function in another calculation.

Getting Information from Repeating Fields

While repeating fields are excellent for storing data, in the past it's been diffi-cult to isolate the information with FileMaker calculations and scripts. Luck-ily, the new version of FileMaker includes two new Repeating functions: GetRepetition and Last. The GetRepetition function returns the value of a specific repeating field while the Last function returns the last non-blank value in a repeating field. You can use these functions to greatly simplify your database development. For example, you could create a repeating field called Marketing Costs that includes all the costs for the sale of a product. With the GetRepetition function, you could then isolate individual cost values from this repeating field. So for this example, use the following calculation to obtain the value of the third repetition in the repeating field Marketing Cost.

```
GetRepetition(Marketing Cost, 3)
```

The Last function returns the last non-blank value in a repeating field. So to return the last value in the Marketing Cost repeating field, simply use the calculation:

```
Last(Marketing Cost)
```

Monitoring Your Databases with Status Functions

Status functions allow you to design scripts and create calculations that perform functions based on the status of the current database. These added functions are especially helpful to the FileMaker developer who's creating database for others to use. By carefully anticipating the changes in the operating environment, the developer can use the Status functions to alter the database to best suit the users needs. In the section, "Working with Logical Functions," earlier in this chapter, you learned how to use the Status(CurrentMessageChoice) to return the user's choice in a dialog box. Now you will learn a few of the other Status functions and how you can use them to improve your databases.

Building Error Traps

If you create a script to automate a function and an error occurs, FileMaker will display an error message. For users unfamiliar to FileMaker, these mes-sages might be confusing. To avoid this situation, use Status(CurrentError) to display customized error messages when the problem occurs. Unfortunately, FileMaker captures only the error codes—not the error explanations—and there's no explanation of these codes in the user's manual. Without knowing the meaning to the error codes, you really can't create usable error message dialog boxes. Therefore, I listed the error codes you might encounter and their meaning in the following table.

–1	Unknown error
0	No error
1	User canceled action
2	Memory error
3	Command is unavailable (such as, wrong operating system, wrong mode, and so on)
4	Command is unknown
5	Command is invalid (such as, a Set Field script step does not have a calculation specified)
100	File is missing
101	Record is missing
102	Field is missing
103	Relation is missing
104	Script is missing
105	Layout is missing
200	Record access is denied
201	Field cannot be modified
202	Field access is denied
203	No records in file to print or password doesn't allow print access
204	No access to field(s) in sort order
205	Cannot create new records; import will overwrite existing data
300	The file is locked or in use
301	Record is in use by another user
302	Script definitions are in use by another user
303	Paper size is in use by another user
304	Password definitions are in use by another user
305	Relationship or value list definitions are locked by another user
400	Find criteria is empty
401	No records match the request
402	Not a match field for a lookup
403	Exceeding maximum record limit for demo
404	Sort order is invalid
405	Number of records specified exceeds number of records that can be omitted

II

Enhancing Databases

406	Replace/Re-serialize criteria is invalid
407	One or both key fields are missing (invalid relation)
408	Specified field has inappropriate data type for this operation
409	Import order is invalid
410	Export order is invalid
411	Cannot perform delete because related records cannot be deleted
412	Wrong version of FileMaker used to recover file
500	Date value does not meet validation entry options
501	Time value does not meet validation entry options
502	Number value does not meet validation entry options
503	Value in field does not meet range validation entry options
504	Value in field does not meet unique value validation entry options
505	Value in field failed existing value validation test
506	Value in field is not a member value of the validation entry option value list
507	Value in field failed calculation test of validation entry option
508	Value in field failed query value test of validation entry option
509	Field requires a valid value
510	Related value is empty or unavailable
600	Print error has occurred
601	Combined header and footer exceed one page
602	Body doesn't fit on a page for current column setup
603	Print connection lost
700	File is of the wrong file type for import
701	Data Access Manager can't find database extension file
702	The Data Access Manager was unable to open the session
703	The Data Access Manager was unable to open the session; try later
704	Data Access Manager failed when sending a query
705	Data Access Manager failed when executing a query
706	EPSF file has no preview image
707	Graphic translator cannot be found

708	Can't import the file or need color machine to import file
709	QuickTime movie import failed
710	Unable to update QuickTime file reference because the database is read-only
711	Import translator cannot be found
712	XTND version is incompatible
713	Couldn't initialize the XTND system
714	Insufficient password privileges do not allow the operation
800	Unable to create file on disk
801	Unable to create temporary file on System disk
802	Unable to open file
803	File is single user or host cannot be found
804	File cannot be opened as read-only in its current state
805	File is damaged; use Recover command
806	File cannot be opened with this version of FileMaker
807	File is not a FileMaker file or is severely damaged
808	Cannot open file because of damaged access privileges
809	Disk/volume is full
810	Disk/volume is locked
811	Temporary file cannot be opened as FileMaker file
812	Cannot open the file because it exceeds host capacity
813	Record Synchronization error on network
814	File(s) cannot be opened because maximum number is open
815	Couldn't open lookup file
816	Unable to convert file
900	General spelling engine error
901	Main spelling dictionary not installed
902	Could not launch the Help system
903	Command cannot be used in a shared file

Many of the error messages are very specific. For example, if you try to perform a lookup on a field not defined as a lookup, FileMaker sends an error code 402. With that information, build an example that performs a relookup on a non-lookup field to demonstrate how you can use the Status(CurrentError) function to display customized error messages:

Enhancing Databases

1. Choose File, New to open the New Database dialog box.

2. Type **Errors** in the Create a New File text box and click Save.

3. In the Define Fields dialog box, create a new Text field called Note and click Done.

4. Choose Script, ScriptMaker and in the dialog box that appears, type **Relookup Field** in the Script Name text box. Click Create.

5. The Script Definition dialog box opens. Click Clear All to remove the sample script from the Script Definition list box.

6. Locate the Set Error Capture command in the Available Steps section and double-click it to add it to the script.

7. At this point, you want to add an invalid step to the script in order to capture the error code. Because the Note field isn't defined as a lookup field, the Relookup command will work. Locate Relookup in the Available Steps section and double-click it to add it to the script.

8. Select the Perform Without Dialog check box and click Specify Field. Select the Note field and click OK.

9. Add an If command to the script and click Specify to open the Specify Calculation dialog box. Choose Status Functions from the View pop-up menu.

10. Double-click the Status(CurrentError) function to add it to the formula box. Then type **= 402** after the function so your calculation looks like the one shown in figure 5.19. When you finish, click OK.

Fig. 5.19
This calculation determines whether the current error code is 402.

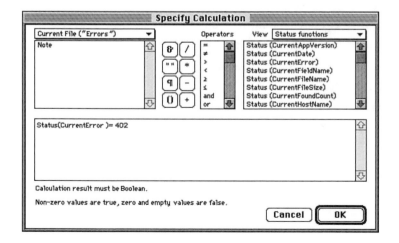

11. Add a Beep command to the script and move it above the End If command.

> **Tip**
>
> To move a script command, select it, press and hold down the ⌘ key and use the up or down arrow keys.

12. Locate Show Message and add it to the script. Position it just above the End If command. Click Specify to open the Specify Message dialog box. Enter the following text in the Message Text list box:

You can't perform a lookup on this field. Please advance to another field and try again.

13. Tab to the Second text box in the Button Captions area and remove `Cancel` from the Second text box. Click OK to close the dialog box.

14. Add an Else command to the script and move it directly above the End If command.

15. Insert another Show Message command to the script and click Specify to open the Specify Message dialog box. Enter the following text in the Message Text list box:

An undefined error occurred. Please try the script again.

16. Again, delete `Cancel` from the Second text box in the Button Captions area and click OK. Position the command above the End If statement. When you finish, the final script should look like the one shown in figure 5.20.

17. Click OK to close the Script Definition dialog box and click Done to close the Define Scripts window.

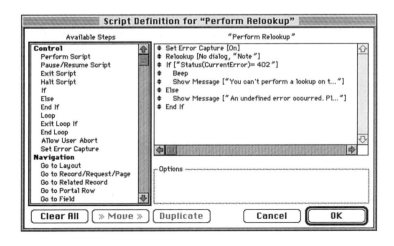

Fig. 5.20
This script tests for a lookup error and displays a custom error message.

At this point, you're ready to test the script and the Status(CurrentError) function. To do so, press the Tab key to enter the Note field and choose Script, Relookup Field. When you do, FileMaker determines that the Note field is not a valid lookup field and displays the dialog box shown in figure 5.21. Now, take a look at another use for the Status Calculation functions.

Fig. 5.21
When your script detects an error, it will display this dialog box.

You can't perform a lookup on this field. Please advance to another field and try again.

OK

Getting Computer Settings with Status Calculations

You can also use Status Calculations to get important information about the user's working environment. For example, you could use Status functions to create a calculation that tells you who created a record, on what platform, and when. Such a calculation would be a good way to create an audit trail for a database.

To build a calculation that uses the various Status functions to create an audit field, follow these steps:

1. Create a database named Info that contains the Calculation field Entry Info.

2. Click Create then click Options to open the Specify Calculation dialog box.

   At this point, you need to define the calculation's formula. To do so, you could use the point-and-click method or type the formula in directly. Because the formula contains so many operators and functions, you'll probably find it easier to type it in.

3. Enter the following formula into the formula text box.

   ```
   "Host Name: " & Status(CurrentHostName) & "¶Working on a " &
   If(Status(CurrentPlatform) = 1,"Macintosh platform","Windows
   platform") & "¶" & "Created/changed by: " &
   Status(CurrentUserName) & " at " &
   TimeToText(Status(CurrentTime)) & " on " &
   DateToText(Status(CurrentDate))
   ```

> **Tip**
>
> If you make a mistake when entering the formula, FileMaker will display a message box that tells you there's a problem, as well as highlight where the error occurs.

4. Click OK to close the dialog box. Click Done to close the Define Fields dialog box.

5. Choose Mode, Layout and select the Entry Info field.

6. Using the lower-right selection handle, enlarge the field to display at least four lines of information.

7. Choose Mode, Browse. You're now ready to test the calculation.

Create a new record. When you do, the calculation uses the Status functions to obtain the system information and displays it in the Errors window (see fig. 5.22).

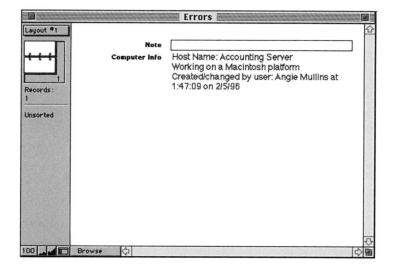

Fig. 5.22
You can use the Status functions to record information about each database entry.

As you continue working with FileMaker, you'll find the Status function invaluable when automating database operations. Appendix C, "Functions Reference," lists other Status functions and briefly explains them.

Special Calculation Considerations

In the past, the more calculation fields you included in a database, the longer it took to update that record. This was especially evident if your database included a calculation that used the Today function: FileMaker would update each record when you opened the database. Now, you can customize the storage and indexing of all your calculations fields.

When you create a calculation, you'll notice the Storage Options button at the bottom of the Specify Calculation dialog box. When you click this button, FileMaker opens the Storage Options dialog. The options in this dialog box let you improve the performance of your database, and allow you to keep your file size to a minimum. When you're designing the database, it's important to choose your setting appropriately.

Storing the Results of Your Calculation Fields

By default, the resulting values of calculation fields are written to the file. This makes the information readily available when you want to display it. However, because this data is stored, it also increases the size of the file. As your database grows in size, its performance can become sluggish. As previously noted, stored results can often change. That means you have to wait while FileMaker recalculates the field values.

To reduce the size of your database, you can activate the Do Not Store Calculation Results option. Because the file no longer contains the calculated values, it is much smaller. Also, because the values aren't stored in the file, FileMaker doesn't need to update those calculations, thus making typical database operations quicker.

Indexing Your Fields

Choosing not to index your database can increase performance. The previous versions of FileMaker indexed every field. That meant that when you wanted to display all records that matched a certain criteria, FileMaker could quickly review the index and go directly to those records. However, because the program indexed every field of every record, it reduced the speed of many database operations.

The new version of FileMaker lets *you* decide whether to index a field. By default, the Indexing option is deselected and the Automatically Turn Indexing On If Needed option is selected. When you use this default setting, FileMaker only indexes the data in the field when you perform certain database operations. You'll find that most fields in your database don't require indexing—just those you use for find and sort operations.

> **Tip**
>
> Don't be afraid to index fields. You'll only experience decreased performance if you have a large number of indexed fields.

From Here...

At this point, you should have a good handle on text calculations or know where to look when you need to pull text apart. You should also understand the basics of the other calculation functions.

From here, you might want to read the following chapters:

- Chapter 15, "Scripting with ScriptMaker" includes using calculations in the ScriptMaker.

- Appendix C, "Functions Reference," is a comprehensive list of all the calculations available in FileMaker Pro.

II

Enhancing Databases

CHAPTER 6
Value Lists

It's fine to have a database that works the way that you—the database author—work, but several people often have to work with the same database. A well-designed database should be easy to work with and easy to understand. You'll know you're a success if someone who has never seen your system before can sit down and immediately figure out what they're supposed to do.

There are many things you can do to achieve this, as explained in this and other chapters. Think about the problem of someone not knowing what customer code to enter on an invoice when a customer calls. It might happen that the person doing the data entry only knows the name of the customer. It would be nice if they could have a pop-up menu attached to the Customer ID field that gave them a current list of customer names and IDs to choose from.

Choosing from a menu like this, or selecting check boxes or radio buttons on a form, speeds up data entry, reduces the possibility of data entry errors, and makes the database easier to work with. All of these are possible through a feature in FileMaker called Value Lists.

In this chapter, you learn about all aspects of Value Lists, including how to:

- Create new value lists
- Use value lists for automating data entry
- Validate field entries with value lists
- Make a value list dynamically use values from another database
- Create conditional value lists

Creating Value Lists

Value lists are predefined sets of choices that a user can choose from when entering data in a field. You can type these choices in by hand, or they can dynamically reflect the contents of another field.

Value lists existed as a feature in earlier versions of FileMaker Pro, but they behaved differently. In FileMaker Pro 2.1 v3 and earlier versions, a value list was an option you could attach to a field when you defined fields. In FileMaker Pro 3.0, a value list is independent of any field. You can attach the same value list to as many fields as you want.

Think about what can happen when you have different people using a database. Even if they know what information to enter, they might enter it differently. An invoice usually shows payment terms, but you might have one employee entering Net 30, another entering 30 days, and so forth. One valuable thing about value lists is that by forcing users to pick from a selection of possible entries, they standardize data entry and they prevent mistakes like misspelled words.

Creating a Value List to Check Entries

You can create value lists from different places in FileMaker Pro 3.0. One of them is in the define fields process. This section shows you how to create a value list for payment terms in an invoice. The value list is set up so you can force a user to enter only values you specify.

1. Choose File, Define Fields.

2. In the Define Fields dialog box, create a new field called Payment Terms (see fig. 6.1).

Fig. 6.1
You need to be in the Define Fields dialog box to add a new field.

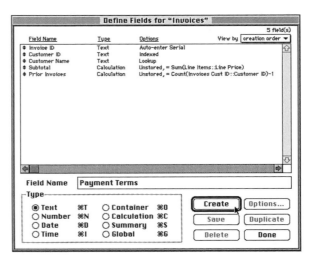

3. Click Options to open the Entry Options dialog box.

4. Choose Validation from the pop-up menu at the top of the dialog box (see fig. 6.2).

Fig. 6.2
You can switch between the Auto Enter to Validation options by using the pop-up menu.

5. In the Validation entry options, select the Member of Value List check box, then choose Define Value Lists from the No Lists Defined pop-up menu (see fig. 6.3). The Define Value Lists dialog box appears.

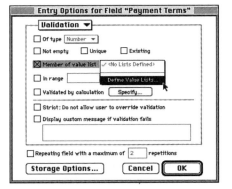

Fig. 6.3
Define a value list from the Valida-tion Entry Options dialog box.

6. Because value lists are now independent of any one field, you must name them. Type **Payment Terms** in the Value List Name text box and click Create (see fig. 6.4).

7. Select the Use Custom Values radio button, and then click in the list box to the right.

8. Type **Net 30** and press Return. Type **Net 10** and press Return. Type - (a dash) and press Return, then type **COD**. Click Save. The Define Value Lists dialog box should look similar to figure 6.5. The dash in the list

will create a dividing line when the list is used on a database layout. (You can see the effect later in figure 6.10.)

9. Click Done.

Fig. 6.4
A value list does not have to have the same name as the field that uses it.

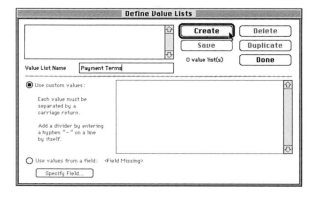

Fig. 6.5
This is how the completed Payment Terms value list should look.

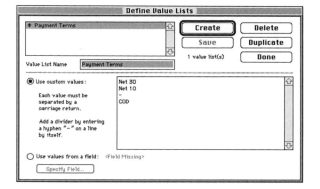

Now when a user enters information into this field, FileMaker will check to see if the information entered is in the specified value list. To test this, click OK to close the Entry Options dialog box, and then click Done to close the Define Fields dialog box.

Ordinarily, the new Payment Terms field should appear at the bottom of your layout. If it isn't there, that means the preferences in FileMaker (under the Edit menu) have been set so FileMaker doesn't automatically add new fields to the current layout. If that's the case and the new Payment Terms field wasn't automatically added to the bottom of your layout, you have to add it manually. To do this, just follow these steps:

1. Choose Mode, Layout.

2. Drag the Field tool onto your layout. When the Specify Field dialog box appears, select Payment Terms and click OK.

3. Choose Mode, Browse.

Because the Payment Terms field is probably the last field on your layout, you can easily move to it by holding down the Shift key and pressing the Tab key once. Pressing Shift+Tab allows you move through the field order backwards.

If you type **Mustard** in the Payment Terms field and move out of the field, FileMaker warns you that the field is defined to contain specific values (see fig. 6.6).

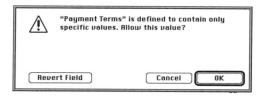

Fig. 6.6
When a user enters invalid information into a field and you haven't specified a custom validation message, FileMaker displays this generic warning.

You have three options: you can revert the field to its prior state, which is empty for this example; you can click Cancel, which lets you modify your entry; or you can click OK to override the warning.

If you click OK, you'll have Mustard going out on invoices to your customers (probably a bad idea). However, in some cases, you might want people to be able to override a validation warning. Sometimes all you want to do is bring something to attention. Maybe a salesperson is selling a product below cost, so you want a warning to pop up. But, maybe the salesperson is giving away a product as part of taking a huge order for some other product, so the below cost product is just a courtesy. In that situation, you need to be able to override the validation.

Preventing Users from Overriding a Validation

If you want to prevent users from overriding a validation, follow these steps:

1. Choose File, Define Fields.

2. Select the Payment Terms field and click Options to open the Validation Options dialog box.

3. Select the Strict: Do Not Allow User to Override Validation check box.

4. Select the Display Custom Message If Validation Fails check box.

5. Click in the text box below the Display Custom Message If Validation Fails check box and enter **You must enter Net 30, Net 10, or COD** (see fig. 6.7).

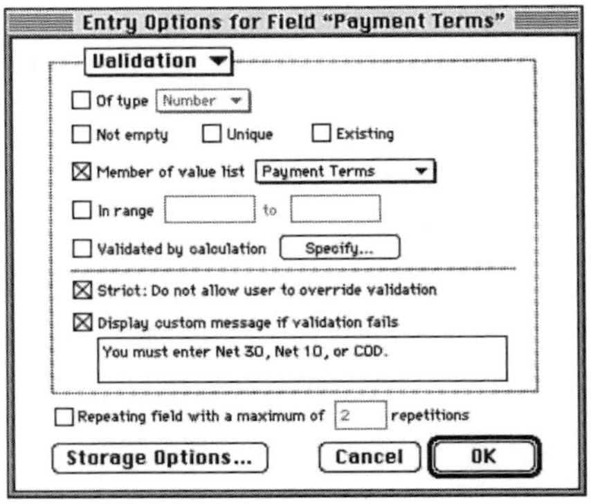

Fig. 6.7
FileMaker uses whatever you type in this text box in place of its generic validation warning.

6. Click OK to exit the Entry Options dialog box.

7. Click Done to exit the Define Fields dialog box.

If you Shift-Tab to the Payment Terms field again, it still has Mustard entered. Tab out of the field and nothing happens. If you Shift-Tab back to the field, select the entire field, retype **Mustard**, and Tab out, you get the new validation message. However, you also get the option to revert the field to its prior state and unfortunately, that prior state was wrong.

This is something to think about. If you create a field without strict validation and then modify the field to have strict validation, any invalid values in the records will remain—even if you Tab in and out of the field. You only trigger the new validation if you try to change the contents of the field. Even then, it's possible to revert back to the original invalid entry. This is another reason why you should think through your design *before* you deploy your database system.

If you change the data in the Payment Options field to Net 30 and Tab out of the field, you don't trigger the warning. However, if you Shift-Tab back to the field and change it to Net30 and Tab out of the field, even though the entry is close, it still triggers the validation warning. This is good. People do make typing mistakes, and this warning ensures that someone using the database will enter information exactly as you want them to.

Creating a Value List with Custom Values

The best way to get users to make correct entries is to set up the database so they don't have to type anything at all; let them choose their selections from a list. Such choice-based data entry is usually faster than typing, and it has an added benefit: it's impossible for someone using the database to make typing mistakes. Here's how you set this up:

1. Choose Mode, Layout.

2. Select the field (Payment Terms in this example) by clicking it once, and then choose Format, Field Format to open the Field Format dialog box.

3. In the Style section, click the Pop-Up List radio button.

> **Tip**
>
> The Field Format dialog box is the second place where you can create value lists. Define Fields was the first.

4. Click OK to exit the Field Format dialog box and choose Mode, Browse.

Now when you want to enter data, Shift-Tab to the Payment Terms field. This time, a list containing the Payment Terms value list pops up. Notice how the COD terms are boxed off from the other two. That's the result of the dash put in the value list in the previous section.

> **Troubleshooting**
>
> *Although I used the Field Format dialog box to attach a value list to a field, the field doesn't display the list.*
>
> Because it's possible to open the Field Format dialog box without having a field selected, a common mistake is forgetting to select the field you want to attach a value list to before specifying a value list in the Field Format dialog box. In Layout mode, select the desired field and choose Format, Field Format. Assign the value list in the Field Format dialog box.

To move to a specific entry, type the initial letter (such as **c**) and the selection jumps to COD. Type **N** and it jumps to the first entry that starts with N (in this case Net 30). You can also use the up- and down-arrow keys on your keyboard to move through the list. If you Tab out of the field when you have an item selected, that item will not automatically get entered. You need to use the Return or Enter keys to enter a selected item in the list.

This is good, as far as it goes. But what if you want to create a value list that constantly changes? You have two options: you can allow the database user to modify the value list, or you can have the value list dynamically display the contents of another database (such as the database of values).

Allowing Additions to the Value List

Try the first option first. To allow a user to modify a value list, follow these steps:

1. Choose Mode, Layout and select the Payment Terms field.

2. Choose Format, Field Format to open the Field Format dialog box.

3. Select the Include "Edit" Item to Allow Editing of Value List check box (see fig. 6.8).

Fig. 6.8
Allow a user to edit the value list by selecting the check box.

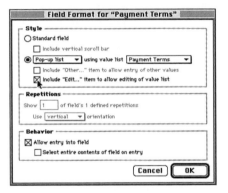

4. Click OK, and then choose Mode, Browse.

Now when you Shift-Tab to the Payment Terms field your screen should look similar to figure 6.9.

If you click Edit, you get the Edit Value List dialog box (see fig. 6.10). You can add a new value, such as Net 15, and also add another dash right after COD.

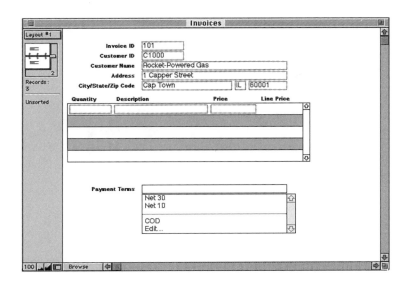

Fig. 6.9
When you enable Edit capability, it appears at the bottom of a value list.

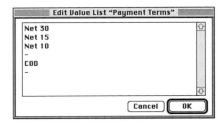

Fig. 6.10
After you modify a value list, you need to click Save for the change to take effect.

II

Enhancing Databases

Click OK and Shift-Tab back to the field. Now your screen should look similar to figure 6.11.

In general, you probably don't want your users changing values in a value list. That kind of capability would be appropriate for an administrator, and you would probably set up a special administrative layout for an administrator to use. For more information on controlling file access and setting up password-protected layouts, see Chapter 12, "Controlling File Access."

Fig. 6.11
When you change
a value list, any
fields using that
list will automati-
cally use the
updated list.

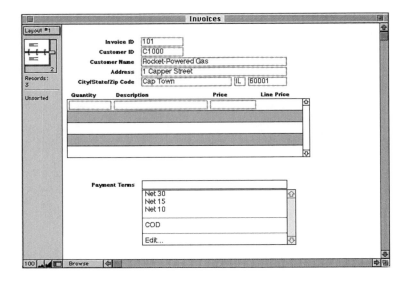

There still might be special circumstances where a user needs to be able to
enter a nonstandard (not in the value list) value. You can allow a user to do
this without having them actually change the contents of the value list. Before you do, you need to turn off your validation for Payment Terms. You
didn't need to do this when a user modified the actual value list because what
they entered became a member of the value list, so it was valid. This isn't the
case for the next option.

To disable the value list validation, do the following:

1. Choose File, Define Fields to open the Define Fields dialog box.

2. Select the Payment Terms field and click Options to open the Entry
Options dialog box.

3. Choose Validation from the pop-up menu.

4. Deselect the Member of Value List check box and click OK to close the
Entry Options dialog box.

5. Click Done to close the Define Fields dialog box.

Now, because you will value listsuse a pop-up list, you can add nonstandard
values. Click in the Payment Terms field. If the list pops up, click on the field
again. Now you can type anything you want. The pop-up list format is the
only format that allows this kind of an override. If you use pop-up menus
(different from a list), radio buttons, or check boxes, you need to modify the
field format to allow for non-value list values.

This is the process for allowing a non-pop-up list field to accommodate non-value list values:

1. Choose Mode, Layout and select the Payment Terms field.

2. Choose Format, Field Format to open the Field Format dialog box.

3. Deselect the Include "Edit" Item to Allow Editing of Value List check box.

4. Choose Pop-up Menu from the pop-up and select the Include "Other" Item to Allow Entry of Other Values check box (see fig. 6.12).

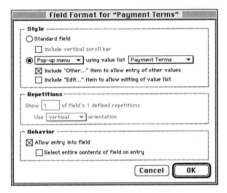

Fig. 6.12
The only way to allow a user to enter non-value list entries into a pop-up menu is with the Other option.

5. Click OK to close the Field Format dialog box, and then choose Mode, Browse.

Shift-Tab to the Payment Terms field. Your screen should look similar to figure 6.13.

Unlike a pop-up list, a pop-up menu format forces a user to choose one of the options. That's why, if you want to enable the user to enter non-standard values, you have to use the Other option. Choose Other from the menu to open the Other dialog box.

Imagine that you're feeling generous and type in **Net 90**. Click OK. This value is actually searchable in the Find mode. If you need to search the database for a record where you entered some nonstandard value in the Other dialog box, you can. To find information that has been typed into the Other dialog box, follow these steps:

1. Choose Mode, Find.

2. Choose Other from the Payment Terms field. Type **90** and click OK.

3. Click Find and look at the Status area. Under the book it tells you how many records were found.

Fig. 6.13
The Other option appears at the bottom of the pop-up menu.

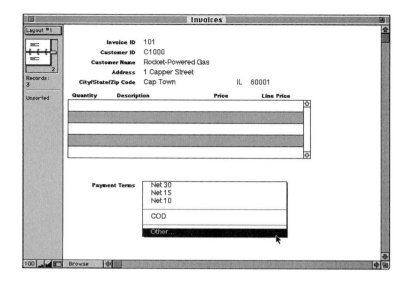

That's one way to have changing information used with value lists. The other way is actually more powerful; you have a database supply your value list values.

Creating a Value List Using Values from a Field

Return to the scenario outlined at the beginning of this chapter. You have a new employee who has no idea who your customers are or what their customer ID's are. What you need to do is create a value list that contains all of your customer ID codes. The problem is that you add new customers all the time, so keeping that value list current is a heavy administrative chore. By tying the contents of a value list to another database, the list becomes a living thing, changing as the database itself changes.

The following steps demonstrate how to make the contents of a value list, in this case the Customer ID field in an Invoices database, change depending on the values in a second database for Customers:

1. In the Invoices database, choose Mode, Layout and then select the Customer ID field.

2. Choose Format, Field Format to open the Field Format dialog box.

3. Select the Pop-up List menu radio button.

4. Click the Using Value List pop-up and choose Define Value Lists.

5. In the Value List Name field, type **Customer ID's** and click Create.

6. Select the Use Values from a Field check box to open the Specify Fields for Value List dialog box.

7. Click Specify File. The Open dialog box appears.

8. Choose Customers and click Open (see fig. 6.14).

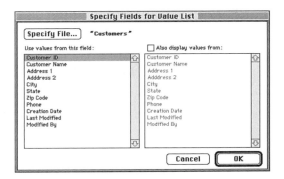

Fig. 6.14
Lists that use field values draw the values from the field's index.

9. Click OK to close the Specify Fields for Value List dialog box.

10. Click Save, then click Done to close the Define Value Lists dialog box.

11. Click OK to close the Field Format dialog box.

Choose Mode, Browse and Tab to the Customer ID field. You should get a scrolling list of customer ID codes as shown in figure 6.15.

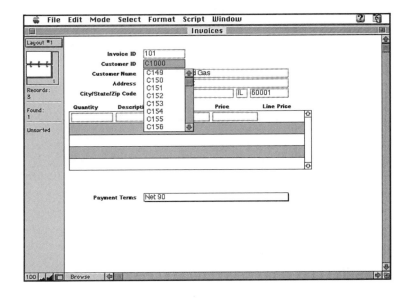

Fig. 6.15
If a pop-up list is long enough, it automatically gets a scroll bar.

II

Enhancing Databases

This is somewhat useful. You can see a list of all the customer ID codes, but how would a new employee know which code went with which customer? They wouldn't. You need to show them who the customers are. To do this, follow these steps:

1. In the Invoices database, choose Mode, Layout, and select the Customer ID field.

2. Choose Format, Field Format to open the Field Format dialog box.

3. Choose Define Value Lists from the Customer ID's pop-up menu.

4. Click Specify Field to open the Specify Fields for Value List dialog box.

5. Make sure Customer ID is selected in the list on the left. The field on the left contains the values that will actually be entered when the value list is used. Select the Also Display Values From check box and select Customer Name from the list below the check box (see fig. 6.16). The field on the right contains values that can only be used for labeling purposes in the value list. The data will only be displayed in the list; it won't be used for field entry.

Fig. 6.16
This value list will change as the field values in the database that it references change.

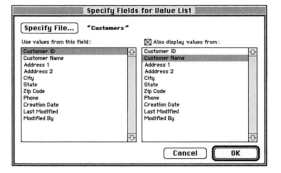

6. Click OK to close the Specify Fields for Value List dialog box.

7. Click Save, and then click Done to close the Define Value Lists dialog box.

8. Click OK to close the Field Format dialog box and choose Mode, Browse.

When you Tab to the Customer ID field, you should see a pop-up list that looks similar to the one in figure 6.17.

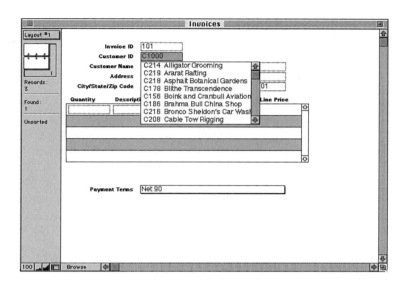

Fig. 6.17
This value list is
displaying values
from another
database.

Notice that the list is alphabetical by Customer Name. If you type different letters, various customer names highlight. Notice also that because the customer names are alphabetized, the Customer IDs are not in any kind of order. If you prefer to have your IDs in order and the customer names out of order, you can do that.

Changing the Order with the Index

The customer IDs and names are coming from the *index* in the Customers database. What's an index? Good question. Look at the index in the back of this book. Regardless of the order in which words appear in the book, an index displays them in some kind of order (usually alphabetical). The index also displays the pages on which you can find a particular word, because a word might be referenced on several pages.

A database works the same way. Each name in the Customers database has been indexed. This means that like a book, the name has been stored once in the record that contains it, and once in the index. It's stored twice. That sounds like a waste of space, doesn't it? An index is actually useful. In the same way you use an index to quickly go to the page you're looking for, a database uses an index to quickly go to the record or records it's looking for. Indexes speed up searches. It's kind of a trade-off between size of the database and performance of searches.

II

Enhancing Databases

FileMaker actually stores two indexes for indexed fields. One is a single word index. In this type of index, New York get two separate index entries: New and York. The other index is a paragraph index. Each index entry runs from the beginning of a paragraph to the first carriage return. New York would look normal in this index. You can actually see the two index types by following these steps:

1. Choose Window and select a database.

2. Click a field and choose Edit, Paste Special, From Index. The View Index dialog box appears (see fig. 6.18).

3. Select the Show Individual Words check box and note the effect (see fig. 6.19). When you finish looking, click Cancel.

Fig. 6.18
The paragraph index contains multiple words and spaces.

Fig. 6.19
Select or deselect the check box to switch between the two indexes.

In FileMaker Pro 3.0, you can turn indexing on and off. In earlier versions of FileMaker, indexing was automatically on for every field.

Choose File, Define Fields to see that indexing has automatically been turned on for certain fields in your database (see fig. 6.20). For example, a customer ID field will probably be indexed because any field that's used in a relationship has to be indexed. That's the law, not just for FileMaker, but for other database systems as well.

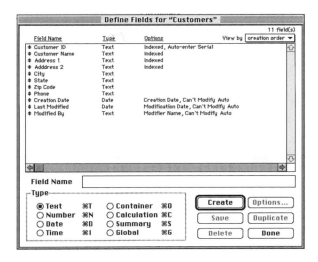

Fig. 6.20
The Define Fields
dialog box will
show if a field is
indexed or not.

In the previous example, the Customer Name field was indexed when it was used in the value list in Invoices. If you want to sort your value list by a different field, such as Customer ID, just turn the indexing off for Customer Name.

> **Note**
>
> If you use two fields in a value list, at least one of the fields has to be indexed or the value list won't display anything.

To turn indexing off for a particular field, follow these steps:

1. Choose File, Define Fields to open the Define Fields dialog box. Select the field you want to work with and click Options.
2. In the Entry Options dialog box, click Storage Options. The Storage Options dialog box appears.
3. Select the Off radio button and deselect the Automatically Turn Indexing On If Needed check box (see fig. 6.21).
4. Click OK to close the Storage Options dialog box.
5. Click OK to close the Entry Options dialog box and click Done to close the Define Fields dialog box.

Fig. 6.21
The Storage Options dialog box is where you control the indexing for a particular field.

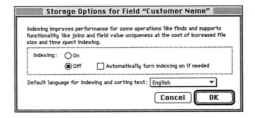

> ## Troubleshooting
>
> *A value list that uses values from a field isn't displaying anything, even though there are values in that field.*
>
> Value lists that use values from a field use that field's index to populate the value list. Go to the database that contains the field and choose File, Define Fields. Select the field in question and note its field type. If it's a container, global, or summary field, it can't be indexed, and therefore can't be used to create a value list. If it's any other type, click Options. Click Storage Options at the bottom of the Entry Options or Specify Calculation dialog box and turn indexing on in the Storage Options dialog box. Your value list should now work properly.

In this example, the field list is sorted by Customer ID, not by Customer Name (see fig. 6.22).

Fig. 6.22
Because indexing was turned off for the Customer Name field, the Customer ID value list is sorted by Customer ID.

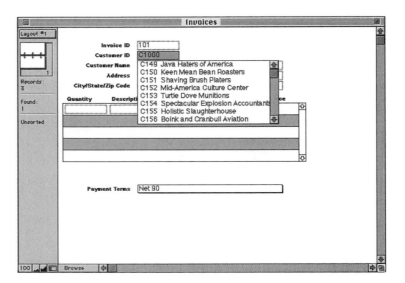

Because you can have a value list that draws values from an external database file, you might wonder if you can also display only part of that file. If you type **Illinois**, can you get a list that only includes customers from Illinois? The answer is sort of. FileMaker isn't designed to do this, but there is a work-around.

Creating a Conditional Value List

Imagine a scenario where you have several sales regions. When you choose a value from a value list of regions, you only see a list of the salespeople from that specific region when you view a value list of salespeople. Maybe you want a value list of all your parts and part numbers. First pick a manufacturer, then view only the parts for that manufacturer in a different value list.

Such conditional value lists aren't easily done in FileMaker, but they are possible. It seems like there should be a few ways to get this done, but you wind up running into a few brick walls in unexpected places. First, I'll show you the method that works. After that, I'll explain why other methods don't work. This will save you a lot of time if you're looking for a better solution, and it will also illustrate some of the idiosyncrasies of global fields and indexing.

The following example demonstrates how you can set up a field in your database (called Invoices in this example) that will show you only a list of the salespeople from a specific region when you view a value list of salespeople.

1. With the Invoices database open, choose File, Define Fields, and create two new text fields: Region and Sales Rep.

2. Choose File, New and create a database called Salespeople. Define two text fields: Rep ID and Rep Name. Enter the following sample data in the database:

Rep ID	Rep Name
East1	Edna East
East2	Edith East
East3	Eric East
West1	Will West
West2	Wynona West
West3	Wallis West
North1	Nancy North
North2	Nora North

North3	Nathan North
South1	Sarah South
South2	Susan South
South3	Sam South

3. Create one more database called Rep List and create a global text field called Region.

4. Create a number field called Serial. Click Options to open the Entry Options dialog box. Select the Serial Number radio button. Set the next value to 1 and increment by 1. Click OK to close the Entry Options dialog box.

5. Create a calculation field called List Key. When you click Create, the Specify Calculation dialog box opens. Double-click Region into the calculation area and click the concatenation button (upper-left button). Double-click the Serial field into the calculation area. Make sure the result is formatted as text, then click OK to close the Specify Calculation dialog box.

6. Create a text field called Rep Name. Click Options to open the Entry Options dialog box (see fig. 6.23). Select the Looked-Up Value radio button to open the Lookup dialog box (see fig. 6.24).

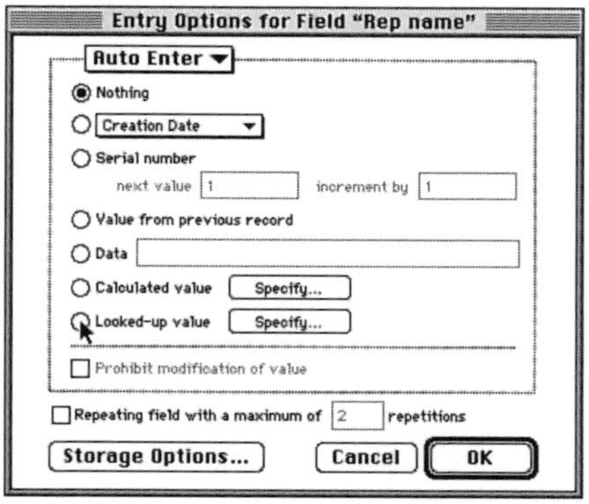

Fig. 6.23
Set a lookup in the Auto Enter options.

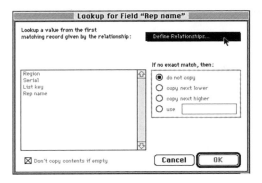

Fig. 6.24
You can't create a lookup without a relationship.

7. Choose Define Relationships from the pop-up menu in the upper-right corner of the dialog box.

8. In the Define Relationships dialog box, click New to open the Edit Relationship dialog box (see fig. 6.25).

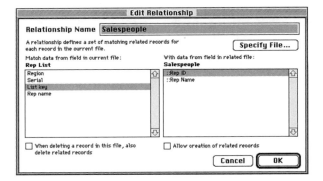

Fig. 6.25
Match fields should be the same field type, in this case text.

9. In the Edit Relationship dialog box, select List key and ::Rep ID as your two match fields.

10. Click OK to close the Edit Relationship dialog box and click Done to close the Define Relationships dialog box.

11. In the Lookup dialog box, select the ::Rep Name field. Deselect the Don't Copy Contents If Empty check box. Click OK to close the Lookup dialog box.

12. Click OK to close the Entry Options dialog box.

13. Click Done to close the Define Fields dialog box.

Now you have databases named Invoices, Salespeople, and Rep List. What you're trying to do is enter a region in the Region field and have a value list display showing only the salespeople for that region. The problem is, when you have a value list that draws from field values, the list will show every value in the database. There's no way to restrict it to a found set of the data. The only answer is to have an intermediate database that holds the subset of data you're looking for.

In this example, when you enter a region name in the Region field in Invoices, you want the Rep List database to load up only those sales representatives who work in that region from the Salespeople database. The Sales Rep value list in Invoices will then show the values in the Rep List database.

The actual mechanics of this process are as follows:

1. Enter a region value in Invoices.

2. Copy that region value and switch to the Rep List database. Paste the region value in the Region global field.

Pasting the region value into the global region field causes the List Key calculation field to recalculate, generating new Rep ID values.

You might think this recalculation would trigger a relookup automatically, but because one of the arguments of the calculation is a global field, the calculation has to be an unstored calculation. Because it's an unstored calculation, you have to manually trigger the lookup. When you trigger a re-lookup, the new values get copied into the Rep Name. These values are then used in the Sales Rep value list in Invoices.

To do this, you need to set up a script scriptsin Rep List that pastes the region information into the Region global field. Follow these steps:

1. Choose Script, ScriptMaker to open the Define Scripts dialog box (see fig. 6.26).

2. Type **Region Update** in the Script Name text box and click Create. The Script Definition dialog box appears (see fig. 6.27).

3. Click Clear All to remove the default script steps.

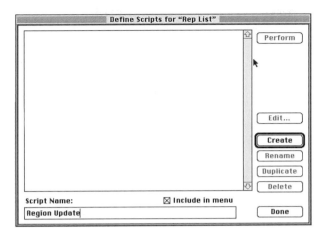

Fig. 6.26
The first step in creating a script is to give it a name.

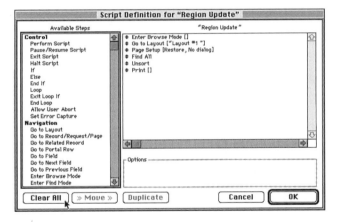

Fig. 6.27
The second step in just about every script is clearing the default script steps.

II

Enhancing Databases

4. Scroll through the Available Steps list until you find the Paste command. Select it and click Move (or double-click it) to move it to the Region Update list on the right.

5. Click Specify Field to open the Specify Field dialog box (see fig. 6.28).

6. Select the Region field and click OK to close the Specify Field dialog box.

7. From the Available Steps list, select the Relookup script step and click OK (or double-click it) to move it to the Region Update list.

Fig. 6.28
When you paste
the region into the
Region Field, the
List Key field
recalculates.

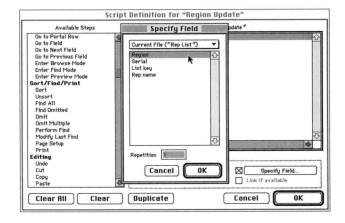

8. Select the Perform Without Dialog check box and click Specify Field to open the Specify Field dialog box.

9. Select the Region field and click OK to close the Specify Field dialog box. Your script should now look similar to figure 6.29.

Fig. 6.29
You have to
relookup the
Region field to
trigger the Rep
Name field.

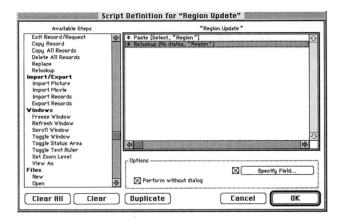

10. Click OK to close the Script Definition dialog box.

11. Click Done to close the Define Scripts dialog box.

12. Choose Window, Invoices to switch to the Invoices database.

13. In Invoices, choose Script, ScriptMaker to open the Define Scripts dialog box.

14. Name the new script Trigger Rep List. Click Create.

15. Click Clear All to remove the default script steps.

16. Scroll through the Available Steps list to find Copy. Double-click to move it to the list on the right.

17. Click Specify Field to open the Specify Field dialog box.

18. Select the Region field and click OK to close the Specify Field dialog box.

19. Scroll through the Available Steps list to find the Perform script. Double-click to move it to the list on the right.

20. Click the Specify pop-up menu and choose External Script to open the External Script dialog box.

21. Click Change File to open the Open dialog box.

22. Select the Rep List database and click Open.

23. In the Specify External Script dialog box, choose Region Update from the Script pop-up menu (see fig. 6.30).

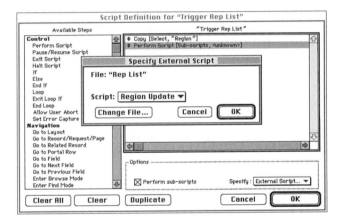

Fig. 6.30
The Trigger Rep List script launches the Region Update script.

24. Click OK to close the External Script dialog box.

25. Select the Go To Field script step on the left and move it to the right side.

26. Click Specify Field to open the Specify Field dialog box.

27. Select the Sales Rep field and click OK. Your completed script should now look like figure 6.31.

28. Click OK to close the Script Definition dialog box.

29. Click Done to close the Define Scripts dialog box.

30. Choose Mode, Layout and select the Region field.

Fig. 6.31
The Trigger Rep
List Script
generates a
conditional list in
the Rep List file.

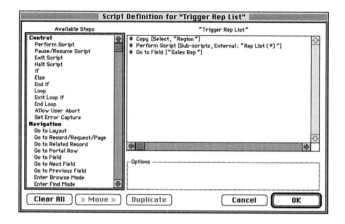

31. Choose Format, Field Format to open the Field Format dialog box.

32. Select the Pop-up List Menu radio button.

33. Choose Define Value Lists from the Using Value List pop-up menu (see fig. 6.32). The Define Value Lists dialog box comes up.

Fig. 6.32
You can define
value lists from
the Field Format
dialog box.

34. Type **Regions** and click Create.

35. In the value list box, type **East**, press Return, type **West**, press Return, type **North**, press Return, and type **South**. Click Save. Your completed list should look similar to figure 6.33.

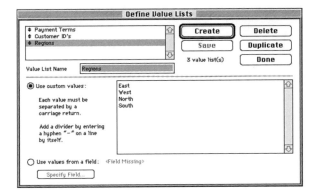

Fig. 6.33
The Regions value
list is static, so it
can be hard-coded.

36. Type a new value list named **Sales Reps** and click Create.

37. Select the Use Values From a Field radio button to open the Specify Fields for Value List dialog box.

38. Click Specify File and in the Open dialog box, select Rep List. Click Open.

39. Select the Rep Name field and click OK to close the Specify Fields for Value List dialog box.

40. Click Save, then click Done to close the Define Value Lists dialog box.

41. Choose Regions from the Using Value List pop-up list, and then click OK to close the Field Format dialog box.

42. Select the Button tool and create a new button next to the Region field (see fig. 6.34).

43. In the Specify Button dialog box, select Perform Script, and then choose Trigger Rep List in the pop-up menu (see fig. 6.35).

44. Type **Rep List** in the button.

45. Choose Mode, Browse.

Choose a region from the Region pop-up list, then click the Rep List button. Presto! A conditional value list.

This may seem like a convoluted technique, and it is. It would be simplest to make the Region field the match field, but global fields can't be match fields. Try it for yourself.

II

Enhancing Databases

Fig. 6.34
Drag the button
out near the
Region Field.

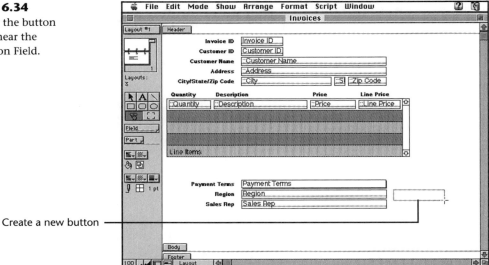

Create a new button

Fig. 6.35
The button now
triggers the
conditional list.

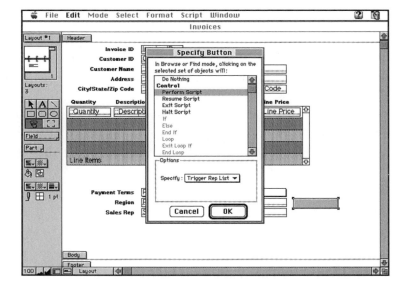

FileMaker also acts a little strange when global fields are involved with lookup triggers. If you go to the Rep List database and try changing the Region value manually, the List Key calculation works okay, but only the record that you edited does a proper relookup. Hypothetically, all records should relookup when the List Key recalculates.

Why is that? I have no idea. All I can offer is that global fields don't behave like ordinary FileMaker fields. Try variations on this technique and note the results.

Value Lists—Pitfalls to Avoid

Value lists are a great convenience when it comes to streamlining data entry, but they have their dark side as well. Check boxes, for example, are a handy thing. There are some things to watch out for, though.

Suppose you have a company that makes hard drives, and your tech support department logs customer calls in a database. Customers call in with various symptoms of their hard drive ailment, and it often happens that a hard drive can have more than one symptom. For example, the drive light might be flashing and the drive could be making a grinding noise. To allow the service representatives to be able to capture the various symptoms, you allow them to use check boxes to capture more than one symptom. Follow these steps to cook up a quick Service Call database:

1. Choose File, New to create a new database called Service Calls.

2. Create a text field called Symptoms, and then click Done to close the Define Fields dialog box.

3. Choose Mode, Layout and click the Symptoms field to select it. Choose Format, Field Format to open the Field Format dialog box.

4. Select the radio button in front of the pop-up list menu, and then choose Check Boxes from the menu. Choose Define Value Lists from the other pop-up menu to open the Define Value Lists dialog box.

5. Type **Symptoms** in the Value List Name text box and click Create. Your cursor should already be in the Custom Values text box. Enter the following values:

   Internal Drive

   External Drive

   Grindig Noise

   Whining Sound

   Clicking

   Blinking Light

I know that Internal Drive and External Drive don't belong in this list, but play along for a while. It sometimes happens that you have to clean up a database someone else designed poorly. You're intentionally designing this poorly so you can go through the process of fixing it later. The word *grinding* is also intentionally misspelled as `Grindig`, again, so you can fix it later.

Click Save, and then click Done to close the Define Value Lists dialog box. Click OK to return to the layout.

6. Resize the Symptoms field so it looks like figure 6.36.

Fig. 6.36

Resize the Symptoms field so it just contains the check boxes.

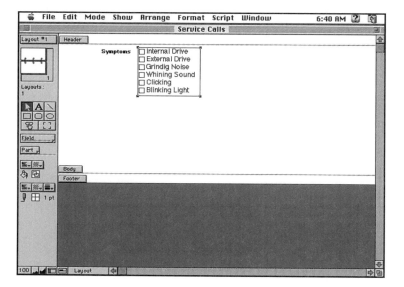

Choose Mode, Browse and try selecting some of the check boxes. Select two or three of them, and make sure to select either internal or external drive. Choose Mode, New Record to create a new record. Select some more check boxes. Make another new record and repeat this process until you have about ten records. Make sure you select Grindig Noise in a few records and that you have selected either internal or external drive on every record. Choose Mode, Duplicate Record so you know you have at least two records that are the same.

Now it's time to take a look at where the problems come in. You're going to create a report that counts each of the symptoms so you can see what the most common symptoms are. Follow these steps:

1. Choose File, Define Fields and create a new summary field called Count. In the Options for Summary dialog box, set it to be a Count of Symptoms. Click OK to close the Options for Summary dialog box. Click Done to close the Define Fields dialog box.

2. Choose Mode, Layout, then choose Mode, New Layout. Name the new layout List and select the Columnar Report radio button. Click OK to open the Specify Field Order dialog box.

3. Click Move All, and then click OK to close the Specify Field Order dialog box. Double-click the Body part label as shown in figure 6.37.

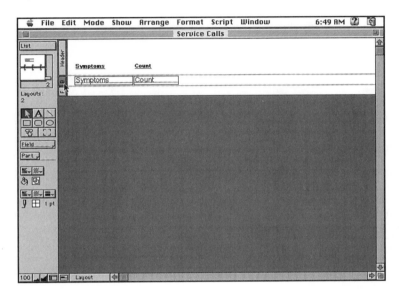

Fig. 6.37
Double-click the Body part label to open the Define Parts dialog box.

4. In the Define Parts dialog box, select the Sub-Summary When Sorted By radio button and select the Symptoms field. Click OK to close the Define Parts dialog box, then select Print Above or Print Below in the dialog box that follows (it doesn't matter which one you select).

5. Choose Mode, Browse, then choose Mode, Sort and sort the database by Symptoms. Choose Mode, Preview to view your report sub-summarized by Symptoms.

Note

Unlike earlier versions of FileMaker Pro, you can't sort while you're in Layout mode. If you're a veteran FileMaker user, it's a little disconcerting at first.

Do you notice anything unusual? Take a look at figure 6.38. Notice that even though you're summarizing by Symptoms, you're getting the same values repeating on several lines. This report is wrong, but FileMaker is doing exactly what you told it to do: summarize by unique values. Although several of these values look the same, each one is actually unique.

II

Enhancing Databases

Fig. 6.38
The Symptoms
Report shows the
same values being
counted in
separate summa-
ries.

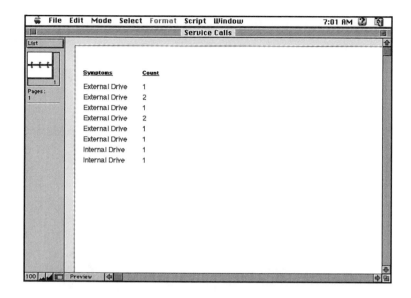

Choose Mode, Layout and resize the subsummary part as shown in figure
6.39. Resize the Symptoms field as well.

Fig. 6.39
Resize the
subsummary part
and the Symptoms
field so that you
can see multiple
lines in each field.

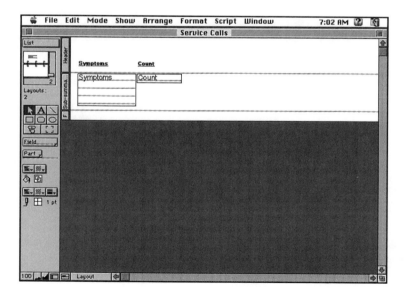

Choose Mode, Preview. Now you can see that each field is actually unique. Although now you can understand why the report was acting so strangely, that doesn't get you any closer to making the report work properly. This is a problem inherent in trying to report on fields that allow multiple values, as is the case with check boxes.

The proper solution for this problem is to convert this check box field into a portal where each checked item is actually a record in the portal. Chapter 10, "More on Conversion Issues," covers this conversion process at length.

There's another problem, though. The values Internal Drive and External Drive don't even belong in this value list. They're not symptoms at all— they're drive types. The drive type information should be broken out into its own field. This makes sense and it enhances the reporting capabilities of your database. Now you can see whether internal and external drives have different types of problems.

The drive type problem is a good one to start with. What you want is a new Drive Type field. You can use a calculated replace to load the appropriate information from the Symptoms field. If you need to break out items in an inappropriate value list, follow these steps, changing the instructions to suit your own database:

1. Choose File, Define Fields to open the Define Fields dialog box. Type **Drive Type** in the Field Name text box, make sure it's formatted as a text field, and click Create. Click Done to close the Define Fields dialog box.

2. If the field isn't on the layout where you want it, choose Mode, Layout to switch to Layout mode. Click and drag the field tool onto the layout. When you release the field tool, the Specify Field dialog box appears. Select the Drive Type field and click OK to close the Specify Field dialog box. Choose Mode, Browse to return to Browse mode.

3. Click in the Drive Type field. Choose Mode, Replace to open the Replace dialog box. Select the Replace with Calculated Result radio button to open the Specify Calculation dialog box.

4. Double-click the Case function to move it into the Calculation area. The Case function evaluates a series of tests to see whether any of them are true. You use the Case function instead of nesting a bunch of If functions inside of each other.

5. Double-click the test1 argument to select it. Choose Text Functions from the View pop-up above the Functions list. Scroll down and double-click the Position function to make it replace the test1 argument in the Calculation area. The Position function returns the position of a string of text in another string of text. For example, the position of "h" in "the" is 2. The test arguments in the Case function only require that something be true or false. FileMaker considers zero, n, or f to be false, and any non-zero number, y, or t to be true. In this example, if the word "internal" is in the field value somewhere, the Position function will return a non-zero value. You don't care what that value is, because if it's greater than zero, then the Case function will consider it true, which means the drive type is internal. The logic is that if the word "internal" is in the Symptoms field, then you're going to replace whatever is in the Drive Type field with the word "Internal."

6. Double-click the text argument of the Position function (which is now inside the Case function), and then double-click the Symptoms field to make it replace the text argument. Double-click the search string argument to select it, click the quotes button, then type **Internal**. Double-click the start argument and type **1**. Double-click the occurrence argument and type **1**. Double-click the result1 argument (this selects result 1 and [ ), click the quotes button, and then type **Internal**.

7. Double-click the test2 argument to select it. Double-click the Position function to make it replace the test2 argument in the Calculation area. Double-click the text argument of the second Position function, then double-click the Symptoms field to make it replace the text argument. Double-click the search string argument to select it, click the quotes button, and type **External**. Double-click the start argument and type **1**. Double-click the occurrence argument and type **1**. Double-click the result2 argument, click the quotes button, and type **External**.

8. Select default result]..., click the quotes button, and type **No Drive Type**. The default result is what gets returned if none of the previous tests evaluate to true. In this example, if neither internal nor external was selected in Symptoms, both tests would fail, so the No Drive Type result should be returned. Figure 6.40 shows what your finished calculation should look like. Click OK to close the Specify Calculation dialog box and to return to the Replace dialog box. Click Replace to run the replace operation using the calculation you just specified.

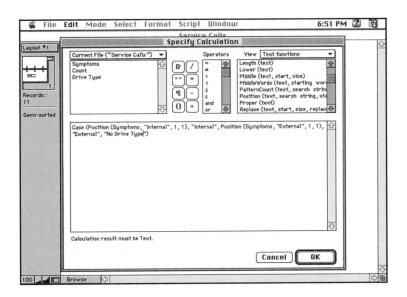

Fig. 6.40
This Case function
uses the Position
functions as
Boolean calcula-
tions (true or
false).

The replace operation takes care of breaking the drive type information out
into an appropriate field, but you still have other problems. Grindig Noise is
misspelled, and the compound values don't allow you to properly report the
actual symptoms.

It seems like the problem of the misspelled symptom is easily fixed. All you
have to do is change the spelling in the value list, right? Wrong. It almost
makes things more complicated. First, follow these steps to correct the misspelled value in the value list:

1. Choose Mode, Layout to switch to Layout mode.

2. Select the field that uses the value list, in this case Symptoms, and
   choose Format, Field Format to open the Field Format dialog box.

3. Choose Define Value Lists from the pop-up menu on the right. The
   Define Value Lists dialog box opens. Select the Symptoms Value list.
   The list pops into the list entry box. Locate the misspelled value and
   correct it. In this case, change Grindig Noise to Grinding Noise. While
   you're in there, you can remove the Internal Drive and External Drive
   values as well. Click Save to save the change, and then click Done to
   close the Define Value Lists dialog box.

4. Click OK to close the Field Format dialog box. Choose Mode, Browse to
   return to Browse mode.

II

Enhancing Databases

Now if you go through your database, you'll notice that none of the records have Grinding Noise selected, even though you previously selected Grindig Noise. To get a better understanding of what's going on, create a duplicate of your Symptoms field and format it as a Standard field. To do this, follow these steps:

1. Choose Mode, Layout to switch to Layout mode.

2. Select the Symptoms field and choose Edit, Duplicate. This duplicates the field and opens the Specify Field dialog box. Click OK to close the Specify Field dialog box, and then drag the new field to an open area on the layout.

3. With the duplicated Symptoms field still selected, choose Format, Field Format to open the Field Format dialog box. Select the Standard field radio button and click OK to close the Field Format dialog box.

4. Choose Mode, Browse to switch back to Browse mode.

Now if you switch to a record that had Grindig Noise selected, you should see something like figure 6.41. Notice that when the field is formatted to use check boxes, Grinding Noise isn't selected. That's because the actual value is Grindig Noise. You should notice also that even though you removed the Internal Drive and External Drive values from the value list, those values are still in the Symptoms field. Changing an item in a value only affects data entry done after the change. Value lists are only entry options, so changing them has no effect on existing data.

Fig. 6.41
Even if you correct an item in a misspelled value list, it has no affect on records that have already been entered.

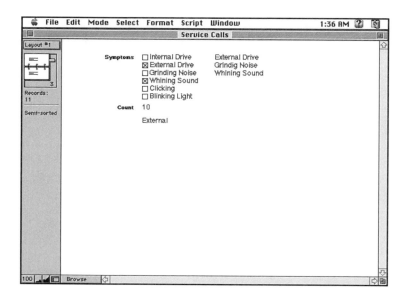

Fixing a problem like this was difficult in earlier versions of FileMaker. The new calculated replace feature makes something like this pretty easy to fix. To fix a database where several records have a single misspelled value, follow these steps:

1. Click in the Symptoms field. Choose Mode, Replace to open the Replace dialog box. Select the Replace with Calculated Result radio button to open the Specify Calculation dialog box.

2. Choose Text Functions from the Functions pop-up menu and double-click the Substitute function into the Calculation area. The Substitute function allows you to replace parts of a text string with a different text string. In this example, replace every instance of Grindig with Grinding, leaving everything else alone. Double-click the text argument to select it, then double-click the Symptoms field to replace the text argument with Symptoms. Double-click the search string argument to select it. Click the quotes button and type **Grindig**. Double-click the replace string argument to select it. Click the quotes button and type **Grinding**. Click OK to close the Specify Calculation dialog box.

3. Click Replace to run the replace operation using the calculation you just specified. Every instance of Grindig should have been replaced with Grinding.

You can run a similar replace to remove the Internal Drive and External Drive values from the Symptoms field (replace the values with nothing). In this case, remember to remove the carriage return as well.

The last problem is the incapability to report on a field that contains multiple values. Reports will only summarize properly when the fields contain single values. This issue turns out to be a conversion issue. You need to take a field with multiple values and convert it to a portal containing those same multiple values as individual records. Chapter 10 covers this process in detail.

From Here...

At this point, you should have a pretty good working knowledge of value lists. From here, you might want to read the following chapters:

■ Chapter 10, "More on Conversion Issues," covers converting check box fields to related portal rows.

II

Enhancing Databases

- Chapter 12, "Controlling File Access," teaches you how to create password-protected databases so you can set up secured layouts where administrators can have value list editing privileges. This chapter also covers other methods of controlling access to a file.

- Chapter 14, "Refining Your Database Design," clearly explains problems with check box fields. You also learn more about relational database design and normalization.

CHAPTER 7

Scripting—The Basics

Like a lot of other databases, FileMaker Pro has a programming language. Unlike a lot of other databases, FileMaker's ScriptMaker is extremely easy to use. There are no programming commands to memorize and no syntax errors to worry about. In fact, you can't help but successfully program in FileMaker Pro. Your scripts might not always do exactly what you want them to, but they'll always run.

This chapter uses an Invoices database system to demonstrate how to do the following:

- Automate reporting
- Create a main menu
- Create routines to do sorts and finds
- Automate lists
- Add speech to your database

Automating Reports

If you're not familiar with reporting in FileMaker Pro, take a look at Chapter 3, which covers reporting in depth.

Almost all reports use a sort order to break out categories. You might sort by City, State, or Company to report by those categories. Reporting also requires that you use a layout that uses the sort order to summarize the data into categories. That layout will only display the report properly when viewed in Preview mode. So, if you were to run a report manually, you would sort the database, switch to the report layout, and change to Preview mode to view your report. After you preview it, you might decide to print it. Whether you just view it or view and print the report, your last steps are to switch back to Browse mode, then switch back to the layout you started from.

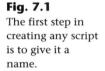

◄ See "Creating Sub-Summary and Grand Summary Fields," p. 71

There are a lot of steps to running a report; because you look at reports often, it makes sense to automate the process. To automate a process in FileMaker, you must use the ScriptMaker (although sometimes a button can perform simple operations, such as creating a new record or switching to a different layout).

The ScriptMaker is very easy to use. You don't have to remember any commands. All you have to do is choose the command you want from a list. Programming doesn't get any easier!

With ScriptMaker, you can automate this entire process. Any time you want to view the report, you can run the script from the Script menu or press a button right on a layout. Here's the process to create a script that will automatically run a report:

1. With your database open, choose Script, ScriptMaker to open the Define Scripts dialog box (see fig. 7.1).

2. Type a name for your script in the Script Name text box.

Fig. 7.1

The first step in creating any script is to give it a name.

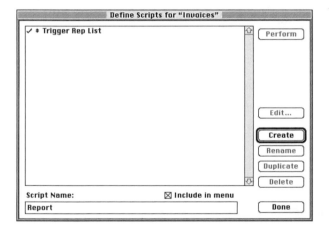

3. Click Create to open the Script Definition dialog box.

    The Available Steps list contains all the scripting steps available in FileMaker Pro 3.0.

4. Click Clear All.

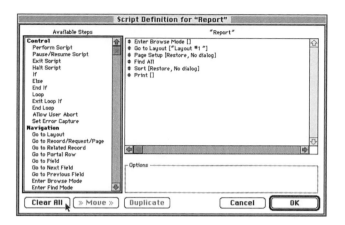

Fig. 7.2
The Available Steps
list contains all the
scripting steps
available in
FileMaker Pro 3.0.

Note

The script steps already in the Report list are default script steps. In early versions of FileMaker, what is now the ScriptMaker consisted of nothing more than a bunch of check boxes. These default steps are the descendants of the early scripting functions. I rarely use them. Consider them a charming relic from FileMaker's long history. You don't need them.

5. The first step in running a report is to switch to the Report layout. In the Available Steps list, select Go To Layout and click OK. This moves it to the list on the right (see fig. 7.3). To move a step to the list on the right, you can also double-click the step or select it and press the space bar.

6. Now you want to sort the database on the fields required to trigger the sub-summary parts in your report layout. Find the Sort script step in the Available Steps list and move it to the right.

7. Switch to Preview mode, find the Enter Preview mode script step in the Available Steps list and move it to the right. One of the options that the Preview step has is the capability to pause. Because you're going to want to look at your report after you take the time to run it, select the Pause check box.

8. Take a look at your report. You'll most likely want to return to the layout you started from. If not, you can switch to a different layout. Either way, you need the Go To Layout script step again. Copy it from the Available Steps list.

Fig. 7.3
Script steps you
move to the list on
the right become
part of the script.

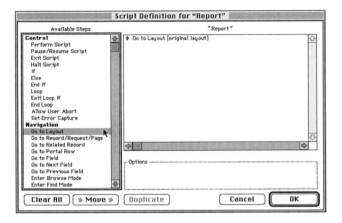

9. Choose Original layout from the Specify pop-up menu. If you want to go to a different layout, specify that one.

10. Click OK to close the Script Definition dialog box and return to the Define Scripts dialog box. Notice that the script you just worked on is automatically selected. You can choose to include or exclude any script from the Script menu by selecting it and selecting the Include in Menu check box in the Define Scripts dialog box. Leave it selected for now and click OK to close the Define Scripts dialog box.

When you run this script, it will do all of the sorting, layout switching, and mode switching for you. All you have to do is look at your report.

Troubleshooting

My report doesn't display properly and sometimes not at all.

One of the crucial things about running a report is making sure your sort order matches the sort order required by the report layout. FileMaker doesn't change its sort order until you tell it to. After you run your script, choose Mode, Sort to open the Sort dialog box. Note the sorting fields in the list on the right. Close the dialog box and choose Mode, Layout to see the report layout. On the left of your report are gray layout part labels. Any labels that begin with Sub-summary by require a certain sort order to display properly. By double-clicking a sub-summary part label, you can find out what field it needs to have sorted. When you know the required sort fields, return to Browse mode, sort the database on those fields, then choose Script, ScriptMaker to open the Define Scripts dialog box. Double-click your report script to open the Script Definition dialog box. Click OK to close the dialog box, and FileMaker will notify you that the sort order has changed. Select the Replace radio button and click OK to close the dialog box. Click Done to close the Define Scripts dialog box.

Automating Finds

Sometimes people using a database have nothing to do with designing it. New employees and temporary workers won't be familiar with the data in a database. For these reasons, it might be worthwhile to automate searching so it's easy to do for someone who isn't familiar with the database.

Here's a scenario that describes how this would work: a user needs to look up a specific record in a data entry layout. He clicks a Find button that puts him in Find mode and takes him to a layout that lists the fields you want him to be able to search. Next to each field is a button that shows him a list of all the data in that particular field. For example, a Company Name field might have a list containing Fred's Scuba Place, Miami Luge Outfitters, and so on. The user can select an item from the list, and it will automatically be pasted into their find request. The user clicks a Find button, and FileMaker shows him the record or records that matched his search criteria.

Using the Paste From Index Command

One of the best ways to automate finds is to use the Paste From Index command. It's a good idea to create a layout for the specific purpose of searching (see fig. 7.4). This type of layout is typically called by a button or script when the user is in another layout. The button or script automatically puts the database in Find mode.

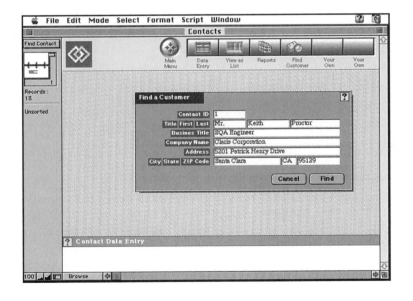

Fig. 7.4
A dedicated find layout can make things easier for users who aren't familiar with your database.

With a layout like this, it's easy to turn the field labels into buttons that will allow a user to paste from the index into that field. Here are the steps to do this:

1. With your database open, choose Mode, Layout to go into Layout mode.

2. Select the first field label.

3. Choose Format, Button to open the Specify Button dialog box (see fig. 7.5).

Fig. 7.5
The Specify Button dialog box allows you to tie a single command or script to a button.

4. Click Specify Field to open the Specify Field dialog box.

5. Locate the field that's associated with the label you're working with and select it.

6. Click OK to close the Specify Field dialog box and OK again to close the Specify Button dialog box.

7. Repeat this process for each item on your Find layout.

8. Choose Mode, Browse to return to the Browse Mode.

Follow these steps to test your script:

1. Choose Mode, Find to enter the Find mode.

2. Click one of your field labels. The View Index dialog box appears (see fig. 7.6). This dialog box displays all of the values from all records for a particular field. Any item a user selects from the View Index dialog box is automatically pasted into the appropriate field. In this way, users who are unfamiliar with the data can be sure to get the spelling in their find requests correct.

Fig. 7.6
The View Index
dialog box allows
a user unfamiliar
with the database
to easily create a
valid find request.

Troubleshooting

When I click a field and choose Edit, Paste Special, the From Index command isn't accessible.

Because global fields have the same value for every record, they aren't indexed. Likewise, any calculation fields that reference global fields cannot be indexed, and you can't paste from the index into these fields.

---

3. Select an item from the Index and click Paste.

This pastes the selected item from your index into the selected field.

4. Click Find to run the search.

Using Buttons

Some other enhancements you might want to make to a dedicated Find layout would be to add buttons to reset the Find and to perform the Find. There are two styles of buttons in FileMaker 3.0: rounded and rectangular. Follow these steps to select a button style:

1. Choose Edit, Preferences to open the Preferences dialog box.

2. Choose Layout from the pop-up menu at the top of the dialog box (see fig. 7.7).

3. Select the button tool radio button of your choice (see fig. 7.8). Click Done to close the Preferences dialog box.

II

Enhancing Databases

Fig. 7.7

Switch to the
Layout Preferences
by selecting
Layout from the
pop-up menu.

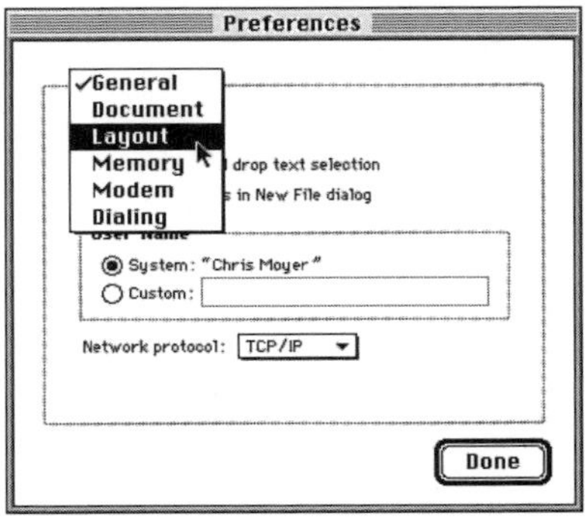

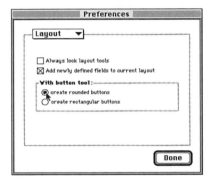

Fig. 7.8

Now any buttons
you create in the
Layout Mode will
have the selected
button style.

If you have users who know how to switch layouts without using buttons you
create, it's possible that they can switch to your find layout and not be in the
Find mode. If that happens, you need to provide a way to put the database
into Find mode so they can enter search criteria. To create a button to reset
the Find layout, follow these steps:

1. Choose Mode, Layout to enter the Layout mode.

2. Select the button tool from the Layout Tools palette.

3. Move the cursor to where you want to draw your button and press and
hold the mouse button. Drag the button to the desired size (see fig. 7.9).
When you release the mouse button, the Specify Button dialog box
appears (see fig. 7.10).

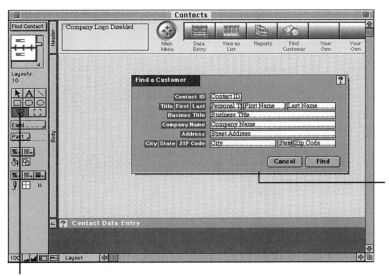

Fig. 7.9
If you inadvertently make your button too small, it will resize automatically to fit the button label.

Drag to the desired size

Button tool

Fig. 7.10
You need to scroll down the list to see the Enter Find Mode command.

4. Select Enter Find Mode from the list and click OK to close the Specify Button dialog box.

5. Type **Reset Find** as the button name (see fig. 7.11).

6. Choose Mode, Browse to return to Browse mode.

Fig. 7.11
The cursor automatically appears in the button so you can label it.

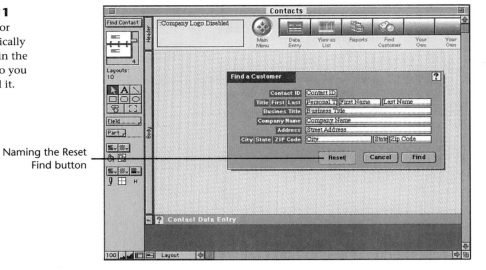

Naming the Reset Find button

Click your new Reset Find button to test it. It should automatically put you in Find mode. Try typing something in a Search field, then click the Reset button again. It should clear the Find.

To create a button that performs the Find after you enter Find criteria, follow these steps:

1. Choose Mode, Layout to enter Layout mode.

2. Select the Button tool from the Layout Tools palette.

3. Move the cursor to where you want to draw your button, and press and hold the mouse button. Drag the button to the desired size. The Specify Button dialog box appears.

4. Select Perform Find from the list (see fig. 7.12). Then click OK to close the Specify Button dialog box.

5. Type **Find** as the button name.

6. Choose Mode, Browse to return to Browse mode.

To test the new Find button, choose Mode, Find, or click the Reset button to enter Find mode. Type some search criteria into any of the fields and click the Find button. The number of resulting records will appear in the Status Area on the left. You can switch to a list view or a data entry view to see the results of your find.

Fig. 7.12
Perform Find will execute any find requests the user enters.

Automating Lists

It's always useful to have a list view in any database you create. You can use it to see the results of your finds, or to look for a specific record when the database is sorted alphabetically. In a list view, such as the one in figure 7.13, you might want to sort by city, state, or customer name. One of the nice things you can do to automate sorting and save some space on the layout is to turn the column headers into sorting buttons.

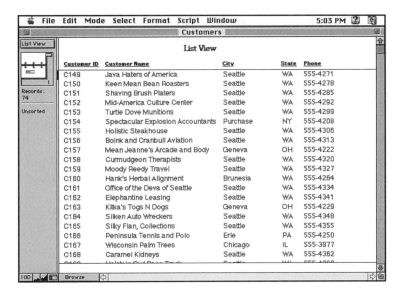

Fig. 7.13
A simple list view like this can be more useful with automated sort buttons.

II

Enhancing Databases

If you sort a database, enter ScriptMaker, and use a sort script step, then you have the option to restore the existing sort order. In this way, ScriptMaker scripts can "remember" sort orders.

To create a sorting script:

1. With the database open, choose Mode, Sort to open the Sort Records dialog box (see fig. 7.14).

Fig. 7.14
If you specify a sort order and click Sort or Done, that sort order can then be recalled by a script.

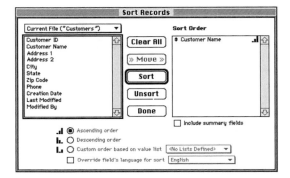

2. Click Clear All to clear the existing sort order.

3. Select the field you want to sort by from the list on the left and click Move.

4. Select the field in the list on the right and notice that you can sort the field in ascending or descending order, or even on an order based on the contents of a value list (see Chapter 6 for more information on value lists). Notice also that you can sort the field using sorting rules from several languages by selecting the Override Field's Language For Sort check box. Choose your appropriate sort order and click Sort.

5. Choose Script, ScriptMaker to open the Define Scripts dialog box. In the Script Name text box, type an appropriate name and click Create (see fig. 7.15).

6. There is a list of default script steps in the list on the right. You don't need these, so click Clear All.

7. Select the sort script step in the Available Steps list and do one of the following to move it to the list on the right: double-click it, select it, and press the space bar; or select it and click Move.

8. Select the Restore Sort Order and Perform Without Dialog check boxes (see fig. 7.16).

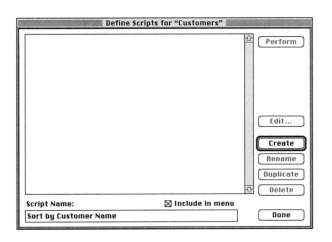

Fig. 7.15
Create a new sort
script by giving it a
name.

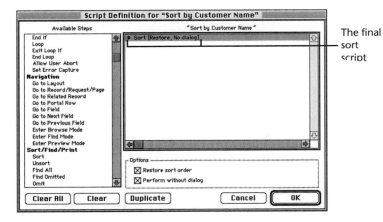

The final
sort
script

Fig. 7.16
When you restore
a sort order in a
script, you capture
the current sort
criteria in the Sort
Records dialog
box.

II

Enhancing Databases

9. Click OK to close the Script Definition dialog box.

10. Click Done to close the Define Scripts dialog box.

Follow these steps to see if this really works:

1. Choose Mode, Sort to open the Sort Records dialog box.

2. Click Unsort to undo the last sort. Unsort puts the records in creation
order.

3. Choose your new script from the Script menu.

It should automatically sort the database, and the Status Area should
reflect this: the word Sorted should appear under the Book.

To tie a script to a button, follow these steps:

1. Choose Mode, Layout to enter Layout mode.

2. Drag the label for the field that's used in the sort script up about 1/2 inch.

3. Select the Text tool from the Layout Tools palette.

4. Double-click the label of the field the script sorts by to select it. For example, if the script sorts by customer name, select the text of the customer label.

5. Choose Edit, Copy to copy the selected text.

6. Select the Button tool from the Tools palette.

7. Drag the button so that it fills the space immediately above the sort field (see fig. 7.17). The Specify Button dialog box appears.

Fig. 7.17
Create the sort button directly above the field it sorts.

New sort button

Text tool

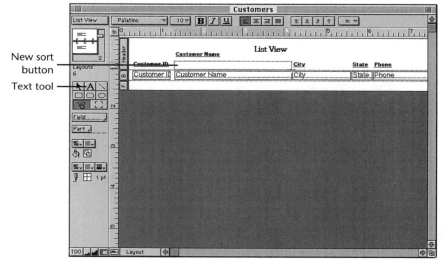

8. Select Perform Script and, in the Options area, specify the sort script (see fig. 7.18).

9. Click OK to close the Specify Button dialog box.

10. Choose Edit, Paste to paste the field label text into the button name.

11. Choose Edit, Select All to select the entire button name.

12. Choose Format and format the button as you choose (see fig. 7.19).

Fig. 7.18
The completed
Specify Button
dialog box.

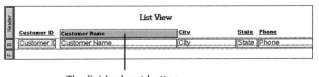

The finished sort button

Fig. 7.19
Format the button
so it stands out.

13. Choose Mode, Browse to return to Browse mode.

14. Repeat this process for any other fields you want to sort by.

FileMaker Speaks—A Word from Our Sponsor!

FileMaker 3.0 has a fun new feature that allows a database to talk to its users. You access this capability through ScriptMaker with a script step called Speak. For the Speak feature to work, you need to install the Speech Manager extension. Unfortunately, the speech technology on the Macintosh is less than crystal clear.

Regardless, this feature has a lot of appeal, and it certainly won't hurt your demonstrations if you need to pitch a database project. There are some fun things you can do with this capability. One of them is to have a database greet each user as they open it.

To have a database greet a user when they open the database, follow these steps:

1. In the database of your choice, choose File, Define Fields to open the Define Fields dialog box.

2. Create a new global field called User and click Create. The Options dialog box appears.

3. Make sure the data type is set to Text and click OK.

4. Create a calculation field called Greeting and click Create. The Specify Calculation dialog box appears.

5. Click the Quotes button.

6. Type **Good Morning** with a space after it.

7. Move the cursor to the right of the closing quotation marks and click the Concatenation button. The concatenation symbol is used when you want to put two pieces of text together. Think of it as a plus sign for words.

8. From the field list in the upper left corner, double-click the User field. The Specify Calculation dialog box should look similar to figure 7.20.

Fig. 7.20
This calculation creates a greeting that's customized for each user.

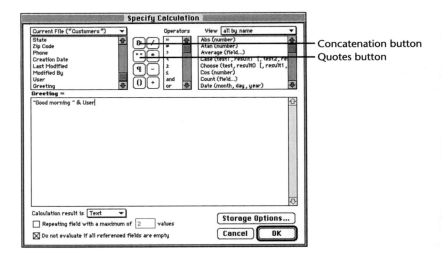

9. Click OK to close the Specify Calculation dialog box.

10. Click Done to close the Find Fields dialog box.

11. Choose Script, ScriptMaker to open the Defined Scripts dialog box.

12. Create a new script called Greetings, Earthling and click Create (see fig. 7.21). The Script Definition dialog box appears.

13. Click Clear All to delete the default script steps.

14. In the Available Steps list, scroll to the Fields category and double-click the Set Field script step.

15. Click Specify Field to open the Specify Field dialog box.

16. Select the User field and click OK (see fig. 7.22).

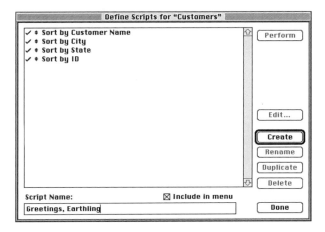

Fig. 7.21
Create a script that will speak the greeting message.

Fig. 7.22
The key to the customized greeting is getting the user's name into the User field.

17. Click Specify to open the Specify Calculations dialog box.

18. Select Status functions from the Functions pop-up menu, as shown in figure 7.23.

19. Scroll to the bottom of the Status functions list and double-click the Status (CurrentUserName) function (see fig. 7.24).

Enhancing Databases

Fig. 7.23
Use the Functions
pop-up menu to
view the Status
functions.

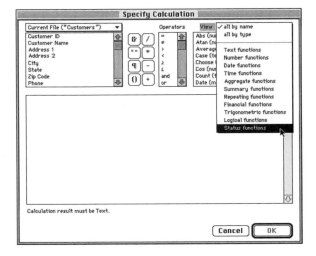

Fig. 7.24
The calculation
captures the name
of the current user
and puts it
together with a
greeting.

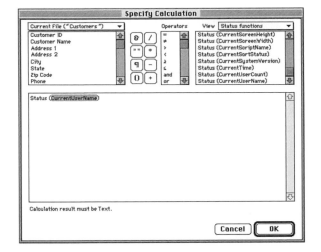

20. Click OK to close the Specify Calculation dialog box.

21. In the Script Definition dialog box, scroll to the bottom of the Available Steps list and double-click Speak.

22. Click Specify to open the Specify Text to Speak dialog box.

23. Select the Field radio button to open the Specify Field dialog box.

24. Select the Greeting field and click OK. The completed Specify Text to Speak dialog box should look similar to figure 7.25.

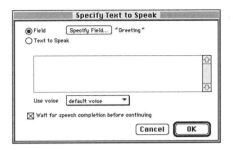

Fig. 7.25
The Specify Text to
Speak dialog box
allows you to use
text from a field or
from the dialog
box.

25. Click OK to close the Specify Text to Speak dialog box.

26. Click OK to close the Script Definition dialog box.

27. Choose Edit, Preferences to open the Preferences dialog box.

28. Choose Document from the pop-up menu (see fig. 7.26).

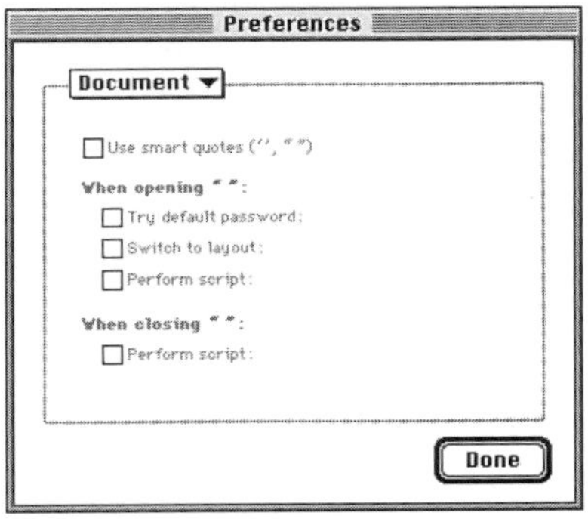

Fig. 7.26
Choose from these
options in the
Preferences dialog
box.

29. In the When Opening category, select the Perform Script check box.

30. Choose the Greetings, Earthling script from the pop-up.

31. Click Done to close the Preferences dialog box.

Every time a user opens his database, the Greetings, Earthling script will automatically run. This will copy the user name to the user global field, and the script will say, `Hello <user name>`.

To test this, close the database and open it again. Remember, for this script to work properly, you need to have your Speech Manager extension installed.

II

Enhancing Databases

From Here...

In this chapter, you learned how to do some basic scripting with ScriptMaker. You learned how to automate reports and finds, as well as how to make a database talk to you. Other chapters that might interest you are:

- Chapter 3, "Creating and Printing Reports," teaches you more about reporting. It also goes into detail about how to find and sort information in a FileMaker database.

- Chapter 11, "Designing Layouts that Work," gives additional information about creating and formatting buttons.

- Chapter 15, "Scripting with ScriptMaker," addresses more advanced issues in scripting.

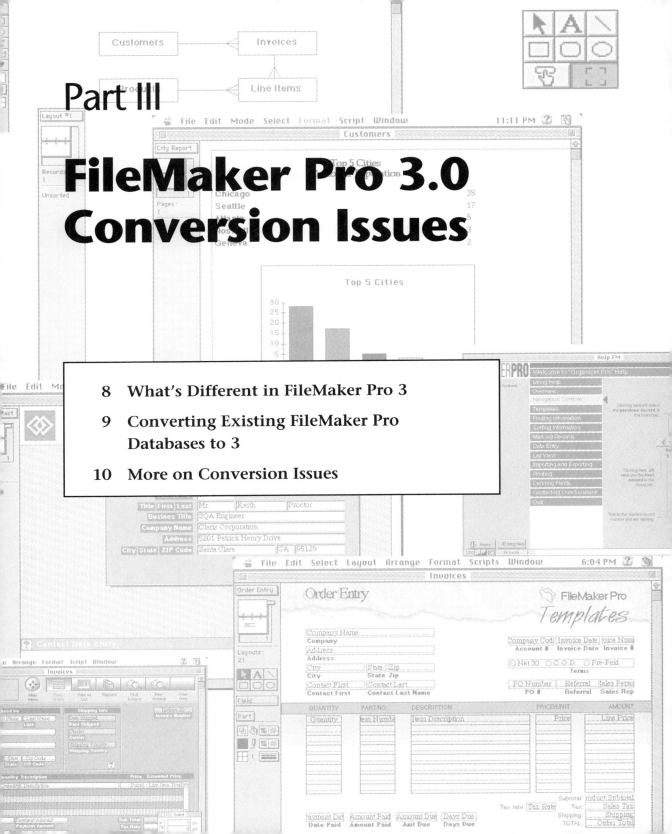

Part III

FileMaker Pro 3.0 Conversion Issues

CHAPTER 8

What's Different in FileMaker Pro 3

This chapter explains some of the basics about the new features in FileMaker 3.0 and what significance these changes have in developing databases with the 3.0 version as opposed to the 2.0 version. It's just intended to be a quick overview of the new features, so if you need detailed information about specific features, see the chapter that covers that feature.

Some of the new features described are:

- Relational capabilities and portals
- ScriptMaker enhancements
- New layout tools
- Global and calculation fields
- Easier networking setup

Relationality!

This is probably *the* most asked-for feature in the history of FileMaker Pro, and it's finally here. There is a significant difference in the functionality of a flat-file database, which FileMaker Pro 2.x was, and a relational database, which FileMaker Pro 3.0 is. The implications of this change (especially in designing relational database systems) are so significant that an entire section of this book has been devoted to this topic alone.

Problems with Flat-File Databases

Why is relationality a big deal? Because it solves the major problems of working with a flat-file database. What problems? Here are a few examples.

The Consistency Problem

In the 2.x version of FileMaker Pro, one of the sample databases that shipped with the product was an invoice template. It contained everything you would expect to find on an invoice: customer information, line items of products, and so on. The invoice template was linked to a Customer database via a lookup. When a user entered a customer number code on the invoice template, the database opened the Customer database in the background, checked for a match on the customer number code, and if it found one, it *copied* the customer name and address information into the corresponding name and address fields in the Invoice database.

This copying meant there were now two copies of the same information floating around: a customer name was stored in the customer name field in the Customer database, and the customer name was also being stored in the customer name field in the Invoice database for as many invoices as the customer had. If the customer had five invoices, the name was stored five times in addition to the one time it was stored in the Customer database. The information was not only redundant, but the invoice data wasn't really linked back to the source data in the Customer database.

Does that sound trivial? What if someone was working with the Invoice database and noticed an error in the address? They could make the change, but information changed in the Invoice database didn't affect information in the Customer database because it was only a copy of the original. Now there'd be two (or three or four) different versions of the same customer information. How do you reconcile them? Which version should you use? It would be a mess, and it would be a bigger mess when you have hundreds or thousands of records with this problem.

Worse still, if someone did a relookup to the Customer database, any changes that had been made to the customer information in the Invoice database would be overwritten. This could be a bad thing (it could also be a great thing), depending on which version of the customer data was the right one.

The bottom line is this: without being able to have relationships between databases, there was no assurance that multiple copies of the same information would stay consistent. To be sure, with the flexibility of the ScriptMaker, you could implement procedures to protect against this, but you would have to have a manually triggered process that might or might not be run when it should be. Regardless, this possibility for multiple versions of data is a significant problem with redundant information.

The Storage Problem

Another problem with redundant information involves storage. If you had a database full of 50,000 invoices (lucky you!) and only 100 customers, that meant that for each customer you would have an average of 500 extra copies of your customer name and address information taking up hard drive space. Because FileMaker Pro 2.x was restricted to a physical file size limit of 32M, having all of that redundant information meant that you couldn't have as many records in your database as you could if you had not duplicated that customer information over and over. Because big databases don't run as fast as small ones, this duplicate information also affects performance.

The Repeating Field Problem

Yet one more significant issue concerns repeating fields. Repeating fields are very useful, and for backwards-compatibility reasons, they're still in FileMaker 3.0, so you can still use them if they suit your needs.

For the uninitiated, a repeating field is a special type of text, number, date, time, or calculation field that can hold multiple values (see fig. 8.1). You use it to handle a one-to-many relationship. Invoices and purchase orders are classic examples where you have *one* invoice or purchase order containing *many* line items of products.

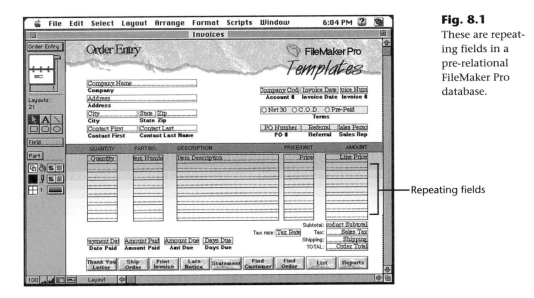

Fig. 8.1
These are repeating fields in a pre-relational FileMaker Pro database.

Repeating fields

For an invoice containing ten line items, you can create one field with ten repetitions for quantity instead of creating ten separate fields for quantity line 1, quantity line 2, and so on. This saves a lot of work. One of the nice things about repeating fields is that you can do math across all repetitions of a repeating field, so you can total a ten-repetition field to get your invoice total.

▶ See "Opening 2.x Files in FileMaker 3.0," p. 225

The problems come in when you need to do reporting on the individual line items of a repeating field. What if you need to find out how many widgets were sold last month? If widgets can be entered on any line of a repeating field, there's no graceful way to count them. There are a few work-arounds—these are covered in the discussion on converting 2.x files into 3.0 files. For now, in FileMaker 2.x, reporting on information contained in repeating fields was less than straightforward.

Okay, so now you might agree that having flat-file databases with lookups, multiple copies of information, and repeating fields is not the best of all possible worlds. How are relational databases better? Relational databases are designed so that only one copy of a piece of information is stored. Well, that's the ideal. The facts of life are that you'll need to have a customer number code in both the Invoice database and the Customer database, but the actual customer name and address information is only stored in one place—the Customer database.

In FileMaker Pro 3.0, that Invoice database has been retooled. Now when you look at the invoice, it still looks the same, but the customer information is actually only in the Customer database. There are no customer information fields in the Invoice database. How can this be? This is possible because of relationships.

How Relationships Work

◀ See "Creating a Relationship," p. 79

FileMaker Pro 3.0 has a new option under the File menu called Define Relationships. Choosing this option opens the Define Relationships dialog box (see fig. 8.2). Every relationship gets a name, and after it's named, the user goes through the process of setting up the details of the relationship. The basic process is a little like creating a lookup was in 2.x, but a lot more understandable.

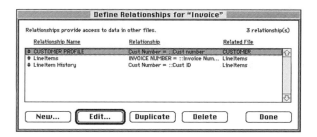

Fig. 8.2
Relationships are
easy to create and
edit in FileMaker
Pro 3.

All you have to do is identify another database file to link to, then pick the
key fields in both databases. For example, if you want to link your Invoice
database to your Customer database, from the Invoice database, you create a
new relationship, select the Customer database as your linked file, and then
choose the fields on which to base the link. In this case, select Customer
Number in the Invoice database and Customer Number in the Customer
database (see fig. 8.3).

After you set up the relationship, you can view the related information
through something called an external field. This is similar to the 2.x concept
of running an external script, but in this case, when you drag a new field
onto a layout, you can either use a field from the current database or you can
use a field from a database that you have a relationship for, such as customers
(see fig. 8.4).

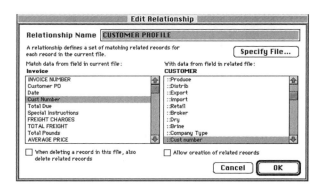

Fig. 8.3
Select the fields
from the files you
want to relate in
the Edit Relation-
ship dialog.

Fig. 8.4
You can place
fields from other
related files on a
layout.

When you view an external field in the Browse mode, it's as if you cut a hole in the Invoice layout and place the Customer database behind the hole. Imagine you're looking *through* the Invoice database at the Customer database.

The end result is that functionally similar databases will be smaller in FileMaker Pro 3.0 than they were in 2.x, which means 3.0 databases will be faster than 2.x databases as the number of records increases. An additional benefit is that you won't have to worry about multiple versions of a particular piece of information and whether the version you're working with is the accurate one.

 ## Viewing Multiple Records through Portals

In FileMaker Pro 2.x, if you had a lookup from one database to another, say Invoices looked up to Customers, and you had more than one match for your lookup trigger, say Company ID, you would only get data from the first record that matched. FileMaker Pro 2.x just wasn't equipped to handle anything more than a one-to-one relationship.

In FileMaker Pro 3.0, you can have one-to-many relationships to accommodate many line items on one invoice, and each of the line items will be an individual record in another file. When each line item is an individual record, it becomes very easy to find out things like how many widgets got sold last month and what the average selling price was.

The way these line items get viewed on one layout is via a portal. Portals will largely replace the use of repeating fields in FileMaker Pro 3.0. They're very different, though. Information in a portal is actually stored in a different database than the one the portal is in. So what is a portal? A *portal* is a new type of layout object that can show multiple corresponding records. When I said a relational layout in FileMaker 3.0 was like a hole cut in the layout, I wasn't kidding. The portal tool creates that hole, that view onto another database (see fig. 8.5).

—Portal tool

Fig. 8.5
Use the portal tool to add multiple related records to a database.

A portal requires a relationship to work properly, so if you try to create a new portal when no relationships have been defined, you will have the option of creating a relationship before proceeding (see fig. 8.6).

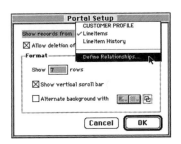

Fig. 8.6
A portal is dependent on a relationship and can have multiple rows as well as scroll bars.

After you tell the portal which relationship to use and you place the portal on a layout, you just choose the external fields (in the related database) to display. Figure 8.7 shows an Invoice database that has a portal containing Line Item fields from a Line Items database. Note the field names in the portal. When you're in Layout mode, you can always tell if a field is an external field by the double colon at the beginning of the name, such as ::Quantity.

Fig. 8.7

This is a completed portal with related fields from another file (Layout mode).

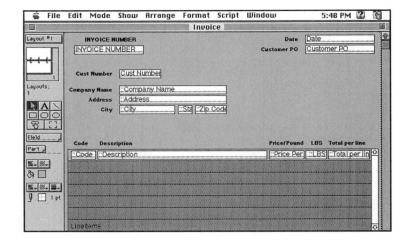

In Browse mode, the portal uses its relationship to display data (see fig. 8.8). For example, this portal uses the Line Items relationship, which has Invoice ID as its key field. When you enter an Invoice ID in the Invoice database, FileMaker checks the Line Items database to see if any of the line items live on that invoice. If it finds a match or several matches, it displays as many matching records as will fit in the portal. If the portal has been defined to display four rows and only three are found, the last row is blank. If ten are found, all four are filled.

Fig. 8.8

In Browse mode, a portal shows data from another file.

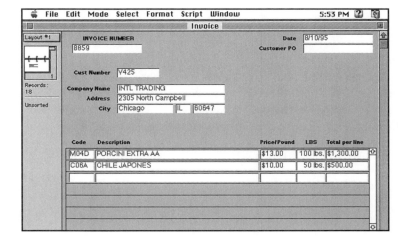

So now you've stumbled onto your first relational design issue. When you're designing this database, you will want to know the typical number of line items that are likely to be entered. You might also want to know the maximum number. When you set up the portal, you can make scrolling available or not (at last—a scrolling repeating field). If you know for a fact that there will never be more than five line items, leave it disabled and no one will get confused and try to scroll to information that isn't there.

You also have the option to make available the creation of new line items. When this is turned on, there will always be a blank line item at the end of the list, whether you have to scroll to it or not. If you click in this empty line item and begin entering information, you will create a new record in the Line Item database. Wild, huh?

ScriptMaker Enhancements

While the scripting capabilities of FileMaker Pro 2.x were already pretty rich, there were things missing that would have made the automation of certain tasks easier and more elegant. For example, if you wanted to reuse a script step several times in the same script, you didn't just set it up once and then duplicate the step. If you needed a bunch of steps to go to Layout #2, you had to set a bunch of individual steps over and over again. You'll be happy to know that you can now duplicate script steps (see fig. 8.9).

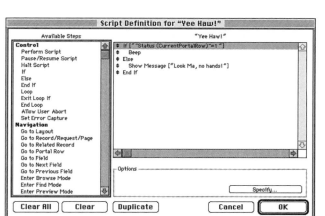

Fig. 8.9
The new Script Definition dialog box has new features, such as the Duplicate button.

III

Conversion Issues

In fact, the entire ScriptMaker has been completely redesigned for 1996. In FileMaker Pro 2.x, the various script steps were blocked off into little groups. In 3.0, the scripts are now listed in functionally similar, labeled categories. Those categories and the new script commands they contain are described in the following sections.

The New Commands

The following sections describe in detail the new commands in FileMaker Pro 3.

Control

These commands manage script actions.

- *Halt Script*: This obviously allows you to stop a script. It could be very handy when combined with If/Else/End If.
- *If []*
- *Else*
- *End If*: Ahhh. True control structures at last. Now with all of the new status functions (see Chapter 16 for more information), you can do stuff like test for what monitor depth the user's computer is set for and then switch to an appropriate black and white or color layout.
- *Allow User Abort*: This script step can prevent a user from canceling a script by typing ⌘-. (period).
- *Set Error Capture*: This allows error trapping.
- *Loop*
- *Exit Loop If []*
- *End Loop*: In FileMaker 2.x, the only way to make a loop was to have a script call itself until it ran into the last record. With looping controls, you can do things like sort all of your records and then loop a process through until you hit a certain threshold value, such as exit loop if invoice age < 30.
- *Set Error Capture []*: If you don't like the error dialog boxes that FileMaker uses, you can intercept errors, such as no records found, and put up more appropriate dialog boxes of your own.

Navigation

These commands manage field, layout, and mode access.

- *Go to First Record/Request*
- *Go to Last Record/Request*: These are just nicer methods than were in FileMaker Pro 2.x. In the old days, to get to the last record of an un-known quantity of records, you had to tell FileMaker to go to some

ridiculously large record number and have it settle for the next closest record. And you had to remember to set this to perform without dialog, or it wouldn't work. This is a nice improvement.

- *Go to Related Record*
- *Go to Portal Row*

Fields

These commands manage field data.

- *Set Field []*: This is similar to a paste command. Unlike a paste command, however, the target field does not have to be on the current layout to receive the value.
- *Paste Result []*: This allows you to paste the result of a calculation without that calculation actually having to be part of a field definition.

Sort/Find/Print

These commands manage sorting, finding, and printing.

- *Modify Last Find*: This allows you to recreate the last find criteria and modify them.

Windows

These commands manage window's specific actions.

- *Freeze Window*: This allows you to lock the screen so the user can't see your script jumping around to various layouts as it runs through a process.
- *Refresh Window*: This is now a separate command, no longer attached to the Go to Layout script step.
- *Scroll Window []*: In general, you should avoid layouts that require scrolling for reasons of good interface design. If you can't avoid them, you now have the option of scriptable scrolling.
- *Toggle Text Ruler []*: Displays the new word-processing style text ruler so the user can set tabs and such.

Files

These commands manage file actions.

- *New*: FileMaker Pro 2.x did not allow the ScriptMaker to create new FileMaker files. This is now possible in 3.0.
- *Change Password*: This opens the Change Password dialog box. This is very useful if you want the user to change his or her password every 30 days or so.

III

Conversion Issues

- *Set Multi-User []*: If you have a database that needs to be shared and some pesky user forgets to set it back to multi-user, you'll be glad to have this.

- *Set Use System Formats []*

Miscellaneous

These commands don't fall into any other category.

- *Send AppleScript []*: You can actually embed long AppleScripts in this script step or you can have it execute scripts that are stored in fields. This is an extremely significant capability and is covered in later chapters.

- *Dial Phone []*: This script step can dial a phone number through a modem.

- *Speak []*: This causes FileMaker Pro 3.0 to say out loud, using the Apple Speech Manager, either what you type in a dialog box in the script step or the text you type into a field.

- *Set Disable User Abort []*: This allows you to prevent a user from stopping your script while it's executing. Use caution: if you combine this with an infinite loop, you can have real problems.

- *Show Message []*: This allows you to use dialog boxes in FileMaker Pro.

- *Comment []*: Now you can actually add notes on what a script is doing for future reference.

- *Beep*: This just runs the system beep, but it can be useful to test conditional scripts or just to signal an error. For example, if you need to make sure a test in your If script step is working right, you might try the following:

```
If SortStatus =1
        Beep
Else
        Beep
        Beep
End If
```

- *Open ScriptMaker*: This does exactly what it says.

- *Open Define Relationships*: This does exactly what it says.

- *Flush cache to disk*: Equivalent to Save in FileMaker.

So, there are 40 new scripting commands in FileMaker Pro 3.0. They offer a variety of new capabilities, which are described in the following sections.

Conditional Scripting

The only way to do conditional scripting in FileMaker Pro 2.x was to use the Go to Layout based on Field Number script. It wasn't exactly the ideal foundation for power programming. The If and Loop commands are a huge improvement. Instead of having to create a whole batch of calculation fields to test for certain conditions, you can now implement such tests in a script process.

Error Trapping

Another problem in FileMaker Pro 2.x, was that when a script executed a find and didn't find anything, an error dialog box asked the user what to do. If the script was searching on some kind of hidden or flag field, the user would have no idea what to do to get things going again. This, in general, is a bad thing. Or, if an impatient user decided that a script was taking too long, they could halt the script by pressing ⌘-. (period). Sometimes, that would leave data in disarray. With FileMaker Pro 3.0's new Set Error Capture and Set Disable User Abort commands, this kind of occurrence can be planned so the user isn't left looking at an error message or a mess.

Commenting

Some scripts can be quite complex, and because people do come and go in companies, it often happens that the person who wrote a database is nowhere to be found and another person has to untangle what a script is trying to accomplish. In FileMaker 2.x, there was no way for a programmer to let future programmers know what they were thinking or why a certain process was even being done. Now, you can leave comments in scripts for the sake of posterity.

Embedded AppleScript

AppleScript was already a nice tool to have with FileMaker 2.x. Able to interact with the Macintosh Finder, it often was just the thing to solve that sticky problem. The one drawback was that AppleScript scripts or applets were separate files, and if they were part of a total solution, they were extra pieces that could get misplaced as an application got moved around. With FileMaker 3.0, you can actually write AppleScript code right inside the ScriptMaker. Now, if you want to have the Finder get a list of files in a folder, a FileMaker script can handle the request without having to launch the Script Editor or an external applet. FileMaker and AppleScript hybrid solutions will now be able to run with less RAM overhead.

Shutdown Scripts

Perhaps a minor thing, but FileMaker Pro 2.x could only automatically run a script when the database started up. In 3.0, you can also have a script automatically execute at shutdown. This can be very handy for running cleanup activities or exporting data for a spreadsheet or the mainframe to pick up and is accessed in Document Preferences.

New Layout Tools

 The actual look and feel of FileMaker 3.0 is different: menus were moved around, there are new menu items to accompany the new features, and the layout tools themselves have some new additions. There are two new graphics tools at the bottom of the Layout tool palette: a Button tool and a Portal tool (see fig. 8.10). Using the Portal tool depends on a relationship, as explained previously.

Fig. 8.10
Two new layout
tools in FileMaker
Pro 3.0.

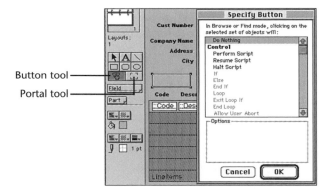

In addition to portals, buttons, and relationships, FileMaker 3.0 brings the capability of hidden layouts. In FileMaker 2.x, every layout in the database was visible in the layout pop-up list in the upper-left corner of a database. Sometimes, it's useful to have a "throwaway" layout that scripts use for searching and copying information around. Having layouts like that in 2.x were problematic; programmers had to password-protect them to prevent users from accessing the layout, or they had to make everything invisible and hope that a curious user didn't wander into the layout and get confused. This has been addressed in 3.0, and simply, too (see fig. 8.11).

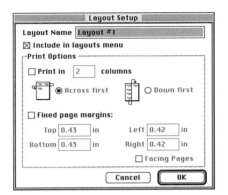

Fig. 8.11
The new Layout
Setup dialog box
has margins and
the capability to
exclude a layout in
the layout pop-up
menu.

As if that weren't enough, FileMaker 3.0 now has a word-processing style text ruler. Previously, you could not use tabs in FileMaker layouts. Now you can. Better still, you can even merge fields right into layout text. Putting field values in the middle of a canned form letter is now a snap.

Maximum File Size Increased

This is a commonly asked for feature in FileMaker Pro. FileMaker Pro 2.x had a physical file size limit of 32M. That meant no database file could be larger than that. At some point, FileMaker 2.x just couldn't handle making the file any larger and it crashed the database—sometimes so the database couldn't be recovered. If there was no backup, all the data was lost. FileMaker Pro 3.0 supports file sizes up to 2G.

The combination of the new larger file size and the capability to relate files to each other will make for much larger FileMaker database systems. While this is a good thing, it will make good design much more important to FileMaker developers because these systems are also likely to be much more mission-critical to the institutions that use them. For that reason, a substantial portion of this book covers relational database design considerations.

Field Definition Enhancements

While the Define Fields dialog box has undergone a face-lift with a larger area for viewing field definitions and a horizontal scroll bar, the real story is in the new and modified field types (see fig. 8.12).

Fig. 8.12
The new Define
Fields dialog box
has more room to
see field options
plus Global fields.

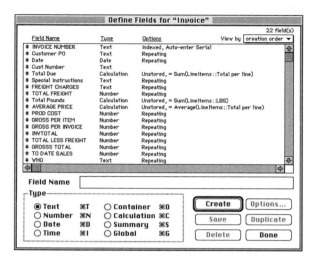

 The FileMaker veteran will immediately notice the Global Field dialog box (see fig. 8.13). Global fields are like variables. They're single instance fields. If I have a calculation involving a global field and I enter a value in that global field, that value will be used as an argument for every record in the database. Users who have had to suffer through the Today function (it calculates the current date every time the database is opened) plodding through thousands of records in FileMaker pro 2.x will rejoice.

Fig. 8.13
Global fields
contain one value
for every record in
a database.

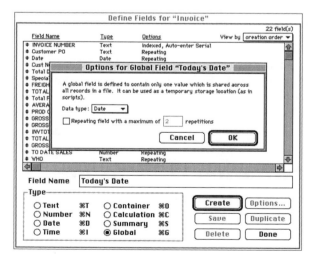

New Features for Performing Calculations

Calculation fields are radically different in version 3.0. First, they have new functions they can use. Users had to deal with some pretty complicated formulas in FileMaker 2.x to do things like parsing a last name from a full name when there may or may not be a middle name. FileMaker Pro 3.0 has improved text functions, so now you can find left, right, or middle words (FileMaker 2.x only did characters).

Second, there's an entirely new class of functions called Status Functions. These are mostly Boolean functions (they evaluate to true or false), but some will give you nice things like which version of FileMaker a user is running, what bit depth their monitor is set to, what layout number they're on, and so on. There's a lot of power when you combine these with the If and Loop conditional scripting functions.

The Specify Calculation dialog box has been expanded so you can see 16 lines of a calculation without having to scroll down (see fig. 8.14). FileMaker Pro 2.x could only show five lines at a time, and the lines were shorter.

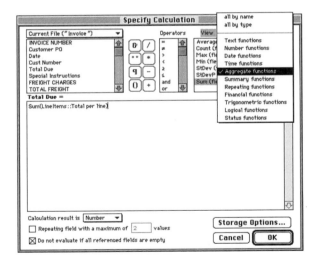

Fig. 8.14
The Specify Calculation dialog box showing functions, which are now grouped by type.

III

Conversion Issues

Unstored Calculations and Indexing

A completely new feature is the concept of unstored calculations. To conserve hard drive space, you have the option of making calculation results unstored. Values will be calculated only when needed; that is, when they're viewed on a layout or used in a Find.

The Storage Options dialog box also allows calculations to be unindexed (see fig. 8.15). Most FileMaker users aren't familiar with indexing because they never had to be. FileMaker Pro 2.x indexed every word of every field. So what is indexing? Think of any index in the back of a book. It's an alphabetized list of items. In books, important terms get indexed. When you index a field, every piece of information in every record gets alphabetized and the contents are actually stored twice: once in the field, and once in the index.

Fig. 8.15
You control the indexing of fields in the Storage Options dialog box.

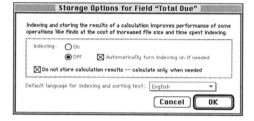

Indexes are good and bad. By having an index in a book, you can quickly find what page the indexed item is on. By having an index in a database, you can quickly find what record a piece of information is in. Indexed fields yield faster search times than unindexed fields. The problem is, the indexes take up space and make the database larger—and larger databases run slower than smaller databases.

Indexes also take time to build. If you ever made a complex calculation in FileMaker Pro 2.x and then had to wait awhile for the calculation to crunch through, part of that wait time was for the building of the index on the new values.

For these reasons, you can now turn off indexing on a field-by-field basis. Now, if you have long comment or note fields that you probably won't search, you can turn indexing off for those fields and save storage space. All you have to do is select the radio button in the Storage Options dialog box. Notice, that you can choose what language to create your index with.

Container Fields

Container fields are the new version of picture, sound, and video fields. In the Windows version, these fields can also store OLE objects.

Easier Network Protocol Selection

So what is a network protocol? It's best to start off by talking about networks. A network is a collection of computers and peripherals connected by some means of communication. In most cases, this means that cabling is strung between the equipment, but it could also mean that wireless radio transmitters are broadcasting the network traffic, or a cellular phone modem may even be dialing into a network modem. For the sake of simplicity, I'll keep it to two computers with a cable running between them.

For example, imagine you only speak English and you are talking on the telephone to someone who only speaks German. You have a good connection, information is physically traveling back and forth between the two phones, but neither of you understands the other, so that information is not being truly received at either end. In this case, the language you speak on the line is roughly equivalent to a network protocol. It is the language that computers speak on a network. Just as different languages are used in different countries, different protocols are used with different Network Operating Systems.

A network operating system is just like a regular operating system such as DOS or Mac OS; however, instead of just running the computer, it runs the network. Perhaps you've heard of Novell. They make a network operating system called NetWare. The usual protocol "spoken" by NetWare is IPX— although, like a cosmopolitan world traveler, it can speak other languages as well. Another network operating system is Windows NT. It uses a protocol called NETBEUI, which conforms to a specification called NETBIOS. The same goes for Windows for Workgroups, LANtastic, and VINES. The Macintosh protocol is AppleTalk. FileMaker Pro 2.1v3 already supported IPX for Novell networks, NETBEUI for Windows NT, Windows for Workgroups, LANtastic, and VINES networks, and it supported AppleTalk for Macintosh networks.

This means that FileMaker can utilize different network protocols. In version 2.x, the only way to change the protocol FileMaker used was to swap out the FileMaker Network file in the Claris Folder (which was usually in the System Folder). In FileMaker Pro 3.0, this can be managed from the Preferences dialog box (see fig. 8.16).

III

Conversion Issues

Fig. 8.16
The network type
is now chosen in
the Preferences
dialog.

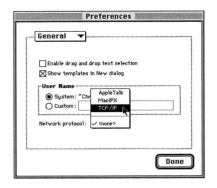

TCP/IP Support

The average person has no idea what TCP/IP even is, much less why they should be excited about FileMaker Pro 3.0 having support for it. TCP/IP is a network protocol that is widely used on UNIX networks. One very large UNIX network you've probably heard of is called the Internet. With FileMaker Pro 3.0, you can connect to the Internet and share your database with users in Australia, Europe, and Japan simultaneously. Granted, it's not the fastest thing in the world, but it works. For certain situations where you need to distribute or assimilate database information from separate parts of the world, there's nothing quite like it.

From Here...

Now that you know the new features in FileMaker Pro 3.0 (and there are a lot of them), you might want to read the following chapters for more information.

- Chapter 4, "Using Lookups and Relationships," describes how to use relational features.

- Chapter 5, "Working with Calculation Fields," gives you more information on using calculations.

- Chapter 15, "Scripting with ScriptMaker," teaches you how to use advanced scripting.

CHAPTER 9

Converting Existing FileMaker Pro Databases to 3

Because FileMaker has been around since 1986, a lot of systems have been built around this easy-to-use database. Many projects you'll do in FileMaker Pro 3.0 will probably build on a system that was created in a 2.x version. This can actually be much more work than starting from scratch. This chapter covers all possible scenarios, so the extra steps won't be difficult.

Because many people used FileMaker Pro's 2.x Invoice template, with slight modifications or as the starting point for a more extensive system, the venerable Invoice template will be the poster child for conversion issues, as well as the starting point for a much more elaborate system.

The chapter looks at the following conversion issues:

■ Converting lookup fields to related fields

■ Converting redundant data to single-instance data

■ Converting repeating fields to related portal records

Opening 2.x Files in FileMaker Pro 3.0

The basic process of converting a FileMaker 2.x file to a FileMaker Pro 3.0 file is very straightforward. Just launch FileMaker and, in the Open dialog box, select the FileMaker Pro 2.x version of the file, and click Open.

Fortunately, FileMaker Pro 3.0 is a wily software application. It knows that most users won't think of the ramifications of converting their database files. One such ramification might be that if you convert the database to a newer format and you still have users working with the old version of FileMaker, you've just ruined their day. To protect against something like that happening, FileMaker Pro 3.0 creates a brand new file from the old version, leaving the original unharmed.

> **Tip**
>
> You don't have to rename the old file. In fact, if others are still using that version, you definitely don't want to rename the file, especially if you're using lookups or external scripts that refer to specifically named files. Before beginning a conversion like this, it's a good idea to create a new folder to hold your new 3.0 files. That way, you won't have to choose different names for either your old or your new files, and any lookups or external scripts will come through the conversion still working.

If you continue by naming and saving the file, it will be converted to FileMaker Pro 3.0.

> **Caution**
>
> If you don't rename your original file, the Save dialog box defaults to the original name and adds the word "Converted" at the end. If the database is part of a system of databases and this file is referenced in another file's lookup, that lookup won't work properly if the file name is changed. Use the original name and save the file to a different folder so you don't overwrite the original file.

To convert the Invoices database to FileMaker Pro 3.0 follow these steps:

1. Choose File, Open.

2. In the Open dialog box, choose the Invoices database and click Open.

   The Conversion dialog box opens with a prompt to rename the old file as Invoices Old (see fig. 9.1).

Fig. 9.1
FileMaker Pro 3.0 prompts you to rename the original FileMaker 2.x files when you convert a file.

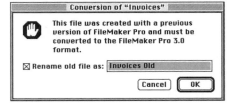

3. Deselect the Rename Old File As check box and click OK. When you do, FileMaker Pro displays the Save dialog box.

4. In the Save dialog box, leave the name Invoices and click the New Folder button. Name the new folder FMPro 3.0 and click Create. Click Save to store the converted file in the FMPro 3.0 folder.

The Invoices database will be converted and opened in FileMaker
Pro 3.0.

Congratulations! Invoices is now a FileMaker Pro 3.0 database. It looks exactly the same, doesn't it? Actually, there is a wrinkle. Choose File, Define
Relationships (see fig. 9.2). FileMaker asks you to locate files. Why? Because
in the 2.x version, Invoices had lookups to two other files: Contacts and
Products. Lookups now work via the relationship mechanism, so even though
you were going to the relationships dialog (as opposed to lookups), FileMaker
3.0 still needs to locate the two files used in the lookups. Take a minute and
convert Contacts and Products to FileMaker 3.0 files, being careful to store
them in the FMPro 3.0 folder. Also, make sure the new files have the same
names.

Fig. 9.2
You have to link
your related files
together with the
Define Relation-
ship command.

Relationships from Lookups

After you convert the files, you can access the Define Relationships dialog
box without problem. Sure enough, even though you might not understand
relationships yet, you already have two of them set up. You should see something like figure 9.3.

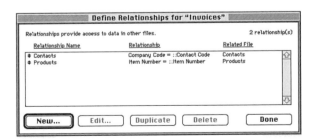

Fig. 9.3
The Define
Relationships
dialog box gives
you an overview
of the current
database's data
relationships.

III

Conversion Issues

Double-click the first relationship, Contacts. This opens the Edit Relationship dialog box (see fig. 9.4). This is similar to how you set up lookups in FileMaker Pro 2.x, but this is much clearer than the old lookup setup.

Fig. 9.4
The Edit Relation-ship dialog box allows you to change the data relationship between the related files.

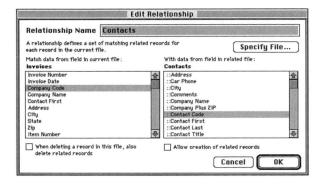

The list on the left contains the names of all the fields in the current data-base, in this case the Invoices database. The list on the right contains the names of all of the fields in the related database, in this case the Contacts database. How does the lookup work? There isn't a place to select the field that the related information gets copied to. You need to look elsewhere for the actual lookup dialog, but because lookups utilize relationships to do the work of finding the related information, I wanted to show you the relation-ships first. It's time to take a look at the field definitions for Invoices.

New Features for Defining Fields

Choose File, Define Fields to open the Define Fields dialog box (see fig. 9.5). If you're a veteran FileMaker user, you should notice several differences in the Define Fields dialog box.

You can see more fields at one time. The old version of FileMaker only displayed 10 fields at once. FileMaker Pro 3.0 can show 18 fields. You can also see the entire field definition without having to go into the Options or Specify Calculation dialog boxes. You can scroll horizontally to see long formulas right in the Define Fields dialog box.

Also note the field types. The Picture or Sound field has been replaced by the Container field. If you import a graphic to a Container field, you get an op-tion to only store a reference to the graphic. That way, if you want to build a large graphics database, you can do so without worrying about maxing out your file size. All you'll be storing are pointers to the graphics files. On a Win-dows machine, a Container field has the additional capability to hold OLE 2.0 objects.

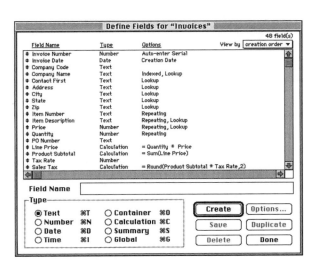

The Global field is also new. A Global field is a single-instance field. If you paste a value into a Global field, that one value will display in every record in the database. You can use it in calculations and showing aging (just paste today's date and every record will calculate invoice age or a person's birthday).

Lookups versus Related Fields

Scroll to the top of the field list and find the field Company Name. It's a lookup field, so take a look at how lookups are set up in FileMaker Pro 3.0. Double-click the Company Name field (you can also select it with a single click and click Options) to open the Entry Options dialog box (see fig. 9.6).

As you can see, the Entry Options dialog box has changed significantly. Note the pop-up menu at the top. It allows you to toggle between Validation options and Auto Entry options. For now, stay in Auto Entry options. Click the Looked-up Value Specify button to open the Lookup dialog box (see fig. 9.7).

Fig. 9.7
While the Lookup dialog box has changed a lot, its function is still straightforward.

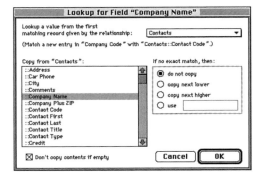

Again, lookups use relationships for the link to the lookup source file. If you have not created relationships yet, the only option available in the Lookup a Value from the First Matching Record Given by the Relationship pop-up menu would be to create a new relationship. You cannot establish a lookup without a relationship.

Lookups have their uses, but for this particular set of company information fields, it would be better to display this information in related fields. (You'll see what this means in a minute.) In Chapter 1, you learn that one of the problems of using lookups in a flat file database is that you can end up having several versions of the same information. Worse yet, you might not be able to tell which version is the correct one.

The easy way to make this conversion is to just delete all of the company information fields (except for the Company Code—you need that to make the relationship) and add the external fields to all layouts where the old fields used to be. In fact, you will do exactly that, but to prepare you to handle the worst possible scenario, I made it harder.

Suppose that instead of having Invoices look up the customer information from the Contacts database, a user just duplicated an existing record (for an existing customer) or entered new customer information for a new customer. There's no Contacts database at all, but now you need to take this single file with multiple records for each customer and derive from it a Contacts database with only one record for each customer. You also need to modify the original Invoices database by adding a relationship to this new Contacts database.

Creating Subsets of Your Database

Often, when converting databases, you'll find that many records contain duplicate information. For example, you might include a customer's name and address in every record of an invoice database. In the following example, you learn how to separate these duplicates into smaller subsets and import them back into your database. This technique is extremely useful any time you need to take multiple entry databases and convert them to single entry databases. To create the subsets of a database, follow these steps:

1. Identify a field that has an entry for every record and corresponds in some way to the information you're trying to isolate. Call it your break field. In this case, you're breaking out customer information, so a good candidate might be Company Code.

2. Create a summary field that counts the occurrences of your break field. For the Invoices database, create a summary field called Count that creates a count of Company Code. To do so, choose File, Define Fields and type **Count** in the Field Name text box. Select the Summary field type and click Create. The Options for Summary Field dialog box opens (see fig. 9.8). Select the Count option and the Company Code field and then click OK.

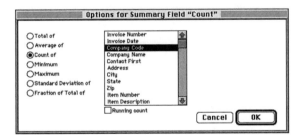

Fig. 9.8

You want the Summary field to count the occurrences of the Company Code field.

3. Choose Select, Find All so you're working with the entire database, then choose Mode, Sort to open the Sort dialog box. For the Summary field to work correctly, you need to sort the database by the break field. Double-click the Company Code to move it to the Sort Order list box and click Sort (see fig. 9.9).

Fig. 9.9
You want to sort
the database by
the break field,
Company Code.

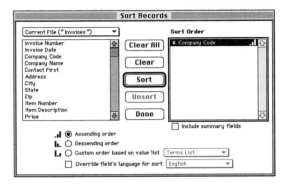

> ### Note
>
> There are some changes to the Sort Records dialog box. First, value lists are no
> longer attached to specific fields in FileMaker Pro 3.0. They exist indepen-
> dently, and one or several fields can make use of the same value list. You'll
> look at this more closely later, but the implications to sorting are that you can
> sort any field based on the order of values in a value list.
>
> Second, you can sort based on the sorting rules for several languages. If you
> have a database of Swedish phrases, you can sort them according to Swedish
> sorting rules, or you can override the language of the field and sort according
> to English language sorting rules.

4. Choose File, Import/Export, Export Records. This opens the Save dialog
box.

5. Type **Customers** in the Save As text box.

6. Click the Type pop-up menu and select FileMaker Pro (see fig. 9.10).

Fig. 9.10
Choose FileMaker
Pro as the export
file type in the
Save As dialog
box.

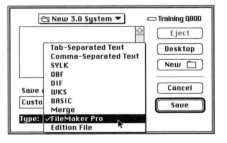

7. Click Save. The Export Field Order dialog box appears.

   The fields listed on the left are the fields in the current file and the fields listed on the right are the fields you're going to export into the new file. The default is every field.

8. Click Clear All to clear the right side, then move the following fields over: Company Code, Company Name, Contact First, Address, City, State, Zip, Ship Address, Ship City, Ship State, Ship Zip, Ship Attn, Contact Last, Contact Name, and Count.

9. Select the Count field and click the Summarize By button. The Summarize By dialog box appears (see fig. 9.11).

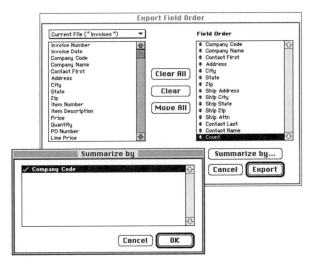

Fig. 9.11
The Export Field Order dialog box lets you summarize the exported data by summary fields.

10. Move the cursor in front of Company Code, and click. A check mark appears. Click OK and Export to create the new Customers database.

> **Note**
>
> If you don't sort the database before exporting, you can't do a summarized export. Only fields that were used in the last sort will be included in the Summarize By list.

Take a look at the new file you just created. First, note the number of records in Invoices. Next, choose File, Open and open the Customers file. There should be fewer records in the Customers file than there were in the Invoices file. Also, no two records should be the same company.

11. After you make sure your summarized export worked correctly, choose File, Define Fields in the Customers database and delete the Count field. The Count field's only purpose in life was to facilitate a summarized export, so you can delete it now. Go back to the Invoices database and do the same.

In the past, you had to do the find, create a clone of the database, open the clone, then import the found set. It was a lot of work. Better still, now you can export databases that don't include all of the fields of the originating database.

For example, imagine you have a large customer database and you want to create a smaller database for each of your salespeople that includes only a few of the fields from the original database. In earlier versions of FileMaker, you had to create a clone of the database, and then go into the Define Fields dialog box and delete the fields you didn't want to include. Finally, you could import the records into the database clone. This was a real drag if you had to do it very often.

 With FileMaker Pro 3.0, you can just choose the fields you want to export and you're off to the races. This has other uses as well. If someone creates a system close to what you need for a different task, you can export what you need. It used to be that if someone had 100 fields in his or her database and only 50 applied to what you needed, you had to knock 50 fields out of the database—one at a time. With this export feature, you just export the 50 you need, and you're done. This is a very important feature.

Okay, that's about it for deriving a customer file from an invoice file. Now you can proceed with the basic process of shooting your lookup fields and replacing them with related fields.

Replacing Lookup Fields with Related Fields

With the new relational features, it's often possible to store data only once in the related database, rather than duplicate the date in each record's lookup fields. For example, an invoice database would include a customer address on each invoice, usually a lookup from a customer ID field. The problem is that lookups simply copy the information to the database. That means if a customer has 175 invoices in the database, the address is stored in the database 175 times. An alternative method, which reduces the size and complexity of your database, is to replace the lookup field with a related field. The database then displays the correct information but stores it only once in the related database. Take a look at how easy this is to do.

To replace your lookup fields with related fields, follow these steps:

1. With the Invoices database open, choose File, Define Fields.

2. In the Define Fields dialog box, delete the company information fields you just exported, *except* for Company Code. Delete these fields: Company Name, Contact First, Address, City, State, Zip, Ship Address, Ship City, Ship State, Ship Zip, Ship Attn, Contact Last, and Contact Name.

   Don't be apprehensive about deleting all of these fields. As long as you don't delete Company Code, you still have this information in the form of the relationship.

3. Click Done to exit the Define Fields dialog box.

4. Go to the first layout in Invoices, the Order Entry layout. There should now be a noticeable hole where the customer information used to be. What you need to do now is put in related fields to display the customer information. To do this, use the Field tool.

5. Drag the Field tool onto the layout and release the new field (see fig. 9.12).

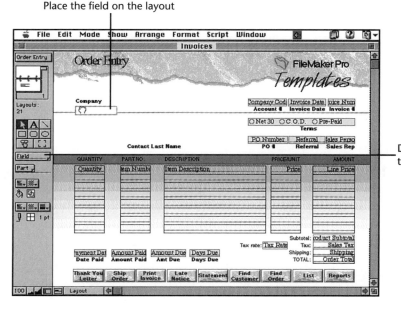

Place the field on the layout

Fig. 9.12
Use the Field tool to drag a field onto the layout.

Drag the Field tool from here

6. The Specify Field dialog box appears. Click the pop-up menu at the top of the dialog box to specify which relationship you want to draw fields from (see fig. 9.13).

Fig. 9.13
Choose the Contacts relationship from the pop-up menu in the Specify Field dialog box.

7. Choose the Contacts relationship. Immediately, the fields in the Contacts database display in the Specify fields dialog box. Notice that each field name is preceded by a double colon (see fig. 9.14). A double colon preceding a field name means the field does not exist in the current database—it's a related field.

Fig. 9.14
After you choose a related database, the Specify Field dialog box displays only fields from that database.

> **Caution**
>
> Because FileMaker uses a double colon to designate the status of related fields, user-defined field names beginning with a double colon are illegal.

8. Repeat the process of dragging the field tool to the appropriate position on the layout until you have Company Name, Address, City, State, and Zip arranged (see fig. 9.15).

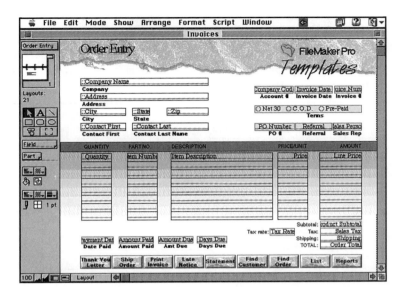

Fig. 9.15
The Order Entry layout includes seven fields from a related database.

9. When you've added the fields, choose Mode, Browse and view the related information. It looks just like it used to. Well, it's not at all the way it used to be.

10. Here's a test you can try to prove it. Resize the Invoices window so it takes up the top of your screen. Choose Window, Contacts and resize the Contacts database so it takes up the bottom of your screen. You need to be able to view the company information in both databases at once (see fig. 9.16).

11. Click in the Company Name field in Contacts and change the name, then click outside the field or press the Enter key to enter the change. Note what happened in the Invoices database. Now try it from the other end. Change the Company Name information in the Invoices database. Again, this changes the information in both databases. That's because the information is only stored in one place, unlike a lookup. When you edit the Company Name information in Invoices, you're actually editing the data in Contacts. This is what's so great about relationships. With related fields, it's impossible to have more than one version of your data, because you can only work on that one version.

Note

You might be nervous about the potential for users to change information in the Contacts database. That's a responsible concern to have. That gets into a

(continues)

(continued)

whole can of worms called relational database design. You'll learn about that in Chapter 10, so hold the thought for now. You still have a lot more to cover in the way of conversion issues.

Fig. 9.16
The order Entry layout includes seven fields from a related database.

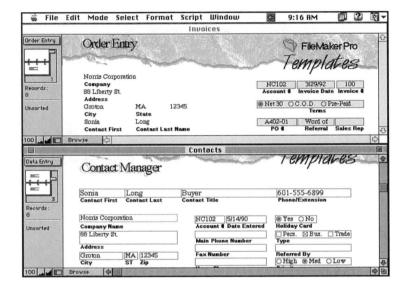

12. Repeat the process of adding related Company information fields (Name, Address, and so on) for the rest of the layouts that need these fields: Order Entry/BW, Shipment Entry, and so on.

After you complete the addition of all these related fields, think about how the relationship is working. An invoice only contains one customer, so from the point of view of an invoice, this is a one to one relationship.

Usually, when you have a one to one relationship between two pieces of information, you put those two pieces of information in the same database file. For example, a company only has one main phone number. If you flip this relationship around, it's still the same: a phone number can only be assigned to one company. In the case of company and phone number, it makes sense to put both pieces of information in the same database. They have a one to one relationship.

If you flip around the invoice/customer relationship, it's different: one company can be on many invoices. This is a one to many relationship. However, you wouldn't want numerous companies listed on a single invoice. Therefore, unlike company and company phone number information, you shouldn't have invoice and customer data in the same database.

Suppose you create a relationship to Invoices based on Company Code in the Contacts database, and then put related invoice fields on the company layout. If you look at the Acme Company and there are seven invoices for the Acme Company in the Invoices database, which one would you see in the related field? You only see the first record (as determined by creation order, not sort order). This is a problem if that isn't the record you were interested in.

So, related fields are fine for displaying data in a one to one relationship (one invoice can only have one customer on it), but they aren't useful for one to many relationships (one customer can appear on many invoices or one invoice can contain many line items).

FileMaker Pro 2.x addressed this issue with repeating fields. A repeating field is similar to a little database in a record. It's a field that could contain multiple values. FileMaker Pro 3.0 handles one to many relationships by combining related fields with a new type of layout object called a portal. A portal allows you to view multiple related records when related fields are placed inside the portal.

Replacing Repeated Fields with Portals

To convert databases with repeating fields into databases that use portals to view multiple related records, you have to break repeating information out into individual records. To do this with the Invoices database, you again have to export a subset of Invoices. This time you're going to export the repeating fields.

This might seem a little backwards, but bear with me. There's a method to my madness.

1. Choose File, Import/Export, Export Records.
2. When the Save dialog box opens, name the new file Line Items, set the type to FileMaker Pro, and click Save.
3. In the Specify Export Order dialog box, clear all fields and then move over the following fields: Invoice Number, Quantity, Item Number, Item Description, Price, and Line Price. Click Export.
4. Choose File, Open and open the new Line Items database.
5. Choose Mode, Delete All and get rid of all of your records.

6. Choose Import/Export, Import Records to open the Open dialog box.

7. Select Invoices as your import source and click Open.

8. In the Import Field Mapping dialog box, the fields will not be matched up properly. Drag the fields in the list on the right so they match figure 9.17.

Fig. 9.17
The Import Field Mapping dialog box lets you select the fields to import.

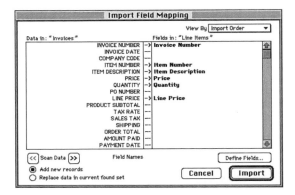

9. Click Import. Click the Splitting Them Into Separate Records radio button and click OK.

That radio button is all-powerful. If you have a lot of databases with repeating fields, you'll get to know this radio button well as you convert databases into FileMaker 3.0.

If you go back to invoices, you can see what breaking out repeating fields does for you. In the following steps, you learn how to modify the Invoices database to accept the repeating fields.

1. In Invoices, choose File, Define Relationships.

2. In the Define Relationships dialog box, click New.

3. In the Specify Database dialog box, select the Line Items database and click Open.

4. In the Edit Relationships dialog box, select Invoice ID from the list of Invoices fields on the left. In the list of Line Items fields on the right, select ::Invoice ID.

5. Select the When Deleting a Record In this File, Also Delete Related Records check box and the Allow Creation of Related Records check box. Click OK and click Done.

6. Open the Order Entry layout. Choose Mode, Layout to go into Layout mode.

7. Choose Show, Graphic Rulers to turn on the rulers. Note the positions of the repeating fields Quantity, Item Number, Item Description, Price, and Line Price, then delete them from the layout.

8. Click the Portal tool and drag a portal to fill the area that was occupied by all of the repeating fields (see fig. 9.18). This opens the Portal Setup dialog box.

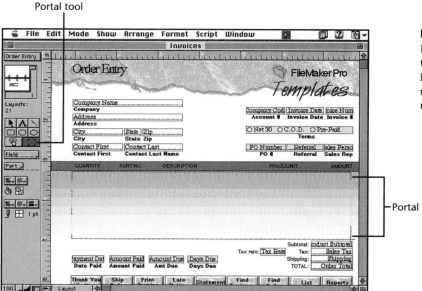

Portal tool

Fig. 9.18
Drag the Portal tool across the layout section that used to hold the repeating fields.

Portal

9. Click the Show Records From pop-up menu and choose your new Line Items relationship (see fig. 9.19).

10. Check the Allow Deletion of Portal Records check box and enter **8** in the Show Rows text box. Click OK. Resize the portal as necessary. Note that the portal displays the relationship that it uses in the lower-left corner.

Now that you have created the portal, you can add related fields to it. This process is the same as the one you used for the customer information.

1. Drag the field tool to the left side of the first row of the portal.

2. Select ::Quantity from the list. Deselect the Create Field Label check box and click OK.

3. Repeat for Item Number, Item Description, Price, and Line Price.

4. Choose Mode, Browse and view the portal information.

III

Conversion Issues

Fig. 9.19
You can display fields from any related database in the database portal.

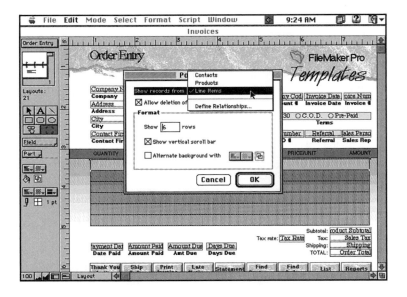

It looks similar to repeating fields, except now each line item is a record, not a value in a repeating field. This distinction is important because now you can easily do reporting on line items. In FileMaker Pro 2.x, you had to go through a lot of contortions to find out how many widgets you sold during the year. This is much nicer.

After you determine that your portal and your Line Items relationship is working properly, you can delete all of your repeating fields. They're no longer necessary.

1. Choose File, Define Fields.
2. In the Define Fields dialog box, delete the repeating fields: Quantity, Item Number, Item Description, Price, and Line Price.
3. Click Done.

Do you notice a trend developing here? When you use related files and related fields, you can whack fields out of your original database. This means that when you use related fields, your databases tend to be smaller. Smaller databases run faster. Again (I can't emphasize this enough), there is only one copy of the data, so you no longer have any issues about which version is the right version. You also save a ton of file and hard drive space by only storing information once. Just for fun, you should notice the total file size of your database system before and after conversion. You're going to be psyched when you see the results.

From Here...

Okay, so now you have a feel for how related fields work in portals and by themselves. You've gone through various techniques for converting flat-file FileMaker 2.x databases into relational FileMaker 3.0 databases, including splitting out repeating information and converting lookup fields into related fields. This really is a radical shift from the way FileMaker used to work. For more information, read the following chapters:

- Chapter 8, "What's Different in FileMaker Pro 3," explains the basics of the new features in FileMaker Pro 3.0 and what significance these changes have in developing databases.

- Chapter 10, "More on Conversion Issues," looks at how you should go about designing relational database systems to exploit the new features you learned about in this chapter.

More on Conversion Issues

This chapter is a sampler of FileMaker Pro 2.x workarounds. If you have to convert a FileMaker 2.x database that you didn't build to FileMaker 3.0, there might be some funky processes lurking in there. This chapter has the rhythm of a tennis match. The 2.x workaround is described, then the 3.0 version of the same process is described.

This chapter covers the following topics:

- How to hide layouts from users
- Working around data relationships
- Finding and exporting data

Hiding Layouts

You'll probably run into a lot of databases that have *utility* layouts. These are layouts that the user is not supposed to see. They exist so a script can copy and paste information into various fields.

Hiding and Switching Layouts in 2.x

In FileMaker Pro 2.x, there was no way to completely hide a layout. The best you could do was name the layout with a hyphen, as shown in figure 10.1. These layouts then appeared as separators in the Layout pop-up menu in the Status area (see fig. 10.2).

Fig. 10.1

If you insert a hyphen (-) in the Layout Option's Name text box, it will appear as a menu separator in the Layout menu.

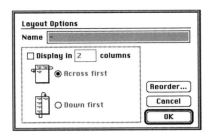

Fig. 10.2

Because the layout appears as a menu separator, the user can't switch to that layout.

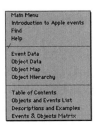

This strategy worked well enough, but there were a couple of problems:

- When you needed to use a Go to Layout script step in ScriptMaker, you couldn't just select the layout by name; the hyphen made it appear as a separator in the Layout pop-up menu in ScriptMaker (see fig. 10.3). The only way to switch to a layout named with a hyphen was by using the Layout Number Given By Field option in the Specify pop-up menu. This, however, required an extra field in the database just to switch to those layouts.

Fig. 10.3

You can't use the Go To Layout command to go to a layout named with a hyphen.

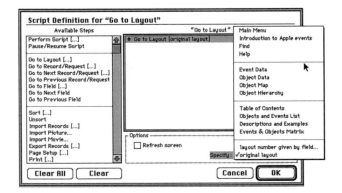

■ When you referenced layouts by layout number, you had to be careful about not changing the order of your layouts. Sometimes when a FileMaker database crashed and was then recovered, the custom layout order reverted back to the layout creation order. That means that after a good hard crash, you probably had to reset your custom layout order.

Converting to 3.0

It's not a big deal to have that extra field in your database, but you do have to watch out for your layout order getting changed by a crash or a user. Because you can now identify specific layout names with the CurrentLayoutName Status function, and because you can perform calculations inside scripts in ScriptMaker, a better way to deal with this entire issue is to use conditional scripting to navigate to a specific layout based on some criteria. This technique has several advantages.

> **Tip**
>
> The Status Calculation functions give the FileMaker Pro developer the capability to customize database applications and make databases more fail-safe.

If you have a database being shared on a network, you can't get access to the field definitions without kicking all users off. You might want to make a minor change to the database without bringing the whole system down. If you switch layouts based on some calculated field value, you can only modify this functionality by changing the field definition. If you build your logic into a script instead, you can change the functionality while the database is up and being shared by any number of users.

Because you can have hidden layouts with regular names, you can switch to specific layouts using name references instead of the layout number given by a field. This means that if your layout order changes or needs to change, your layout changing scripts will still work properly. A big disadvantage of changing layouts based on a number in a field was that once you set a calculation up, you were virtually handcuffed to that particular layout order. If you had to change your layout order, you also had to change what was usually a complicated calculation to make the layout numbers match your new layout order. It was cumbersome in the best of times.

Calculated layout numbers were necessary in FileMaker Pro 2.x, but they're not in 3.0. It's worth going over an example to see how you can use calculations in ScriptMaker as an alternative to a calculation field.

Suppose you have a customer database you use for generating correspondence. If you want to conditionally switch to a "Thank you for your order" letter layout or a "Here's a special sale you might be interested in" layout, you could modify the conditional switch to layout script as follows:

1. Choose Script, ScriptMaker to open the Define Scripts dialog box.

2. Select your script that changes layouts based on a number given by a field value and click Edit to open the Script Definition dialog box. The script can be as simple as the one shown in figure 10.4.

   Figure 10.5 shows the calculation for the field value. You can print or write down the formula for the field. You need it to set up your conditional scripts.

Fig. 10.4
This script goes to the layout specified by the value in the Layout Number field.

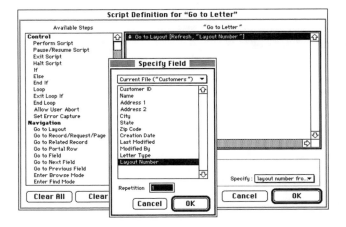

Fig. 10.5
This calculation will switch to the third layout if the value in the Letter Type field is Thanks and the fourth layout if the value in the Letter Type field is Special Sale.

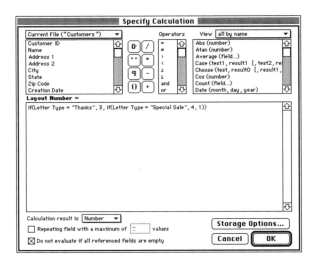

3. Double-click the If script step to move it to the list on the right.

4. Click Specify to open the Specify Calculation dialog box.

Take a look at the formula for your layout number field. Take the first calculation test and enter it in the If calculation (see fig. 10.6). Remember that in an If calculation, the result must be Boolean (true or false). Click OK to close the Specify Calculation dialog box.

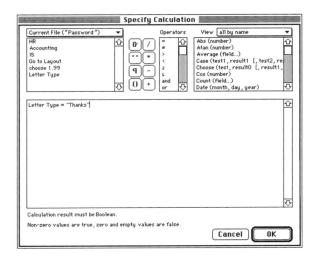

Fig. 10.6
This calculation will return a true value if the value in the Letter Type field is Thanks. Otherwise, it will return a false value.

5. Double-click the Go to Layout script step to move it to the list on the right. Drag it above the End If step. Choose the appropriate layout from the Specify pop-up list (see fig. 10.7).

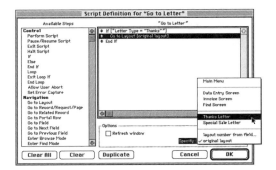

Fig. 10.7
You must specify the layout you want the script to switch to in the Go to Layout pop-up menu.

III

Conversion Issues

6. Double-click the Else script step to move it to the list on the right. Drag it above the End If step.

7. Double-click another If script step to move it to the list on the right. Drag it above the first End If script step.

> **Tip**
>
> You can also duplicate the first If script step, but remember to add another End If script step.

8. Click Specify to open the Specify Calculation dialog box. Take the second calculation test and enter it in the If calculation. Click OK to close the Specify Calculation dialog box.

9. Select the first Go to Layout script step and click Duplicate. Reset the layout specification to go to the appropriate layout.

10. Add as many Else/If combinations as you need to accommodate your layout changes. You might want to add one final Else condition to give the user a message when the trigger field contains no value. Your final script should look similar to figure 10.8.

Fig. 10.8
This script uses FileMaker's new conditional scripting functions to determine which layout it switches to.

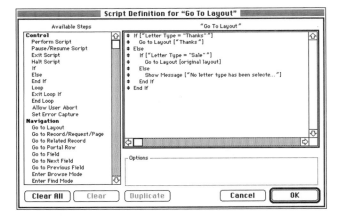

You can use this type of script in place of a layout number calculation field.

Pretending to Be Relational

Although FileMaker 2.x wasn't relational, some people had to have that kind of functionality. It's especially important in inventory systems. When you sell something, at your point of sale, you need the quantity deducted from your inventory so you know when to order more inventory. This really requires a relational database, but you could make it work (slowly) with lookups. Lookups create something that resembles relational functionality, but lookups are a one-way transaction.

When a lookup is triggered, information is copied from one database to another. A user can then change that looked up information, but the changes aren't relayed back to the original database. To have the lookup work both ways, you need to have a lookup in both databases. This provides something like relational functionality, but it's pretty slow.

There are many variations on the theme, but that's the basic concept. To identify this workaround, look for scripts that run a relookup and call an external script that also runs a relookup in the other database.

Converting to 3.0

The first step is to take all lookup fields and convert them to related fields using the process described in Chapter 9. Relationships in FileMaker Pro 3.0 are dynamic and don't require any relookup type of operation. After you implement related fields and discard the lookup fields, you can delete the scripts that run the relookups.

◀ See "Replacing Lookup Fields with Related Fields," p. 234

Using Value Lists

Neither dynamic value lists or value list labels were possible with FileMaker Pro 2.x. In 3.0, you can have a value list that will dynamically reflect the values in another database, and the list can actually display a value for label purposes only. If you have a value list of Customer ID codes, it's much more useful if you can see which customer the ID code corresponds to.

Using Lookups

Lookups in general are no longer necessary in FileMaker Pro 3.0. Because a lookup field copies information from another file, having a lookup field in a database means you have multiple versions of the same information floating around. This can lead to confusion (which version is the right one?), and it takes up a lot of space on the hard drive. You have larger and slower files when you use lookups. There are, however, two good reasons to use lookup fields in FileMaker Pro 3.0:

■ When you need to freeze information in time, which you might do to make price information in a line items database not update every time the price changes (it would with a related field), you can use lookup fields. Lookups are static unless you manually go in and run a relookup.

■ Related fields in FileMaker Pro 3.0 can only show information from one relationship away. Imagine a situation where you had a customer's file, an invoices file, and a line items file, with relationships between customers and invoices and between invoices and line items. If you want to put a portal in your Customers database so you can see the products as customers order, you can't just create a relationship between customers and line items because the Customer ID field isn't in the line items database. If you want to make a direct relationship between customers and line items, you have to add the Customer ID field to line items.

The Old No Records Found Trick

In FileMaker Pro 2.x, if you performed a find and got no matches, you got an error dialog box. If this happened in the middle of a script, the user got the option to cancel out of the rest of the script. This sometimes left users in the middle of the woods—parked in some utility layout with no obvious way to return to the layout they started from. To prevent the display of the error dialog box when no records were found, a funky workaround was devised. Here's how it works in case you run into it.

The only way to prevent the error dialog box that FileMaker presents when no records are found is to make sure a record is always found. One way to do this is to have a dummy record with a value like "XXX" in the database. When the Find portion of the script is run, it restores a find for the record containing the "XXX" value, as well as an empty find request for the user to type their own find criteria. This method has a major drawback in that the database always contains a record with no meaningful data. This can throw off summary functions that count or average data. Another drawback is that the user can delete the record and then the error dialog box is back.

A better way to make sure a record is always found is to create a dummy record just before the find script is run, then delete it after the find is completed. The record is never around long enough to get counted in summaries, and the user can't stumble across it and delete it. This step is still not foolproof, because a user could still cancel while the find operation is in progress.

 In FileMaker Pro 3.0, you don't have to worry about users canceling your scripts in mid-stream—all you have to do is deactivate the Allow User Abort option in ScriptMaker. For example, imagine you have a script that performs a find and then beeps one time (see fig. 10.9). If you run this script and there's no matching record found, FileMaker will display an error dialog box (see fig. 10.10). To avoid this, you can modify the script to turn off the Allow

User Abort option at the beginning of the script and turn it back on when the script finishes (see fig. 10.11). FileMaker still displays the error dialog box, but removes the option to cancel the script (see fig. 10.12).

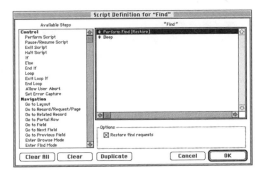

Fig. 10.9
This script will perform the stored find request and then beep once.

Fig. 10.10
If FileMaker finds no matching records, it gives the user the option to cancel the script.

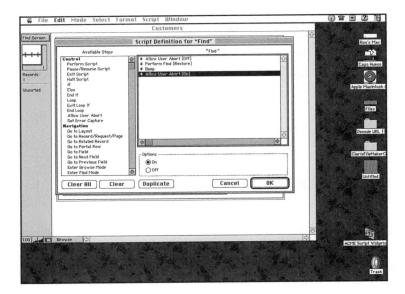

Fig. 10.11
If you don't want the user to be able to cancel a script, deactivate the Allow User Abort option in ScriptMaker.

III

Conversion Issues

Fig. 10.12
Now the user can't
cancel a script.

Tip

When you create a script that temporarily moves to another script, it's a good idea to turn off the Allow User Abort option.

From Here...

In this chapter, you reviewed some of the common workarounds found in databases developed in FileMaker 2.x. You learned what to look for to determine if a particular workaround had been used, and you also learned how to implement the same or better functionality using FileMaker Pro 3.0.

From here, you might want to read the following chapters:

■ Chapter 9, "Converting Existing FileMaker Pro Databases to 3," teaches you how to convert your existing databases.

■ Chapter 15, "Scripting with ScriptMaker," describes how to use ScriptMaker. ScriptMaker is at the heart of any special functionality you might want to add to your databases.

■ Chapter 16, "Using AppleScript," covers AppleScript and how to use it to extend the functionality of FileMaker beyond what you can do with ScriptMaker.

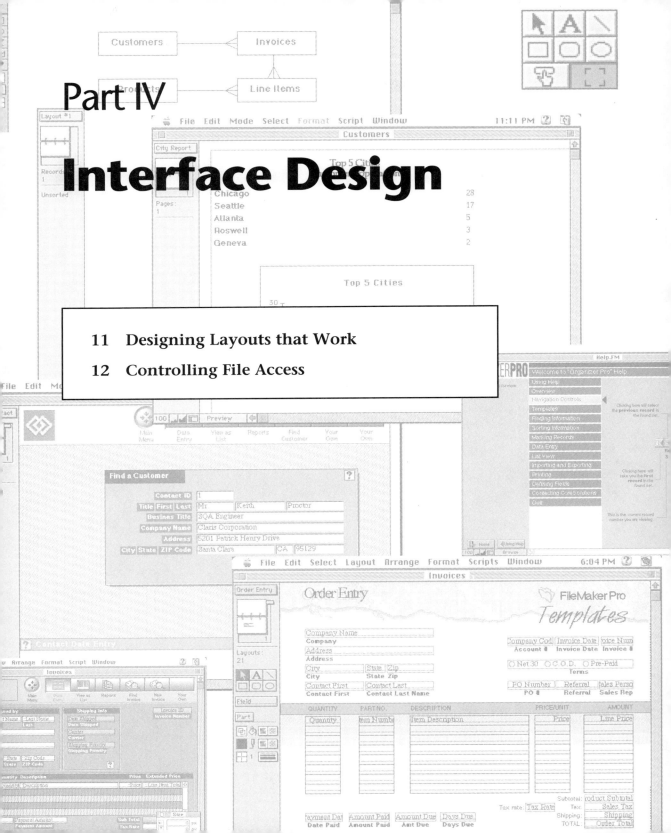

Part IV

Interface Design

CHAPTER 11

Designing Layouts that Work

I recently asked a class I was teaching which of two databases their clients would be happiest with: a perfectly designed database with a mediocre look or a mediocre database with drop-dead graphics. The overwhelming winner was the mediocre database with drop-dead graphics.

This is significant because it means that even if you do a great job as a database designer and you only have a so-so interface, your clients won't appreciate the value of your work. It's very important to have good graphical design in your database projects.

In this chapter, you learn the following:

- Rules of thumb for designing database layouts
- Sample interface schemes
- Three-dimensional layout tricks
- Things to keep in mind if your database ever goes cross-platform

Guiding Principles

Think about the things you have to interact with on a regular basis. If you drive a car, use an ATM, and hey, if you're reading this book, I'll bet you use a computer. When you move from one car to another, or one ATM to another, or one computer to another, you still know what to do. Cars all have steering wheels and gas pedals, ATMs have number pads, and computers have keyboards and monitors. All of these gizmos have consistency among different versions. After you learn how to use one machine, you can use that knowledge on others.

You should strive for the same kind of consistency across layouts and across database files in the systems you develop in FileMaker Pro. You should have clear, understandable layouts; and once a user learns where your button controls are and how they work, they should find them in a consistent location throughout the database system. You might even want to create something like a navigation bar that contains all of your buttons. You want to create an expectation that a user can count on certain things just being there. Do this with consistent use of color, placement, and functionality.

By having consistency across your database, you make the database easier to use and understand. Always try to eliminate anything that might confuse or disorient a user.

Here's a classic example: you, the database designer, get asked by a client to build a database. The client gives you a bunch of forms the client currently uses to conduct business. Your client asks you to reproduce those forms so the users will have minimal confusion in moving to the new system. Mimicking an interface (in this case, a form) that the user already knows can be a good idea. Their familiarity with the layout will reduce training time on the new system.

There are a couple of problems with this assumption. First, is the form well-designed? It could be busy and cramped or it might have bad work flow. Take the time to see how users actually get their work done before you design the layouts in your database. Often, as you go over the forms with your client, the conversation is peppered with remarks like "Ignore this part, it doesn't apply to this department." or "This part is old. We don't do this anymore."

The moral of the story is this: always question forms. Usually, someone has been meaning to revise them for some time, so forms are often out of date. You need to carefully review the content of a form. When you know the functional work flow across a process or an organization, then you can begin designing the flow of the database layouts.

Data entry layouts should be whole screen layouts; avoid making scrollable forms at all costs. It is very disconcerting for a new database user to tab out of the last field on a layout and have the cursor jump to the top of the page. The whole screen jumps and changes. The user has no idea what just happened and might think he did something wrong.

> **Tip**
>
> Break long forms into several full screen layouts—don't jam all the items from a full form onto a single scrolling layout.

It's fine if you need to reproduce a form for printed output. Make it easy for a user to enter and modify information, then package that information into printing layouts. Separate printing and data entry forms bring up another topic: graphics. Your printer and monitor have different resolutions.

The computer screen can only display 72 dpi. That means if you put a graphic of a logo on a data entry layout, any resolution greater than 72 dpi is wasted and it takes extra time to display—FileMaker has to spend some clock cycles converting the image down to 72 dpi. Also, because higher resolution graphics are physically larger, they slow down performance on a network. If you have graphics with a resolution greater than 72 dpi, put them into an image editing program like PhotoShop and knock the resolution down to 72.

It's different for printing layouts. Because your end product is a printed page, you should optimize printed graphics for that. Find out what the resolution of your printer is. If it's a laser printer, it's probably 300 dpi or better. If it's an ink jet printer, it will be less. Whatever the resolution of the output device is, set your printing graphics to that same resolution.

3D Layout Tricks

Everyone likes to use a snappy looking database. It's easy to find great looking graphics and paste them in your FileMaker database. You can do that, but make sure you optimize the graphics to a resolution of 72 dpi for data entry layouts or 300 dpi (depending on your printer) for printing layouts. One problem with pasting in graphics is that when you use the database over a network, all of those graphics have to get shipped over the network as well. The more time FileMaker spends sending graphics around, the slower your database will be.

The alternative is to draw the graphics in FileMaker. When you create graphics with FileMaker's layout tools, they don't need to get sent over the network. Because they're FileMaker objects, the local copy of FileMaker can recreate them from the specifications (for example, a line starts at point A and ends at point B). Basically, if the database is used on a network, use FileMaker graphic objects instead of imported graphic objects.

This means you need to learn how to make great looking layouts with FileMaker's layout tools. The place to start for inspiration is FileMaker's own interface. Take a look at the Status Area and the buttons at the bottom of a FileMaker window (see fig. 11.1).

Fig. 11.1

The Status Area shows the number of records in a database; you control zooming at the bottom of the Status Area.

In figure 11.1, notice the shading around the Layout pop-up button. The shadow falls to the right and down, meaning the virtual light source is coming from the upper left. Look at the line between the number of records and the sort status. There's a white highlight just below the line itself. This gives the line a kind of carved-in look. The lower edge of the Book box has the same highlight, while the upper edge has a gray shadow. The combined effect makes the Book box appear to be inset in the Status Area.

If you look closely at the Zoom buttons, each has a highlight on the top and left edges, and a shadow on the right and bottom edges. This highlighting and shadowing give the buttons a raised bevel look. Also, notice that these highlights and shadows are inside the button object, while the highlights and shadows on the Book box are outside of the box. Slight differences in the placement of light or dark lines give a different effect.

Consistency is an important aspect of any interface scheme. If you look at the layout tools or the layout part tags while you're in Layout mode, you see that this subtle 3D look runs throughout FileMaker. Figure 11.2 shows the layout tools in the Status Area.

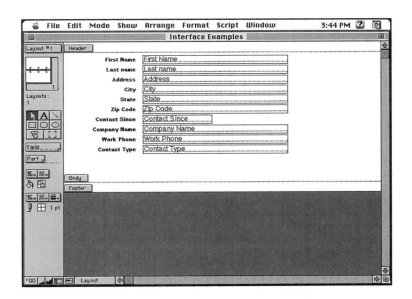

Fig. 11.2
Use FileMaker's
layout tools to
create layout
objects.

While it's certainly not mandatory, your layouts will have a more unified look and "be one with FileMaker" if they follow the basic look of FileMaker's interface elements. Shadows and highlights should indicate a light source coming from the upper-left corner of the window. Most FileMaker elements are not "tall" on the screen. They're usually only one or two lines deep. I've seen layouts that completely ignore this and they look fantastic, so take it as a reference point, not a rule.

The following sections cover how you can create attractive layouts using only FileMaker layout tools.

Creating a Layout Background

When you create a printing layout, you usually need to recreate an existing physical document—so you play with the look and feel of it. On data entry layouts though, you're free to make them look however you want. Because data entry layouts don't get printed, you're not constrained by the printed appearance of the layouts. To minimize confusion for data entry people, you also want to create data entry forms that can't scroll. That way, someone won't accidentally click the scroll bar and make the screen jump.

It's easiest to create shadows and highlights against a non-white background. Notice that the Status Area of FileMaker is light gray. To create a gray background (or another color you like) for a non-scrolling layout, follow these steps:

1. Choose Mode, Layout to switch to Layout mode.

2. Delete the Header and Footer layout parts. To delete a part, click the tag to select it, then press the Delete key.

Because this is a non-printing layout, these layout parts have no use. First, make sure you move any fields or graphics into the Body part before you delete parts.

3. Resize the Body so it's the same size as your screen (see fig. 11.3).

Fig. 11.3

You can resize the Body of a layout to fit the screen.

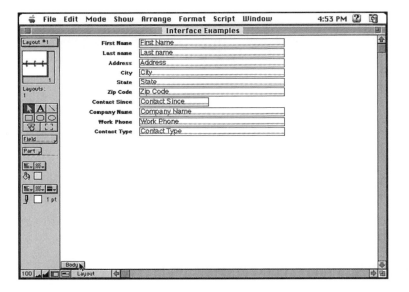

Tip

FileMaker uses the AutoGrid to help you create objects in Layout mode. When AutoGrid is on (it is by default), items you drag and drop snap to specific screen increments. When you drag the Body tag to the exact bottom of the screen, it will probably snap to a point just a little too low or too high. If you press ⌘ as you drag, you temporarily disable AutoGrid. You can also choose Arrange, AutoGrid to turn it off permanently. AutoGrid is useful when you're trying to line objects up, so if you're going to work on a layout later, you might want to leave it on.

You can test to see if you got the Body tag at exactly the right spot by switching back to Browse mode. Choose Mode, Browse and your screen should look similar to figure 11.4. When you have it just right, the vertical and horizontal scroll bars will be empty—you can't scroll at all. If you have a horizontal scroll bar, that means you have a layout object, text, field, or graphic to the right of your screen. Scroll to it, switch back to Layout mode, and move it to the left.

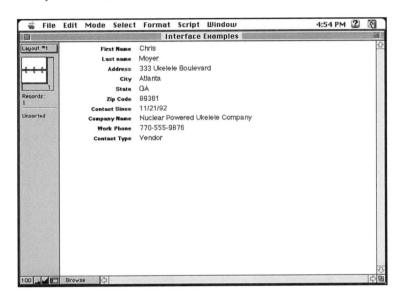

Fig. 11.4
No scroll boxes appear in the scroll bars when you're in Browse mode and the layout fits the screen size.

4. In Layout mode, select the third gray from the bottom of the fill color palette by clicking the Fill tool, as shown in figure 11.5.

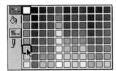

Fig. 11.5
Select a color from the large range available.

5. After you have the layout height correct, make sure you're in Layout mode and click the Rectangle tool (see fig. 11.6). Don't try to drag the tool—just click once.

Fig. 11.6
Use the Rectangle
tool to draw
squares and
rectangles.

Rectangle Tool ——————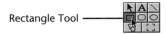

6. Move the mouse onto the layout, click, and drag a rectangle.

   Click and drag the rectangle so it's as far into the upper left corner of the screen as possible (see fig. 11.7).

Fig. 11.7
Stretch the lower-
right corner of the
rectangle into the
upper-left corner
to make a colored
background.

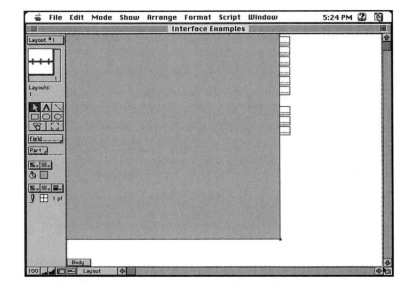

7. Click the rectangle once to select it. Click the lower-right handle and drag it to the exact lower-right corner of the screen. Press ⌘ to disable AutoGrid. Remember, you can switch to Browse mode to make sure you get it sized exactly right.

8. Your screen should look similar to figure 11.8. There's a black line around the rectangle. For it to be a true background, you need to change the line color so it matches the fill color. To do this, make sure the rectangle is selected by clicking it once, then select the third gray from the bottom in the line color palette (see fig. 11.9).

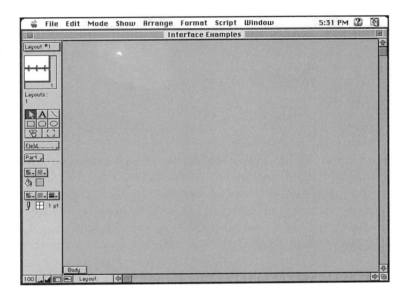

Fig. 11.8
Here is the final rectangle size for a colored background in Layout mode.

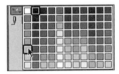

Fig. 11.9
Choose a color for the background.

9. Click the rectangle once to make sure it's selected, then choose Arrange, Send to Back to move it behind any fields on the layout.

10. With the rectangle still selected, choose Arrange, Lock to lock the background rectangle. When the rectangle is locked, you can't accidentally drag it out of position when you're moving other objects.

11. Choose Mode, Browse to view the finished background. Your horizontal and vertical scroll bars should be empty.

Now you have a layout with gray background and no scrolling capability.

Tip

I taught a class some time ago in which one of my students mentioned that he had to make sure he built databases that could be used by people who are color blind. By doing some informal research, he found that people who are color blind can more easily see light gray and soft pastel colors. If someone in your user population is color blind, test your layout color schemes with him to make sure he can use them.

Because it's kind of a drag (no pun intended) to create these backgrounds, create one and duplicate it when you make new layouts. You can also copy and paste your precisely sized rectangle into existing layouts, then drag the Body tag to the bottom of the rectangle. That should give you the right layout size. If you often create new databases, create a boilerplate database that has layout backgrounds, field styles, and layout titles already set up without any fields. Every time you create a new database, just duplicate the empty database and start creating fields.

When the layout is set, you can give your fields a 3D appearance.

Making 3D Fields

Field appearance is very important. Because fields are the real point of interaction between a user and FileMaker Pro, you need to give some thought to what you want to communicate to a user. For example, users can't enter information in a calculation field. You might want to make calculation fields (or auto entered fields) have a different look from standard data entry fields. Also, if you have fields that are to be filled in at a later time, you can designate them by using a different field style or color. As always, when you use a distinctive look to convey meaning, you need to use that look consistently throughout your database. If you don't, you might confuse your users.

To give fields a 3D look on a gray (or colored) background, follow these steps:

1. Choose Mode, Layout to switch to Layout mode.

2. Select all the fields you want to change. If you want to change every field on the layout, select one field, then press ⌘-Option-A to select the rest.

3. Choose a white or light gray fill color from the fill color palette by clicking the Fill tool (see fig. 11.10).

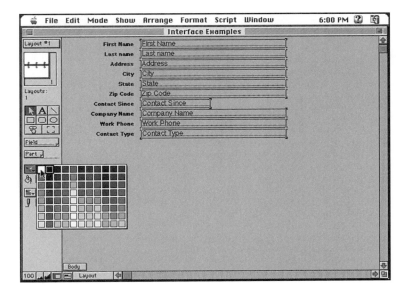

Fig. 11.10
Select a white or
light gray fill for
the background.

4. With the fields selected, choose Format, Field Borders to open the Field
   Borders dialog box.

5. Select the Top and Left check boxes (see fig. 11.11).

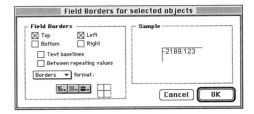

Fig. 11.11
Create a 3D effect
by showing two
field borders.

6. Click OK to close the Field Borders dialog box.

7. Choose Mode, Browse to return to Browse mode. Your screen should
   look similar to figure 11.12.

Fig. 11.12
You can achieve
the basic 3D field
look by showing
only two borders.

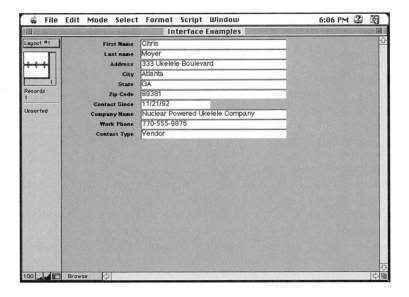

This is a basic 3D look. It's not flashy, but it's okay and it doesn't take much time for FileMaker to render the layout. That's a consideration if the database will be used heavily over a network. If you want more pizzazz, follow these steps and substitute the colors or shades of your preference:

1. Choose Mode, Layout to switch to Layout mode.

2. Select the background rectangle and choose Arrange, Unlock. Give the rectangle a darker fill and outline color, perhaps the gray that's two or three positions below the white color in the color palette. When you're done, choose Arrange, Lock.

3. Select all the fields you want to change.

4. Choose a light gray fill color from the fill color palette, perhaps the third from the bottom.

5. Choose the white color from the line color palette (see fig. 11.13).

Fig. 11.13
Select a white line
color from the
color palette to
draw a white line.

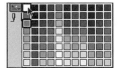

6. Select the Line tool (see fig. 11.14).

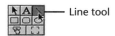 —— Line tool

Fig. 11.14
Select the Line tool to draw a line on the layout.

IV

Interface Design

7. Draw a line the length of your first field, as shown in figure 11.15.

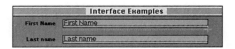

Fig. 11.15
Draw a white line the same length as the field for a more advanced 3D effect.

8. Use the arrow keys to nudge the line up next to the lower edge of the field (see fig. 11.16).

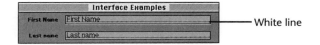 —— White line

Fig. 11.16
Move the white line against the bottom edge of the field.

9. Select the Line tool again and draw another line along the right edge of the field. It might help to press the ⌘ key as you do this to temporarily disable AutoGrid. If you don't, it can be difficult to make the line the correct length. Make the line run from one pixel above the field to one pixel below, aligning with the end of your horizontal line. Again, use the arrow keys to place it right next to the edge of the field.

10. Select the vertical line and choose Edit, Duplicate. Move the duplicated line to the left end of the field. Use the arrow keys to move it against the left edge. Duplicate the horizontal line and move it to just above the top edge. Press the Shift key and select the left vertical line so you have both the top and left lines selected.

11. With the lines selected, change the color in the line color palette to a dark gray (see fig. 11.17).

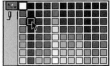

Fig. 11.17
Select a dark gray from the line color palette.

12. Choose Mode, Browse to see the final effect (see fig. 11.18).

Fig. 11.18
This shows a more
advanced 3D
effect.

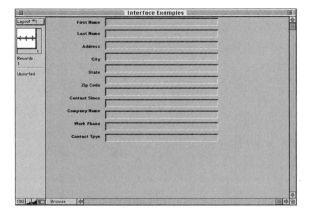

13. Repeat this process for each field. If your fields are the same length, you can duplicate all four lines and just move them to the next field.

Try experimenting with different shades or colors, or even not drawing two lines and using Field Borders for those two lines. For example, you could draw the bottom and right lines in white, then select the field and turn on black or gray field borders for the top and left sides.

You could also try experimenting with multiple lines of progressively lighter or darker colors. It gives your field edges a rounded look. If you use thicker lines, you can't dovetail your corners as nicely as you can using multiple thin lines. Your corners won't look right. If you do use multiple thin lines, vary the lengths so your corners come together (see fig. 11.19).

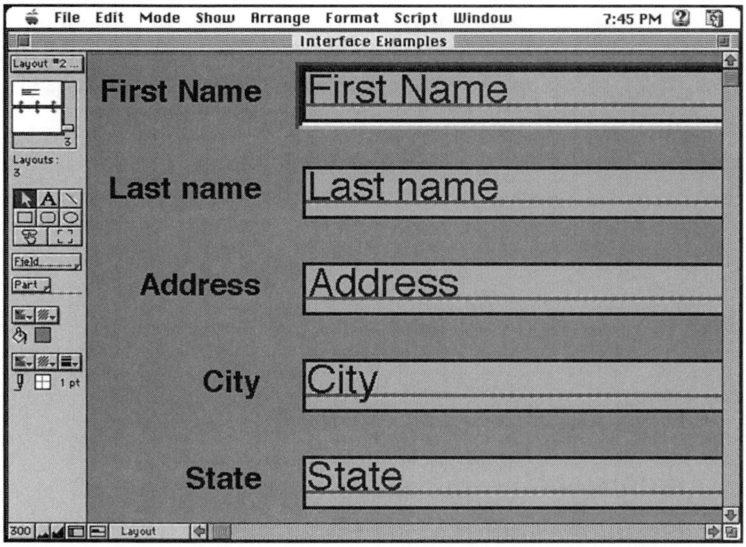

Fig. 11.19
Adding highlights
with colored lines
give a great 3D
appearance.

IV

Interface Design

Creating 3D Boxes

Now you have nice looking fields. It makes sense to group fields into logically similar clusters. When you do this, you might want to box these groups off in their own area.

To create a 3D box, follow these steps:

1. Choose Mode, Layout to switch to Layout mode.
2. Select the white color from the line color palette.
3. Select the Line tool and draw a vertical line.
4. Select the Line tool again and draw a horizontal line, starting at the top of the vertical line. Your screen should look similar to figure 11.20.

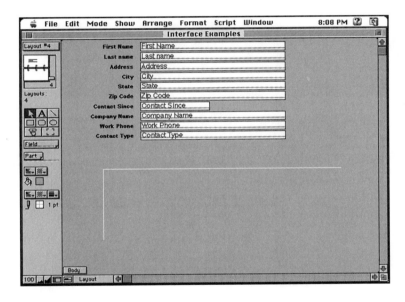

Fig. 11.20
To make a 3D box, start by drawing vertical and horizontal lines.

5. Select both lines and choose Edit, Duplicate.
6. With the lines still selected, choose the black color from the line color palette.
7. Move the lines to form a rectangle (see fig. 11.21). The rectangle appears embossed on the background.

Fig. 11.21
Make a rectangle
out of the four
lines.

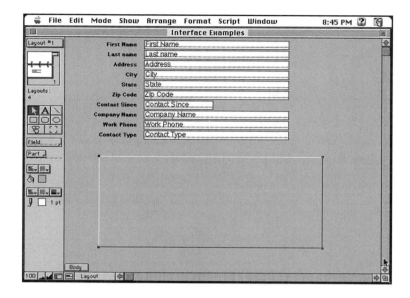

8. Select all four lines. When you do, it looks like nothing is selected because the handles overlap.

9. Choose Arrange, Group. Now you can drag the rectangle around and
resize it. Resize it so it's about the size of the rectangle shown in figure
11.22.

Fig. 11.22
Resize a 3D box to
fit your layout.

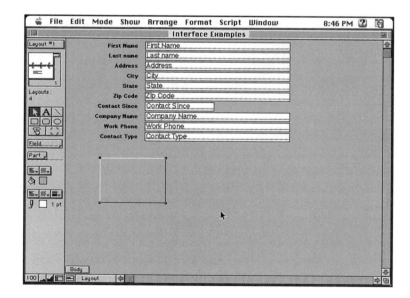

10. Click the upper-left handle and drag it down and to the right of the lower-right handle (see fig. 11.23). The rectangle will now look like the one shown in figure 11.24. The flipped rectangle appears inset into the background.

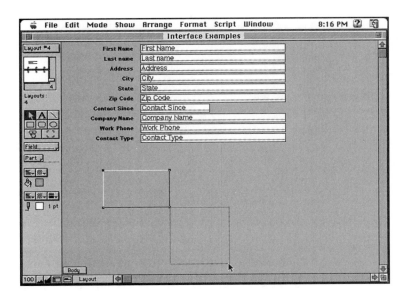

Fig. 11.23
This is the direction the 3D box will flip.

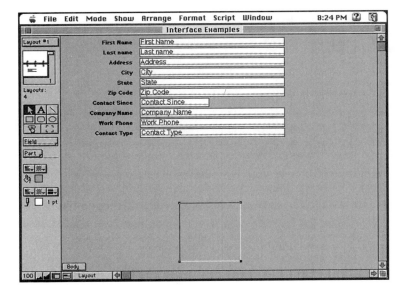

Fig. 11.24
The flipped 3D box looks inset into the background.

11. Pick the rectangle style of your choice, duplicate, resize, then box off your fields into functional areas, as shown in figure 11.25.

Fig. 11.25

This is a great looking 3D layout.

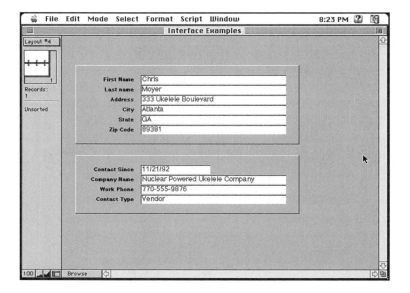

These rectangles can be used around fields, to improve button appearance, or just for breaking up layouts. They're handy things. Now you have everything looking good, but you need a layout title.

Creating 3D Text

To create 3D text, follow these steps:

1. Choose Mode, Layout to switch to Layout mode.

2. Select the text you want to work with. Make it bold and a large point size, at least 14 points or higher.

3. Choose Edit, Duplicate.

   When you duplicate an item, it gets offset by six "nudges." If you press the left arrow key six times and the up arrow key six times, the item will be exactly on top of its original. You want a slight offset in the other direction. Press the up arrow key seven times and the left arrow key seven times.

4. With the text still selected, choose Format, Text Color and choose the white color from the color palette. Your screen should look similar to figure 11.26.

Fig. 11.26
By placing white over black text, you can achieve a 3D effect.

5. If you like the effect, you can leave it. If you want, select the white text and choose Arrange, Send to Back. This will move the text behind the background. Make sure you don't deselect the text. Choose Arrange, Bring Forward. Press the down-arrow keys twice and press the right arrow key twice. Your screen should look similar to figure 11.27.

Contact Database

Fig. 11.27
By placing black over white text, you can achieve a 3D effect that looks inset into the background.

Design Issues in a Cross-Platform Environment

The two things to remember when designing layouts that will be used on both the Mac and Windows platforms are screen size and text fonts.

Because the screen sizes of Windows users are different (usually larger) than Macs, you might end up with more blank space on your layout on a Windows screen. One solution is to have two layouts, one for each platform, that are custom designed for each screen size.

You should always use a font that looks good on both platforms when in a cross-platform environment. Some Mac fonts don't read very well on a Windows screen, so pick one that does. Also, text tends to take up more room on a Windows screen and might look truncated at first—resizing the text object to be a little larger will fix this problem.

From Here...

In this chapter, you learned basic interface guidelines and how to create 3D effects using FileMaker Pro's layout tools. From here, you might want to read the following chapters:

- Chapter 3, "Creating and Printing Reports," describes how to create reports. It also goes into detail about finding and sorting information in a FileMaker database.

- Chapter 12, "Controlling File Access," explains how to set up access privileges and build password systems, and teaches developers how to create time bombs to protect demo versions of their databases.

Controlling File Access

FileMaker Pro has had password protection built-in for a long time now. Passwords enable you to control two things: actions that a user can perform on the database, and fields or layouts that a user can access. This combination of privileges allows you to create extremely customized access restrictions. The password features have been enhanced in FileMaker Pro 3.0, so they're even tighter now.

Not only can passwords be used to control access to layouts and fields in a database, they can also be used to control what a user can edit. This chapter covers how to do the following:

- Use the access privileges in FileMaker Pro
- Turn off access to FileMaker menus
- Hide layouts from users
- Create an alternate password system
- Time-bomb a database if you need to distribute sample templates of your work

Using FileMaker Access Privileges

The whole access privileges feature set, ncluding password protection, is one of the least understood features of FileMaker Pro because the area seems complicated at first glance. It's important that you have a good working knowledge of how to implement password protection for the databases you develop.

Access is controlled through the use of *groups* and *passwords*. You can restrict groups to certain layouts and fields in the database. Through groups, you control what parts of the database a user can access. Passwords control whether a user can print, edit records, create new records, and so on. Through passwords, you control the kinds of actions a user can perform. You can assign passwords to groups; by combining the two control structures, you can have a flexible security system.

To set up access privileges for any FileMaker database, follow these steps:

1. In the database you want to protect, choose File, Access Privileges, Define Groups to open the Define Groups dialog box.

2. In the Group Name text box, type in a new group name (for example, **Accounting**). Click Create. Repeat this process for as many different groups as you have (see fig. 12.1).

Fig. 12.1
Groups of
passwords are
created in the
Define Groups
dialog box.

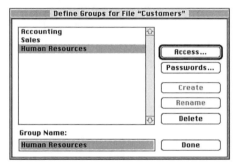

3. After you define your groups, click Access to open the Access Privileges dialog box. If you have a group selected when you click Access, you also will have that group selected in the Access Privileges dialog box (see fig. 12.2).

If you don't have a group selected, click a group name. Notice the key at the bottom of the dialog box. A solid bullet means a field or layout is fully accessible. A gray bullet means the field or layout is completely inaccessible. If a user tries to switch to a layout for which they don't have access, the entire layout appears gray. The same goes for a field. A hollow bullet means the field or layout is read-only; a user can view information in the layout or field, but can't edit anything.

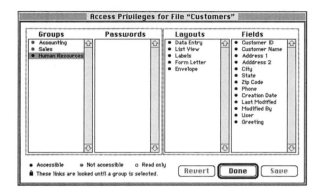

Fig. 12.2
The Human Resources group is selected in the Access Privileges dialog box.

IV

Interface Design

4. To change the layout access for the selected group, move the mouse over the bullet in front of a particular layout in the Layouts list. The cursor changes to a check mark. Click to cycle through the bullet accessibility options. A solid bullet will turn hollow, then gray, then solid again with each click. Figure 12.3 shows a layout that has been changed to Not Accessible.

The cursor changes to a check mark

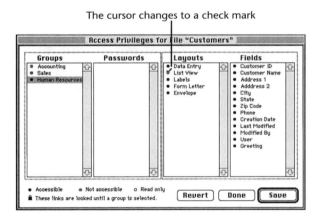

Fig. 12.3
Making the layout not accessible for a group.

5. When you finish making the access settings for a specific group, click Save. You can then work on the access privileges for a different group.

6. To work on a different group, just click the group name in the Groups list.

7. Set the access privileges for each group, clicking Save after you finish each group. When you finish all groups, click Done. You return to the dialog box you were in last. In this case, it's the Define Groups dialog box.

8. Click Passwords to open the Define Passwords dialog box (see fig. 12.4).

Fig. 12.4
You can hide menu items for certain passwords.

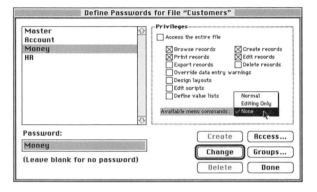

9. To create a new password, type it in the Password text box and click Create. Repeat this step for other passwords.

> **Tip**
>
> Create a master password first. Make it something that you can easily remember. Because the master password doesn't need any access restrictions, it's finished as soon as you create it. Master passwords work across all groups.

10. If you need to be able to assign a password to a specific group (you might want to give a user full database privileges, but restrict them to certain layouts), deselect the Access the Entire File check box.

11. To control menu access for a particular password, choose the appropriate setting from the Available Menu Commands pop-up menu. When you select Editing Only, a user can edit existing records only—they cannot create new records. Browse mode is the only mode available. If you select None, no changes can be made to the database.

12. Make as many passwords as you need. When you finish, the Define Passwords dialog box should look similar to figure 12.5.

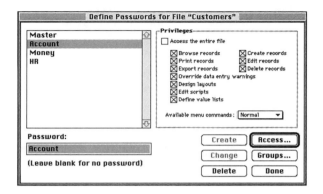

Fig. 12.5
Create passwords
to limit access to
users of the
database.

13. When you finish editing the password privileges, click Access to open the Access Privileges dialog box.

14. To assign a password to a specific group, first select the group you want to work with, then click the bullet for the associated password to make it solid (see fig. 12.6). You can't unassign a master password to any group. Master passwords, by their nature, work across all groups.

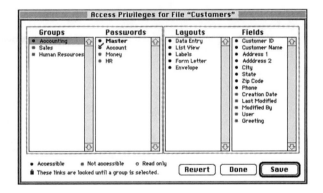

Fig. 12.6
Assign passwords
to a group, where
layout and field
access is con-
trolled.

15. When you finish editing the access privileges, click Done. You return to the Define Passwords dialog box. Click Done to close the Define Passwords dialog box. The Confirm dialog box appears (see fig. 12.7).

A nice thing about FileMaker is that it makes sure you don't accidentally lock yourself out of your own database.

Fig. 12.7
The Confirm
dialog box ensures
you know the
master password.

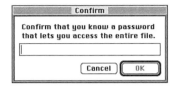

> 16. Enter your master password and click OK.

Try closing the database and opening it again. You are prompted for a
password in the Password dialog box. Enter a password you assigned to a
group with no access to a specific layout. When you switch to a layout that
is not accessible with your current access privileges, your access should be
denied (see fig. 12.8). Figure 12.9 shows a layout where only certain fields are
inaccessible.

Fig. 12.8
Access to an entire
layout can be
blocked to certain
groups.

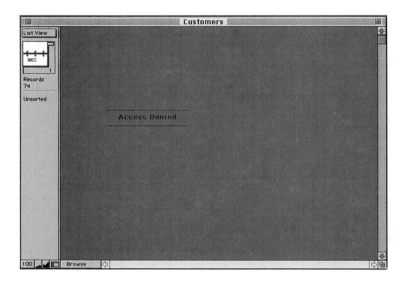

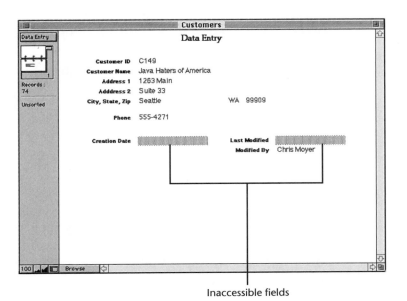

Fig. 12.9
Fields can be made
inaccessible to
hide information.

Inaccessible fields

Tip

If you have trouble changing Layout or Field access in the Access Privileges dialog
box, make sure you have a group selected first.

You should have a good idea of how to work with FileMaker's access privileges now. Keep reading to learn about other ways to restrict access to a file.

Controlling Layout Access

Take a look at one of the files that ships with FileMaker Pro. In the FileMaker
Examples folder is the Integrated Solution folder. In the Integrated Solution
folder is a file named Invoices (see fig. 12.10).

Fig. 12.10
Sample files such
as the Integrated
Solution files
are located in
the FileMaker
Examples folder.

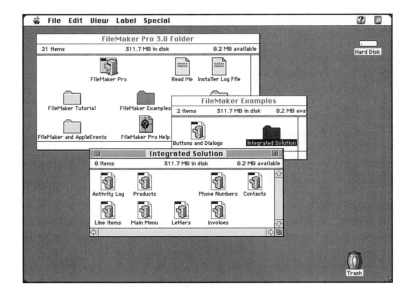

Open the Invoices database to see that this database already has a level of
access control set up. Look at the layout pop-up menu in the Status Area. It
says you're currently on the Invoice Entry layout. Click and hold the layout
pop-up menu (see fig. 12.11).

Fig. 12.11
You can hide
layouts from users
in Browse mode.

Layout pop-up menu—

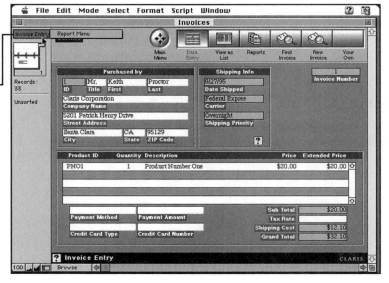

Only one layout is showing: the Report Menu layout. You know that there are at least two layouts, because you're currently on the Invoice Entry layout—but it doesn't show up in the layout list. This database actually has 14 layouts, all but one of which are hidden. Why would you want to hide layouts?

If you have scripted operations that depend on certain fields being on a layout, you need to disable a user's ability to move from layout to layout on their own. Also, if you need to make sure that certain layouts are completed before a user can advance to the next layout, you need to force the user to navigate with your buttons and scripts. If they can just switch layouts through the layout pop-up menu, they defeat data entry rules you're trying to enforce.

There are several good reasons for restricting user access to layouts in Browse mode. If you need to work with a layout, though, you need to access and view the layouts. To view the layouts in this database, choose Mode, Layout. Now click the layout pop-up menu (see fig. 12.12).

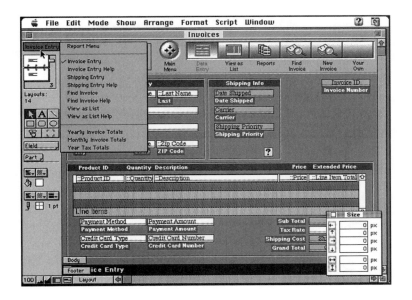

Fig. 12.12
All of the layouts are always shown in Layout mode.

If you count the actual layout names, you only see 12. However, you're currently on Invoice Entry, which appears to be the second layout. Look at the layout number in the Book. It shows that you're on layout three. There's only one way to get to layout two. Click the top page of the Book (see fig. 12.13).

Fig. 12.13
Use the Book to move to layouts named dash, which appear as a dashed line in the layout pop-up menu.

Click the top page

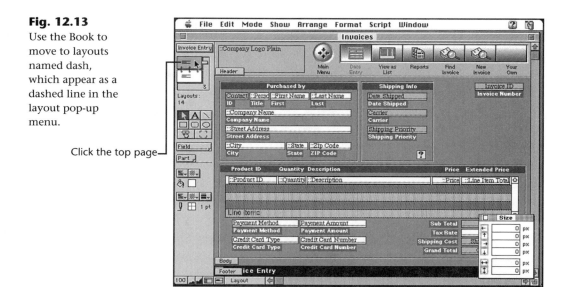

Figure 12.14 shows layout two. Notice that the layout is blank. It's a throw-away layout, if you will. The one significant thing about this layout is its name: it's a dash. Click the layout pop-up menu again to see what effect this has. The dash appears as a separator in the layout list.

Fig. 12.14
A blank layout named dash is used as a separator in the layout pop-up menu.

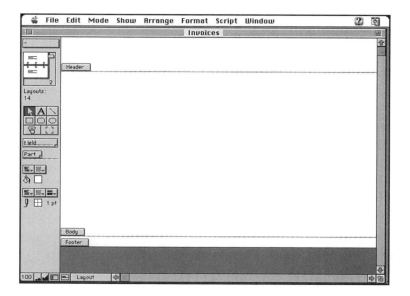

Dash layouts are probably best used only as separators in the layout list and not to hide layouts from a user. If you need to navigate to a layout in a script, it should be properly named for clarity.

If you need to hide layouts, there's a better way. In fact, there are two methods. Here's how to hide a single layout:

1. Choose Mode, Layout to get into Layout mode.
2. Choose Mode, Layout Setup to open the Layout Setup dialog box.
3. Deselect the Include in Layouts Menu check box (see fig. 12.15). If you need to show the layout, select the check box.

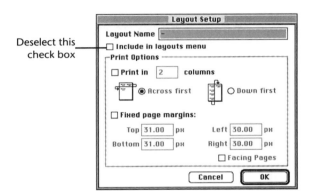

Fig. 12.15
You can exclude each layout from the Layout pop-up menu in Browse mode.

4. Click OK to close the Layout Setup dialog box.

> **Note**
>
> If you hide a layout that is named with a dash, a separator layout, then the separator will not appear in the layout pop-up menu when you're in Browse mode.

Here's how to hide or show multiple layouts at one time:

1. Choose Mode, Layout to go to Layout mode.
2. Choose Mode, Set Layout Order to open the Set Layout Order dialog box.
3. Select the layout you want to hide.
4. Deselect the Include in Layouts Menu check box (see fig. 12.16). You can do this for multiple layouts by holding the cursor over a check mark next to a layout name and dragging the check mark cursor down the list.

Fig. 12.16
You can hide multiple layouts at one time and re-order the layouts in the Set Layout Order dialog box.

5. Click OK to close the Set Layout Order dialog box.

Creating an Alternate Password System

An alternate password system is available in FileMaker Pro that does not apply to all of the records in a given database.

Imagine you have a purchase order system. A purchasing agent needs to be able to complete a purchase order. After it's been approved, though, you don't want any more changes on that particular record. (It would be bad if someone got a purchase order for a box of pens approved, and then changed the purchase order line items to a new computer for their desk.) With FileMaker's built-in password protections, it is possible to deny access to existing records but allow any new records created to be edited. If the Edit check box in the Define Passwords dialog box is not selected, this is the result. This feature works on a per-session basis, every time the database is closed and opened again the existing records cannot be edited.

Time-Bombing Database Templates

If you're a database developer who writes templates, you probably have to "seed" the market by sending out demonstration versions of your databases. The problem is, when someone has a demo version of your template, why should they pay for the real thing?

You only have two options. You can send out a version of your template with a limited feature set (a *crippled* version) or you can send out a full-featured version that has an expiration date. The crippled version has the disadvantage that it can't show off the things it can do. Some might not like your template because they're only getting to try a few of the features.

The best solution is to have a full-featured demo version that expires after a
certain period of time. You can easily implement a "time bomb" scheme with
the ScriptMaker. To build a 30-day time bomb script, follow these steps:

1. Open the database you want to time-bomb and choose File, Define
   Fields to open the Define Fields dialog box.

2. Create a new global date field called TBDate. Click Done to close the
   Define Fields dialog box.

3. Choose Script, ScriptMaker to open the Define Scripts dialog box.

4. Enter a new script name called Time Bomb and click Create.

5. Click Clear All to remove the default script steps.

6. From the Available Steps list, move the If script step to the script list on
   the right and click Specify. The Specify Calculation dialog box appears.

7. Choose Logical Functions from the View pop-up menu and double-click
   the IsEmpty (field) function. It moves to the calculation area.

8. In the Current File list, double-click the TBDate field. It moves to the
   IsEmpty argument (see fig. 12.17).

◀ See "Working
with Logical
Functions,"
p. 128

▶ See "Logical
Functions,"
p. 513

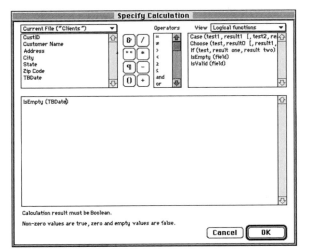

Fig. 12.17
A field can be
checked to see if it
is empty using the
IsEmpty function.

9. Click OK to close the Specify Calculation dialog box.

10. From the Available Steps list in the Script Definitions dialog box,
    double-click the Set Field script step to move it to the list on the right.
    Drag it up so it's between the If and End If script steps.

11. Click Specify Field to open the Specify Field dialog box.

12. Select TBDate and click OK to close the Specify Field dialog box.

13. Click Specify to open the Specify Calculation dialog box.

14. Choose Status Functions from the View pop-up menu and double-click the Status(CurrentDate) function. It moves to the calculation area.

15. Click OK to close the Specify Calculation dialog box.

16. From the Available Steps list in the Script Definitions dialog box, double-click the Else script step. It moves to the list on the right. Drag it above the End If script step.

17. Double-click another If script step into the list on the right and drag it above the first End If script step.

18. Click Specify to open the Specify Calculation dialog box.

19. Choose Status Functions from the View pop-up menu and double-click the Status(CurrentDate) function. It moves to the calculation area.

20. Click to the right of the function and click the minus button.

21. Double-click TBDate into the calculation area.

22. From the Operators list, double-click the   operator. It moves to the calculation area.

23. Type **30**. The finished calculation should look like figure 12.18.

Fig. 12.18
Use this simple calculation in a script to time bomb a file after 30 days.

Time bomb calculation ———

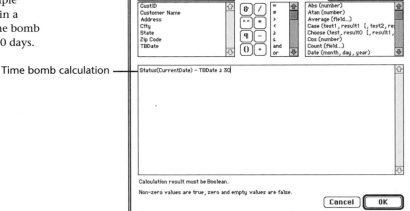

24. Click OK to close the Specify Calculation dialog box.

25. Double-click the Show Message script step in the Script Definitions dialog box, and drag it above the two End If script steps.

IV

26. Click Specify to open the Specify Message dialog box.

27. In the Message text box, type **This demo template has expired after 30 days of trial use! Please contact the person you received this template from to obtain a licensed version. When you click OK, this template will automatically close.**

28. Delete Cancel from the Second Button Captions text box (see fig. 12.19).

Fig. 12.19
You can place custom messages in scripts to let users know what is going on.

29. Click OK to close the Specify Message dialog box.

30. From the Available Steps list in the Script Definitions dialog box, double-click the Close script step. It moves to the script list on the right. Drag it above both End If script steps.

31. Click Specify File and select the database you're working in. Click Open. Figure 12.20 shows what the finished time bomb script should look like.

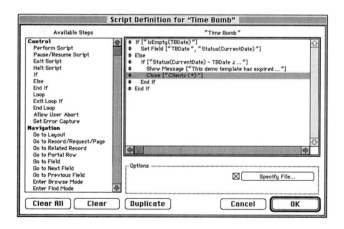

Fig. 12.20
Here is what a script that time-bombs a file after 30 days looks like.

32. Click OK to close the Script Definition dialog box.

33. Click Done to close the Define Scripts dialog box.

I purposely did not tell you to make this the startup script for the database. The following are a few points that will make the time bomb airtight:

- Make a backup copy of your database before installing a time bomb! The last thing you need is to time-bomb yourself out of your only copy of your database.

- To make this a true bomb, you need to have this script automatically run when the database starts up.

- Because this script uses the Set Field command to load the TBDate field, it doesn't need to be on any layout. Make sure the field isn't on a layout where a user can manually reset the date.

- For the time bomb to be effective, you have to make sure the user can't turn it off. When you distribute your templates, you need to lock people out of the Define Fields dialog box, the Preferences dialog box, and ScriptMaker. If users have access to any of these areas, they could delete the field the script uses, cause the script to not run at startup, or delete the script entirely. You can prevent access to all of these areas by creating a blank user password that doesn't have access to the entire file. It's a piece of cake.

Caution

Make a backup of your database before you install a time bomb.

You might look at that time bomb script and say, "No problem. I could get around that." Everyone knows the old trick of setting back the system clock. That gets around a lot of time-bombed software. The other thing you could do to defeat this script is to press ⌘-. (period) when the database starts. That cancels execution of the time bomb script.

Now that I've warned you to back up your database twice, I'm going to tell you how to modify this script to make it airtight. Again, back up your database before you do this, or else you can kiss this database good-bye. To make the time bomb unbeatable, follow these steps:

1. ·Choose File, Define Fields to open the Define Fields dialog box.

2. Create a new global text field called Expired.

3. Click Done to close the Define Fields dialog box.

4. Choose Script, ScriptMaker to open the Define Scripts dialog box.

5. Double-click the Time Bomb script to open the Script Definition dialog box.

6. Double-click the If script step that immediately follows the Else script step to open the Specify Calculation dialog box.

7. Double-click the or operator to move it to the calculation area.

8. Double-click the Expired field to move it to the calculation area.

9. Double-click the = operator to move it to the calculation area.

10. Click the quotes button and type the letter **E**. Figure 12.21 shows the finished calculation.

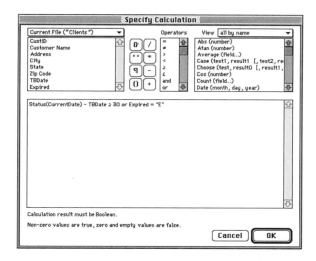

Fig. 12.21
Make the time bomb calculation airtight.

11. Click OK to close the Specify Calculation dialog box.

12. Select the Set Field script step and click Duplicate.

13. Drag the duplicated Set Field script step so it's just above the Show Message script step.

14. Click Specify Field and select Expired. Click OK to close the Specify Field dialog box.

15. Click Specify to open the Specify Calculation dialog box.

16. Select the Status(CurrentDate) function and delete it.

17. Click the quotes button and type the letter **E**. Figure 12.22 shows the final calculation.

Interface Design

IV

Fig. 12.22
This is the finished
Set Field calcula-
tion.

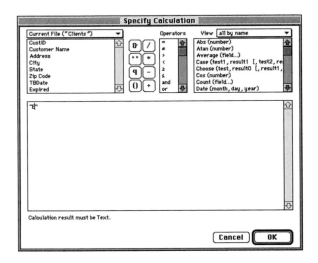

18. Click OK to close the Specify Calculation dialog box.

19. And now for the silver bullet. Double-click the Allow User Abort script
step into the script list on the right. Drag it to the top of the list. Select
the Off radio button (see fig. 12.23).

Fig. 12.23
This is the
improved time
bomb script.

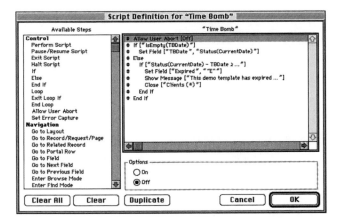

20. Click OK to close the Script Definition dialog box.
21. Click Done to close the Define Scripts dialog box.

Okay, so how is this improved? Well, because you disabled user abort, the script can't be canceled. You also locked down the expiration. The first time the template expires will be the last—even if the user sets the system clock back, the Expired field still has an E in it. Because both the TBDate, which holds the starting date, and the Expired field are evaluated by the Time Bomb script, expiration is permanent.

The *only* way to defeat this script is to set the system clock back before the template expires. Most people don't think to do that until after something has already expired. Besides, that strategy would defeat any kind of time bomb, not just this one. It's also a huge inconvenience. If I liked a template, I'd rather pay the money for the real thing than go through the system clock hassles.

From Here...

Now you know how to lock people out of databases in several ways. You can use FileMaker's access privileges to control user access to layouts, fields, and menus. If you're a template author, you might find the time bomb script useful as well. From here, you might want to read the following chapters:

- Chapter 5, "Working with Calculation Fields," gives you more information on how to perform calculations across multiple related records. This is useful in totaling line items on an invoice.

- Chapter 7, "Scripting—The Basics," provides in-depth information on everything you need to know about the elements of scripting.

- Chapter 15, "Scripting with ScriptMaker," teaches you the process of advanced scripting.

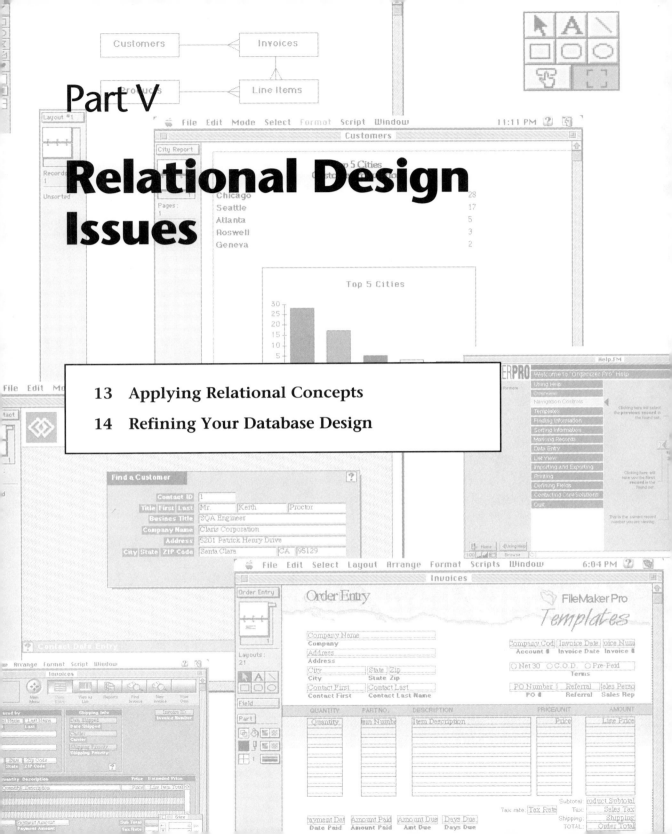

Part V

Relational Design Issues

CHAPTER 13

Applying Relational Concepts

Relational databases such as FileMaker Pro 3.0 are inherently flexible in terms of design. You can develop a database in a variety of ways to address the same problem. That's the good news. The bad news is that not all of those designs will enable you to do what you want to do. Some of the designs are inefficient and will make your database performance crawl. To avoid these negative possibilities, you need to put some thought into your database system before you start to build it. Effort applied up front on the design of your database will pay off in benefits down the road.

This chapter covers the following topics:

- The importance of data normalization
- Database design problems and solutions
- A design process anyone can use to create a successful relational database
- Referential integrity

Understanding Relational Database Design

The terms "rows" and "columns" are often tossed about in the relational database world. Because this might be your first experience with a relational database, I will use "records" and "fields" interchangeably with "rows" and "columns" (respectively). In Chapter 16, you found that the AppleScript Dictionary also references records and fields in a row and column fashion. If you imagine a List view in FileMaker Pro, the columns are the fields, and the rows are record instances of the fields.

I will also refer to a FileMaker database as a table. In other relational database systems, a single database can consist of several tables—what FileMaker users call a database or file. Just for fun, here's more jargon. Impress your friends with this stuff:

tuple = row = record

relation = table = database

attribute = column = vector = field

match field = key field

Suppose a friend has an extensive collection of CDs and has asked you to create a database system for him so he can manage his collection. Because this is just a learning example, forget all the bells and whistles. This will be a basic example with just enough to show the impact that the design has on the usefulness of the final product.

As a starting point, your friend has given you a list he created using his word processor. This list breaks out into the following fields:

CD Title

Artist/Group Name

Musical Category

Track 1 Title

Track 2 Title

Track 3 Title

and so on

Right now, all the data is in a single table. It is possible to make a database with this single table structure and put both title and track information in that table, but that would be extremely awkward to work with.

Think about it. How many fields do you set up for track titles? Ten? Twenty? Any time you run into a CD that goes beyond your maximum number of tracks, you need to redesign the database and add more track fields. Just as it makes sense to have invoice line items in a separate file (because the number of line items varies from invoice to invoice), it also makes sense to put the individual track information in its own file.

In general, you don't want to have multiple fields in a given database that capture the same type of information. In this database, Track 1 Title, Track 2 Title, and Track 3 Title are all capturing the same kind of information: track titles. If you have databases where you have this kind of structure, move those fields and that information to a separate table where each item becomes its own record. In this example, each track will be a single record in the new table.

So you create two tables in FileMaker Pro, calling one the CD Header table and the other the CD Tracks table. Load the first table with the information on the CD Title line of your friend's list, and load the other table with the Track Title information from the list.

How will you know which tracks go with which CD titles? You need to establish a link between the two tables so you can find all the track data for a given CD. You need a match field for a relationship in FileMaker. Why not the CD Title field? Define the columns in the CD Header table to be:

> CD Title
>
> Artist/Group Name
>
> Musical Category

Then you define the columns in the CD Tracks table to be:

> CD Title
>
> Track Title

Because you have many tracks that correspond to a single CD title (a many to one relationship), you need to use a portal in the CD Header table to view the tracks. When you have a many to one relationship, you always use a portal on the one side of the relationship. Because portals allow you to see multiple, related records, it doesn't make sense to put it on the many side. If you put a portal in the CD Tracks table, the portal would be in each track record. Because a track can only belong to one CD, you would only have one item—the CD title—appearing in your portal. When you put the portal on the CD Header side, you see every related track record. One CD can have many tracks. Just remember that the portal always goes on the one side of a one to many relationship. Figure 13.1 shows the result.

Fig. 13.1

Each row of a portal corresponds to a single record in the related table.

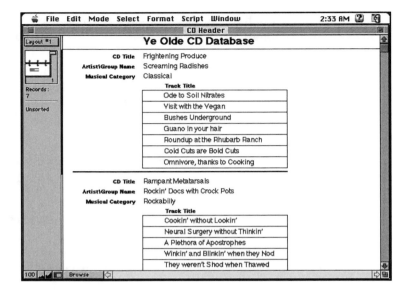

Now here's a problem. You can load the track information into the table as it's shown on your friend's list, but how do you identify the order of the tracks? If you wanted to see a report showing only Track 3 titles, you need to be able to identify specific tracks. No problem. Just modify the CD Tracks table to look like this:

CD Title

Track Number

Track Title

This additional field gives you sufficient information to uniquely identify any row in the CD Tracks table. Big deal, right? It's a very big deal. If you can't uniquely identify a single row in your table, how can you be sure you have the right match? If two rows are identical across all fields, does that mean they both belong to one CD that has a duplicate track, or does that mean one belongs to one CD and the other belongs to a different CD? It makes a difference if you need to print a list of CD's and what tracks they contain.

FileMaker uses an *index* to display records in a portal. An index in FileMaker is very similar to an index in the back of a book. If you look in a book's index and locate a specific word or term, you'll see the pages that the word or term appears on, in order. For example, a word might appear on pages 2, 16, 37, and 90. The index would never list them as being on pages 37, 90, 2, 16. The references are always in order.

FileMaker is the same way. The first time a word, say the CD title, appears in the database, it gets put into the index and the record number it appears in (FileMaker's internal record number) gets noted as well. The next time it appears, because the word has already been put in the index, only the new record reference is added. To FileMaker, the index entry in the CD Tracks table for a happening CD like Shaking Down the Mangrove Spaceship might look like this:

Shaking Down the Mangrove Spaceship, 7, 8, 9, 10, 11, 12

Because the CD tracks were probably all entered at the same time, the record numbers would probably be sequential, as shown above. If they were entered in a random order, with tracks from another CD interspersed, then there would be gaps in the order.

So, because FileMaker uses the index to display items in a portal, portal items appear in the order they were created. In this example, if you want your CD tracks to be in order, enter them in the proper order. If you need to sort items in a portal, Chapter 16 covers how you can create a script to reset the creation order.

There's another problem in your friend's list: some CD's have the same title! Because you have CD Title as the match field between your two tables, this isn't going to work properly for those cases. This means that one CD will show its track information as well as the track information for the other CD. Figure 13.2 shows the effect when two tracks from different CD's have the same match field.

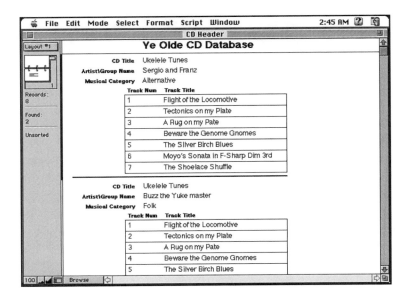

Fig. 13.2
When two database records have the same ID, all related records will match both of them.

Each CD shows all the tracks for both CDs. That's not correct, and because good database design is all about having a database system accurately reflect the real world system it models, you can't allow this.

One possible fix is to use the title plus the artist as the link. In FileMaker, though, only a single field can be a match field, so you would have to create a calculation field to put the two fields together (this is called *concatenation*). This calculation field containing information from both the CD Title and Artist/Group Name fields would then be your match field. This would make the CD Tracks table look like this:

> CD Title
>
> Artist\Group Name
>
> Title\Artist Match Calculation
>
> Track Number
>
> Track Title

The final calculation would look like figure 13.3.

Tip

If you use a field in a calculation, the field cannot contain math operators (such as +, −, *, /). The field also cannot begin with a number. If you need to use a slash in a field, such as Artist/Group Name, use a backslash—the field reads Artist\Group Name.

Fig. 13.3
This is the new calculation for the CD Tracks table.

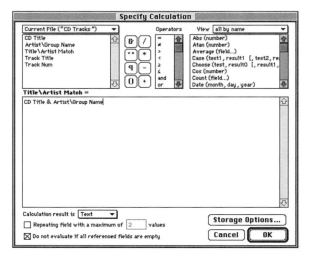

The calculated match field might work, but you might want to consider adding a CD Number field in both tables and using that as the link. The problem with match fields is that you not only need to worry about whether the values in the field are unique now, but that they will be unique always. Because you're probably not psychic, you need to look for values that have some guarantee of permanent uniqueness.

A CD Number could be the manufacturer's number that's printed on the CD label, it could be the CD serial number that's usually etched around the hole in the CD, or it could be a unique ID number that FileMaker Pro creates when you create the CD Header row. The important thing is that the link be unique so there's no ambiguity about which tracks in the CD Track table belong to a given row in the CD Header table.

It's not a bad habit to have the first field that you create in any new database be a unique ID field. Because the match field in this example is CD Number, you'd set it up as an auto-entered serial number in the CD Header table. The CD Number field in the CD Tracks table would be filled in automatically when you created new tracks in a the CD Tracks portal.

To set up a serial number, follow these steps:

1. Choose File, Define Fields to open the Define Fields dialog box.
2. Type in the serial number field name and click Create.
3. Click Options to open the Entry Options dialog box.
4. Select the Serial Number radio button. Enter a number for Next Value and Increment By.

> **Tip**
>
> For serial numbers, you can set the beginning value to anything you want, but you should probably increment them by one. If you make a large gap, say 15 or 20, your serial numbers will get very large after a few hundred records. This will require a large field on your layouts. Also, if you increment serial numbers by one, it's easier to spot when a record has been deleted. If your database skips a number, a record's been deleted. This requires more thinking when you have gaps built in to your serial number scheme.

5. Select the Prohibit Modification of Value check box. This prevents anyone from intentionally or unintentionally changing serial numbers. If you allow serial numbers to be changed, it's possible you might duplicate an existing serial number. The previous example shows that if you have duplicate match fields, your related data will show up for both records. The Entry Options dialog box should look similar to figure 13.4.

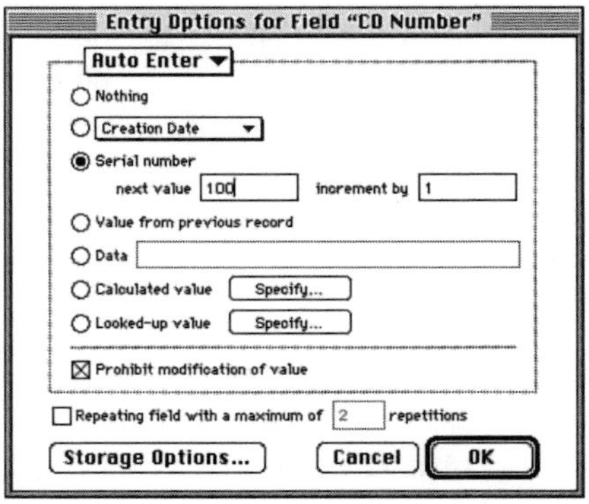

Fig. 13.4
About the only
way you can
guarantee unique
ID numbers is to
let FileMaker make
them for you.

6. Click OK to close the Entry Options dialog box.

7. Click Done to close the Define Fields dialog box.

The table layouts look like this:

CD Header table:

CD Number

CD Title

Artist/Group Name

Musical Category

CD Tracks table:

CD Number

Track Number

Track Title

CD Number is now the match field for the relationship between the two tables. Remember, if you create records in a portal, the match field is automatically entered in the portal record. You don't need to show the match field on the portal row. In this example, you would have a portal in the CD Header table, and the portal would only be showing the Track Number and Track Title fields.

At this point, you have a basic design for your CD database system. After you work out a design, manually run through some of your incoming data. No matter how much you plan, there are always some unusual cases that inevitably appear. In this CD example, there are two unusual cases: a compilation CD that has a different artist/group on every track and a CD that is really two CDs in one case. Your database design can't handle either of these situations.

If you chose to use the CD number printed on the label as your unique ID, the multi-disk CD would cause a problem. You could adopt the strategy of allowing -1 , -2 suffixes to the base CD number. This will work, but it's not a great solution. Regardless, the serialized CD Number field wouldn't have a problem with a double CD set.

The other problem shows that you have to modify your CD Track table design. Because every track can have a different group or artist, your table structure needs to look like this:

CD Number

Track Number

Track Title

Artist/Group Name

This solves the initial problem of dealing with a CD that has different artists on each track, but it also means you need to change your CD Header table. Because the Artist/Group Name information is now stored with the track, remove that field from the CD Header table. Also, because it's possible that each track might be a different Musical Category, that information should probably also be stored in the CD Tracks table.

The new layout would look like this:

CD Header table:

CD Number

CD Title

CD Tracks table:

CD Number

Track Number

Track Title

Artist/Group Name

Musical Category

Things have really switched around, but there's a good reason: attributes such as Group Name and Musical Category should be in the table with the object they pertain to. In this case, that object is the track. The attribute Artist/ Group Name usually applies to an entire CD, meaning it would go in the CD Header table, but because you found a CD where this isn't the case, that rule is wrong. The rule that an Artist/Group Name applies to a track does not exclude the possibility of it applying to an entire CD. Because it addresses all CD's, it's a better rule. The same holds true for Musical Category.

The idea of encoding rules into a database is fundamental of database design. You might have heard the term *business rules*. A business rule might be that if a product level drops below a two week supply, it should be reordered. Another might be that if a customer is more than 90 days past due on an invoice, no orders can be shipped to them until they pay their bill. Try and identify the rules, business or otherwise, as you work on your database design.

Back to the decision to move the Musical Category field from the CD Headers table to the CD Tracks table. There are several ways you can arrive at this conclusion, but one very effective method is to think ahead to the time when you're trying to find information in your database. How would you identify a CD as being a Jazz selection if the CD is categorized as Miscellaneous? With the Musical Category field associated with the track rather than with the CD, this problem disappears.

Has the CD Header table been reduced to the point where it's no longer needed? Not at all. It represents the "handle" for your data—the starting point for finding out all the rest of the information you want to know about a specific CD. You can find a particular CD and get the track information, or you can find a specific track and get the CD the track is a part of. It's the ultimate in flexibility.

You might wonder if it's typical to have such an important table with so few columns in it. Remember that this is a bare bones example. Think about where you would put the fields to store such information like price of the CD, date of purchase, last time used. Remember, attributes belong in the table that describes the object they pertain to. These pieces of information would be defined in the CD Header table because they describe the whole CD, not the individual tracks.

Now that you have things pretty well set on the design of your friend's database, it's time for the *WIBNI* (pronounced wib ney) to kick in. What's a WIBNI? Over time, you'll discover that it's an integral part of the database design process. Here's how it usually happens. You go over the details of the design with the end user and they say something like, "Wouldn't it be nice if we could identify each CD as a vocal or instrumental, and if it's an instrumental, wouldn't it be nice if we could identify what the primary solo instrument is? That shouldn't be hard to do, should it?" WIBNI stands for "wouldn't it be nice if."

If you have worked with FileMaker Pro for a while, you're probably familiar with this phenomenon. Fool that you are, you say, "Piece of cake," and mosey back to your drawing board. You little suspect that the more you let people know how easy it is to change a FileMaker database, the more changes you'll be asked for.

> **Tip**
>
> You might want to tell your end user that changes will take some effort, but they can usually be done. If you keep telling them that every change is a piece of cake, the next thing you know you'll be looking at 50 new features, which isn't necessarily a piece of cake.

You start by modifying the CD Header table:

> CD Number
>
> CD Title
>
> Vocal/Instrumental
>
> Solo Instrument

Does this look familiar? You just created the same problem you had before—different tracks on a CD might have different categories. Here it is the second time:

> **CD Header table:**
>
> CD Number
>
> CD Title
>
> **CD Tracks table:**
>
> CD Number
>
> Track Number
>
> Track Title
>
> Artist/Group Name
>
> Musical Category
>
> Vocal/Instrumental
>
> Solo Instrument

Maybe you could put "Voice" for the Solo Instrument on a Vocal and then you could eliminate the Vocal/Instrumental field. Time for a new design:

CD Tracks table:

CD Number

Track Number

Track Title

Artist/Group Name

Musical Category

Solo Instrument

Done at last! Time to start loading data.

But then, another WIBNI: it seems your friend has such an extensive CD collection that all his friends come to him to borrow CD's. He goes along with this practice reluctantly. His only method of keeping track of loaned CD's is a bunch of notes taped to his CD racks. There has to be a better way. "Wouldn't it be nice if the computer could keep track of things?"

This leads to another new layout:

CD Header table:

CD Number

CD Title

Loaned To

Loan Date

It's obvious why the new columns were added to the CD Header table rather than the CD Tracks table, right? It's pretty tough to loan different tracks on the same CD to different people at the same time.

This looks like it will satisfy all your friend's needs, until he asks "How will I be able to find out who I've loaned each CD to?" or "How many CD's have I loaned to each person?" You could probably generate some reports to answer these questions. By breaking the borrower information into a separate table, you get some additional benefits. Time for a new design:

CD Header table:

CD Number

CD Title

Borrower ID

Loan Date

Borrower table:

Borrower ID

Name

Phone Number

Address

CD Tracks table:

CD Number

Track Number

Track Title

Artist/Group Name

Musical Category

Solo Instrument

Now you can run through the entries in the Borrower table counting all the matching Borrower ID's in the CD Header table and come up with the information your friend wants very easily. As an added bonus, if Sara Jones becomes Sara Smith, you can make the change in one place and all her outstanding loans are instantly updated.

The Basic Design Process

FileMaker is very forgiving of design changes, even when the database is full of data. If, after deploying a database system and filling it with data, you need a few more calculation fields or a summary field, it's no problem. Few database systems tolerate being redesigned when they're full of data. FileMaker's forgiving nature leads thousands of inexperienced users into becoming amateur database designers. You don't really have to know what you're doing to get good results from it.

To an extent, that's still true of FileMaker Pro 3.0. If you need to add a calculation on the fly, you still can. With a relational system, however, individual fields are likely to spread out over several databases. If you need to make a change to accommodate some redesign, the change might involve moving a field from one database to another, not to mention moving all the data in that field from one database to another. While that's certainly possible, it can be time-consuming. The point is that it makes a lot of sense to spend more time doing up-front design work than you ever had to do in older versions of FileMaker. Redesigning a complex relational system will be more expensive in terms of time and anguish than it used to be, so it's worthwhile to try to avoid lots of tweaking later on.

FileMaker database designers are optimists. Everything is so easy to do in FileMaker that everything takes about five minutes to implement—half an hour at the most. Because database designers think everything takes only a few minutes to do, they have a tendency to underestimate the time required to complete a database project.

To be fair, though, I've seen very few database projects that have come in on time, regardless of the program they were written with. This is usually due to several factors (which makes it easy for everyone to shift all the blame to everyone else), but it is often that the designers didn't appreciate the full ramifications of implementing a feature. Adding a new layout that's almost the same as an existing layout is easy, but then a button for it needs to be included in the main menu, scripts have to be written for it, and so on. FileMaker projects are typically faster than identical projects on other systems, but that doesn't mean they take only fifteen minutes to write.

A well-written statement of objectives lets everybody know the score, and will probably make for a smoother project in terms of client relationship.

If you're revising an existing database system, define exactly what revisions you're going to make: what changes you'll make to existing layouts, new layouts that will have to be created, and what buttons and scripts will have to be changed or added. Specifically identifying all the changes up front will enable you to better estimate the time required to complete a project.

Here's part of a sample project estimation:

> XYZ Corporation
>
> Invoicing System Conversion
>
> Project Objective:
>
> XYZ Corporation has an invoicing system written in FileMaker Pro 2.1 v3. The invoicing system is to be converted to FileMaker Pro 3.0 and redesigned to take advantage of the new relational database and conditional scripting features in FileMaker Pro 3.0.
>
> Specific Goals:
>
> A startup script will be added that conditionally branches and puts the user into a layout that has been optimized for Windows or Macintosh, depending on the machine the user is running.

This is the final product that you want to end up with. Before you can ever know this much about a database project, you need to do some research.

Research

The first step in any database project is to define what your goals are. If you don't know where you're going, how will you know whether you arrive? Goals need to be specific.

Because a database project usually impacts some kind of business process, your goals need to incorporate the before and after picture. Specifically state how the process or system works at the beginning of the project and how it will work at the end of the project. Incorporate as many measurable milestones as possible. For example, instead of vaguely mentioning the redesign of a reporting process, you want to be able to be specific and say:

> Fifteen new reports will be added, and each report can be run with the push of a button. The first report will show customer activity broken down by Region, State, and City, with the City breakout showing specific customer volumes. The second report...

When you're as specific as you can be, it's very clear to you and your client what the scope of the project is. When clients ask for something extra, it should be obvious to all concerned that the something extra is not included under the vague goal of "redesigning the reporting process." Being specific makes everyone accountable. You're accountable to do exactly what you say you will, and the client is accountable when they ask for features that are outside the description of the scope of work.

You can't get into any specifics until you've done your research. Research should consist of more than a twenty minute conversation with the person who asked you to work on the database. To get the before picture of the business process you need to talk to everyone involved, bearing in mind what the stated objective of the project is.

There are three scenarios you're likely to run into as a FileMaker database designer. The first scenario is where nothing has been automated and people have been moving paper around. The database system you write will simply automate an existing manual process. These are usually dream projects because everyone is so relieved to not be doing things manually that you almost can't help but look like a hero.

The second scenario is where you're either rewriting or tweaking an existing database system. You would probably rewrite it if you're converting the system to FileMaker Pro from another database system for performance or flexibility reasons. If it's already in FileMaker Pro and you're just tweaking it, odds are you're just smoothing out some rough spots or adding features. Either way, your odds of implementing a successful project are high. You'll either be giving everyone better performance or new features—or both. The system will be a clear improvement over what they had.

The third scenario is the one to watch out for. Often, when you and the client are working out how the business process works, the client decides that now is the time to improve the process. It's always good to fix a bad process, but there are several ways this kind of project can fail:

- If your client is changing the process without getting feedback from the end users, the end users might resent the changes.

- If your client is changing the process without getting feedback from the end users and there are details the project manager doesn't know about, these shortcomings will show up in the final system. It will give the end users ample opportunity to reject the new system. If this happens, it's easy for the database designer to be made into the scapegoat. This is probably the worst possible scenario.

- If you do get participation from the users and they give input on the new system, you can still run into problems if you don't implement the new system properly. If you just put the system online with minimal or no training, users will get lost because they'll have to learn your database system without the old business process as a frame of reference. They're learning both a new process and a new database. You'll need to spend extra time on training in these situations, or your implementation will be bumpy.

Be aware that if you work on a project similar to the third scenario, the project will take much longer to complete than one similar to one of the first scenarios. Revamping the existing process properly will require lots of meetings with all of the players. You should probably sit in on these meetings so you'll be familiar with how the process ran in the past. You need to be familiar with the reasoning behind the changes so you can structure the logic of the database system properly, and because you'll have credibility with the users if they know you understand their work.

Another reason to sit in on the process change meetings is because you're the database expert. Some of the process issues that come up might require your input. There are hardware, networking, and capacity issues they will probably look to you for answers on.

Just getting through the ordeal of restructuring the process will take a large amount of time, but you should definitely wait until the new process specification is carved in stone before you start to build anything. If you start working on the database too soon, you'll have lots of last minute changes that will cost you time. Make it clear to your client that the new process has to be fixed before you can start work. It will motivate them to reach final decisions.

> **Tip**
>
> If you see that end users aren't being consulted on process changes, try to get them in the loop. Don't try to build a database without talking to the ultimate users of the database. If you don't get their input, you'll probably be sorry.

When you have a fixed business process, you can document it in your research. You need to make note of every place information comes into the process, where information is modified or processed in some way by users (an approval process, for example), and where information needs to come out or be viewed. Typical information outputs might be reports, lists, or printed forms. Itemized output lists will be very useful to you when you need to build the layouts in your databases. The final product of your research should be a detailed process description. Here's a simple process description to give you an idea of the kind of detail you want:

XYZ Corporation conducts seminars out of several facilities around the country. When a client wants to conduct a seminar, they contact a seminar coordinator who takes all of the seminar information. Seminar information includes date, start and end times, facility location, seminar name and subject, a minimum number of attendees, and presenter information. Seminar information needs to be available to all facilities around the country, because coordinators can schedule seminars at any facility and need to know about scheduling conflicts.

After a seminar is scheduled, it gets assigned to a seminar host. The host will be responsible for the production of the seminar. The host arranges publicity for the seminar, arranges for any necessary equipment, and coordinates with all presenters.

When a seminar has been marketed, attendees reserve seats in the seminar. If a seminar doesn't have enough reservations one week before the seminar, the host will cancel the seminar. After a seminar is given, the number of attendees is captured. Every month, management needs to see a report showing the number of seminars presented, the number of attendees in each seminar, the average number of attendees for the seminars held that month, and the number of canceled seminars for that month. This information needs to be broken down by each facility. Management also needs reports showing facilities ranked by the number of seminars held and the total number of attendees for the month.

The objective for the database project is to capture the monthly activity and attendance metrics so reporting can be more timely than it has been with a manual process.

Write a process description similar to this, then go over it with your client and the users to make sure they agree on the process. It's much easier to correct mistakes at this stage than it is after the database system has been built.

When you have a good process description, you can begin the process of diagramming your database system structure.

Creating an Entity-Relationship Diagram

Unless you're a hard-core database jockey, you probably have no idea what an *entity-relationship diagram* is. If you want to show off for MIS types, just refer to these things as E-R diagrams. An E-R diagram is a simple chart made of boxes and arrows. Figure 13.5 shows a sample E-R diagram.

Fig. 13.5
You can easily create an entity-relationship diagram with almost any graphics program.

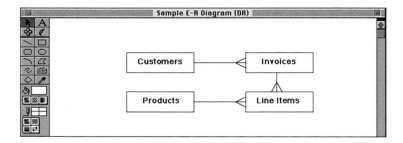

E-R diagramming starts with your process description. In your process description, identify a list of possible entities. An entity is a thing required to conduct the business process. Typical entities are customers and products. Go through your process description and look for nouns. Ignore proper names; they might not be entities. Right now you're just compiling a list of candidates.

The process description of the previous example would yield the following list of candidate entities:

> seminars
>
> facilities
>
> country
>
> client
>
> seminar coordinator
>
> attendees
>
> presenters
>
> seminar host
>
> publicity
>
> equipment

reservations

management

report

Entities are usually plural—you're looking for things in multiples. If there's only one type of thing, then you don't need to track it in a database. For example, all facilities are in one country, so it doesn't make sense to track what country a facility is in.

Even though client, seminar coordinator, and seminar host are singular, it is implied that one out of a population of several was chosen. If you have any questions, you can always ask your client.

Publicity is less clear. You need to refer to your objective and see if publicity is relevant to the project. Because attendance and activity levels are main points of interest, publicity information isn't really relevant to the gathering of those numbers. Even if that is the case, you need to point out that once they start getting good monthly comparisons of facility performance, the client might want to track publicity efforts to see the correlation between publicity and facility goal achievement. There are probably good reasons to track publicity methods and seminar host publicity effectiveness, but for the sake of this example, publicity isn't relevant to the project at hand.

Equipment falls into the same category as publicity: it isn't germane to the final reports. Management is a singular noun, and because they don't show up in the final reports, they come off the list. Reports are an output of the system, so they don't need to be tracked. No one is going to be measured on how many reports they put out.

The revised list now reads as follows:

seminars

facilities

clients

seminar coordinators

attendees

presenters

seminar hosts

reservations

Now you have a good list of entities. The next step is to determine the relationships between the entities. When you have the right entities picked, this is very straight forward. If you have difficulty establishing relationships for a particular entity, that could be a signal that it's not a valid entity.

V

Relational Design Issues

It's easiest to begin at the beginning of the process flow and proceed from there. The seminar example would yield the following relationships:

> **clients** book **seminars** with **seminar coordinators**
>
> **seminars** take place in **facilities**
>
> **seminar hosts** produce **seminars**
>
> **attendees** make **reservations** for **seminars**
>
> **presenters** present at **seminars**
>
> **attendees** attend **seminars**

Then code these relationships into a basic entity-relationship diagram (see fig. 13.6).

Fig. 13.6
This entity-relationship diagram graphically represents the relationships found in the process description.

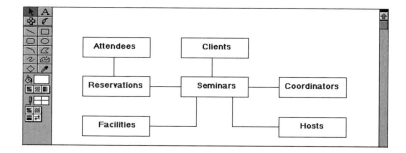

You can refine E-R diagrams still further. Take a look at each relationship and determine whether the relationship is one to one, one to many, or many to many. One client can have many seminars, but each seminar is put on by only one client. One seminar coordinator books many seminars. One seminar host produces many seminars. Many attendees attend many seminars, and so on.

These types of relationships are designated by special symbols in the E-R diagram (see fig. 13.7).

Fig. 13.7
Symbols designate the kind of relationship between two entities.

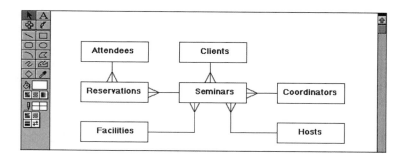

A single line going to an entity designates the one side of a relationship. Three branches going to an entity represent the many side of a relationship. As you've probably noticed, one to many and many to one relationships are the most common. You also might have guessed that these entities are ultimately going to become databases.

The next step is to identify the attributes for each entity. An *attribute* is a field. Attributes describe an entity. For example, date is an attribute of seminars, as is seminar name. The trick in identifying attributes is getting enough information about the entity, but not more than you need. Shoe size could be an attribute of seminar coordinator or seminar host, but it has nothing to do with the seminar process. Figure 13.8 shows the E-R diagram with attributes identified. Attributes can be identified by asking the database user what they need to know about a specific entity.

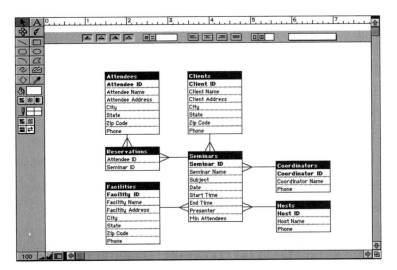

Fig. 13.8
Attributes describe all relevant information about an entity.

The next step is extremely important. Identify the key field for each entity. A *key field* uniquely identifies each record in a database. Imagine if your company couldn't uniquely identify your record in their payroll file. Your paycheck would go to someone with the same last name, or the same street name, or with the same whatever that they used as the key field.

Again, the easiest way to guarantee the uniqueness of a key field is to set it up as a serial number. If each entity gets its own serialized ID number, no two ID numbers in the same database will be the same.

After you identify key fields, you can reference the entities against each other. To do this, take a copy of the key field in one database and add it to a related database. Add a Host ID attribute to the Seminars entity, and now you can assign a host to a seminar. You can know that seminar 876 was assigned to host 31. Host 31 also produced seminars 456, 502, and 637.

When a key field is referenced like this in another database, it's called a *foreign key*. Host ID does not uniquely identify a seminar in Seminars, but it does uniquely identify a host in the foreign Hosts database. Figure 13.9 shows the revised E-R diagram with foreign keys.

Fig. 13.9

In this E-R diagram, foreign keys are identified with italics.

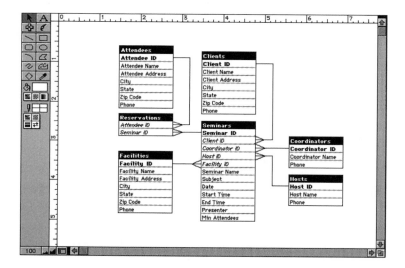

At this point, you have the basic file structure for your database system.

Now comes an issue that is fundamental to relational database design. What happens if host 31 leaves the company? Should she be deleted from the Hosts database? If she *is* deleted from the Hosts database, then Seminars will contain references to information that no longer exists in the Hosts database. When this happens, the validity of your data is compromised. Your database no longer mirrors the process it was designed to model, and information coming out of it will be wrong. If you run a report showing the number of hosts who produced seminars last quarter, the report will be wrong because one of the hosts will be missing.

Go over the logic of your file structure with your client. For each relationship, you need to ask what should happen if a record on one side of the relationship is deleted or updated. For example, if a seminar gets deleted, delete any reservations for that seminar—if you don't, people will have reservations for an event that doesn't exist.

This particular problem is part of a larger issue called referential integrity.

Referential Integrity

Referential integrity basically means that when you have databases relating to each other, information in one database that references information in another database has to reference information that exists.

There are two parts to this issue: maintaining referential integrity when data is deleted, and maintaining referential integrity when data is updated. For example, if client A bought client B, all the seminars for client B need to be re-assigned to client A.

The basic concept isn't too complex, but maintaining referential integrity in a complicated database system can get challenging. It's easier to think of database relationships in terms of parents, children, grandchildren, and so on. The client database is the parent database that might have child records in the seminars database, and these child records might have grandchild records in the reservations database.

To maintain referential integrity when you delete data, you can allow one of two scenarios:

- *Restricted Delete.* You can only delete a parent record when there are no child records in another database. Otherwise, you can't delete the parent record.
- *Cascading Delete.* When you delete a parent record, any child records also get deleted, any grandchild records associated with those child records get deleted, and so on.

To maintain referential integrity when you update data, you can allow one of two scenarios:

- *Restricted Update.* You can only change a parent record when there are no child records.
- *Cascading Update.* When you change a parent record, any child records also get changed, any grandchild records associated with those child records get updated, and so on.

As you can see, this can get complicated in a hurry. Before you begin building databases, you need to work out the integrity relationships between the databases.

FileMaker has all the tools you need to maintain referential integrity in your database systems. The options relating to referential integrity are in a few places.

Cascading Delete. In the Edit Relationship dialog box, there is a check box labeled, When Deleting a Record in this File, Also Delete Related Records (see fig. 13.10). By selecting this check box in each of your parent/child/ grandchild databases, you can implement a cascading delete. In the previous example, you need a relationship from client to seminars and one from seminars to reservations. In each of these relationships, you need to select the check box. These relationships are only for implementing cascading deletes. To view client data in the seminars database, you need a relationship from seminars to clients. Your delete relationships will probably always be on the other end of your viewing relationships.

Fig. 13.10
The Edit Relationship dialog box allows you to implement a cascading delete.

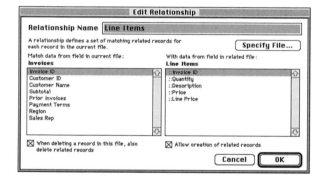

Restricted Delete. With a restricted delete, you need to prevent the user from deleting a record if it has any child records in another database. The only way to implement this is to prevent users from using FileMaker's menus. If users can use menus, then they can choose Mode, Delete Record. You can block menus only by using FileMaker's Access Privileges. To turn off user access to the menus, follow these steps:

1. In the parent database (where you implement the restricted delete), choose File, Access Privileges, Define Passwords to open the Define Passwords dialog box.

2. Create a master password that gives you full access to the file by entering the password and clicking Create.

3. Create a blank user password that has no menu access by deleting the password, choosing None from the Available Menu Commands pop-up menu, then clicking Create. Your final Define Passwords dialog box should look similar to figure 13.11.

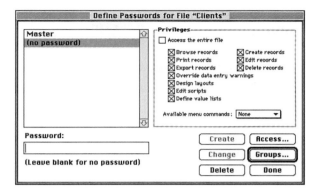

Fig. 13.11
This is the
completed Define
Passwords dialog
box.

4. Click Done to exit the Define Passwords dialog box.

When you restrict access to the menus, you take on a large responsibility. Because the users can't access the menus, you need to provide buttons and scripts to replace the lost functionality of the menus. The nice thing about this is that users are forced to run your scripts when they want to do anything. This control gives you the capability to implement restricted deletes.

A given record can have child records in any database that has a relationship back to the parent or that the parent database has a relationship to. Think of an Invoice example. The real parent database would be the Customer file, but it probably doesn't have a relationship to Invoices. Invoices has a relationship to it.

If the parent record has relationships to or from four databases, check for child records in all four databases. The easiest way to do this is to use the Count aggregate function. Ordinarily, you use this function to count the line items in a portal. You don't have to have a portal to get the count of items that would be in a portal. The aggregate function will work whether a portal is there or not. If you don't have a relationship to a database where the current database is referenced with a foreign field, you'll need to create a relationship to that database.

You need to create a script that will determine whether child records exist in a given child database. If none exist, the parent record was deleted. If any exist, a message box tells the user that the record cannot be deleted because it has related records in another database.

To create this script, follow these steps:

1. Choose Script, ScriptMaker to open the Define Scripts dialog box.

2. Create a new script called Delete Record and click Create.

3. Click Clear All to remove the default script steps.

4. Double-click the If script step into the list on the right.

5. Click Specify to open the Specify Calculation dialog box. Note that the result of this calculation is Boolean. If it's a zero, it will be treated as false; if it's anything else, it will be treated as true. That means that you need to format this calculation as a true or false equation.

6. Choose Aggregate Functions from the Functions pop-up menu.

7. Double-click the Count function into the calculation area.

8. Choose the relationship you want to check from the pop-up menu above the field listing.

9. Double-click the foreign key field in the other database. For example, if you're in Customers and you're viewing fields for the Invoices database, you want to count ::Customer ID.

10. If you have more than one child database to check, insert a plus sign, then add another count function for each child database, adding each new count function to all of the others. If there is a child record in any of the related databases, this calculation will total at least 1, and will therefore evaluate to true.

11. Click OK to close the Specify Calculation dialog box.

12. If there are child records, you need to tell the user that they can't delete the record and why. Double-click the Show Message script step and drag it below the If statement.

13. Click Specify to open the Specify Message dialog box. Type **This record has one or more related records in another database and can't be deleted.** Delete Cancel from the second button and click OK.

14. Double-click the Else script step into the list on the right and drag it above End If.

15. Double-click the Delete Record/Request script step into the list on the right. Drag it above the End If script step.

16. Click OK to close the Script Definition dialog box.

17. Click Done to close the Define Scripts dialog box.

Tie this script to a delete button or just leave it in the Script menu. You now have a restricted delete.

Restricted Update. Implementing a restricted update isn't hard, but it can take some time if your database has a lot of fields. In general, FileMaker's automatic cascading update should be fine for most of the work you do, but a restricted update can be extremely useful. Imagine a purchase order system where you need to make sure that after a line item has been added to the order, no one can go in and change destination or recipient information. In FileMaker, you can actually restrict updates on a field-by-field basis. That's the great news. The not-so-great news is that to do a true record-level restricted update, you need to implement it for every field. That's a lot of time if you have a database with lots of fields. Restricted updates are implemented through FileMaker 3.0's new calculated validation option.

To implement a restricted update for one field, follow these steps:

1. Choose File, Define Fields to open the Define Fields dialog box.

2. Select the field you want to restrict and click Options to open the Entry Options dialog box. If you're not there already, switch to Validation Entry Options using the pop-up at the top of the dialog box.

3. Click the Validated By Calculation check box to open the Specify Calculation dialog box.

4. Double-click the Count function to move it into the calculation area. Choose the relationship to the appropriate child database. In the previous purchase order example, it would be Purchase Order Line Items. Double-click the foreign key field in the other database. In the Purchase Order Line Items database, it would be the Purchase Order Number field. Click the cursor to the right of the function. In the operators list, double-click the equal sign to move it into the calculation area. Type a zero to complete the calculation. Your Specify Calculation dialog box should look like figure 13.12. Click OK to exit the Specify Calculation dialog box.

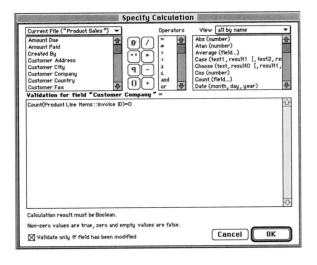

Fig. 13.12
This calculation triggers a validation dialog box if any related records exist.

5. In the Entry Options dialog box, select the Strict: Do Not Allow User to Override Validation check box. Also select the Display Custom Message if Validation Fails check box. In the text box beneath it, type **This record has one or more related records in another database and can't be changed.** Click OK to exit the Entry Options dialog box.

6. Click Done to exit the Define Fields dialog box.

Repeat steps 2 through 5 for as many fields as you want to set up. To try this out, create a new record and type some information in one of the fields you just set up. You should be able to tab out of the field without any problems. Now create a related record in the portal or related field that uses the same relationship you just used for your count validation. After you create the record, go back and try to change the first field. You should see something that looks like figure 13.13.

Troubleshooting

I can't create a new record in the portal.

Being able to create related records is controlled by the relationship. To edit the relationship, choose File, Define Relationships to open the Define Relationships dialog box. Double-click the relationship in question to open the Edit Relationship dialog box. Check the Allow Creation of Related Records check box. Click OK to exit the Edit Relationship dialog box. Click Done to exit the Define Relationships dialog box.

Fig. 13.13
This message box will only allow users to restore previous information, effectively implementing a restricted update.

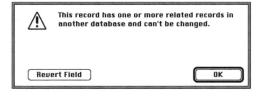

To "unlock" the record, delete the record in the portal. Try changing the field again, and this time it should let you.

Caution

Pay close attention to the message you get when you delete a portal record. If you're in a field in a portal row and you choose Mode, Delete Record, you'll actually be deleting the entire record, not just the one portal record. To make sure you're only deleting the single related record, click inside the portal row, but not in any field in that row. When you do, the entire portal row is highlighted. When the entire row is selected, then you can delete that row only.

Troubleshooting

I can't delete a record in the portal.

The capability to delete records in a portal is controlled in the Portal Setup dialog box. To access this dialog box, choose Mode, Layout. Double-click the portal to open the Portal Setup dialog box. Select the Allow Deletion of Portal Records check box. Click OK to exit the Portal Setup dialog box. Choose Mode, Browse to return to Browse mode.

Cascading Update. In a cascading update, when you change information in a parent database, that change should be reflected in any child databases or grandchild databases. Because FileMaker can only display a related field from one relationship away, any information in a grandchild database that originated in a parent database could only come by way of a lookup field or an unstored calculation field (usually the better method) in the child database. An unstored calculation is automatically based on changes in related fields; so, in a typical implementation, cascading updates are automatic.

Lookup fields are a bit problematic, but you would typically only use them in cases where you wanted to capture information at a point in time (like prices on old invoices) and didn't want data to update. If a lookup field becomes a stumbling block to a necessary cascading update, you can easily implement a scripted relookup, which will refresh the lookup field with current information. After the lookup is refreshed, then referential integrity is restored.

Before you can create a relookup script, you need to know which field is the trigger for your lookup field. To find out, follow these steps:

1. Choose File, Define Fields to open the Define Fields dialog box.
2. Select the appropriate lookup field and click Options to open the Entry Options dialog box.
3. If you're not looking at it already, switch to the Auto Enter options using the pop-up menu at the top of the dialog box.
4. Select the Specify button to the right of Looked-Up Value. The Lookup dialog box appears.

5. At the top of the Lookup dialog box is a pop-up showing the name of the relationship the lookup is using. Note the name of the relationship and choose Define Relationships from that same pop-up. The Define Relationships dialog box opens.

6. In the Define Relationships dialog box, select the relationship you just noted, and select Edit to open the Edit Relationship dialog box. The list on the right displays fields in the related database, the list on the left displays fields in the current database. The selected field in the list on the left is the trigger for your lookup field. Click Cancel to exit the Edit Relationship dialog box.

7. Click Done to exit the Define Relationships dialog box. Click Cancel to exit the Lookup dialog box. Click Cancel to exit the Entry Options dialog box. Click Done to exit the Define Fields dialog box.

Now that you know what your lookup trigger field is, you can create a script that will refresh your lookup fields whenever you want. To create a relookup script, follow these steps:

1. Choose Script, ScriptMaker to open the Define Scripts dialog box.

2. Type **Relookup** as the script name and click Create to open the Script Definition dialog box.

3. Scroll about halfway down the Available Steps list and double-click the Relookup script step into the list on the right.

4. Select the Perform Without Dialog check box and click Specify Field to open the Specify Field dialog box. Select your lookup trigger field and click OK.

5. Click OK to exit the Script Definition dialog box. Click Done to exit the Define Scripts dialog box.

Any time you run this script, all lookup fields (that use the specified lookup trigger field) in all records of your current found set will be updated with current information.

From Here...

This chapter covered a typical twisted route to a final database design. Along the way, several examples of flawed database designs were presented and the problems were identified and corrected. You also learned a basic process for designing relational databases and how to implement referential integrity in FileMaker Pro.

The following chapters provide more insight into database design and scripting:

- Chapter 7, "Scripting—The Basics," teaches you how to use the ScriptMaker in FileMaker Pro.

- Chapter 14, "Refining Your Database Design," describes another refinement you can make to a relational design. While it isn't a design methodology in and of itself, normalization is a necessary polishing step to refine or verify the final file structure.

- Chapter 15, "Scripting with ScriptMaker," provides examples of more complicated scripting problems.

V

Relational Design Issues

Refining Your Database Design

This chapter covers a process called *normalization*. Normalization isn't really a design process—it's a final check that verifies that you have proper file structure. This chapter applies the normalization process to the FileMaker Pro 2.x Invoice database. Chapter 9 explained how to convert a database from a flat file structure to a relational structure. This chapter covers why the particular file structures were chosen and presents a methodology for checking the soundness of your relational designs.

This chapter covers the following topics:

- Understanding functional dependencies
- Developing first, second, and third normal forms
- Applying relational rules to FileMaker databases

Functional Dependencies

Relational database theory has its roots in set theory. That might sound arcane, but Chapter 13 proved there's something wrong with an improperly structured database. The methodology in Chapter 13 was similar to bumping into a wall, turning around, and bumping into another wall—eventually muddling through to the end. Normalization techniques are a more formal way of accomplishing what was done by trial and error in Chapter 13. Before you get into normalization techniques though, you need to learn about functional dependencies.

When you have a functional dependency, it means a field or fields are dependent on another field or fields. This is best illustrated by the Invoice template that shipped with FileMaker 2.0 and 2.1. Feel free to juxtapose the instructions to your own databases.

The FileMaker 2.x Invoice database contains the following fields:

Invoice Number

Invoice Date

Company Code

Company Name

Contact First

Address

City

State

Zip

Item Number

Item Description

Price

Quantity

PO Number

Line Price   Quantity * Price

Product Subtotal   Sum (Line Price)

Tax Rate

Sales Tax   Round (Product Subtotal * Tax Rate,2)

Shipping

Order Total   Product Subtotal + Sales Tax + Shipping

Amount Paid

Payment Date

Amount Due   Order Total – Amount Paid

Terms

Referral

Ship Address

Ship City

Ship State

Ship Zip

Ship Attn

No Boxes

Qty per Box

Qty Last Box

Ship Via	
Weight	
Days Due	If (Amount Paid<Order Total,Today – Invoice Date,0)
Contact Last	
Contact Name	Contact First & " " & Contact Last
Total Due	
Year	Year (Invoice Date)
Month Number	Month (Invoice Date)
Month	MonthName (Invoice Date)
Total Invoiced	
Include find	If (Amount Due > 0, "Include", "")
Total Paid	
Sales Person	
Aging Calc	If (Days Due > 90, "Over 90 days due", If (Days Due > 60, "Over 60 days due", If (Days Due > 30, "Over 30 days due", If (Days Due > 0, "Less than 30 days due",""))))
Total Tax	

You can cluster these fields into a few distinct groups. One group of fields pertain specifically to an individual invoice:

Invoice Number	
Invoice Date	
PO Number	
Product Subtotal	Sum (Line Price)
Tax Rate	
Sales Tax	Round (Product Subtotal * Tax Rate,2)
Shipping	
Order Total	Product Subtotal + Sales Tax + Shipping
Amount Paid	
Payment Date	
Amount Due	Order Total – Amount Paid
Terms	
No Boxes	

Qty per Box

Qty Last Box

Ship Via

Weight

Days Due   If (Amount Paid<Order Total, Today – Invoice Date,0)

Total Due

Year   Year (Invoice Date)

Month Number   Month (Invoice Date)

Month   MonthName (Invoice Date)

Total Invoiced

Include find   If (Amount Due > 0, "Include", "")

Total Paid

Sales Person

Aging Calc   If (Days Due > 90, "Over 90 days due", If (Days Due > 60, "Over 60 days due", If (Days Due > 30, "Over 30 days due", If (Days Due > 0, "Less than 30 days due","""))))

Total Tax

Another group of fields pertain to the customer on the invoice:

Company Code

Company Name

Contact First

Address

City

State

Zip

Referral

Ship Address

Ship City

Ship State

Ship Zip

Ship Attn

Contact Last

Contact Name   Contact First & " " & Contact Last

The last group of fields pertain to the individual line items on a particular invoice:

Item Number

Item Description

Price

Quantity

Line Price   Quantity * Price

For each one of these groups, the first field is an ID number: the Invoice Number, the Company Code, and the Item Number. The Invoice Number is the primary key for the Invoices database. Each Invoice Number is the unique identifier for a particular record. You use the Company Code to look up company information from the Contacts database. In the Contacts database, Company Code is the primary key. In the Products database, Item Number is the primary key.

Because these fields are primary keys, the other fields in their groups are dependent on them. If you change the Company Code, you'll have different company information in the Company Name and Address fields, but the change won't effect information in the line item fields such as Item Description or Price. That's because these fields aren't dependent on the Company Code field. These types of relationships are called *functional dependencies*. In the Invoices database, City and State are functionally dependent on Contact Code, while Invoice Date and Amount Paid are dependent on Invoice Number.

Now that you understand functional dependencies, it's time to discuss the normalization process.

Normal Forms

Normal forms are standards for good database structure. There are several normal forms, but most people concern themselves only with forms one through three. Each higher normal form is a superset of all of the lower normal forms. That means that a database in the third normal form is automatically in first and second normal forms. First normal form is the least rigorous.

Creating a First Normal Form

You reduce an entity to first normal form by removing repeating or multi-valued attributes (fields) to another child entity. Don't confuse repeating attributes with FileMaker's repeating fields. You have repeating attributes when more than one field captures the same type of information in a given record. When your database is structured this way, it can be difficult to query and report on the data associated with the repeating or multivalued attributes.

Imagine you have a contact database where each record contains company information. To capture each person who works at a given company, you create Contact 1 field, Contact 2 field, and so on. If you need to find out where Eric Smith works, you look for him in the Contact 1 field, the Contact 2 field, and so on. While data entry might be a little quicker, working with the database after it's filled with information is very cumbersome. These multiple contact fields are repeating values; you need to put them in a child database and relate them back to the parent.

You can store more than one piece of data in one field; this is called a *multivalued field*. Repeating fields are an obvious example of multivalued fields, but FileMaker has a couple of ways of storing data you should watch out for. One you might not expect is a field that has data entered by a value list formatted as check boxes. When you check more than one item, FileMaker stores the multiple values on different lines in the same field. Again, the values are delimited by returns. To see this, take a field that's formatted as a check box entry field and duplicate it in Layout mode. Change it to a standard field (not using a value list) and stretch it so you can see three or four lines. If you have more than one check box checked, you see multiple lines of data (see fig. 14.1).

Fig. 14.1
When you format a field as a check box and click multiple check boxes, FileMaker stores multiple values separated by return characters. As you can see in this figure, the Symptoms field contains four values in the same field.

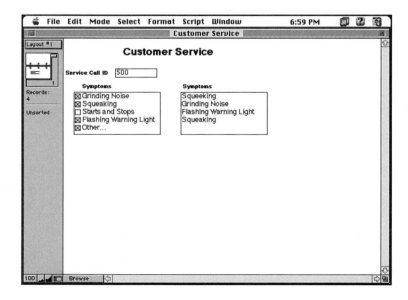

If you ever tried to do reporting on a check box field, you can understand why this is a bad thing. First normal form dictates that you move such a field to its own separate database. There are several reasons to do this. Figure 14.2 shows a report generated using data stored in the check box entry field shown in figure 14.1.

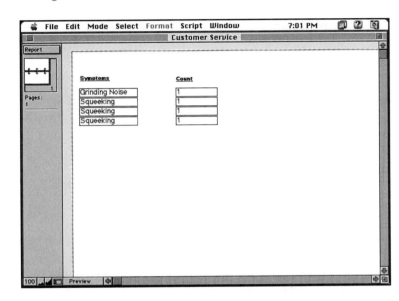

Fig. 14.2
When a field contains multiple values, it's extremely difficult to generate reports. In this case, you're only viewing the first value in each of the four records in the database.

Notice that some subtotals appear several times on the report. This is very confusing until you change the field format to display several lines of data. Figure 14.3 shows the resulting report. Suddenly it's obvious why the values are repeating: the combined multiline value is actually unique from subsummary to subsummary.

The only way to report on this type of information is to break it up using calculations. Chapter 3 describes this process.

You have a similar problem with repeating fields. If you need to report on the contents of repeating fields, you need to break each repetition out into its own field (Chapter 3 also describes this process).

Fig. 14.3
These fields are bigger so you can see all the data values contained in them. Each record contains different values that make them unique.

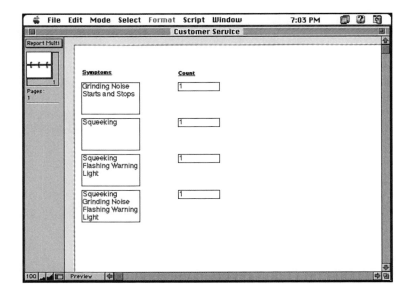

For both of these problems, the final result is a database with repeating attributes, which leaves you only slightly better off than when you started. The bottom line is that databases with these structures lead to great complexities when you need to report your data. Putting these repeating groups and multivalue data fields in a separate database greatly simplifies your life.

To eliminate repeating groups, export each of the repeating group fields out in a separate export. For example, if you have Contact 1 and Contact 2 with Phone 1 and Phone 2, you need to export each logical cluster (such as Contact 2 with Phone 2) for later combining into one related group database (see fig. 14.4).

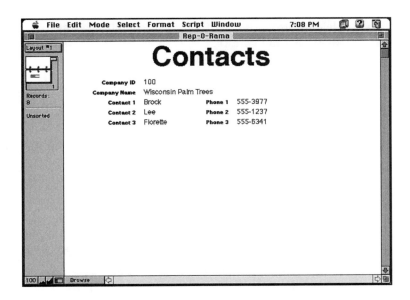

Fig. 14.4
This database was designed to store a maximum of three contacts and three phone numbers. This data needs to be extracted in logical groups before it can be combined in a new related file.

Follow these steps to eliminate repeating groups:

1. Use the design process described in Chapter 13 to construct a data structure diagram.

> **Tip**
>
> Always construct an entity relationship diagram before developing a new database or before you begin conversion from a flat file database structure to a relational model. Be clear on your ultimate data structure before you begin any work on the computer. If you don't know where you're going, it can be hard to get there.

2. Choose File, Import/Export, Export Records to open the Save dialog box. Enter the name of your export database.

Because you're doing an export for all of your field groups, name each export file with the name of the group it belongs to.

3. Choose FileMaker from the Type pop-up menu. The Save dialog box should look similar to figure 14.5.

4. Click Save to open the Export Field Order dialog box.

Fig. 14.5
The Save dialog box shows the FileMaker Pro file type selected.

5. In the Export Field Order dialog box, make sure you export the fields associated with your repeating group and the primary key (see fig. 14.6). If you don't export the primary key, you cannot tell which record your repeating data was associated with.

Fig. 14.6
Export the primary key field with the repeating group fields so the exported data can be related back to the main file using the primary key.

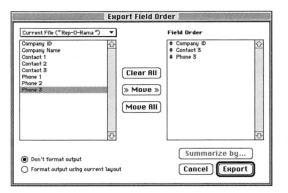

6. Repeat this process for each repeating group.

7. Locate your exported repeating group files (see fig. 14.7). Rename your first group file so it has just the name of the group—don't use numbers.

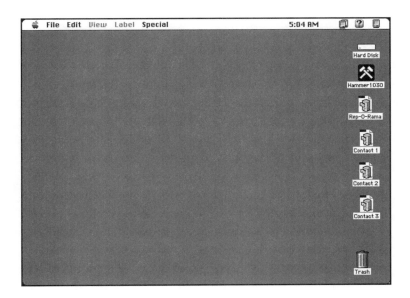

Fig. 14.7
When the export is complete, each of the three exported repeating group files contains the data associated with each group.

8. Open your newly renamed file.

9. Choose File, Import/Export, Import Records to open the Open dialog box.

10. Select your next group file and click Open (see fig. 14.8). The Import Field Mapping dialog box opens.

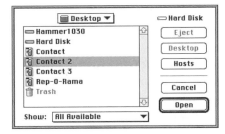

Fig. 14.8
You're now importing the data from the Contact 2 file, which contains the data from the original file for all records that had values in the Contact 2 and Phone 2 fields.

Make sure your incoming fields map to the fields in your database. (If you exported each group the same way, they should line up without you having to drag fields around.)

11. Click Import.

12. Repeat the importing process in steps 9 through 11 for each group file you exported. If you create a list view (which is not required) and find all records, you see something similar to figure 14.9.

Fig. 14.9

This screen shows a list of the records after the data in all three exported files was imported into this file.

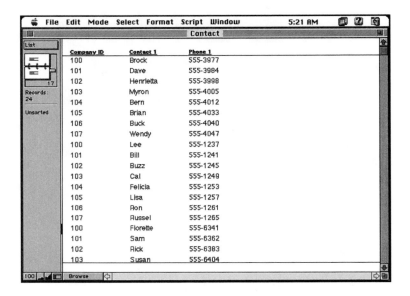

The next stage is to relate this information back to your original file. Resist the temptation to delete your repeating group fields immediately. Keep them around until you complete the relationship and verify that you did everything correctly.

Now set up a relationship between the two files and view the related records from the original file. Return to the file you started with and follow these steps:

1. Choose File, Define Relationships to open the Define Relationships dialog box.

2. Click New to open the Open dialog box.

3. Select your new group file and click Open (see fig. 14.10). The Edit Relationship dialog box opens.

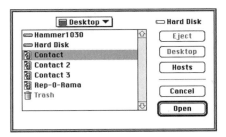

Fig. 14.10
Choose the
Contact file that
contains all of
your exported data
so you can set up a
relationship back
to the original file.

Now you can set up a relationship based on your primary key field, as
shown in figure 14.11. This is why you exported the primary key with
the other data. You'll also want to refer back to your structure diagram
to decide what to do about the check boxes at the bottom of the Edit
Relationship dialog box.

If you click the Allow Creation of Related Records check box, you can
create new related group file records from a portal in the original file.

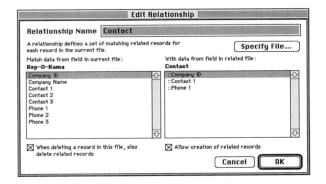

Fig. 14.11
Here you're setting
up a relationship
between two files
based on the
Company ID key.

You might not want to do this if you have a lot of fields to fill out in
your related group file. In that case, you probably can't fit all of the
related fields in a portal row (although you don't need to put the key
field your relationship uses in the portal—FileMaker fills it in automatically). Because you don't want users to create new records without completing all fields, you would be better off creating a button that copies
the primary key, switches to the new group database, and creates a new
record with the primary key. Chapter 7 describes this type of script.

V

Relational Design Issues

Depending on your database system structure, you may or may not want to delete related records when you delete records in the current file. In the example, contacts work at a specific company. If the company record itself gets deleted, it doesn't make sense to keep the contacts for that company, so you select the When Deleting a Record in This File, Also Delete Related Records check box.

If you do not select the check box, you have a referential integrity problem (see Chapter 13). Create a mechanism that goes into your related file and removes the reference to a primary key that no longer exists. In the current example, if you want to delete a company but keep the contact around, make sure the company code in the Contacts database gets removed so the contact isn't assigned to a company that no longer exists in your companies database.

4. When you finish with the settings in the Edit Relationship dialog box, click OK to close the dialog box. Click Done to close the Define Relationships dialog box.

5. Choose Mode, Layout to switch to Layout mode.

6. Select the Portal tool from the layout tools (see fig. 14.12).

Fig. 14.12

Use the Portal tool to create or draw a portal on your layout that will act as a window to the related file.

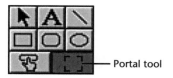

Portal tool

7. Drag a portal large enough to accommodate your existing repeating group fields.

8. In the Portal Setup dialog box, choose your new relationship to the repeating group database (see fig. 14.13).

If you want to permit users to delete the group records from the portal, select the Allow Deletion of Portal Records check box.

9. Click OK to exit the Portal Setup dialog box.

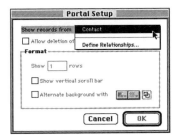

Fig. 14.13
Select the Contact
file in the Portal
Setup dialog box.
Through this
portal, you can
view records in the
Contact file.

10. Click and drag the Field tool into the first row of your portal (see
    fig. 14.14).

    When you release the Field tool, the Specify Field dialog box opens.

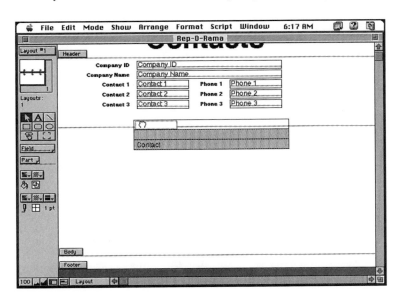

Fig. 14.14
Use the Field tool
to place fields from
the Contact file
inside the top row
of the portal.

V

Relational Design Issues

11. Select the first field (not the primary key) from your related group file
    and click OK (see fig. 14.15). Repeat the process for other fields you
    want to have in your portal. Your final portal arrangement should look
    similar to figure 14.16.

Fig. 14.15
Select the related field through the relationship you created earlier.

Fig. 14.16
This is the completed portal to the Contact database. Two fields from the Contact file were placed in the top row of the portal.

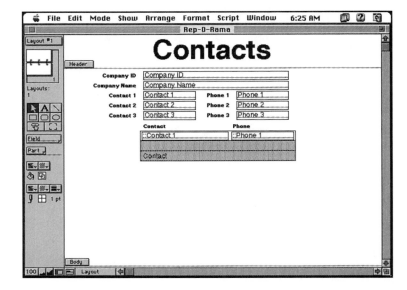

12. Choose Mode, Browse to return to Browse mode.

Compare the information in your portal with the information in your repeating group fields to make sure they match. If they don't match, make sure your related fields aren't touching the sides of the portal. The fields must be completely contained in the first row. If your field position is okay, go back over the process to see if you missed a step. It could be that your relationship isn't matching on the right field.

13. Go through several records to make sure the information in your portal matches the information in your repeating group fields. When you're convinced that all is well, choose File, Define Fields and delete your repeating group fields.

Because the information now resides in another database, you no longer need the fields in the current database. Don't delete your primary key field! If you do, you'll destroy the link that matches records in your repeating group database with the records in your current database. Rearrange your layout accordingly.

This new file structure has several advantages. With the old structure, you were limited in how many related pieces of information you could attach to a record. When you ran out of fields, you either had to add new fields to the database or not add any more information. With the new structure, you can attach an unlimited number of related records. If you want to limit the number of related records you can have, see the section in Chapter 5 covering validation calculations.

Another advantage is that if you want to find a specific related record, you can just switch to Find mode, type your search criteria in the first row of the portal, and find your matching record regardless of what portal row it's in. You had to search each one of your fields with the old structure.

If you need to report on how many records you had for a given set of criteria, you can just run the report in your new related database. With the old structure, you couldn't run the report at all because the information was in separate fields (Well, you might be able to if you did a bunch of cumbersome calculations, but who needs that hassle?).

Creating Second and Third Normal Forms

As you move through the normal forms, you'll find that each higher normal form is a superset of all the lower ones. For a database table to be in second normal form, it needs to be in first normal form, and it also has the additional requirement that any fields not dependent on the primary key must be removed to a separate database. In second normal form, the primary key can be made up of multiple fields that together form a unique key.

Similarly, third normal form requires that a database be in second normal form and that any fields not dependent on the primary key be removed to a separate database. In third normal form, the primary key is a single field that uniquely identifies each record in the file. In the example at the beginning of the chapter, customer information and line items information don't belong in the Invoice database because the data is not dependent on the primary key of Invoice Number. These fields should be moved to a related child database.

From Here...

In this chapter, you learned about functional dependencies and normal forms. Besides sounding impressive in conversation, these terms describe processes that can further refine your database designs. This chapter also touched on a few processes described in other chapters.

From here, you might want to read the following chapters:

- Chapter 5, "Working with Calculation Fields," contains validation calculations that are useful in controlling data entry into related portal records.

- Chapter 9, "Converting Existing FileMaker Pro Databases to 3," describes how to split repeating fields into separate records.

- Chapter 13, "Applying Relational Concepts," covers the design groundwork you need to do before you start thinking about normalization.

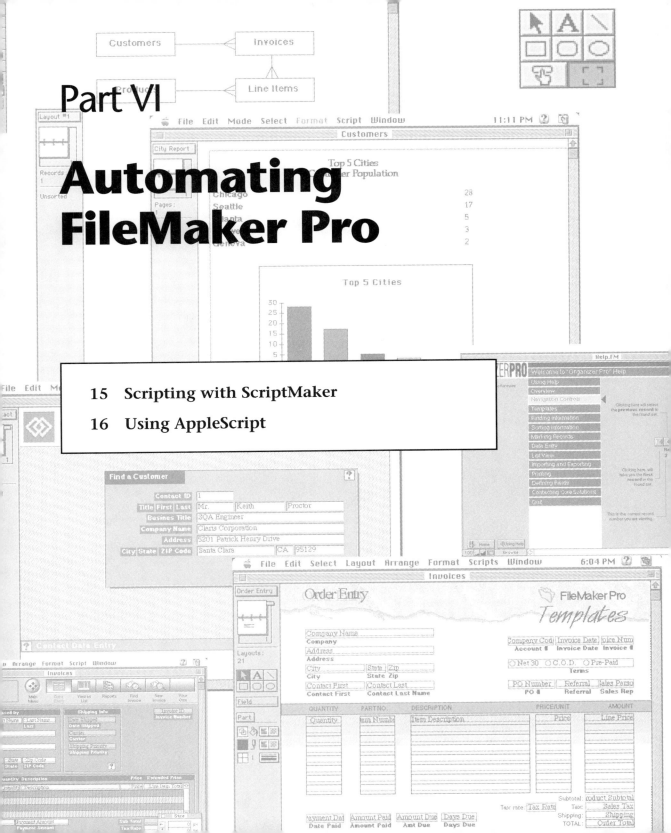

Part VI

Automating FileMaker Pro

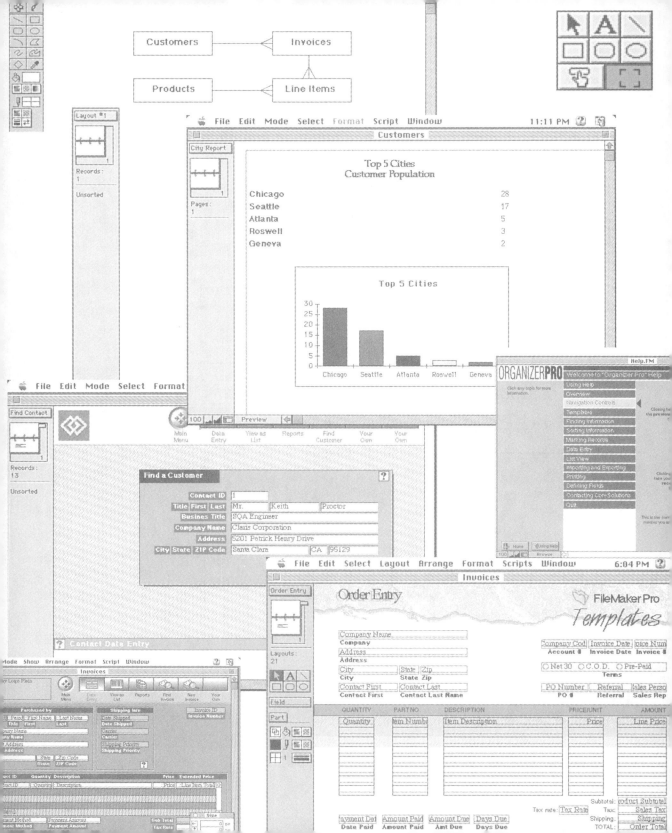

CHAPTER 15

Scripting with ScriptMaker

ScriptMaker is arguably the most powerful feature of FileMaker Pro. It is an amazingly versatile tool, and it's extremely easy to learn to use and work with. Just the same, with the wide array of scripting commands available in ScriptMaker, just learning what everything does is a task.

Rather than being a general reference on ScriptMaker, this chapter focuses on specific practical examples of scripting in FileMaker Pro. The topics covered are:

- Using the Message (dialog box) command
- Creating scripts for error trapping
- Conditional Finds
- Automating page numbering
- Finding and marking duplicate records

Scripting the User Interface

This section focuses heavily on dialog boxes. After learning to create them, you'll learn how to use them to redirect a user when they get database errors.

Creating Standard Issue Dialog Boxes

Dialog boxes are a new feature of FileMaker Pro 3.0. There are a couple of limitations you need to be aware of but, in general, they are handy gizmos to have around. One limitation is that you can't have more than three response buttons in a dialog box. A more significant limitation is that users cannot enter data in a dialog box. FileMaker dialog boxes do not have a response field; however, there is a workaround (isn't there always). You can use AppleScript to generate a dialog box that a user can put information in. To learn how to do this, see Chapter 16, "Using AppleScript."

If you use a dialog box, it's important to determine what button a user clicks. The following example walks you through creating a basic dialog box that displays three buttons: January, February, and March. Then you conditionally branch to different parts of the script and display a different message depending on the button you clicked.

To create a generic dialog box script, follow these steps:

1. Choose Script, ScriptMaker to open the Define Scripts dialog box.

2. In the Script Name text box, type **Message** as the new script name and click Create to open the Script Definition dialog box.

3. Click Clear All to remove the default script steps.

   In steps 4 through 8, you create a dialog box that displays a button for each month in the first quarter.

4. Scroll to the bottom of the Available Steps list and double-click the Show Message script step.

5. Click Specify to open the Specify Message dialog box.

6. Type **Pick a month from the first quarter.** in the Message Text box.

7. In the Button Captions area, change the First (Default) text box to January; change the Second text box to February; and change the Third text box to March (see fig. 15.1).

Fig. 15.1
The text entered in a Button Captions text box labels the button on the dialog box when it's displayed.

8. Click OK to close the Specify Message dialog box.

   In steps 9 through 20, you use an If statement to check if the first button was clicked by the user. If this is true, then a dialog box with the message You picked January appears.

9. From the Available Steps list, double-click the If script step to move it to the list on the right.

Tip

In FileMaker Pro 3.0, the Script Definition dialog box has a new button that allows you to duplicate a script step—this can save you some time. If you hold down the Option button while duplicating an If[] or Loop script step, notice how the duplicated step is indented below the original.

10. Click Specify to open the Specify Calculation dialog box.

11. Choose Status Functions from the Functions pop-up menu.

12. Double-click the Status(CurrentMessageChoice) function into the calculation area.

13. Click an insertion point immediately after the Status (CurrentMessageChoice) function. Double-click the = operator, then type **1**. Your finished calculation should look similar to figure 15.2.

You can find out what button was clicked by checking the value of the Status(CurrentMessageChoice) function. It equals 1 when the first button is clicked, 2 if the second button is clicked, and 3 if the third button is clicked.

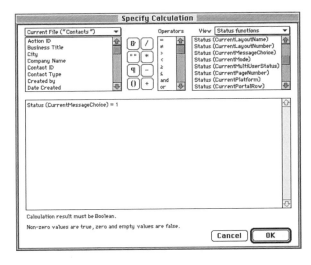

Fig. 15.2
The Status (CurrentMessageChoice) function can be checked in a calculation to find out what button was clicked. Here, you're checking to see whether the first button was clicked by the user.

14. Click OK to close the Specify Calculation dialog box.

15. Scroll to the bottom of the Available Steps list and double-click the Show Message script step.

16. Drag the Show Message script step above the End If script step.

17. Click Specify to open the Specify Message dialog box.

18. Type **You picked January.** in the Message Text box.

19. Leave the First (Default) text box set to OK and delete Cancel from the Second text box. The Specify Message dialog box should look similar to figure 15.3.

Fig. 15.3

Use the Specify Message dialog box to communicate with the user; display a message informing the user that they clicked the January button.

20. Click OK to close the Specify Message dialog box.

    In steps 21 through 33, use an If statement to check if the second button was clicked by the user. If this is true, then display a dialog box with the message You picked February.

21. From the Available Steps list, double-click the Else script step to the list at the right and drag it above the End If script step.

22. Move another If script step to the list at the right and drag it up so it's directly beneath the Else script step.

23. Double-click the new If script step to open the new Specify Calculation dialog box.

24. Again, choose Status Functions from the functions pop-up menu.

25. Double-click the Status(CurrentMessageChoice) to move it to the calculation area.

26. Click an insertion point immediately after the Status (CurrentMessageChoice) function. Double-click the = operator, then type **2**. Your finished calculation should look like figure 15.4.

27. Click OK to close the Specify Calculation dialog box.

28. Scroll to the bottom of the Available Steps list and double-click the Show Message script step.

29. Drag the Show Message script step above both End If script steps.

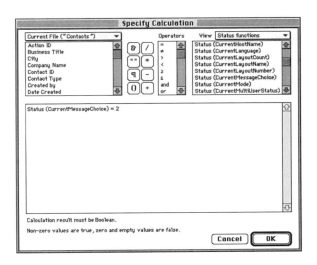

Fig. 15.4
Here you're checking whether the second button was clicked by the user.

30. Click Specify to open the Specify Message dialog box.

31. Type **You picked February.** in the Message Text box.

32. Leave the First (Default) text box set to OK and delete Cancel from the Second text box. Your completed Specify Message dialog box should look similar to figure 15.5.

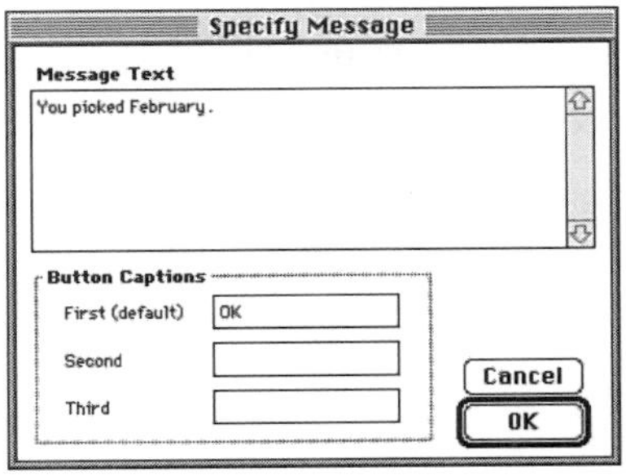

Fig. 15.5
Display a message informing the user that they clicked the February button. This dialog box will display only one button labeled OK.

33. Click OK to close the Specify Message dialog box.

    In steps 34 through 39, check whether the third button was clicked by the user. If this is true, display a dialog box with the message You picked March.

34. From the Available Steps list, double-click the Else script step to the list at the right and drag it above both End If script steps.

35. Move the Show Message script step to the list on the right and drag it above both End If script steps.

36. Double-click the Show Message script step to open the Specify Message dialog box.

37. Type **You picked March.** in the Message Text box.

38. Leave the First (Default) text box set to OK and delete Cancel from the Second text box.

39. Click OK to close the Specify Message dialog box.

    Figure 15.6 shows the final message script.

Fig. 15.6

This script is an example of the new conditional scripting available in FileMaker Pro 3. One of three messages will display depending on what button the user clicked.

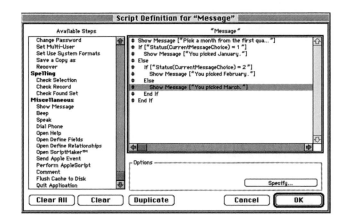

40. Click OK to close the Script Definition dialog box.

41. Click Done to close the Define Scripts dialog box.

Now it's time to test the script. Choose Script, Message to run your new message script. Figure 15.7 shows the dialog box you should receive.

Fig. 15.7

This dialog box appears so the user can pick the appropriate month.

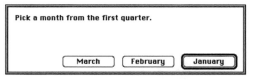

Click any of the month buttons and note the result. Your script "knows" which button you clicked. You could adapt this script to perform specific actions depending on the button the user clicked. For example, you could print a monthly report for the month chosen by the user.

Dealing with Errors

In FileMaker Pro 3, you can implement error-handling routines that were not possible in previous versions of FileMaker. You achieve this in a script by first turning error capture on to suppress the regular FileMaker error message dialogs. If you do this, it is your responsibility to check for and act upon any errors. Before you can perform the appropriate action, you need to know what error occurred. When an error occurs and error capture is turned on, FileMaker returns an error code that can be checked in your script. You can view these error codes in the FileMaker Help system.

Follow these steps:

1. Choose Help, Index. The Index dialog box appears.

2. In the Type the First Few Letters of the Word You Are Looking For text box, enter **St**. This displays an index of help topics that begin with the letters St (see fig. 15.8).

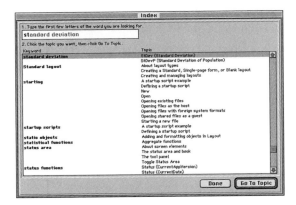

Fig. 15.8
The FileMaker Help system contains an abundant amount of valuable information that is not documented in the manual.

3. Click the down scroll arrow until you see the Status(CurrentError) topic.

4. Highlight the Status(CurrentError) topic and click the Go To Topic button.

5. Scroll down to see a list of error codes.

Tip

It's a good idea to copy these error codes, paste them into your favorite word processor program, format them, and print them. Put them by your computer as a handy reference.

Now that you know how to find an error code number, you can conditionally branch inside your scripts when a certain error code is returned. Typical trouble spots are Find scripts, Go to Record scripts, Import scripts, and basically any script that might reference something not there. The following example uses a Find script.

1. Choose Script, ScriptMaker to open the Define Scripts dialog box.

2. In the Script Name text box, type **Find** as the name for the new script and click the Create button.

3. Click the Clear All button to remove the default script steps.

4. In the Available Steps list, double-click the Set Error Capture script step. It moves to the script list on the right.

5. In the Available Steps list, double-click the Enter Find Mode step and deselect the Restore Find Requests check box.

6. In the Available Steps list, double-click the Perform Find step and deselect the Restore Find Requests check box.

7. Double-click the If[] script step to move it to the right.

8. Click Specify to open the Specify Calculation dialog box.

9. Choose Status Functions from the functions pop-up menu and double-click the Status(CurrentError) function into the calculation area. Then double-click the = operator and enter **401**. What you're doing here is checking for error code 401, which occurs when no records match the find request.

10. Click OK to close the Specify Calculation dialog box.

11. Scroll to the bottom of the Available Steps list and double-click the Show Message step.

12. Click the Specify button and enter **No records were found.** in the Message Text box. In the Button Captions area, remove the word Cancel from the Second text box. Click the OK button.

13. Move the Show Message step above the last End If step.

14. Double-click the Else step in the Available Steps list and move it above the last End If step.

15. Insert another Show Message step and position it between the Else and the last End If step.

16. Click the Specify button and type **Records were found.** in the Message Text box.

17. Your script is now complete. It should look like figure 15.9.

18. Click OK to close the Script Definition dialog box and click Done to close the Define Scripts dialog box.

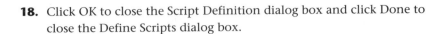
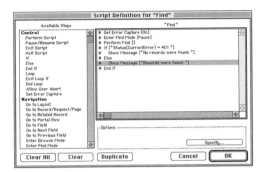

Fig. 15.9
This script turns error capture on to check for error code 401 (no records found). If this is true, a message indicates no records were found; otherwise, a different message indicates that records were found.

Run the script to test it:

1. Make sure you're positioned on a layout where you can perform a find. Choose Script, Find.

2. You are now in Find mode. In any field, enter text that you know does not exist to force a condition where no records are found. For example, enter **xxxxxxx** in a name field.

3. Click the Continue button. The message shown in figure 15.10 appears. Click the OK button.

Fig. 15.10
The Find script displays this message if the error code 401 is returned.

4. Notice that the Found Set contains 0 records. This is something new in FileMaker. Previous versions did not support a found set of zero records.

5. Choose Select, Find All.

6. Run the Find script again but this time enter something you know exists. A different message appears indicating that records were found.

Troubleshooting

I have a problem with one of my scripts. Every time it runs, it never seems to do anything. The only way I can get it to stop is to close the database.

(continues)

> (continued)
>
> You probably used the Allow User Abort [Off] step in your script. You have to be careful with this command. By turning the user abort off, the user cannot abort the script by pressing ⌘-. (period). This is good because it adds an element of control. However, if you have a bug in your script that causes it to continuously loop, there is no way to stop the script from running. The solution is to add the Allow User Abort [Off] step after you test your script and know that it works under all conditions.

Conditional Scripting

One of the most powerful new features of FileMaker Pro 3.0 is the capability to run scripts conditionally. This capability has several applications, one of which is conditional searching. Using this technique, you can improve upon the find script you created in the last section. For example, if a find turns up more than one record, you might want to display the results of that find in a list view. If you only find one record, you might want to see a detailed view of that record. If you don't find any records, either return the user to where they started or allow them to create a new record.

No matter how well you design your database, there's always some user who puts in Find criteria that doesn't get a match. In previous versions of FileMaker, a not found condition resulted in the user getting the message shown in figure 15.11. If the user clicked the Cancel button, the script aborted and could possibly leave the user in an unfamiliar layout. Clicking the Continue button created a found set of all records in the database and performed the remaining steps in the script. If one of those steps included the Delete Found Set step, then all the records in your database were deleted. Not a good thing. Clicking the Modify Find button allowed the user to enter new Find criteria and continued with the script. There were workarounds to this problem, but none of them were pleasant.

Fig. 15.11
In previous versions of FileMaker, this message appeared if no records were found as a result of a find step in a script.

You'll be pleased to know that you can prevent this sort of thing in FileMaker Pro 3.0. From now on, if a user gets this message, it's your fault.

The following example requires that you have a list layout, data entry layout, and a find layout. To set up a conditional search, follow these steps:

1. Choose Script, ScriptMaker to open the Define Scripts dialog box.

2. Create a new script called Find and click Create.

3. Click Clear All to remove the default script steps.

4. Scroll to the bottom of the Available Steps list and double-click the Comment script step.

5. Click Specify to open the Specify dialog box.

6. Type in descriptive comments that explain what the script does (see fig. 15.12).

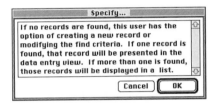

Fig. 15.12
In FileMaker Pro 3, you can enter descriptive comments in your scripts.

7. Move the Set Error Capture [On] script step to the script list on the right. Leave the option set to On.

8. Double-click the Enter Find Mode script step to move it to the list on the right. Deselect the Restore Find Requests check box. Leave the Pause check box selected so the user will have the opportunity to enter their own find criteria.

9. Double-click the Perform Find script step to move it to the list on the right. Again, deselect the Restore Find Requests check box.

10. Double-click the If script step to move it to the list on the right. Notice that two commands, If and End If, came over at the same time (see fig. 15.13).

11. Click Specify to open the Specify Calculation dialog box.

12. Choose Status Functions from the functions pop-up menu (see fig. 15.14).

13. Double-click the Status(CurrentFoundCount) function to move it to the calculation area.

VI

Automating FileMaker Pro

Fig. 15.13

The If script step automatically brings the End If script step with it.

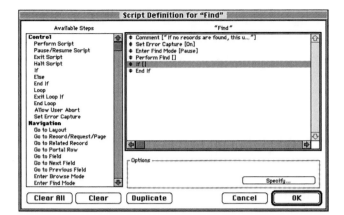

Fig. 15.14

You can use the functions pop-up menu to display a smaller list of functions by choosing a specific group of functions.

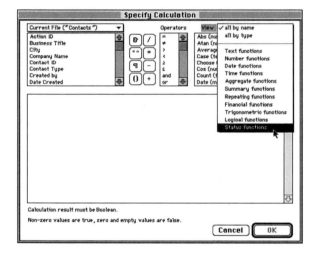

14. Click an insertion point immediately after the Status (CurrentFoundCount) function (make sure the cursor is after the last closing parenthesis). Double-click the = operator, then type a zero. Figure 15.15 shows how your finished calculation should look.

15. Click the OK button to close the Specify Calculation dialog box.

16. Double-click the Show Message script step to move it to the list on the right. You want this step to be between the If and the End If script steps (see fig. 15.16).

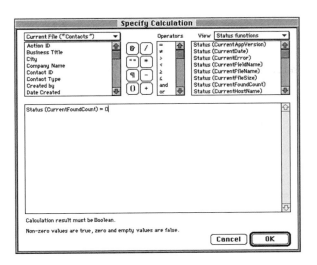

Fig. 15.15
This calculation uses the Status (CurrentFoundCount) function to check if zero records were found.

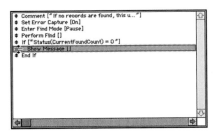

Fig. 15.16
You can change the position of any script step by clicking and dragging the double-headed arrow to the left of the script step.

17. Click Specify to open the Specify Message dialog box.

18. Type **No records were found. You can either create a new record or return to the Data Entry layout.** in the Message Text box.

19. In the First (Default) text box, type **Return**.

20. In the Second text box, type **New Record**. Figure 15.17 shows how your finished Specify Message dialog box should look.

21. Click OK to close the Specify Message dialog box.

22. Double-click the If script step to move it to the script list on the right. Drag it above the End If script step.

23. Click Specify to open the Specify Calculation dialog box.

VI

Automating FileMaker Pro

Fig. 15.17
Here you see how you can display descriptive messages to the user and use custom labels on the buttons.

24. Choose Status Functions from the functions pop-up menu and double-click the Status(CurrentMessageChoice) function into the calculation area.

25. Double-click the = operator and type **2** (see fig. 15.18).

Fig. 15.18
This is how the finished message status calculation will look.

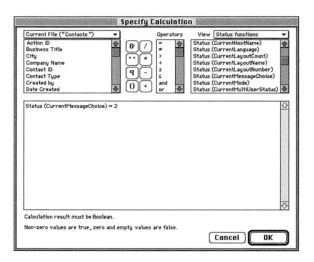

26. Click OK to close the Specify Calculation dialog box.

27. Double-click the New Record/Request script step to move it to the script list on the right. Drag it above both End If script steps.

28. Double-click the Else script step to move it to the script list on the right. Drag it above both End If script steps.

29. Double-click the Find All script step to move it to the script list on the right. Drag it above both End If script steps.

30. Double-click the Go to Layout script step to move it to the script list on the right. Drag it between the two End If script steps.

31. Select the Refresh Window check box. Click the Specify pop-up menu and select your data entry layout (see fig. 15.19).

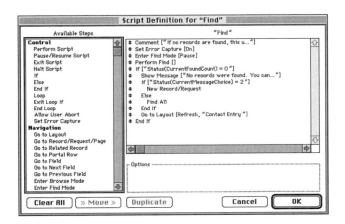

Fig. 15.19
Your script is about halfway complete and should look like this.

32. Double-click the Else script step to move it to the script list on the right. Drag it above the last End If script step.

33. Double-click the If script step to move it to the script list on the right. Drag it between Else and End If.

34. Click Specify to open the Specify Calculation dialog box.

35. Choose Status Functions from the functions pop-up menu and double-click the Status(CurrentFoundCount) function into the calculation area.

36. Click an insertion point immediately after the Status (CurrentFoundCount) function. Double-click the = operator, then type **1**. Your finished calculation should look like figure 15.20.

Fig. 15.20
Here you're checking to see if only one record was found.

37. Click the OK button to close the dialog box.

38. Add another Go to Layout script step and drag it directly under the last If script step.

39. Click the Specify pop-up menu and choose your data entry layout.

40. Add another Else script step and drag it immediately above the last two End If script steps.

41. Add another Go to Layout script step and drag it immediately above the last two End If script steps.

42. Click the Specify pop-up menu and select your list view layout. Your final Find script should look like figure 15.21; however, due to the limited display area, the top three steps are not visible.

Fig. 15.21
This script demonstrates the power of conditional scripting in FileMaker Pro 3. Check for the number of records in the found set and branch to different parts of a script to perform appropriate actions.

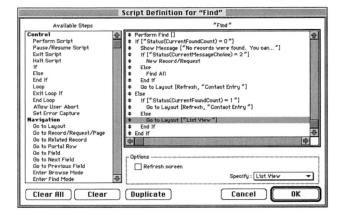

43. Click OK to close the Script Definition dialog box.

44. Click Done to close the Define Scripts dialog box.

Test this script with different kinds of Finds. Try going back into ScriptMaker and changing the Set Error Capture step to Off. Then try running a Find that returns no records and see what happens.

Because this script has two conditions that call for the data entry layout, when no records are found and when one record is found, it could be made a little more efficient. I presented it in a straightforward way for those of you who aren't familiar with conditional programming (see fig. 15.22).

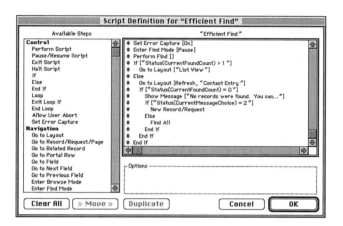

Fig. 15.22
This script is a more efficient version of the script shown in figure 15.21.

Miscellaneous Tricks

The following script examples don't fit neatly into a particular category, but they're useful just the same.

> **Tip**
>
> The new ScriptMaker has two new script steps: Open Define Relationships and Open ScriptMaker. During development you can save countless trips to the menu bar by creating scripts with these steps. You then execute the scripts with keyboard commands.

Determining the Total Number of Pages in a Report

When you need to run long reports, it's a good idea to put page numbers somewhere on the report. The problem with long reports is that sometimes pages get lost. It's nice to know how many pages are supposed to be in the entire report. Page numbers that read "Page 2 of 37" are convenient because you know immediately how many pages you're supposed to have. You never wonder if you have all of your pages.

Page numbering itself is easy for FileMaker to do. Just choose Edit, Paste Special, Page Number to get automatic page numbers. To get the page number to print with the total number of pages, such as Page 2 of 37, is a bit trickier. To calculate the total number of pages for any report, follow these steps:

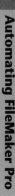

1. Choose File, Define Fields to open the Define Fields dialog box.

2. Create a new Global Number field called Total Pages and click OK to close the Options for Global Field dialog box.

3. Click Done to close the Define Field dialog box.

4. Choose Script, ScriptMaker to open the Define Script dialog box.

5. Make a new script called Find Last Page and click Create.

6. Click Clear All to remove the default script steps.

7. Double-click the Enter Preview Mode script step into the list on the right.

8. Deselect the Pause check box in the Options area.

9. Double-click the Go to Record/Request/Page script step to move it to the script step at the right.

10. Click the Specify pop-up menu and choose Last.

11. Double-click the Set Field script step into the script list on the right.

12. Click Specify Field to open the Specify Field dialog box.

13. Select the Total Pages field and click OK to close the Specify Field dialog box.

14. Click Specify to open the Specify Calculation dialog box.

15. Choose Status Functions from the functions pop-up menu.

16. Double-click the Status(CurrentPageNumber) function into the calculation area. Your finished calculation should look like figure 15.23.

Fig. 15.23
Another handy status function is Status(CurrentPage-Number). It returns the page number of the current page you're on in Preview mode.

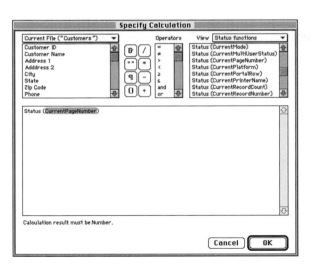

17. Click OK to close the Specify Calculation dialog box. Figure 15.24 shows how the finished script should look.

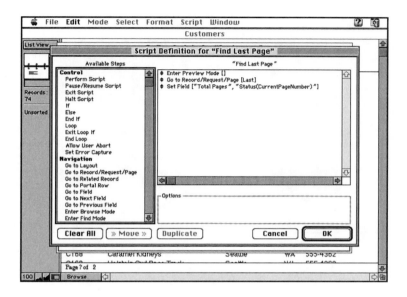

Fig. 15.24
By inserting a Go To Last Page step in a script and setting a Global field to the current page number, the value of the last page in a report is placed in the Global field.

18. Click OK to close the Script Definition dialog box.

19. Click Done to close the Define Script dialog box.

20. Switch to the Report layout in your database and choose Mode, Layout.

21. Select the Text tool from the Layout Tools palette and click an insertion point in the footer. Type **Page** and choose Edit, Paste Special, Page Number (see fig. 15.25).

22. Type a space, and then type **of**.

23. Click the Field tool and drag a new field just to the right of your page number text in the footer (see fig. 15.26).

24. In the Specify Field dialog box, select the Total Pages field and deselect the Create Field Label check box.

25. Click OK to close the Specify Field dialog box. You should now have something that looks like figure 15.27.

26. Choose Mode, Browse to return to Browse mode.

VI

Automating FileMaker Pro

Fig. 15.25
Choose Edit, Paste
Special, Page
Number to paste
the page number
on your layout.

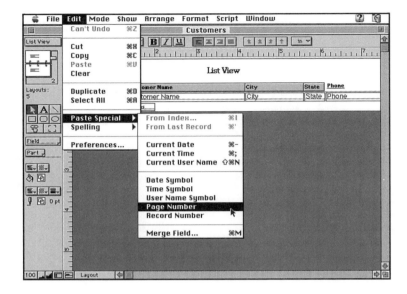

Fig. 15.26
Use the Field tool
to place a new
field on your
layout.

New field ─

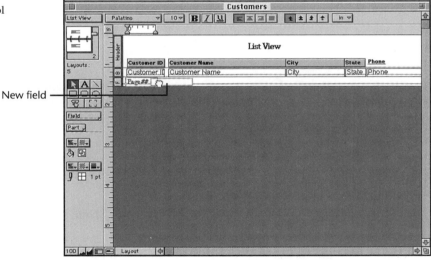

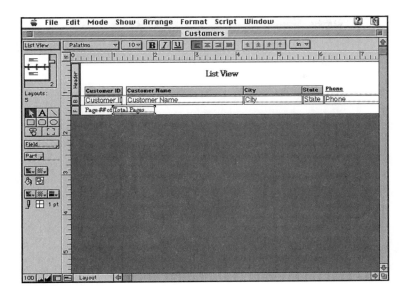

Fig. 15.27
The Global field Total Pages has been placed in the footer of your List View layout.

You can use this script as a subscript in all of your report scripts. If you want to do this, you need to modify all the footers—or whatever layout part you want your page numbers to appear on—of your report layouts using the process just given.

To use this script as a subscript in an existing report script, follow these steps:

1. Choose Script, ScriptMaker to open the Define Scripts dialog box.

2. Double-click your existing reports script to open the Script Definition dialog box.

3. Double-click the Perform Script step into the script list on the right.

4. Drag the Perform Script above the Enter Preview Mode script step in the existing script.

5. Choose the Find Last Page script from the Specify pop-up menu (see fig. 15.28).

6. Click OK to close the Script Definition dialog box.

7. Click Done to close the Define Scripts dialog box.

Fig. 15.28
In this sample report script, you perform a subscript called Find Last Page that calculates the total number of pages in a report.

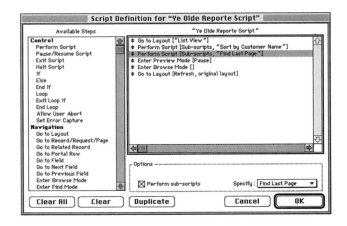

You can use this process to modify all of your report scripts. If you run a three-page report, the bottom of each page will read Page 1 of 3, Page 2 of 3, Page 3 of 3.

Finding and Marking Duplicate Records

This handy script finds and marks duplicate records in a file. For example, say duplicate records were added by mistake to the Contacts database. You don't want to manually find the duplicate records nor do you want to automatically have them deleted by a script. The best solution is to write a script that will mark them. You can view the marked records later and manually delete the ones you don't want. Before you create the script itself, you first need to open a database that contains a Last Name field. To create duplicate records, choose Mode, Duplicate Record a number of times.

Here are the steps:

1. Create two new fields. Choose File, Define Fields.

2. Type **Mark** in the Field Name text box, make sure it's a Text field, and click Create.

3. Type **gLastName** in the Field Name text box, make sure it's a Global field, and click Create.

4. In the Options for Global Field dialog box that appears, select Text from the Data Type list and click OK.

5. Click Done to close the Define Fields dialog box.

6. Now create a new layout. Choose Mode, Layout then choose Mode, New Layout.

7. Type **List** in the Layout Name text box.

8. Select the Columnar Report radio button and click OK.

9. Double-click your Last Name (you might call it by another name), Mark, and gLastName fields to move those fields into the Field Order list on the right. Click the OK button to close the Specify Field Order dialog box. Your layout should look similar to figure 15.29.

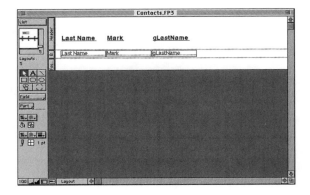

Fig. 15.29
The Last Name, Mark, and gLastName fields are positioned on the List layout. The Mark field will indicate the duplicate records in the database by placing an X in every duplicate record.

10. Choose Mode, Browse to return to Browse mode.

11. Now set the sort order so it can be saved in the new script you will soon create. Choose Mode, Sort. Click the Clear All button to remove any previous sort order steps. Double-click the Last Name field to move it to the list on the right. Click the Done button (you don't have to actually perform the sort).

12. Perform a find so it can be saved in the new script you will soon create. Choose Mode, Find. Enter **X** in the Mark field and click the Find button.

13. Now it's time to write the script itself. Choose Script, ScriptMaker.

14. Name the script. Type **Mark Duplicates** in the Script Name text box and click the Create button.

15. Click the Clear All button to remove the default steps.

    Now choose the new script steps from the Available Steps list on the left by double-clicking the appropriate steps. They will copy to the script area on the right.

16. Double-click the Enter Browse Mode [] step.

17. Double-click the Go to Layout step. In the Specify pop-up menu, choose List.

18. Double-click the Find All step.

19. Double-click the Sort step. Make sure the Restore Sort Order and Restore Without Dialog check boxes are selected.

20. Double-click the Set Field step. Click the Specify Field button, highlight gLastName, and click OK. Next click the Specify button, double-click the Last Name field, and click OK. Your script should look like figure 15.30.

Fig. 15.30
With the addition of these first five steps, your script is almost half complete.

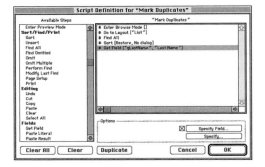

21. Double-click the Loop command. Notice that both the Loop and End Loop steps copy over.

22. Include the Go to Record/Request/Page step. Click the Specify pop-up menu and choose Next. Select the Exit After Last check box. Move the Go to Record/Request/Page step between the Loop and End Loop steps.

23. Double-click the If step. Notice how the If [] and End If steps copy to the right. Position both steps between the Go to Record/Request/Page step and the End Loop step.

24. Click the Specify button. Double-click the Last Name field, double-click the = operator, and double-click the gLastName field. Click the OK button to close the Specify Calculation dialog box.

25. Double-click the Set Field step from the Available Steps area. Move it between the If and End If steps. Click the Specify Field button and double-click the Mark field. Click the Specify button and the Specify Calculation dialog box appears. Click the double quotation marks and type **X**. Click OK.

26. Double-click the Else script step from the Available Steps and move it just above the End If step.

27. Click the Set Field step on the right and click the Duplicate button. This duplicates the step and places it at the end of the script. Drag it up between the Else and the End If.

28. The last step to insert is the Go to Record/Request/Page step. Leave the default choice of First from the Specify pop-up menu selected.

29. The script is now complete. It should look like figure 15.31. Click the OK button to close the Script Definition dialog box. Click Done.

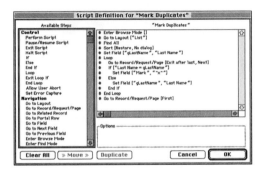

Fig. 15.31
This script will loop through an entire database and mark records that have a duplicate last name by displaying an X in the Mark field. You can easily modify the script to check for any duplicate field.

Now test the script. Choose Script, Mark Duplicates. When the script runs, all the records are sorted by last name. Notice that duplicate records (with the exception of the first record in a group) are all marked. Non-duplicate records are not marked. It's now an easy task to check the records and delete the ones you don't want to keep by finding all records with an X in the Mark field.

From Here...

In this chapter, you learned some good scripting tricks. The advanced scripting features of FileMaker Pro and the conditional scripting capability of the product allow you to implement an element of control in your scripts that was not possible before. You can now discard many of the workarounds you had to develop to overcome the shortcomings of previous versions.

- To find out how to use ScriptMaker to control access to files, see Chapter 12, "Controlling File Access."

- You might also want to look at Chapter 16, "Using AppleScript," to learn how to use AppleScript.

VI

Automating FileMaker Pro

CHAPTER 16

Using AppleScript

AppleScript is a fairly powerful scripting language that not only enables you to hot-wire certain processes in FileMaker Pro, it enables you to move information between FileMaker Pro and other applications, including the Finder. It's ideal for creating integrated solutions involving FileMaker and other AppleScript-savvy applications like MacWrite Pro, Word, or Excel.

With AppleScript, you can change information in specific fields in a FileMaker database. You can take information from a FileMaker database and give it to another program. You can even write and compile your own applications. Because this can get a bit arcane, this chapter shows you several wrong ways to do things and tells you they're wrong. That way, you'll know why a funky line of code has to be that way.

In this chapter, you learn how to:

- Install AppleScript
- Work with the Script Editor
- Find out what AppleScript commands are supported by an application
- Make custom dialog boxes in which users can enter information (you can create a FileMaker layout that looks like a dialog box, but it won't have quite the same behavior as the real thing)
- Write a script that creates documentation for any FileMaker database
- Write a script that indexes any hard drive or folder you tell it to, and uses that information to create a report in FileMaker Pro.

Installing AppleScript and Scripting Additions

AppleScript and the Scriptable Finder come free with Apple's System 7.5. While AppleScript will also work with System 7.1 or System 7.0 and QuickTime 1.6, you'll be unable to interact with the Finder unless you have System 7.5, which you will be doing in this chapter.

After you run the System Installer, you'll find a folder called Apple Extras that contains the AppleScript components. These are the pieces you need, and where they need to be:

- The AppleScript extension, the Apple Event Manager, the Finder Scripting Extension, and the Scripting Additions folder go in your Extensions folder.

- You need the Script Editor 1.1 somewhere on your hard drive.

Using AppleScript

Scripting in AppleScript is a way of harnessing the power of Apple Events, the underlying mechanism Macintosh applications use to communicate with one another (and the Finder). Your gateway to AppleScript is a bare bones editor called Script Editor. With it, you can write stand-alone scripts that request specific services of the Finder or other scriptable applications.

Here's a simple example: turn Sound on. It's one of the scripts that ships with System 7.5; you can run it yourself by choosing Automated Tasks from the Apple Menu.

```
tell application "Finder"
    set volume 5
    beep
    display dialog "Your system sound volume has been turned on."
buttons {"OK"} default button 1
end tell
```

Because AppleScript code is pretty easy to read, I'll dispense with a long-winded explanation, save a few trees, and move on.

Using Additions

Scripting additions are essentially libraries containing commands not supported by AppleScript in its natural state. People are writing new scripting additions all the time—you can find these on bulletin boards and on the Internet. To install a new scripting addition, just drop it into your Scripting Additions folder in the Extensions folder.

When the MacOS loads its extensions at startup, it discovers the core AppleScript commands in the AppleScript extension file. It does not load scripting additions at this time. Later, if the Macintosh is executing a script that uses an addition, it will go looking in the Scripting Additions folder for the code it needs to interpret the script.

From the user's standpoint, scripting additions integrate seamlessly into the AppleScript language. As a scripter, you don't have to care where the command lives in order to make use of it.

> **Tip**
>
> To get the most out of AppleScript, you'll want to build your own collection of scripting additions to extend the capabilities of the language. A wonderful collection of freeware and shareware scripting additions is maintained at the ScriptWeb WWW site on the Internet at **http://www.scriptweb.com/scriptweb/osaxen/default.html**.

Creating Custom Dialog Boxes

One of the scripting additions that comes with AppleScript is called Display Dialog; it enables you to create your own custom dialog boxes. To create a basic dialog box script, follow these steps:

1. Locate the Script Editor on your hard drive and double-click its icon to launch it. A new untitled script document appears, as shown in figure 16.1. You can enter a brief description of your script in the Description text box (optional), and use the larger text box to type in your AppleScript code.

Fig. 16.1
When Script Editor is launched, it creates a new untitled document.

VI

Automating FileMaker Pro

2. In the untitled script document, type the following:

```
display dialog "Hello!"
```

3. Click Check Syntax. If you make a typo, you receive a rude error message and you have to determine where you went wrong. But if everything checks out, the font changes from Courier to Geneva, indicating that the text is valid AppleScript code.

4. Click Run. Your script executes and a dialog box appears (see fig. 16.2).

Fig. 16.2

You created a dialog box that says "Hello!"

5. Click OK to close the Hello dialog box.

A window named The Result appears. You might have to move or resize other windows to see it. The Result is a temporary variable maintained by AppleScript. You can capture this information and put it in a variable of your own. You would do this because the result changes each time a user interacts with the script while your variables keep the same values until you intentionally change them.

6. Add the following two lines to your untitled script:

```
set x to the button returned of the result
display dialog x
```

7. Click Check Syntax to validate what you've typed and notice that some text turns bold. These are AppleScript keywords—the building blocks of the language. The Display Dialog command does not show up in bold because it's a scripting addition. It behaves just like a core AppleScript command, but it's really just an extension to the language.

8. Click Run to display the Hello dialog box and click OK to close it.

You get another dialog box that shows you what button you clicked. If you close the second dialog box and run the script again, this time clicking Cancel instead of OK, nothing happens. This is because the Cancel button tells the operating system that you want to cancel the script. Therefore, the script is canceled before it can report back to you. This, as you might imagine, is a problem. Here comes the workaround.

9. Choose File, Open Dictionary. Choose the Go to "Scripting Additions" Folder button. Scripting additions extend the vocabulary of AppleScript beyond its core set of commands. Some additions allow you to perform numeric functions (Numerics) and string manipulations (String Commands), some give you control over global system settings (Set Volume, MonitorDepth), while others make interactive components of the Finder available for your use in a script (Choose File, Display Dialog).

> **Caution**
>
> If you plan to make your script available for others to use, you must make sure that any non-standard scripting additions you employ are distributed and installed with your script. Otherwise, your script won't run on their machine.

10. Select the Display Dialog scripting addition (you might have to scroll down to find it) and choose Open to open the Display Dialog Dictionary window. You just opened an AppleScript dictionary that describes how a given scripting addition or application will enhance or interact with AppleScript. These dictionaries are created by application programmers to assist you in understanding how to create scripts involving their programs.

11. Click the Display Dialog command on the left side of the window. Figure 16.3 shows the result.

Notice the five command extensions beneath the Display Dialog command on the right. They're in square brackets because they're optional. The one you want to look at is [buttons list], which allows you to assign your own button names. It's telling you that the Display Dialog command can be modified with a buttons parameter, taking a list of up to three elements as arguments. Now that you've discovered how the Display Dialog command behaves, click back to your untitled script to apply some changes.

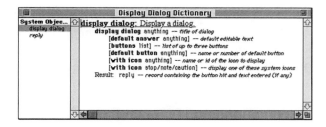

Fig. 16.3
The Display Dialog Dictionary window shows the syntax of the Display Dialog scripting addition command.

Now, you want your dialog box to support the two buttons (Cancel and OK) as before, but you have to be careful how you phrase things. Even if you name the button Cancel, it would still be interpreted as a system-level cancel command, which aborts the script. To get around this, add a space at the beginning and end of the word so it looks the same but doesn't get trapped by the system when it's chosen.

12. Click back into your untitled script and modify the first line so it now reads:

    ```
    display dialog "Hello!" buttons {" Cancel ","OK"}
    ```

13. Run the script again.

    Notice that neither of the buttons is a default button. When you specify your own buttons, you need to specify which one is the default button. You will do this in step 15.

14. Choose Cancel. Because you added the custom Cancel button, your script runs all the way through.

    So far, this dialog box isn't doing anything that FileMaker Pro's Show Message script step can't do. Display Dialog scripting addition has additional capabilities that make it much more useful. The most important difference is that it can take user input in a dialog box.

15. Modify the first line of your untitled script as follows:

    ```
    display dialog "Hello!" buttons {" Cancel ","OK"} default
    button "OK" default answer "Hello yourself..."
    ```

    Type this command as one line. If you don't like scrolling in the Script Editor, you can press Option-L-Return somewhere in the middle to wrap the text to the next line and still have it treated as a single AppleScript command. While you're at it, replace the remaining code with these four lines so you can examine the result more closely:

    ```
    set x to the result
    set y to the text returned of x
    set z to the button returned of x
    display dialog "You entered " & y & return & "You chose " & z
    ```

    This code allows you to capture both the button the user chooses and the text the user enters, and it displays these two pieces in the final dialog box. Notice how character strings are joined together (concatenated) by an ampersand (&). Also note that you can display a character string across two lines by embedding a return in the middle of the string.

16. Run the script. The second display dialog box command should give you the dialog box shown in figure 16.4.

    It's a little difficult to distinguish between what was actually entered and the dialog box text. It would be nice to put the variable values in quotation marks. It seems like a really straightforward thing, but it's not. When you put quotes inside of quotes, AppleScript assumes you're just closing the first quote string. To embed a quotation mark in a text string you need to proceed it with a backslash (\) character.

You entered Hello yourself...
You clicked OK

Cancel   OK

Fig. 16.4
The modified
dialog box shows
what text you
entered and what
button you chose.

17. Modify the last line in your script so it reads:

```
display dialog "You entered \"" & y & "\"" & return &
➥"You chose \"" & z & "\""
```

Again, if you want to break this command over two lines, you can press Option-Return in the middle somewhere (but not in the middle of a string). After the word return would be a good place.

18. Run the script again. Your final dialog box should be formatted nicely, with quotes surrounding the returned expressions.

19. Choose File, Save; or press ⌘-S and name this script Dialog. But don't save it to the Scripting Additions folder. You'll probably want to keep it in a separate folder with other scripts you'll be creating. If this script is meant to accompany a particular FileMaker project you're working on, navigate to that folder.

There are a couple of other things to consider before you choose the Save button to open the Save dialog box (see fig. 16.5). You can pick what kind of file is being saved by selecting a value from the Kind pop-up list. If you want to save the file as raw text, choose Text. If your program passes the syntax check, you can save the file as a Compiled Script. In this form, the script can be run only from the Run button in the Script Editor. If you're expecting this script to work as a stand-alone application or in conjunction with another program, you need to save the file as an Application.

Finally, you need to deselect the Stay Open check box and select the Never Show Startup Screen check box. That way your script will launch without fanfare and quit when it's done.

20. Choose the Save button to save your script as an application. Choose File, Quit to leave the Script Editor, and locate your script in the Finder. Double-click it to ensure that it runs as a stand-alone program.

Now that you can create dialog boxes and capture information a user might enter in them, you can take that information and put it in a FileMaker database.

VI

Automating FileMaker Pro

Fig. 16.5
The Save dialog box lets you choose what kind of script you're saving, and lets you affect how the script behaves when it runs.

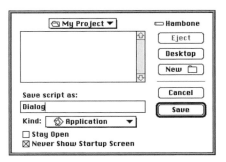

Using AppleScript To Control Applications

After you learn how to run AppleScript by itself, you need to make it talk to FileMaker Pro. In effect, you need to start a conversation with a different application.

To get an idea of the format of that conversation, you can use the Record button. Follow these steps:

1. Launch the Script Editor and an untitled document appears. If the Script Editor is already running, choose File, New Script.

2. Choose Record and switch over to the Finder using the Application menu. Select your hard drive or any folder, and double-click it. Switch back to the Script Editor.

3. Choose Stop. Figure 16.6 shows what your Script Editor window should look like. Notice that the syntax for addressing the Finder (it's the same for any application) consists of the command pair `tell` and `end tell`.

Fig. 16.6
This is the code recorded for you courtesy of AppleScript and System 7.5's Scriptable Finder.

You're probably wondering why you haven't been using the Record button all along if it can produce AppleScript code by itself. Well, there are some severe limitations to Recording. First, the Script Editor can only record steps it can watch you perform. None of the dialog script you created earlier could have been recorded because there's no way to perform those steps interactively. You were creating dialog boxes and manipulating and displaying variables. There's no way for the Script Editor to watch you do those things. Second, not all scriptable applications are recordable—and FileMaker Pro 3.0 falls into that category. You can record all you like, but nobody's watching and taking notes for you. That places a greater burden on you to know how to write AppleScript code. Take heart though: FileMaker 3.0 does offer improvements over previous versions in the way it deals with AppleScript routines. You'll get to those improvements later in the chapter.

If you look at the script you just created, you can see that for the purposes of AppleScript the Finder is just another application. To initiate a conversation with another application, you use the command `tell application`. To close a conversation with another application use the command `end tell`.

Notice the `activate` command. It brings the application to the foreground. Activate also forces an application to launch if it's not running already.

Now, because you can't record a conversation with FileMaker, you should make changes to this script as follows:

- On the first line, replace the word `Finder` with `FileMaker Pro`.
- Remove the third and fourth lines.

You end up with a shell for your new script. Choose Check Syntax to make sure the code is sound.

You need a database for AppleScript to manipulate. Open a database or quickly create one by following these steps:

1. Launch FileMaker Pro and create a new database named Guinea Pig.
2. In the Define Fields dialog box, create a text field called Name.
3. Choose Done to close the Define Fields dialog box.
4. Change the layout to List view and create at least one blank record.
5. Resize the database window so it only takes up 1/3 of your screen. Arrange the window so you can see both FileMaker and the Script Editor window, as shown in figure 16.7.

Fig. 16.7
Resize and
position the
FileMaker window
so it won't hide
the Script Editor.

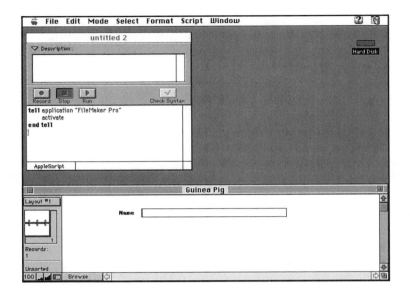

Now you have a database to work with and a script that gets data from a user. The time has come to integrate them. AppleScript thinks of a FileMaker database much as you think of a spreadsheet. The fields in FileMaker correspond to columns in a spreadsheet, and the records in FileMaker correspond to rows in a spreadsheet.

Like a spreadsheet, if you need to refer to a specific row of a field, you refer to a cell. Cell 1 of the Name field would be the first record of the Name field. When you use absolute cell referencing like this, AppleScript doesn't care what the current record is; it will pluck information from anywhere you specify.

Copy the lines from your untitled script and paste them at the end of the Dialog script you created earlier. Then insert this line between the `activate` and `end tell` statements:

```
set Cell 1 of Field "Name" of database 1 to y
```

You can refer to cells, fields, and databases by either their name or their number. Cell 1 would be the first field created on the first record in the database. You can find out the field number by viewing by creation order in the Define Fields dialog box.

Caution

Database 1 is the database currently in the foreground. Because this can change as you use the program, it's safest to reference databases by name.

When you run this script, notice that what you type in your dialog box is inserted in the Name field in the first record. You can experiment using different cell numbers and see what happens. If you use a number greater than the number of records in your database, you encounter the Execution Error dialog box (see fig. 16.8).

If you try to refer to an object that doesn't exist, the Script Editor captures the error from AppleScript and tells you what the problem is.

> **Caution**
>
> When you embed AppleScript code in FileMaker Pro script steps, FileMaker will not return AppleScript errors to you. If your script doesn't work, FileMaker won't tell you why. For that reason, it's always a good idea to test drive your scripts in the Script Editor before you pop them into FileMaker Pro.

What if you want to do something to the current record in FileMaker, regardless of what record that happens to be? AppleScript can retrieve something called "the current record of a given database." First, you need to know what you get when you ask for the current record. To do this, create a new Script Editor document and type in the following script:

```
tell application "FileMaker Pro"
set currec to the current record of database 1
display dialog currec
end tell
```

If you run this script, you'll get another Execution error. This one complains that it can make some data into the expected type.

So what does this mean? The Display Dialog scripting addition requires text information. If you ask it to display a variable that isn't in a text format, it tries to coerce the data into that format. Sometimes it's successful, sometimes it isn't. You can coerce the data into text by changing the script to read as follows:

```
tell application "FileMaker Pro"
set currec to the current record of database 1
display dialog currec as string
end tell
```

By telling the Display Dialog scripting addition to use the variable currec as a string, you drop any non-text elements that might be stored in the variable. This can be good and bad. It's good because it allows you to use Display Dialog to get a glimpse into the variable. It's bad because you're not seeing all of the information and you might make the assumption that you are.

If you run this script, you see the data that's stored in the current record. There's more information, though. You can change the script by commenting out the Display Dialog command as follows:

```
tell application "FileMaker Pro"
set currec to the current record of database 1
--display dialog currec as string
end tell
```

Choose the Check Syntax button and watch the third line become italicized. That's the Script Editor's way of acknowledging that you turned this text into a comment that will be ignored when the script runs.

If you run the script again, The Result window shows the information contained in the variable currec. If you don't have The Result window open, choose Controls, Show Result. The Result window opens (see fig. 16.9).

Fig. 16.9
The Result window shows the value of the variable currec.

Notice that what you see in The Result window doesn't look like what you saw when your script displayed its dialog box. That can happen when you force non-text information (in this case, a record reference) into text string information. You get unpredictable results.

Anyway, now that you know you can at least capture current record information, how do you use it? You can go back to your Dialog script and modify the FileMaker part so it reads as follows:

```
tell application "FileMaker Pro"
activate
set cell "Name" of the current record of database 1 to y
end tell
```

Now when you run the script, whatever you type in the dialog box gets put into the Name field in the selected record. You can try going into FileMaker, changing the current record, and then re-running the script.

To take this script and run it in FileMaker Pro, follow these steps:

1. In the Script Editor, make sure the Dialog script is selected and choose Edit, Select All.

2. Choose Edit, Copy to copy the entire script to the Clipboard.

3. Switch to FileMaker Pro and choose Script, ScriptMaker to open the Define Scripts dialog box.

4. Make a new script called Dialog and choose Create to open the Script Definition dialog box.

5. Choose Clear All to clear the default script steps.

6. Scroll to the bottom of the Available Steps list and double-click the Perform AppleScript script step to move it to the list on the right.

7. Choose Specify to open the Specify AppleScript dialog box.

8. Choose Edit, Paste to paste the script from the Clipboard.

9. Choose OK to close the Specify AppleScript dialog box.

10. Choose OK to close the Script Definition dialog box.

11. Choose Done to close the Define Scripts dialog box.

Try running your new Dialog script from the Script menu. Everything seems to work fine until FileMaker tries to tell itself to set a field value. You receive the error dialog box shown in figure 16.10.

Fig. 16.10
This error dialog box appears when FileMaker tries to access data while running a script.

Welcome to the biggest FileMaker/AppleScript bummer. FileMaker can't execute an AppleScript that accesses its own data. As you saw, it's no problem for FileMaker to call a scripting addition or some external process. You can even put the entire script inside the lines `tell application, "FileMaker Pro"`, and `end tell`. The Display Dialog pieces will still work. The problem comes in when FileMaker tries to access itself at the same time it's running a script. It can't do it.

This is a big downer if you want to move all of your scripts into FileMaker so you don't have all these external scripts floating around and waiting to get misplaced.

There is a workaround, of course. This workaround requires the use of any scripting addition that will allow you to set the Clipboard to some value.

Making FileMaker Pro Access Itself While Running a Script

There's a freeware scripting addition called Jon's Commands that enables you to set the Clipboard much as you would set a variable value. You can find it on the Internet at the ScriptWeb WWW site mentioned earlier, or download it directly from the author from **ftp://iw.cts.com/public/JonPugh/jonscommands.sit.hqx**. To use the addition, you need to put it in your Scripting Additions folder in your Extensions folder in your System folder.

In FileMaker, choose Script, ScriptMaker and double-click your Dialog script to edit the script. Double-click the Perform AppleScript command to edit the AppleScript code, and change the text to the following code. Choose OK when you're done.

```
display dialog "Hello!" buttons {" Cancel ", "OK"} default button
➥"OK" default answer "Hello yourself..."
set x to the result
set y to the text returned of x
set z to the button returned of x
display dialog "You entered \"" & y & "\"" & return & "You chose\
➥"" & z & "\""
tell application "FileMaker Pro"
activate
set the clipboard to y
end tell
```

Tip

ScriptMaker's Specify AppleScript screen doesn't offer the same flexibility as the Script Editor when it comes to editing and testing your script. In most cases, you'll want to develop your script with Script Editor or an even more sophisticated third-party AppleScript debugger and paste it into FileMaker when it's complete.

Caution

If you must resort to editing in ScriptMaker's Specify AppleScript screen, you might have trouble with those commands that span more than one line. Back in the Script Editor, you broke those commands apart by sticking an Option-Return in the middle. Here, that's not possible. You must do one of two things: type your command so it wraps around to subsequent lines (with no Return character between the lines) or use Option-L-Return to generate a line break.

After you modify the AppleScript script step, you need to add another script step. All you've done so far is to set the Clipboard to some value. Now you need to have FileMaker perform a paste command so the data moves from the Clipboard to FileMaker.

1. In the Available Steps list, double-click the Paste script step into the list on the right. Paste is grouped under Editing.

2. Choose Specify Field to open the Specify Field dialog box.

3. Select the Name field and choose OK.

4. Choose OK to close the Script Definition dialog box and choose Done to close the Define Scripts dialog box.

Try the script again, and you'll find that it works properly this time.

Creating Dialog Boxes that Perform Finds

When you have the dialog box working, with some effort, you can make it into a front end for searches. You can have a user type in a month, have AppleScript turn that into a date range, and put the result in a find. Try using the following script as a front end for Find requests. You'll want to create a new script in the Script Editor and copy it to a FileMaker script after you test it for errors. Remember to pad your Cancel button with a space on each end.

```
global range
set range to ""
repeat until the number of characters in range > 0
select_month()
end repeat
display dialog range
on select_month()
display dialog "Enter Month" default answer "January" ¬
buttons {" Cancel ", "OK"} default button "OK"
set temp to the result
if the button returned of the result = "OK" then
set m to the text returned of temp
set y to the year of the (current date)
if m = "January" then
set range to "1/1/" & y & "...1/31/" & y
else if m = "February" then
set range to "2/1/" & y & "...2/28/" & y
else if m = "March" then
set range to "3/1/" & y & "...3/31/" & y
else if m = "April" then
set range to "4/1/" & y & "...4/30/" & y
else if m = "May" then
set range to "5/1/" & y & "...5/31/" & y
else if m = "June" then
set range to "6/1/" & y & "...6/31/" & y
else if m = "July" then
set range to "7/1/" & y & "...7/31/" & y
else if m = "August" then
set range to "8/1/" & y & "...8/31/" & y
else if m = "September" then
set range to "9/1/" & y & "...9/30/" & y
```

```
else if m = "October" then
set range to "10/1/" & y & "...10/31/" & y
else if m = "November" then
set range to "11/1/" & y & "...11/31/" & y
else if m = "December" then
set range to "12/1/" & y & "...12/31/" & y
else
display dialog ¬
"Incorrect date entry. Would you like to try again or cancel?" ¬
buttons {"Try Again", " Cancel "} default button "Try Again"
if the button returned of the result = " Cancel " then set range to "="
end if
set the clipboard to range
end if
end select_month
```

This script asks the user for a month name. If the user enters a valid month, the script creates a month range suitable for pasting into a FileMaker date field in a Find request. If the user enters an invalid date, the script notifies the user that the entry is invalid and asks if they want to try again. If they cancel, the script returns an equal sign. The equal sign finds all records in FileMaker Pro.

Creating Custom FileMaker Menus

FileMaker developers have been asking for the capability to create custom menus in FileMaker for years. While FileMaker offers no facility for doing this in the application (with the exception of scripts showing up as menu items), you can create custom menu items with AppleScript. These custom menus will remain until you quit FileMaker Pro. If you quit and reboot FileMaker, you need to run your menu creation scripts again.

When you create custom menus and menu items, a new menu item called External gets added under the Script menu. When you choose one of the menu items, FileMaker sends an event to the application that created the menu item and notifies it of the selection. This means that if you want to use these kinds of custom menus, you need to create an AppleScript applet that stays open after it's launched. It needs to stay open so it can respond to the menu selection events from FileMaker.

> **Note**
>
> An *applet* is just a working script saved as an application. You can run it by double-clicking it. In contrast, a *droplet* is a script that supports drag-and-drop. You can double-click it to run it, or you can drag a file or folder on top of it to have it act on that selection.

There are other issues when creating menus. If you run your menu creation script more than once without quitting and restarting FileMaker, the same menus will be created again, giving you duplicates of everything. To avoid this, you need to add some lines of code that check to see if the menus are already there. It's not a big deal, just something you need to keep in mind.

To learn more about custom menus, you should look at FileMaker's AppleScript Dictionary. To do this, follow these steps:

1. In the Script Editor, choose File, Open Dictionary to open the Open Dictionary dialog box.

2. Locate the FileMaker Pro 3.0 application and choose Open to open the FileMaker Pro Dictionary.

3. Scroll to the very last item in the Dictionary and select Menu from the FileMaker Suite of commands (see fig. 16.11).

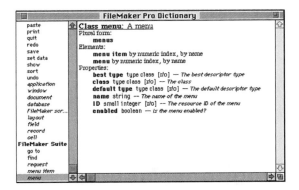

Fig. 16.11
The FileMaker Pro Dictionary describes what commands and objects you can control through AppleScript.

4. When you finish examining the Menu object, look at the Menu Item object above it. Close when you're done.

The Dictionary gives you a lot of information about custom menu items. Looking at the Properties for a menu or menu item, you can see that you have the capability to change a menu's name and to enable or disable a menu. When a menu is disabled, it still appears in the menu, but it's grayed out and does not respond to the mouse.

To create an AppleScript that creates a custom menu and menu item in FileMaker Pro, create a new script in the Script Editor and type the following script:

```
tell application "FileMaker Pro"
activate
if not (exists (document 1)) then
```

```
open (choose file)
end if
create new menu item with properties ¬
{name:"Message", ID:500} at menu "External"
create new menu with properties ¬
{name:"Position", ID:500} at menu "External"
end tell
```

> **Note**
>
> Every program on the Macintosh contains re-usable resources like sounds, icons, windows, dialog boxes, menus, and menu items. To reference these resources, the Macintosh identifies them by resource type and a unique resource ID (per type). In this script, you're creating new menus to be used by FileMaker, but you'll have to be careful that you pick an ID that's not already in use. Menu ID's in the range of 100 to 1,400 are good to use because FileMaker's own menu ID's run from 1 to 52, then jump to 1,500 and beyond, up through 13,001.

After you check the syntax for typos, run the script. If FileMaker isn't currently running, it will launch and prompt you to select a database to open. If FileMaker is running already, the script will act on the current database.

With FileMaker still running, choose Script, External to see the Message menu item and the Position menu you created (see fig. 16.12). These won't do anything yet if you select them, but you will soon attach them to external routines.

Fig. 16.12
You can create your own custom menus and menu items grouped under the External menu.

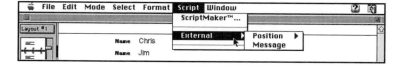

A menu differs from a menu item in that it has a triangle on the right end of the menu. This means that menu items are attached to it. Never create a menu unless you're going to add menu items to it. Instead, just create a menu item.

Menu items appear in the opposite order they are created. It's as if you stack menu items as you create them. The first item you create is at the bottom of the menu, the next item on top of it, and so on. Keep this in mind as you write your scripts.

In the previous script, you added a custom menu and a menu item to FileMaker Pro. To add menu items under the Position menu, try modifying that script so it looks like the following code:

```
tell application "FileMaker Pro"
activate
if not (exists (document 1)) then
open (choose file)
end if
create new menu with properties ¬
{name:"Position", ID:500} at menu "External"
create new menu item with properties ¬
{name:"Bottom", ID:500} at menu "Position"
create new menu item with properties ¬
{name:"Middle", ID:501} at menu "Position"
create new menu item with properties ¬
{name:"Top", ID:502} at menu "Position"
create new menu item with properties ¬
{name:"Message", ID:503} at menu "External"
end tell
```

This script creates hierarchical menus, also known as menus with submenus. To actually have these menus respond to a user selecting them, you need to add the following lines of code:

```
on «event» of theData
tell application "FileMaker Pro"
activate
display dialog "I got the event! The Data is " & (theData as list)
end tell
end «event»
```

To use this script, choose File, Save As and save it as an application. Select the Stay Open and Never Show Startup Screen check boxes. Launch FileMaker, then launch this AppleScript applet. Try running some of the custom menus and see what happens. Instead of displaying dialog boxes, you could have the script run specific AppleScript processes.

Creating Documentation with a Script

You can use AppleScript to make FileMaker document your database for you. This script will ask you to locate a database, then it will generate a profile of all the layouts, fields, and formulas contained in that database.

To get this to work, you need to create two things: a database that the script can send its findings to, and the script itself.

Creating the database is simple:

1. Choose File, New to create a new file named Documenter. Choose Save.

2. In the Define Fields dialog box, you need create only four text fields: Database Name, Layout Name, Field Name, and Formula. Choose Done when you're finished.

3. Keep the fields where they fall on Layout #1. Choose Mode, Layout to switch to Layout mode.

4. Choose Mode, New Layout to create a new layout and call it Field List.

5. Position and resize your fields, field labels, and parts using figure 16.13 as a guide.

6. Choose Mode, Browse to enter Browse mode and choose Select, View as List so the records will display in rows. There's no data to view yet, but there will be when the script runs.

Fig. 16.13
Your completed Field List layout will show Documenter's four fields in columns.

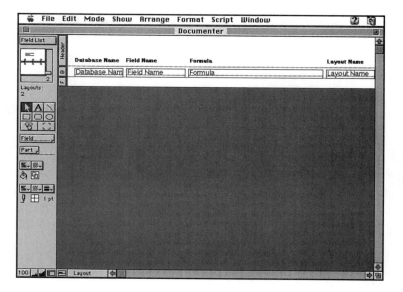

You can close FileMaker now and switch to Script Editor to begin inputting the script. When you catch your breath at the end, I'll review what you typed.

```
set dLayout to {}
set dField to {}
set dForm to {}

tell application "FileMaker Pro"
activate
```

```
open (choose file with prompt ¬
"Please find the Documenter database." of type "FMP3")
open (choose file with prompt ¬
"Please pick a FileMaker database to document." of type "FMP3")
set dName to the name of database 1
repeat with x from 1 to the number of layouts in database 1
show layout x in database 1
repeat with y from 1 to the number of fields in layout x in database 1
set dLayout to dLayout & the name of layout x of database 1
set dField to dField & the name of field y in layout x of database 1
set dForm to dForm & the formula of field y in layout x of database 1
end repeat
end repeat
repeat with z from 1 to the number of items in dField
create new record in database "Documenter"
end repeat
set field "Database Name" of database "Documenter" to dName
set field "Layout Name" of database "Documenter" to dLayout
set field "Field Name" of database "Documenter" to dField
set field "Formula" of database "Documenter" to dForm
close database 1
end tell
```

Save your script as an application under the name Documentary. Select the Never Show Startup Screen check box, but leave the Stay Open check box unselected.

Essentially, what this script does is set up three variables and initialize them as empty lists. Then it opens FileMaker and asks the user to locate two files. The first file is the Documenter database you just created; the second file is the database you want to have documented. It opens these files and goes to work. The script goes through each layout in the database, one at a time, by number. As it visits each layout, it instructs FileMaker to show that layout on the screen so you can watch it as it progresses. While on each layout, it builds a list of properties of each of the fields contained in that layout. It collects the name of the layout, the name of the field, and the formula of the field.

There's something special you need to know about list variables that makes this script work the way it does. A list in AppleScript is a collection of values of arbitrary type. You can have an empty list {}; a list of numbers {1,2,3}; a list of strings {"Bob's", "your", "uncle"}; or a list of lists {{1,2},{2,3}}; or a list of a combination of these {"spatula", {3.14},9}. AppleScript uses the concatenation operator (&) to append elements to a list. So where you see the instruction

```
set dField to dField & the name of field y in layout x of database 1
```

what it's doing is taking what's already in dField, perhaps {"City","State"}, and adding another field name {"Zip"} to the end to yield {"City","State","Zip"}. Because the script is building dLayout and dForm in parallel, when it has exhausted all fields on all layouts, each list will have the same number of elements. The script then counts how many elements it has in dField, and creates that number of blank records in the Documenter database.

The final grouping of set field statements looks odd. When you think of re-placing data in FileMaker, you think in terms of one field in a single record or possibly all fields in a single record. Here, you're replacing one field in all records in the database with successive elements from your amassed list vari-able. Whoa! Perhaps an example will help. Assume that dField has the value {"City","State","Zip"} and three blank records have been created in the Documenter database. The instruction

```
set field "Field Name" of database "Documenter" to dField
```

replaces the Field Name field in record 1 with City; replaces the Field Name field in record 2 with State; and replaces the Field Name field in record 3 with Zip. So in four innocuous statements, the entire Documenter database is filled with the results of its inquiries.

Indexing a Hard Drive or Folder

System 7.5's scriptable Finder opened up all kinds of opportunities for auto-mating and monitoring the desktop. In this script, you are asked to pick a folder on your hard drive that you want to index. The script will collect infor-mation about the name and path of each file in your folder and, when it completes its data collection, it dumps the information into a FileMaker database.

As with the previous script, you need to create two things to get this example to work: a database the script can send its findings to, and the script itself.

You can create the database in the same manner as you did Documenter. Call this one Index and set up two text fields: Name and Path. Create a new lay-out called Field List and format it to look like figure 16.14.

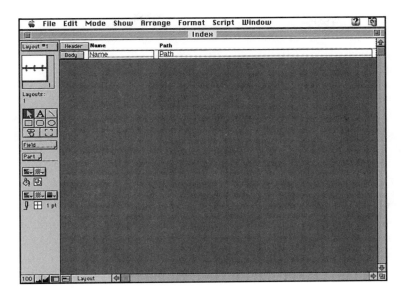

Fig. 16.14
Your completed
Field List layout
will show Index's
two fields in
columns.

Again, I'll let you type the script into Script Editor, and then I'll step through
it.

```
set fileNme to
set fPath to

tell application "Finder"
choose folder with prompt "Pick a folder.  Any folder."
set fName to the result
repeat with x from 1 to the number of files in folder fName
set fileNme to fileNme & the name of file x of folder fName
set tempName to (fName as string) & the name of file x of folder ¬
fName as string
set fPath to fPath & tempName
end repeat
end tell

tell application "FileMaker Pro"
activate
try
show database "Index"
on error
choose file with prompt "Can't find Index.  Can you?" of type "FMP3"
set opName to the result
open opName
end try
repeat with z from 1 to the number of items in fileNme
create new record in database "Index"
end repeat
set field "Name" of database "Index" to fileNme
set field "Path" of database "Index" to fPath
end tell
```

Save your script as an application under the name Indexer. Select the Never Show Startup Screen check box and leave the Stay Open check box unselected.

The Indexer script has a similar structure to Documentary. It first initializes two list variables: `fileNme` for collecting a list of file names, and `fPath` for collecting a parallel list of paths. A *path* is the series of folders you have to follow to travel from your hard drive to a given file. The script tells the Finder to offer you an Open Folder dialog box so you can pick the folder you want indexed. Then for each file in that folder, the script accumulates information into the lists `fileNme` and `fPath`.

When it's done, it activates FileMaker and tries to display the Index database, assuming that it might be open. If it can, great! Otherwise, it prompts you to locate the Index database on your hard drive. By restricting the choices to files of type FMP3, the script shows you nothing but FileMaker Pro 3.0 databases in the Open File dialog box. After you find the file it needs, the script opens it.

The final few steps echo what you saw in the Documentary script, as the script creates blank records in Index for each file it's collected data on. Finally, it fills values into the Name field for all records at once from the ordered list elements in `fileNme`, then it does the same from the `fPath` list into the Path field.

There's plenty of opportunity for you to expand on the power of this script. For example, you could collect the file type of each file into a Type field, and sort the FileMaker database on this field so the files group by the application they were created under. The possibilities are endless!

From Here...

In this chapter, you learned how to install AppleScript and how to use the Script Editor to create and test scripts. You also learned how to embed these scripts into FileMaker's ScriptMaker. The ScriptMaker has some limitations with AppleScript, but there are workarounds.

From here, you might want to investigate the following chapter:

- Chapter 15, "Scripting with ScriptMaker," describes other things you can do with ScriptMaker, such as create dialog boxes and set up conditional scripts

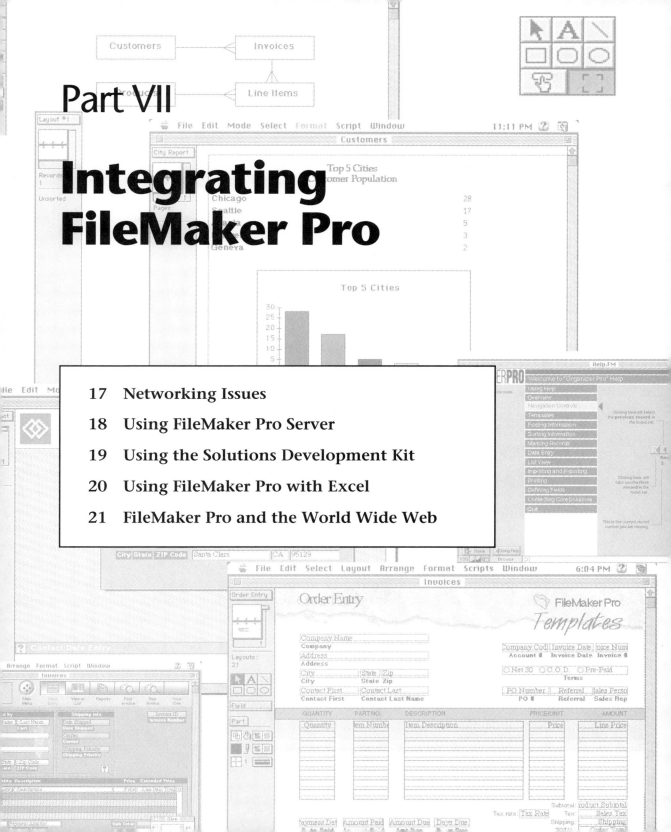

Part VII

Integrating FileMaker Pro

CHAPTER 17

Networking Issues

by Shelly Brisbin

Databases frequently contain information that is needed by several people in an office, often at the same time. FileMaker Pro addresses this need by allowing several users to use a single file (or group of files) simultaneously via a network. Because FileMaker Pro works on Macs and PCs, and because several kinds of networks are used in today's offices, you can network databases over a number of wiring types and conductivity schemes.

With networked databases, one user can perform data entry while others sort or print records. Mac and PC users can view and modify the same files. You can even set access privileges that lock certain layouts or functions away from users or groups of users.

Because network access depends on multiple computers, users, and network interfaces, it is important to understand how to use FileMaker Pro's network access, how it operates, and what to do if something goes wrong.

In this chapter, you learn how to:

- Make databases accessible over a network
- Use networked databases
- Troubleshoot network problems with AppleTalk, IPX, and TCP/IP networks

Sharing Databases

To share FileMaker Pro databases with others, you must have a network in place and copies of FileMaker Pro and its networking support software on each machine that will share files. You also need to tell users where they can find the databases you want to share, and provide any passwords you have established for the files.

> **Note**
>
> You must purchase a copy of FileMaker Pro or obtain a site license covering each computer on which you plan to use FileMaker. This is true even if you are only using FileMaker to access databases stored on other computers. Making unauthorized copies is illegal.

If you used the Easy Install option when you first installed FileMaker Pro, the networking software you need to share databases is already in place. You don't need to activate System 7 File Sharing or place your database on a public file server. To achieve maximum performance and relieve individual users of any overhead associated with hosting databases, you can use the FileMaker Pro server. For more information about FileMaker Pro Server, see Chapter 18, "Using FileMaker Pro Server."

If you used the Custom Install option to place FileMaker on your hard disk, or if you deleted or moved items FileMaker Pro needs, you might be unable to share files. (See the "Network Troubleshooting" section later in this chapter for more details.)

Making Files Accessible

To make a database file available to users via a network, follow these steps:

1. Open the database you want to share.

2. Choose File, Single User. The menu item changes to Multi-User, with a check mark in front of it.

    If the menu item is already labeled Multi-User, proceed to step 3.

3. Decide what (if any) access privileges you want to put in place. See Chapter 12, "Controlling File Access," for details on how to set them.

4. Choose Edit, Preferences to make sure a network connection has been enabled. In most cases, the Network Protocol pop-up menu should say AppleTalk. If no network protocol is selected, choose AppleTalk and click OK.

That's it. Your file is now visible on the network. Leave the database file open as you continue using your computer. If you prefer not to see the database window, choose Application, Hide FileMaker.

Using Shared Files

When a database is available on the network, one or more users can log into it as guests. Unless the owner (or *host*) of the database has restricted access to the file, a guest can work with it as if it were stored on his own computer. Just as with a single user file, changes made to shared files are automatically saved.

To use a FileMaker Pro database stored on another computer, follow these steps:

1. From a Mac that does not contain the shared database, open FileMaker Pro.

2. In the Open dialog box, choose Open an Existing File. If you told FileMaker to bypass this dialog box at launch, choose File, Open.

3. Click the Hosts button to reach a list of databases available on your network (see fig. 17.1).

Fig. 17.1
The Open dialog box shows files on your hard disk. Click Hosts to see those on a network.

4. Choose a shared database from the list in the Hosts dialog box (see fig. 17.2).

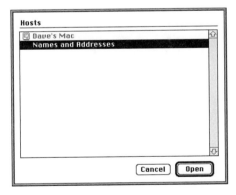

Fig. 17.2
The Hosts dialog looks like this if you're using an AppleTalk network.

If your AppleTalk network contains multiple zones, you might have to click one of them to find the database you are looking for.

If your network uses TCP/IP, choose Local Hosts or Specify Host from the lower pane of the Hosts dialog box (see fig. 17.3). Enter the IP address or domain name of the machine you want to connect to. If you don't have this information, contact the owner of the machine where a database you need is stored and ask for the IP address (in the format: 123.234.45.1) or the machine's domain name (in the format: bob.mycompany.com).

Fig. 17.3
The Hosts dialog box lists all of the computers with shared databases and the files available on each. The Zones dialog box allows you to view other parts of your network.

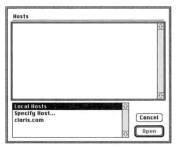

Tip

If the network is very busy, a shared database might not appear in the Hosts dialog box. Press the Option key as you click an AppleTalk zone to force the file to appear.

After you choose a database, FileMaker Pro informs you that you are being logged into it as a guest. If the owner of the file has created a password for the file, you will be asked to enter it.

Guest Access Limitations

In general, guests can perform most functions a host can in Browse mode. This includes finding, sorting, printing, and other data manipulation tasks. All guests can also switch modes, activate scripts from the Scripts menu, and import or export data.

Some functions are limited to one user at a time. That user can be a host or a guest. Actions limited in this way include: editing a record or layout (multiple users can view records or layouts on which others are working, but cannot change them while another user is editing them), opening the ScriptMaker dialog box, and defining or changing relationships between files.

A few functions are completely off limits to guest. Only hosts can do the following:

- Define fields or change their definitions
- Reorder layouts
- Work with access privileges
- Switch files between single- and multi-user
- Save copies of a file with the Save A Copy command
- Check the spelling of a found set
- Close a shared file (guests can leave a shared file, but it remains open on the host machine for others to use)

Note

You can also limit guest access to FileMaker functions by a file's access privileges (see Chapter 12, "Controlling File Access"). If the owner of the file has restricted access to Layout mode, for example, a guest who does not have the proper password cannot switch to that mode.

Network Troubleshooting

Although FileMaker Pro's networking functions are easy to understand and use, problems sometimes occur when networks fail or files are not available to share. If you cannot share files as previously described because you can't locate them on the network, you need to diagnose and correct the problem by taking several logical steps.

Understanding Your Network

First, you should know something about your networking environment. Because FileMaker Pro supports both Mac and Windows formats, it also supports the kinds of networks used to connect the two.

FileMaker supports three different network *protocols*. These protocols are the language each computer uses to communicate with others on the network.

- *AppleTalk.* Used by most all-Mac networks and even on some where there are a few PCs with AppleTalk support installed.
- *IPX.* Used on networks where Novell NetWare file servers are present. IPX can coexist on a network with other protocols. In fact, it's unlikely that you will work with it unless your FileMaker Pro databases are stored on NetWare file servers.

■ *TCP/IP.* Used in many large networks with many kinds of computers. TCP/IP is the network protocol used on the Internet. Many organizations with networks in several buildings or several cities use TCP/IP to link their computers together. Like IPX, TCP/IP can coexist with AppleTalk, and you can only use it to communicate with databases that reside on PCs or on Macs located outside your local network.

> **Tip**
>
> If you're not sure what network protocol you're using, choose Edit, Preferences. The Network Protocol pop-up menu indicates the protocol you are currently using.

Installation Basics

Each network protocol requires different support software. As previously discussed, all of the software you need to use FileMaker Pro on a network is added to your hard disk during the Easy Install process. Most of the software used to support networking is stored in the FileMaker Extensions folder in your FileMaker Pro folder. There are extensions for AppleTalk, IPX, and TCP/IP networks. The installer also adds the MacIPX control panel to the Control Panels Folder in your System Folder.

If you have an AppleTalk or TCP/IP network, you also need Apple networking software (AppleTalk) or MacTCP (TCP/IP). Both are included with System 7.5. If you use system software older than System 7.5 and do not have MacTCP, you need to acquire it if you plan to use FileMaker Pro on a TCP/IP network. Talk to your network administrator if you don't have access to MacTCP.

Common Problems with All Protocols

Most network-related problems fall in general categories. Use the following scenarios to work through your problem. If you don't find one that exactly matches your situation, choose one that's close. If your problems are specific to AppleTalk, TCP/IP, or IPX, read the next three sections, which discuss those protocols specifically.

You Can't See a Particular Host Database

If you try to open a database as a guest, but can't find it on the network, contact the owner of the computer where the database is stored to make sure the machine is on and connected to the network, and that the file you need is open and set to multi-user access.

If the file is available, make sure guest and host are using compatible versions of FileMaker Pro. FileMaker Pro 3.0 guests cannot open databases launched with older versions of the software.

Hosts and guests must be using the same network protocol. Check the Network Protocol pop-up by choosing Edit, Preferences. If protocols for host and guest are different, the parties should agree on one for which both have the proper configuration.

You Can't See Any Host Databases

If several shared databases are available on your network and you cannot locate any of them, the problem is either with the guest machine or with the network—not the host. This situation might occur if the guest machine is using the wrong protocol or is not connected to the network.

Use the Preferences dialog box to check your protocol, and find out which one is being used by machines hosting database files. If the protocols match, check your own network configuration and connection.

You Can't Make Changes to a File

If you are using a database file as a guest and receive an error message saying you cannot edit a value list or change relationships, it's because FileMaker allows only one guest to modify the file in this way. For a more complete list of limitations FileMaker places on guest modifications, see the section "Guest Access Limitations" earlier in this chapter.

AppleTalk Problems

AppleTalk is the most common and simplest protocol for all-Mac networks. In most cases, it just works! If you can't see AppleTalk-based databases in the Hosts dialog box, and you're satisfied that the guests and machines hosting databases you need are using AppleTalk, use the Chooser and Network control panels to check AppleTalk. To do this, follow these steps:

1. Open the Chooser from the Apple menu. If AppleTalk is active and you see network devices and zones as you normally do, AppleTalk is correctly configured.

2. If AppleTalk is inactive, select the Active radio button. You might be told that the change will not take effect until you restart the Mac.

3. If AppleTalk is active, click the AppleShare or Printer icon to see if network devices are visible. (If your network has zones, you don't need to do this.)

4. If no devices appear, open the Network control panel by choosing Control Panels from the Apple menu and selecting Network.

5. You should see one or more icons, one of which is highlighted (see fig. 17.4). If you know what network driver you're using (LocalTalk, EtherTalk, or TokenTalk), choose the correct icon. Most office AppleTalk networks use Ethernet. If you're not sure, ask your system administrator. A dialog box will warn you that changing the AppleTalk driver will interrupt network activity. Because that's what brought you here in the first place, click OK.

Fig. 17.4
Icons in the Network control panel represent drivers the Mac uses to run both built-in and add-on networking hardware

6. If your network contains zones, a pop-up displaying them should appear in the Network control panel, if you've chosen the correct driver. You can confirm that your network connection is working by reopening the Chooser. Close the Chooser and the Network control panel, and try to open the FileMaker Pro database again.

IPX Problems

If you know your network includes Novell NetWare file servers and FileMaker Pro files are stored on one of them, you might be using Novell's IPX and the MacIPX control panel to connect to host databases. If you have difficulty with IPX connections, use this section to diagnose and solve them.

If you don't see hosts or databases in the Hosts dialog box, close it and open the MacIPX control panel by choosing Control Panels from the Apple Menu and double-clicking MacIPX. If Auto-Configure Frame Type is selected, deselect it and choose the correct frame type. If you don't know your server's frame type, ask your system administrator for help. After you reconfigure MacIPX properly, restart your Mac.

TCP/IP Problems

Many problems with shared TCP/IP databases occur because TCP/IP (MacTCP control panel on the Mac) is configured incorrectly. If you use the TCP/IP network to communicate with file servers or to connect to the Internet, TCP/IP configuration problems will affect these applications, as well as FileMaker

Pro. Your system administrator should be able to help you configure MacTCP and will give you the IP addresses you need to make connections. Here are a few situations in which TCP/IP configuration is probably the cause of your FileMaker Pro difficulties.

Specified Hosts Are Not Visible

If you have specified hosts in the past and cannot see them when you open the Hosts dialog box in FileMaker Pro, try specifying the host again by using the IP address (number) rather than the text name you previously assigned to the host. If this doesn't work, then your problem is related to your TCP/IP configuration.

You Cannot Connect to Remote Databases

If you can see and use local databases by clicking Local Hosts in the Hosts dialog box, but cannot use Specify Hosts to locate others, check MacTCP to see whether the Gateway Address is entered correctly. When you open the MacTCP control panel, you'll see your own IP address. Click More to see the Gateway address and other information (see fig. 17.5). If the IP address entered in the control panel is the same as the Gateway Address you see when you click the More button in MacTCP, you should consult your system administrator to obtain a proper Gateway Address.

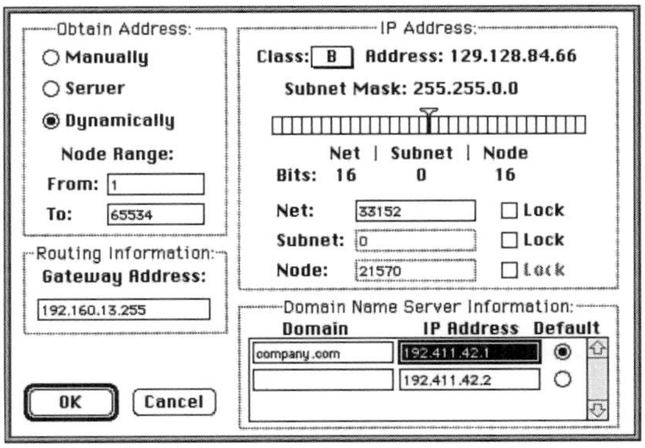

Fig. 17.5
The Gateway Address in the MacTCP dialog box should not be the same as your Mac's IP address.

Your IP Address Is in Use Elsewhere

If you receive an error message indicating that the IP address is in use by another machine on the network, open MacTCP and verify that you are using the address assigned to you. If you aren't sure what address you are using, contact your system administrator, who will either correct the address error or assign you a different address.

From Here...

In this chapter, you learned how to use FileMaker Pro's networking features and how to solve common problems associated with using files over several types of networks.

To learn more about networking topics, read the following chapters:

■ Chapter 12, "Controlling File Access," explains how to create passwords and access restrictions for databases you share over the network.

■ Chapter 18, "Using FileMaker Pro Server," describes the FileMaker Pro Server, an application that is designed to provide high-volume, high-performance access to shared files.

Using FileMaker Pro Server

FileMaker Pro Server is a client server database engine optimized for network file sharing; it speeds up network performance of FileMaker Pro operations. With the new version FileMaker Pro 3.0, there's a new FileMaker Pro Server 3.0. If you want to host databases that were created with FileMaker Pro 3.0, you have to run the 3.0 Server. The 2.1 Server isn't compatible with the new relational file format.

FileMaker Pro Server is not for everyone but, if you're running multi-user databases with generally ten or more users, you'll benefit from the performance boost of FileMaker Pro Server.

In this chapter, you learn about the following:

- Boosting FileMaker Pro Server performance
- How to install FileMaker Pro Server
- FileMaker Pro Server Administration
- Creating a startup database

Factors Affecting FileMaker Pro Server Performance

Before you install FileMaker Pro Server, there are some considerations. First, you need to know when to use FileMaker Pro Server. Many people mistakenly believe that if they host databases with FileMaker Pro Server, the databases will run faster than if the databases were running in single-user mode with a regular copy of FileMaker. If your database runs slow on a regular copy of FileMaker and the database isn't being shared, FileMaker Pro Server is not going to increase the performance. If you run a database in multi-user mode on a regular copy of FileMaker and it's being shared by 20 people, you will get an increase in performance by moving that database to FileMaker Pro Server. Remember that the best possible performance the Server will give you is approximately the speed you would get if you were running your databases in single-user mode—it will never be faster.

FileMaker Pro Server 3.0 is "multilingual." It can share databases with Macintosh guests who are running AppleTalk, IPX (Novell's protocol), or TCP/IP (the protocol used on the Internet) at the same time. You can even have Windows machines running IPX or TCP/IP as guests. AppleTalk isn't supported on Windows.

The following list gives you some factors that contribute to FileMaker performance. This list not only applies to the Server, but also when you're sharing databases with the regular version of FileMaker or with the Server. This list is roughly in order of importance.

- *Hard drive speed on the host machine.* FileMaker Pro makes frequent use of the hard drive. Anytime you change a record and press the Enter key or click outside of a field, that change is written to the hard drive. If you're sharing a database and several people are entering or changing information in the database, that hard drive traffic goes up accordingly. Use the fastest hard drive you can afford on your host machine. To get the maximum throughput on your drive, make sure your hard drive and your machine support asynchronous I/O. *Asynchronous I/O* means that while your hard drive retrieves information, your machine can perform other tasks. It's similar to being able to talk and listen at the same time. Your conversations would go twice as fast. Asynchronous I/O is supported on the Quadra AV and PowerMac machines. If you're using a third-party drive or SCSI card, check to see if it supports asynchronous I/O.

- *Dedicate the host machine to FileMaker.* Many people are tempted to put AppleShare, their calendar server, and their e-mail server on the machine with FileMaker Pro Server. All of these applications, especially AppleShare, need to use the hard drive—so does FileMaker. When you put them on one machine, they all slow down because they stand in line for hard drive access. Besides hard drive access, the applications will be generating competing network traffic and occupying network sockets on the machine. You also want to make sure you don't have personal file sharing turned on. This also generates network traffic and forces FileMaker to share drive access with users coming in over the network. If you're going to take the trouble to get a server for FileMaker, don't defeat the purpose by cluttering up the machine.

> **Tip**
>
> Screen savers also use system resources. If you want to use a screen saver, use one that blacks out or dims the screen. Better yet, turn the monitor brightness down yourself and forget the screen saver. Screen savers that use moving images steal cycles from the Server.

- *Have a fast network.* There's no point in getting FileMaker Pro Server if you're running a LocalTalk network. The network is too slow for FileMaker Pro Server's throughput. You'll have slow performance due to a network bottleneck. You need to run Ethernet or you're wasting money on FileMaker Pro Server.

- *Make your host machine a PowerMac.* The FileMaker Pro Server is a *FAT* binary application: both the PowerPC-optimized code and the 680X0-optimized code are in the same application. (If you're not running a PowerMac, FileMaker Pro Server requires a minimum of a 68030 processor.) When you launch the Server, it checks to see which chip you're running and loads the appropriate code. If you have a PowerMac, FileMaker Pro Server will take advantage of it. (For regular FileMaker Pro 3.0, the Installer installs either a PowerPC or 680x0 version of FileMaker, depending on the chip. This smart installer scheme is different from FAT binary software, where both versions are in the same program.) While processor clock speed isn't as important as hard drive access speed, it also helps to have a fast chip.

- *Give FileMaker Pro Server as much RAM as you can.* The documentation recommends at least 8M of RAM, but FileMaker Pro Server can use all the RAM you give it; 8M of RAM is enough for 25 guests and 50 hosted files, but giving it more RAM will improve performance and allow you to have more guests and open files. Don't use virtual memory to "make" more RAM for FileMaker. Virtual memory uses the hard drive to create additional memory space. Because FileMaker also uses the hard drive, you'll actually slow FileMaker down by using virtual memory. After you install FileMaker Pro Server (see the following section), you can change its RAM allocation by following these steps:

  1. Make sure the application isn't running. If it is, quit FileMaker Pro Server.

  2. Choose About This Macintosh from the Apple menu. The About This Macintosh window appears (see fig. 18.1). Note how much available memory you have when no applications are running (Largest Unused Block). Set the FileMaker Pro Server to use about 500K less than that. Close the About This Macintosh window.

Fig. 18.1
Check the available memory to determine the optimum memory allocation for FileMaker Pro Server.

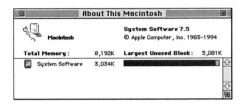

3. Click the FileMaker Pro Server icon to select it. Choose File, Get Info to open the FileMaker Pro Server Info window (see fig. 18.2).

Fig. 18.2
Use the FileMaker Pro Server Info window to allocate the optimum memory requirements to FileMaker Pro Server.

4. In the Memory Requirements area, click in the Preferred Size text box (it says Current Size in some versions of the Mac OS) and enter a number that's about 500K less than your available memory. That 500K is left to give the system enough room to do things like open windows or copy files. Close the FileMaker Pro Server Info window.

Now that you've had a chance to think over the factors affecting performance in FileMaker Pro Server, you're ready to install the software.

Troubleshooting

I'm running FileMaker Pro Server 3.0 on a PowerMac 7200, but I'm having difficulty sharing the files over our network.

Make sure you're running Open Transport 1.0.8 or higher. FileMaker Pro Server 3.0 is not compatible with earlier versions of Open Transport.

Installing FileMaker Pro Server

In FileMaker Pro Server versions 2.1 and 2.0, the Installer automatically created an alias of the FileMaker Pro Server and placed it in the Startup Items folder inside the System Folder. This "startup alias" caused FileMaker Pro Server to automatically launch every time the Macintosh was restarted.

The Installer for FileMaker Pro Server 3.0 does not create a startup alias. If you are installing FileMaker Pro Server 3.0 on a machine that had an older version of FileMaker Pro Server 2.x on it, remove the old 2.x startup alias. If you run FileMaker Pro Server 3.0 on a computer where an older version was used, the old FileMaker Pro Server Preferences file is automatically used by the new version.

Caution

If for any reason you run the older version of FileMaker Pro Server after installing the new version, the old version will reset the Preferences file back to the default values. Any preference changes you made, such as custom server name or maximum number of guests, will be lost.

To install FileMaker Pro Server 3.0, follow these steps:

1. Insert the Installation disk.

2. When the Disk 1 window appears, double-click the Installer icon (see fig. 18.3).

Fig. 18.3

Begin the installation of FileMaker Pro Server by inserting Disk 1 and double-clicking the Installer icon.

3. The splash screen opens. Click Continue to open the Install FileMaker Pro Server dialog box (see fig. 18.4).

4. Leave it set to Easy Install and click Install to start the installation process.

5. When the installation is complete, you are asked to restart your computer (see fig. 18.5). Click Restart.

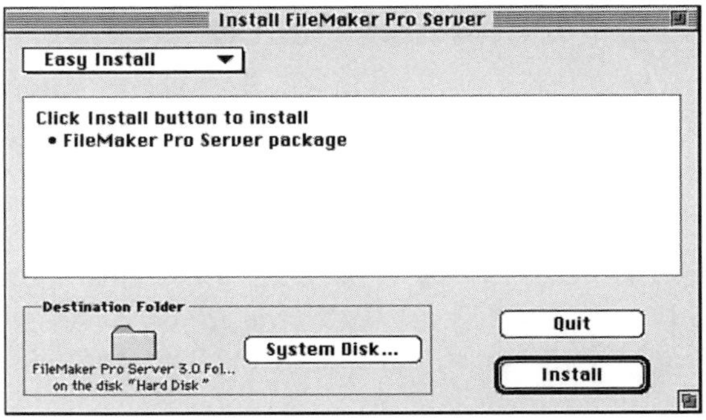

Fig. 18.4
Make sure Easy
Install is selected
and click the
Install button to
install FileMaker
Pro Server on your
hard drive.

Fig. 18.5
When the
installation is
complete, you will
be asked to restart
your computer.

Differences between FileMaker Pro Server and FileMaker

FileMaker Pro Server is very different from the regular version of FileMaker Pro. Here's a list of differences you should know about:

- The Server has no interface. When databases are open under the Server, you can't see them. In fact, the only way to tell what databases are open is to choose File, Administer to open the Administration dialog box. This means you can only host files with the Server. If you need to modify a database in any way, you have to use a regular copy of FileMaker Pro.

- When it starts up, the Server will open any databases or aliases to databases (that have been set to multi-user mode) in the same folder as the Server application, or one folder down from that level. Even if a database is elsewhere on the drive or on another drive, if the alias is in the Server folder, it will be opened.

- The Server will only open databases that have been set to multi-user mode by a regular copy of FileMaker Pro. If you have files in single-user mode in the Server's folder when it launches, the Server tells you it couldn't open the files (see fig. 18.6). You must set the databases to multi-user mode with a regular copy of FileMaker before you can open them with the Server.

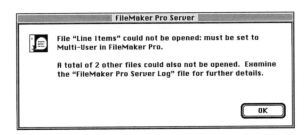

Fig. 18.6
FileMaker Pro Server displays this message if it finds any files that are not set to multi-user; it won't open single-user files because they can't be shared over the network.

- The Server can have 100 files open at a time, while the regular version of FileMaker can only have 50 files open.

- The Server can have 100 guest users at one time, while the regular version of FileMaker can only have 50 guests.

- The server can "speak" the AppleTalk, IPX, and TCP/IP protocols at the same time so it can have guests running any of those protocols. The regular version of FileMaker can only use one protocol at a time, which you select in the Preferences dialog box. When a file is shared by FileMaker, all of its guests must run the same protocol.

- The Server has a different set of supported AppleScript commands. Figures 18.7 and 18.8 show the AppleScript dictionaries for the FileMaker Pro Server and FileMaker, respectively.

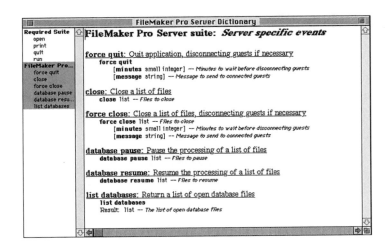

Fig. 18.7
If you use AppleScript with FileMaker Pro Server, check out the AppleScript dictionary—it's different than the regular FileMaker Pro dictionary.

Fig. 18.8
The AppleScript dictionary for the regular version of FileMaker Pro is more extensive than the dictionary for FileMaker Pro Server.

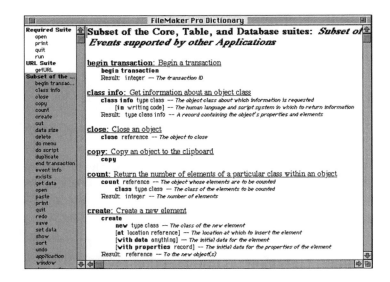

- When the Server is running, you can administer it locally by choosing File, Administer; or you can administer it remotely by using FileMaker Pro. You cannot administer regular FileMaker Pro remotely when it's sharing databases.

Administering FileMaker Pro Server

FileMaker Pro Server contains some powerful database administration functions. You can keep track of users and files on the network, disconnect guests over the network, close network files, send messages to users, monitor usage, and monitor network file operations. To access the administrative functions choose File, Administer. The FileMaker Pro Server "FMP 3.0 Server" dialog box appears (see fig. 18.9).

Fig. 18.9
FileMaker Pro Server supports many useful administrative tasks accessible from a single dialog box.

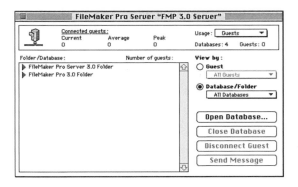

The Usage pop-up menu has seven options that read and monitor as follows:

Transactions	Transactions per second.
Network	Network kilobytes or megabytes per second.
Disk	Disk kilobytes or megabytes per second.
Cache hits	Hit percentage. This should be a high number (75 to 80 percent). If not, you should allocate more memory to FileMaker Pro Server.
Cache swaps	Cache swap percentage. This should be a low number (20 to 25 percent). If not, you should allocate more memory to FileMaker Pro Server.
Databases	Number of open databases.
Guests	Number of connected guests.

You can also switch views between Guest mode and Database mode by selecting the appropriate radio buttons. Select the Guest radio button to enable its pop-up menu. Using the Guest pop-up menu, you can list all guests who currently have databases open on the network. You can also list all databases currently open by a single guest by choosing a guest name from the pop-up menu or by double-clicking a guest name in the list. Notice that you can select the Database/Folder radio button to have FileMaker Pro Server display a Finder-like view of the folders containing open files. You can also limit this view to just one folder by choosing the folder name from the Database/Folder pop-up menu.

Using the buttons at the right of the dialog box, you can open databases, close databases, disconnect guests, and send messages to all guests.

You can get this administration view remotely by using any copy of FileMaker Pro 3.0. To enable remote administration, follow these steps:

1. Choose Edit, Preferences to open the Preferences dialog box.
2. Select the Requires Password radio button or the Requires No Password radio button. If you require a password, type the password.
3. Click OK.
4. Restart the FileMaker Pro Server.

To administer the server remotely, make sure remote administration has been enabled, then follow these steps:

1. Launch FileMaker Pro from a remote machine.
2. Select the Open an Existing File radio button and click OK.

3. Click Hosts to display the list of hosts and their shared databases.

4. Click the host name (not one of the shared databases) and click Open.

5. Type the remote administration password if one is required and click OK.

Using this process, you can open the Administration dialog box from anywhere on the network. You can open and close databases and send messages to users without even being on the server machine.

Troubleshooting

In FileMaker Pro Server 3.0, I set the maximum number of guests to 75 and the maximum number of open files to 75; however, I noticed that these numbers sometimes change by themselves to 25 guests and 50 files.

It sounds like you upgraded from an earlier version of FileMaker Pro Server. The same preferences file can be used by both applications. If you change your preferences in FileMaker Pro Server 3.0 and later launch FileMaker Pro Server 2.0 or 2.1 on the same computer, the preferences file will be reset to the original default values, causing any preferences you may have specified to be replaced.

AppleScript Examples

FileMaker Pro Server ships with six AppleScript scripts located in the AppleScript Examples folder (see fig. 18.10). You will need AppleScript 1.1 and System 7.5 to use these scripts because they require the scriptable Finder. You can modify the scripts to create your own customized solutions for use with FileMaker Pro Server.

Fig. 18.10
You can use the six AppleScript scripts that ship with FileMaker Pro Server as starting points for developing your own custom solutions.

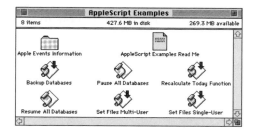

The Backup Databases script is a droplet that backs up all specified databases to the folder it resides in. The Pause All Databases script pauses all databases that FileMaker Pro Server has open and the Resume All Databases script resumes all databases that FileMaker Pro Server has open. When FileMaker Pro files are dragged onto the Set Files Multi-User droplet, it will instruct FileMaker Pro 3.0 to set the files to multi-user and then close the fields. The Set Files Single-User droplet works in a similar way to set files dropped on it to single-user. Finally, the Recalculate Today Function script closes the specified databases in FileMaker Pro Server, opens and closes them in FileMaker Pro, and opens them again in FileMaker Pro Server.

Schedules

A new feature of FileMaker Pro Server is the capability to run activities at specific times. For example, you could set up a schedule to back up your databases at predefined times. Here's how to go about it.

1. Choose Edit, Schedules to open the Schedules dialog box (see fig. 18.11).

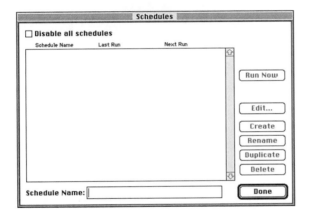

Fig. 18.11
The Schedules dialog box allows you to create, edit, rename, duplicate, delete, and run schedules.

2. In the Schedule Name text box, type **Backup** and click the Create button to open the Edit Schedule dialog box.

3. In the Edit Schedule dialog box, select the Backup to Folder radio button and click its Specify button to choose which folder you want to back up your files to.

4. Select the Run Script radio button and click its Specify button to select the AppleScript you want to run in this schedule (see fig. 18.12).

5. Click the days and times to designate the schedule run times. You can also enter the number of minutes past the hour you want the script to run (see fig. 18.13).

6. Click the OK button to close the Edit Schedule dialog box.

7. Click Done to close the Schedules dialog box.

Fig. 18.12
Click the Backup
Databases script
and click the Open
button to select
the AppleScript
you want to run in
the schedule.

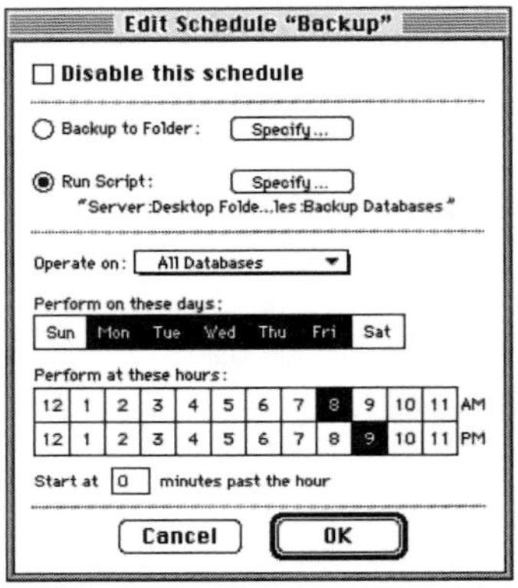

Fig. 18.13
The Edit Schedule
dialog box has
been configured to
run the Backup
Databases script
on weekdays at
8:00 am and
9:00 pm.

Log File

FileMaker Pro Server generates a log each time it is launched. The log is
actually a text file called FileMaker Pro Server Log that you can open with
SimpleText. It is located in the same folder as FileMaker Pro Server. Each time
the Server opens, it generates a new log and saves the previous log as a text
file called FileMaker Pro Server Last Log. FileMaker Pro Server time stamps
many types of activities in the log, such as Server startup and shutdown dates
and times, error messages, opening and closing of files, guest connections,
and guest messages (see fig. 18.14).

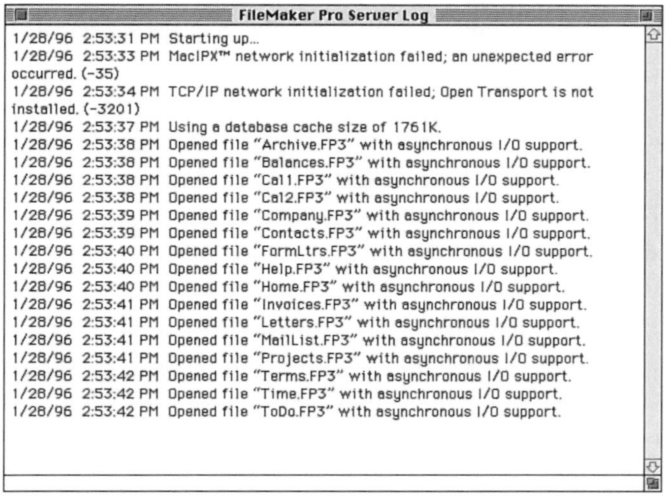

```
┌─────────────────────────────────────────────────────────────────┐
│ ▤            FileMaker Pro Server Log                         ▤   │
├─────────────────────────────────────────────────────────────────┤
│ 1/28/96  2:53:31 PM  Starting up...                          ⬆   │
│ 1/28/96  2:53:33 PM  MacIPX™ network initialization failed; an unexpected error │
│ occurred. (-35)                                                   │
│ 1/28/96  2:53:34 PM  TCP/IP network initialization failed; Open Transport is not │
│ installed. (-3201)                                                │
│ 1/28/96  2:53:37 PM  Using a database cache size of 1761K.       │
│ 1/28/96  2:53:38 PM  Opened file "Archive.FP3" with asynchronous I/O support.  │
│ 1/28/96  2:53:38 PM  Opened file "Balances.FP3" with asynchronous I/O support. │
│ 1/28/96  2:53:38 PM  Opened file "Cal1.FP3" with asynchronous I/O support.     │
│ 1/28/96  2:53:38 PM  Opened file "Cal2.FP3" with asynchronous I/O support.     │
│ 1/28/96  2:53:39 PM  Opened file "Company.FP3" with asynchronous I/O support.  │
│ 1/28/96  2:53:39 PM  Opened file "Contacts.FP3" with asynchronous I/O support. │
│ 1/28/96  2:53:40 PM  Opened file "FormLtrs.FP3" with asynchronous I/O support. │
│ 1/28/96  2:53:40 PM  Opened file "Help.FP3" with asynchronous I/O support.     │
│ 1/28/96  2:53:40 PM  Opened file "Home.FP3" with asynchronous I/O support.     │
│ 1/28/96  2:53:41 PM  Opened file "Invoices.FP3" with asynchronous I/O support. │
│ 1/28/96  2:53:41 PM  Opened file "Letters.FP3" with asynchronous I/O support.  │
│ 1/28/96  2:53:41 PM  Opened file "MailList.FP3" with asynchronous I/O support. │
│ 1/28/96  2:53:41 PM  Opened file "Projects.FP3" with asynchronous I/O support. │
│ 1/28/96  2:53:42 PM  Opened file "Terms.FP3" with asynchronous I/O support.    │
│ 1/28/96  2:53:42 PM  Opened file "Time.FP3" with asynchronous I/O support.     │
│ 1/28/96  2:53:42 PM  Opened file "ToDo.FP3" with asynchronous I/O support.     │
│                                                              ⬇   │
└─────────────────────────────────────────────────────────────────┘
```

Fig. 18.14
You can see when FileMaker Pro Server started up, errors that occurred, the database cache size, and the names of all files that were opened. Each entry is date and time stamped.

Creating a Startup Script for Served Databases

If you are a guest of a shared database that has relationships to other databases, those other databases will open automatically after you open the first database. When you have a database system that spans several databases and you don't have relationships between all files, it can be time consuming to use the host button repeatedly to open all of the files.

One solution to this problem is to create a *startup* database, a database with no fields that has a startup script that opens the shared databases you need then closes itself. You can build the startup database quickly and distribute it to your end users. They can put it in their Apple menu and run it as a launching utility.

To build a startup database, follow these steps:

1. Make sure all of the databases in your system are open under the FileMaker Pro Server. You can open them all at once by putting them in the FileMaker Pro Server folder and launching the Server, or by selecting and dragging them onto the Server icon.

2. From a remote machine, launch FileMaker Pro.

3. Select the Create a New Empty File radio button and click OK.

4. Type **Startup** in the Create a New File Named text box and click Save.

5. Click Done to close the Define Fields dialog box without creating any fields.

6. Choose Script, ScriptMaker to open the Define Scripts dialog box.

7. Type the script name **Open All** and click Create to open the Script Definition dialog box.

8. Click Clear All to clear the default script steps.

9. Scroll through the Available Steps list and double-click the Open script step to move it to the list on the right.

10. Click Specify File to open the Open dialog box.

11. Click Hosts to open the Hosts dialog box. If your databases are shared on a network with multiple zones, select the zone your server is located in. Your host machine and a list of the open databases appears in the top of the dialog box. Select your first database and click Open.

12. Repeat steps 9 through 11 for each database you need to connect to.

13. Scroll through the Available Steps list and double-click the Close script step to move it to the list on the right. Leave it unspecified.

14. Click OK to close the Script Definition dialog box.

15. Click Done to close the Define Scripts dialog box.

16. Choose Edit, Preferences to open the Preferences dialog box.

17. Choose Document from the pop-up at the top of the dialog box.

18. Select the Perform Script check box in the When Opening "Startup" area. Choose Open All from that Perform Script pop-up menu. The Preferences dialog box should look similar to figure 18.15.

Fig. 18.15
Using the Preferences dialog box, you can perform a startup script that opens all the files you need.

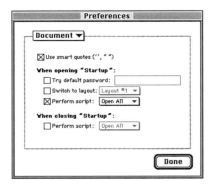

19. Click Done to close the Preferences dialog box.

To test your Startup database, quit FileMaker Pro, then double-click the Startup database. It should launch FileMaker, open all of the networked databases, then close itself, leaving the networked databases open.

From Here...

In this chapter, you learned about the factors that affect performance for the FileMaker Pro Server. You learned how to install the application and how to administer it locally and remotely. Also, some of the differences in functionality between FileMaker Pro Server and FileMaker Pro were discussed.

From here, you might want to look at the following chapters:

- In Chapter 15, "Scripting with ScriptMaker," you learn about the advanced scripting features of FileMaker Pro and the conditional scripting capability of the product, which allow you to better control your scripts.
- Chapter 17, "Networking Issues," describes more about networking, which has a large impact on the smooth operation of FileMaker Pro Server.

CHAPTER 19

Using the Solutions Development Kit

It is important to note that as of the writing of this book the current version of FileMaker Pro Solutions Development Kit (SDK) was 2.1v1. Claris is planning to release FileMaker Pro SDK 3.0 in March 1996, about three months after the release of FileMaker Pro 3.0. Remember that FileMaker Pro SDK 3.0 will have all the features of FileMaker Pro version 3.0 with the added capability of being able to bind files.

Topics covered in this chapter include:

- What to consider before you bind
- Setting up password protection
- Creating splash screens
- How to bind primary and auxiliary files
- Running, updating, and distributing your solution

What Is the SDK?

The FileMaker Pro Solutions Development Kit helps members of the Claris Solutions Alliance to distribute their FileMaker Pro solutions commercially. Using the SDK, you can create unlimited, royalty-free, runtime versions of FileMaker Pro databases for both the Macintosh and Windows environments. The SDK also provides a mechanism that protects the developer's solution by preventing others from modifying layouts, scripts, and field definitions.

The SDK is made up of two components: the FileMaker Pro SDK application and the FileMaker Pro User application. The FileMaker Pro SDK application is simply a modified version of FileMaker Pro 2.1v3. An extra menu item is added to the menu bar and, using the commands in this menu, you can bind or attach your own database solution to a copy of FileMaker Pro User. The FileMaker Pro User application is a scaled-down version of FileMaker Pro that only opens files you choose to bind to it. Think of the SDK application as the glue you use to attach your database files to the FileMaker Pro User runtime engine.

What's on the CD-ROM?

The CD-ROM contains over 300 files totaling approximately 14.9M in size. How you view the CD-ROM depends on whether you are using a Macintosh or Windows computer. This has been written from the perspective of a Macintosh user.

The root level of the CD-ROM contains the three folders shown in figure 19.1.

Fig. 19.1
This window has three folders that contain files for both Macintosh and Windows platforms.

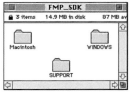

Opening the Macintosh folder reveals two additional folders. The first one, FileMaker Pro SDK, contains the installation files for the SDK application it-self. You can find the installation files in two folders: Install 1 and Install 2. These folders contain help files, networking files, Apple Event examples, Claris Translators, the Claris XTND System, example templates, tutorial files, spelling dictionaries, and the SDK application itself. In fact, most of the files mentioned here are also part of the regular FileMaker Pro installation. The second folder, labeled FileMaker User, contains its installation files, which are comprised of networking files, Claris Translators, the Claris XTND System, spelling dictionaries, and the FileMaker Pro User application. Note that there are no help files, example templates, or tutorial files. There is good reason for this, as you'll see later in the chapter.

If you are a Windows user, you will find that the second folder (or directory) containing the Windows files are organized in the same fashion, an SDK directory and a User directory. While the files provided for both platforms are of course different, they achieve the same purpose. Additional filter and support files are provided for the Windows platform.

The third folder, Support, contains valuable support files for FileMaker developers (see fig. 19.2). It includes the following:

- AppleScript 1.1 (for Macintosh users only)
- Script Editor (for Macintosh users only)
- AppleScript examples (for Macintosh users only)
- Q & A Translator
- A sample Help database
- A sample splash screen
- FileMaker databases containing cross platform buttons and backgrounds
- Helpful information on developing cross platform solutions

Fig. 19.2
Macintosh developers should check out the Macintosh Support and X-PLAT folders; they contain many helpful resources including database examples, sample dialogs, help files, and buttons.

You'll find the information and examples in these files very helpful. For faster access, copy the support files applicable for your platform to your hard disk. Macintosh users should copy the Macintosh Support (2M) and X_PLAT (3.9M) folders.

Installing FileMaker Pro SDK for Macintosh

If you installed FileMaker Pro before, you will find the installation of the SDK to be very similar. Turn off any virus protection software and disable any extensions you have running before installation. You must also quit any open applications or you will get a message from the Installer asking you to do so.

There are two types of installs you can do:

1. Choose the Easy installation if you use AppleTalk file sharing and want to install all files and folders in their preferred locations.

2. Choose the Custom installation if you want to:

   - Selectively pick the files you want to install. For example, you might not want to install the tutorial files.
   - Install only the FileMaker Pro SDK application.
   - Install support files for the MacIPX networking protocol.

To install using the Easy option, open the Macintosh and FileMaker SDK folders, double-click the Installer icon, and follow the prompts.

The installer displays the names of the files as it installs them. Some files are automatically uncompressed by the installer; you'll see messages appear to this effect. A dialog box appears when the installer is done.

If you turned off any extensions, turn them back on and restart your computer. During the installation, the Installer creates a Claris folder inside your System Folder and puts the necessary files inside it. If you already have a Claris folder, the Installer prompts you to replace any duplicate files.

To install the Custom installation, click the Customize button and select items from the dialog box that appears. Click Install.

During a custom installation, the Installer puts all the files inside a folder called FileMaker Pro SDK 2.1 Folder. It is up to you to move these files to their correct locations.

If you installed the MacIPX files, move them to the locations as shown in the following table.

File Name	Move to This Location
MacIPX	Control Panels folder
MacIPX AppleTalk	Extensions folder
MacIPX Token Ring	Extensions folder
MacIPX Ethernet	Extensions folder
FileMaker Network	Claris folder

Caution

If you're upgrading from an older version of MacIPX, make sure you remove the old MacIPX file from your Control Panels folder and delete it.

Preparing to Bind

Now that you have successfully installed FileMaker Pro SDK, you're probably champing at the bit to bind your solution. Before you rush ahead, there are some things to consider and some work to do before your solution is ready for binding.

While you can always make changes after binding your solution, you might save yourself some time and frustration by first considering the issues raised in this section. You should also be aware that FileMaker Pro User is a scaled-down version of the regular FileMaker Pro. Some of the menu commands have been disabled. Claris also removed the FileMaker Pro splash screen and help system—it's your responsibility to provide your own. It's also your responsibility to provide technical support for your solution.

Choosing a Primary File

You must choose a primary file before you can bind a file to FileMaker Pro User. In situations where you have only one database file, picking the primary file is straightforward. However, some developer solutions can consist of many databases. In these cases, your primary file should be the central file of your entire solution. Think of the primary file as the hub of a wheel containing buttons and scripts (spokes) that are attached to the auxiliary files (the rim). You can use the primary file for many purposes: to open other files that are part of the solution, to store your customized splash screen, to run custom scripts to import data from other files, or to store information that could be accessed from other databases in the solution.

Tip

Provide a preferences layout in the primary file so your end-user can enter constant information (such as name, address, and phone numbers). This data can then be used in other databases; for example, you could use this method to create report headers that end-users could update at any time and without your assistance.

Selecting Single-User or Multi-User Access

If your solution is going to be shared over a network, you must set the file to Multi-User access before you bind the primary file. To do this, choose File, Single-User. This toggles the file from Single-User access to Multi-User access (see fig. 19.3).

Fig. 19.3

You can change the file access from Single-User to Multi-User by choosing the Single-User command from the File menu.

If all the files in your solution are to be shared, then each file must be set to Multi-User access. You must also ensure that the correct network support files are installed in their proper folders on each of the computers running your solution. After you bind a solution, you cannot change the file access from Single-User to Multi-User without rebinding the solution.

Cross-Platform Issues

If you are planning to run your solution on Macintosh and Windows platforms, all the things you need to consider for the regular version of FileMaker Pro should also be considered for the SDK. If you are running on Windows 3.x, your file name must conform to DOS naming conventions (eight characters followed by a period and extension). FileMaker Pro 2.x files should end with the FM extension and FileMaker Pro 3.0 files should end with the FP3 extension. If you are planning to run on Windows 95, your file name can be the same on both platforms but the extension should be FP3. Other considerations include fonts, layout size, use of color, printing, and character sets. These issues and some cross-platform tips are discussed in a file called XPLATHLP.FM located in the X_PLAT folder on the SDK CD-ROM.

> **Tip**
>
> While you can bind more than 16 files in a solution, FileMaker Pro User can only open 16 at one time.

Opening Auxiliary Files

Claris disabled the Open and Close menu items in FileMaker Pro User so your end-users have no way to open auxiliary files. You must provide scripts and buttons in your solution to do that.

It's good practice to open all your files in a startup script and provide buttons in a central database that performs this function. In all of my commercial solutions, I use a primary file and usually name it HOME.FM. This is the central database from where all others are accessed via buttons by the end-user. Figure 19.4 shows the HOME.FM menu layout from one of those solutions. Clicking any of the buttons opens the corresponding file. Although lookup files open automatically when they are needed, it's good practice to open all your files from a central database when the solution is started. This is important if you're running the solution on a server because you usually want the server to be the host and not another computer on the network. Remember that the first computer that opens the files acts as the host for those files.

> **Tip**
>
> If your solution requires multi-user access, this is an excellent layout in which to place your company logo. This layout will probably be displayed all day for all to see if your solution runs on a server. Free advertising is good.

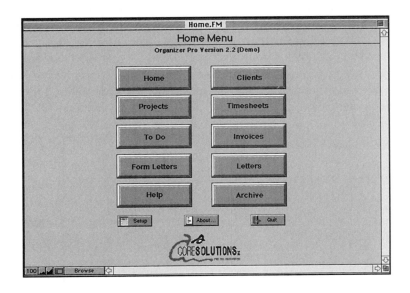

Fig. 19.4
This is the main menu of a typical primary file.

Planning for Updates

When you update your solution files, you must decide how you will provide the update to end-users. One solution is to develop scripts to allow the end-user to easily export data from the old database to the revised database. The primary file is the perfect location to store these housekeeping scripts.

Printing Issues

With such a variety of printers available, it's nearly impossible to design layouts that will always print correctly on every printer. Remember, the end-user will be unable to make revisions to your layouts after you bind your solution. Design layouts for the most popular printers—you cover most of the bases. It's also nearly impossible to design a layout that will suit every customer's letterhead. Offer your end-users some level of customization at a reasonable cost. You might even want to build this into the cost of your solution.

Updating Value Lists

◀ See "Creating Value Lists," p. 146

In previous versions of FileMaker Pro, the capability to update value lists was not possible. After you bound a database, there was no way for the end-user to update value lists. This problem has been solved in version 3.0; the end-user can now update value lists.

Password Protection

You have made a considerable investment in the research and development of your solution. However, if you don't password protect your files, anyone with a regular version of FileMaker Pro can open your database and access the scripts, layouts, and field definitions. If you make a living as a FileMaker developer, protect your investment by password protecting your files. Set up a master password that gives you full access to your database. Figure 19.5 shows that the master password "ocean" gives access to the entire file.

Fig. 19.5
Set up a master password by selecting the Access the Entire File check box, which selects all the other check boxes. You must then enter your password in the Password text box.

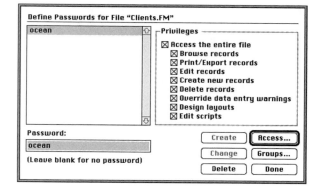

When you open a database with FileMaker Pro User, there is a way you can choose not to display the Define Passwords for File dialog box to the end-user. You select this option during the binding process. When the database opens, the user is not asked to enter any password—the database simply opens. In addition to a master password, you should set up a no-password entry so your users don't have to enter a password when the file opens.

Here's how to set up no-password entry:

1. Choose File, Access Privileges, Define Passwords.

The Define Passwords for File dialog box appears.

2. Leave the Password text box empty.

3. Deselect the Design Layouts check box.

This stops the end-user from going to Layout mode when the file is opened with a regular version of FileMaker Pro.

4. Deselect the Edit Scripts check box.

This disables the Scripts menu when the file is opened with a regular version of FileMaker Pro.

5. Click the Create button.

The words (no password) are entered in the dialog box (see fig. 19.6).

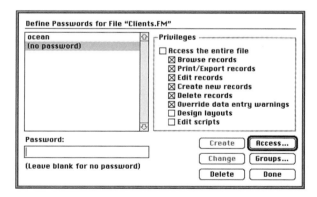

Fig. 19.6
You can set up a no-entry password by leaving the Password text box empty and clicking the Create button.

6. Click Done to close the Define Passwords for File dialog box. A confirmation dialog box appears (see fig. 19.7). Enter a password that allows you to access the entire file before you can close the file.

Fig. 19.7
FileMaker asks you
to enter a master
password.

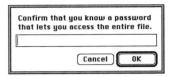

When a database with a no-password entry is opened in the regular version of FileMaker Pro, you are asked to enter a password. You can disable this request with FileMaker Pro User. The next section describes how to do this.

> **Tip**
>
> Set up the same password scheme for every file in your solution. By doing this, auxiliary files can be opened without having to type additional passwords.

Creating a Splash Screen

Claris removed the familiar FileMaker Pro splash screen from FileMaker Pro User. Consequently, the responsibility to provide one falls to you. However, it is easy for you to create your own splash screen. On the SDK CD-ROM, Claris provided a sample splash screen that you can copy and paste into your own solution. Here's how you do it:

1. If you haven't already copied the support files from the SDK CD-ROM to your hard drive, do so now.

   If you are low on hard disk space, do the following. On the SDK CD-ROM, open the Support folder then open the X_PLAT folder. Inside the X_PLAT folder, you will find a FileMaker file called SDK_MAIN.FM. Copy only this file to your hard disk.

2. Open the file SDK_MAIN.FM. A sample splash screen appears (see fig. 19.8).

3. Select the entire layout and copy it. Enter Layout mode and choose Edit, Select All. Choose Edit, Copy.

4. Open your primary file. This will be the main file in your solution from where all other files get opened.

5. Create a new blank layout and paste the sample splash screen into the blank layout. Call the layout Splash Screen.

Fig. 19.8
You can use this sample splash screen provided by Claris as a model for creating your own splash screen.

6. Now replace components of the sample splash screen with your own information. For example, change Solution Name to the name of your own solution, replace the logo place holder with your own logo. Also, include your company name, address, phone numbers, fax number, online addresses, and technical support information so users can contact you for technical support.

7. Each time your database is opened, you want to ensure that the splash screen displays. There are two ways to do this. The first is to write a script that displays the splash screen each time the database is opened. The second is to choose File, Preferences, click Document to set the document preferences, select the Switch to Layout check box, then select Splash Screen from the Layout pop-up menu.

Figure 19.9 shows the customized splash screen for a commercial solution.

Fig. 19.9
This is a commercial splash screen that contains helpful contact information for the end-user. This example also contains a copyright notice and an ISBN number.

Adding Customized Help

Claris removed the FileMaker Pro Help application from FileMaker Pro User. This had to be done because many of the menu commands and features of the regular FileMaker Pro just don't exist in FileMaker Pro User. Again, it's your responsibility to provide a help system. You should provide help on the functionality of your own solution and on all of the FileMaker Pro User commands and features. Remember that the end-user isn't purchasing FileMaker Pro and therefore has no manual. All of the basic features you take for granted must be explained to the new user. On the SDK CD-ROM, Claris provided a sample help database you can modify to suit your own solution. Here's how you go about it.

1. Find the SDK_HELP.FM file on the CD-ROM in the X_PLAT folder.
2. Open SDK_HELP.FM. A sample help database appears (see fig. 19.10).

Fig. 19.10
You can use this sample help database provided by Claris as a model for developing your own help systems.

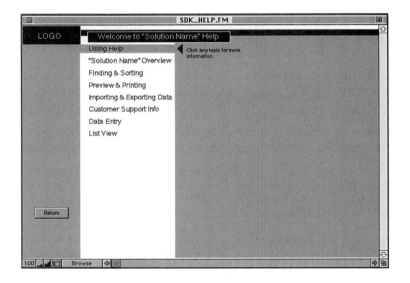

3. Enter Layout mode.
4. Edit the topic name on the left and revise the help information on the right as necessary. Each topic has its own layout; you will have to go to each layout and revise as necessary. You will also have to add new layouts specific to your solution.
5. Add or modify buttons and scripts to integrate the help database into your own solution.

Figure 19.11 shows the customized help database for Organizer Pro.

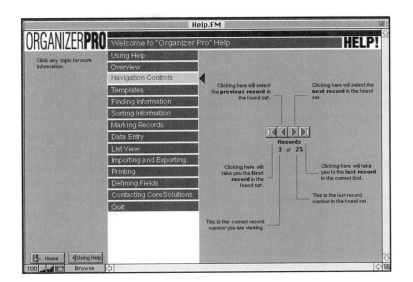

Fig. 19.11
This is the help
system for a
commercial
solution. It was
created by the
developer from the
model provided by
Claris.

Binding Your Solution

When you first launch FileMaker Pro SDK, it looks remarkably similar to the
regular version of FileMaker Pro. In fact, the only differences are the splash
screen and the addition of a new menu item. Have a look at the menu bar
and you'll see that to the right of the Window menu there is now a new
menu called SDK. Examining the SDK menu reveals only two menu items:
Bind Primary File and Add Files. These are the commands you use to create
your runtime solution. I'll explain the process, then I'll give you the steps
involved.

After launching the FileMaker Pro SDK application, choose SDK, Bind Primary
File. You are asked to provide a unique key that will bind the Primary file
to a FileMaker Pro User application. After entering the key, you are then
prompted to locate the FileMaker Pro User application and the primary file.
During this process, the SDK application embeds the key you specified into
the file structure of both the FileMaker Pro User application and the primary
file. It also embeds the name of the primary file into the file structure of the
FileMaker Pro User application. When you launch the FileMaker Pro User application, it knows what file to look for. Before opening the file, it checks the
keys to make sure they match and, if they don't, it doesn't open the primary
file. You can then add other files (auxiliary files) to the solution by choosing
SDK, Add Files. When asked, provide the same key code you did earlier, and
locate and select each auxiliary file you want to "stamp" with the key code.
This links all the database files into one solution.

Follow these steps to bind the primary file:

1. Launch FileMaker Pro SDK if it is not already running.

2. Choose SDK, Bind Primary File.

3. Enter a unique identification key between 6 and 31 characters in the dialog box that appears (see fig. 19.12). In the figure, I entered masterkey as the unique key. Click the OK button.

Fig. 19.12
Enter a unique binding key.

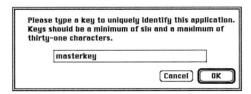

4. Now you have to locate the FileMaker Pro User application (see fig. 19.13). Navigate to the location of the FileMaker Pro User application on your own hard disk. Click the application name then click the Select button.

Fig. 19.13
When the FileMaker Pro User application is selected, the unique key is attached to the application.

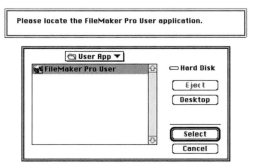

5. You are then prompted to locate the primary file for this application (see fig. 19.14). In the figure, the primary file is called HOME.FM. Locate the primary file on your hard disk and click it. Select the Do Not Ask User for Password When Opened check box (the Password dialog box won't display when the primary file is opened by FileMaker Pro User). Click the Select button.

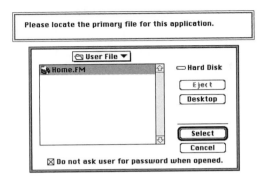

Fig. 19.14
Selecting the primary file binds it to the FileMaker Pro User application with the unique key.

6. The SDK application then confirms the binding (see fig. 19.15). Click OK to continue.

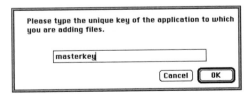

Fig. 19.15
If all works well, a dialog box confirms that the primary file was bound to the FileMaker Pro User application. The unique key used to bind the files is also displayed here.

If your solution contains only one file, then you're finished. But most solutions contain multiple files and they must also be bound to the FileMaker Pro User application. These additional files are sometimes referred to as auxiliary files. Follow these steps to add them to your solution.

1. Choose SDK, Add Files.

2. Enter the same unique key you entered when you bound the primary file to FileMaker Pro User (see fig. 19.16).

Fig. 19.16
Make sure the unique key is spelled exactly the same as the key you entered for the primary file.

3. Now locate additional files for this application (see fig. 19.17). Locate the additional files on your hard disk, click a file to highlight it, then click the Add button. Repeat this sequence for each file you want to add to the solution.

Fig. 19.17
Each auxiliary file must be highlighted and added to the solution by clicking the Add button.

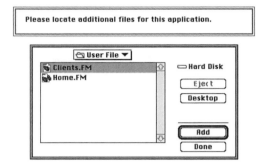

4. Click the Done button.

That's it. You successfully created a bound solution.

Tip

Instead of using the mouse, it's faster to highlight the auxiliary file names using the direction arrows on your keyboard and pressing Return instead of clicking the Add button.

Running Your Solution

It's time to see the result of all the work you've done. To run your solution, double-click the bound FileMaker Pro User application. Your primary file will open and your splash screen will appear (if you created one).

Tip

You can change the name of the FileMaker Pro User application to the name of your solution. You can do this after the binding is complete, but not before.

Troubleshooting

I want to share my Contacts database over the network with another user. I use FileMaker Pro User and my colleague uses the regular version of FileMaker Pro. I copied an alias of my Contacts database to his computer, but every time he launches it the alias opens a different FileMaker Pro User application on his computer.

The problem resides in the creator type assigned to the Contacts database. When you bind a database to FileMaker Pro User, the creator type is changed from FMPR (the creator type for the regular version of FileMaker Pro) to FMPU (the creator type for FileMaker Pro User). When your colleague launches the alias from his computer, the Macintosh system looks for an application on his hard drive that matches the creator type. It could find another FileMaker Pro User application that resides on his computer.

There are a couple of ways to solve this problem. First, give your colleague a copy of the FileMaker Pro User application that is bound to your Contacts file. When he opens it on his computer, it will look for the Contacts database over the network and open it. Your colleague can still use his regular version of FileMaker to open the file if he wants. Ask him to choose File, Open and then click the Network button. The Network Access dialog box appears and he can open the file from there.

Now take a look at some of the differences between FileMaker Pro User and the regular version of FileMaker.

The most visible change is that your database windows have no Close boxes. The Open and Close commands have been removed from the File menu. There's no way for an end-user to close your database or open another one. You must control this (through scripting) and you must provide buttons to perform the appropriate commands.

The menu items in the following table have been changed, removed, or behave differently.

Menu Items	Means...
File Menu	
New	New databases cannot be created.
Preferences	After choosing this menu item, you'll notice that the document preferences cannot be changed.
Multi-/Single-User	After you bind a file, networking access cannot be modified.

(continues)

(continued)

Menu Items	Means...
File Menu	
Recover	There is no recover menu item in the File menu.
Quitting	You see a dialog box every time you quit FileMaker Pro User. Unfortunately, there is no way to prevent this friendly and constant reminder from Claris.
Select Menu	
Layout	End-users cannot make any revisions to your layouts or create new ones.
Define Fields	End-users cannot revise or create field definitions.
Format Menu	
Align Text	End-users can only change the font, font size, font style, and color. All other menu items have been removed from the Format menu.

> **Note**
>
> The entire Scripts menu has been removed. End-users cannot create or edit scripts.

Updating Your Solution

If you add new features, make modifications to your solution, or add additional files, you need a way to update your solution and make it easy for your end-users to add their data to the new solution.

To update the primary file, follow these steps:

1. Open the primary file with FileMaker Pro SDK.

2. Make your changes.

    As long as you don't change the key or the file name, you don't need to rebind the file.

3. Save the primary file as a clone and send it to your end-user.

4. Develop a script to import all the data from the user's old file into the new clone and document this process for the end-user.

To update or add new auxiliary files, follow these steps:

1. Open the auxiliary file with FileMaker Pro SDK and make your changes.

2. Close the file.

3. Choose SDK, Add Files and enter the original key code used to bind the primary file. Click OK.

4. Locate and add the new or updated files.

5. When you're finished adding files, click Done.

Troubleshooting

After binding my solution, I made some revisions to an auxiliary file called Invoices, added the file to the solution again, and now I get a message saying The application FileMaker Pro User is unable to open the file 'Invoices'.

There are a couple of things you need to check. First, make sure you haven't re-named the Invoices file to something else. It's also possible that you entered the wrong key when you added the Invoices file again. When adding auxiliary files, the SDK will let you enter a different key than the original key that was used. You don't encounter an error until the FileMaker Pro User tries to open the file and realizes the key is different. To correct the problem, add the auxiliary files using the original key you used to bind the primary file to FileMaker Pro User. Remember that the key is case-sensitive; a change in case when adding auxiliary files will cause the same error.

This error can also appear if you open the solution by double-clicking the primary file and you have more than one FileMaker Pro User on your hard drive. What can hap-pen is that the wrong FileMaker Pro User application gets opened and the auxiliary files won't open because the application running has a different key. To solve the problem, remove the extra FileMaker Pro User from your hard drive.

Installing Your Solution

You might find this to be more time consuming than you originally plan. The ultimate goal here is to make the installation as easy as possible for the user and reduce the number of errors that can occur. You have two choices:

- Use the Claris Installer provided on the SDK CD-ROM to install the FileMaker Pro User application and all its associated files. You also need to find a way to install your own solution files.

- Create a custom installation using a third-party installer program.

Using the Claris Installer

The Claris Installer automatically installs the FileMaker Pro User application and all support files including networking options, translators, dictionaries, and so on in their preferred locations. For example, on a Macintosh, the

Claris Translators and Networking files are installed inside the Claris folder located inside the System Folder. If these files already exist from a previous installation of some other Claris program, the Installer detects this and offers the end-user the options to either replace or skip the duplicate files. So, using the Claris Installer does offer some advantages. Bind your solution as previously discussed and follow these steps;

1. Get three 1.4M disks and name them Disk1, Disk2, and Disk3.

2. From the SDK CD-ROM, copy the contents of the FileMaker Pro User Disk1 folder to the Disk1 disk.

3. Copy the bound FileMaker Pro User application to Disk2.

> **Caution**
>
> Do not rename it first. During the install process, the Claris Installer program looks for the FileMaker Pro User file. If you change its name, the Installer won't find it and the install will fail.

4. Copy all your solution files to Disk3.

> **Note**
>
> On a network, the solution files need to be installed on the computer that acts as the host only once. Use the Claris Installer to install the bound FileMaker Pro User application and support files on all other computers. Solutions can be run cross-platform by distributing separate FileMaker Pro User applications that were bound on their respective platforms. Your solution files only need to be installed in one location.

While the Claris Installer does an excellent job of installing the FileMaker Pro User and support files, it does not install your solution files. Here are some things you might want to consider before you select this option:

■ If you use the Claris Installer, you will have to distribute three disks. Disk 1 and Disk 2 will contain the FileMaker Pro User application and support files and Disk 3 your own solution files.

■ You will have to document the installation instructions for your end-user.

- Users will need to use a combination of the Claris Installer and manual copying of your solution files to perform a complete installation.

- When all files have been installed, the user must copy the FileMaker Pro User application to the same folder as the solution files. Otherwise, the FileMaker Pro User application might not be able to find your primary file. All solution files should reside in the same folder.

- You might also want the user to rename the FileMaker Pro User application to the name of your solution.

- There might be too many steps involved for your end-users and therefore potential for error.

Using a Custom Installation

From experience, I recommend using a custom installation. Some of the reasons are as follows:

- You can reduce the installation process to a click of the mouse.

- You can control where each file gets installed.

- You can get to installation help in the installer splash screen (see fig. 19.18).

- You will reduce the number of disks required to distribute your solution.

- You will make life easier for your end-user.

- It's a more professional and efficient way for distributing demos of your templates.

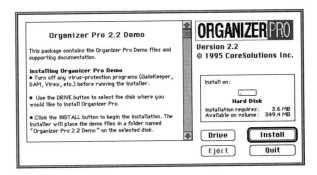

Fig. 19.18
This commercial template uses Smaller Installer to install its solution files. Use a third-party installer to simplify the installation process for the end-user.

The following is a list of third-party installation programs:

- Apple Installer by Apple Computer, Inc.
  Telephone: (408) 974-4667
  AppleLink: **SW.LICENSE**

- DeveloperVISE by MindVision Software
  P.O. Box 81886
  Lincoln, Nebraska, 68501
  Telephone: (402) 477-3269
  Fax: (402) 477-1395
  AOL, AppleLink: **MindVision**
  CompuServe: **70253,143**
  Internet: **http://www.mindvision.com/**

- DragInstall by Ray Sauers Associates
  1187 Main Avenue, Suite 1B
  Clifton, New Jersey, 07011
  Telephone: (201) 478-1970
  AOL: **Sauers**
  CompuServe: **70731,2326**
  AppleLink: **D1922**

- ScriptGen Pro and InstallerPack by StepUp Software
  710 Glendora Avenue
  Dallas, Texas 75230-5428
  Telephone: (214) 360-9301
  Fax: (214) 360-0127
  AppleLink: **StepUp**
  AOL: **StepUp1**
  CompuServe: **73607,3630**

- Script-Ease by Glen Canyon Software
  921 Shasta View
  Eugene, OR. 97405
  Telephone: (800) 477-6947 or (503) 345-6360
  AppleLink: **GlenCanyon**

- Smaller Installer by Cyclos
  P.O. Box 31417
  San Francisco, CA 94131-0417
  Telephone: (415) 821-1448
  AppleLink: **CYCLOS**
  CompuServe: **71101,204**
  Internet: **http://www.cyclos.com/**

- Stuffit InstallerMaker by Aladdin Systems
  165 Westridge Drive
  Watsonville, CA 95076
  Telephone: (408) 761-6200
  Fax: (408) 761-6206
  AOL, AppleLink: **Aladdin**
  CompuServe: **75300,1666**

A review on all of these installers is available in the form of a TechInfo from Claris. It's called "Guide to Software Installers," TechInfo No. JOAGU9426234942. The TechInfo database is available at the Claris Web site at **http://www.claris.com**.

From Here...

This chapter covered how to create commercial quality, runtime solutions using the Solutions Development Kit, including how to install FileMaker Pro SDK, the issues to be considered, and how to run the binding process. You now have the tools and skills required to create stand-alone solutions, with a professional looking splash screen and integrated help system. If you're a professional FileMaker developer, you'll appreciate this powerful tool set.

If you need more help with scripting, read the following chapters:

- Chapter 15, "Scripting with ScriptMaker," describes the advanced scripting features of FileMaker Pro and the conditional scripting capability of the product, which you can use to take better control of your scripts.

- Chapter 16, "Using AppleScript," shows how to install AppleScript and how to use the Script Editor to create and test scripts. You also learn how to embed those scripts into FileMaker's ScriptMaker.

VII

Integrating FileMaker Pro

CHAPTER 20

Using FileMaker Pro with Excel

This chapter covers the steps involved in making FileMaker Pro share data with other applications. One consideration with using multiple applications like this is to make sure you have enough memory (RAM) to run both FileMaker and the other application at the same time.

This chapter covers the following topics:

■ Exporting summarized data to Excel

■ Creating charts from FileMaker data in Excel

■ Placing exported charts in FileMaker

Charting FileMaker Data in Microsoft Excel

One shortcoming of FileMaker Pro is that it cannot gracefully chart its own data. Especially when you're summarizing data, it is helpful to have a charted representation of summarized report results. If you have a database with a report layout that looks similar to figure 20.1, you can create a simple script in FileMaker that calls a macro in Excel to chart your data and copy it to the Clipboard so you can paste it back in FileMaker. (Try saying *that* ten times fast.)

Fig. 20.1

Here's a simple report you can create in FileMaker, showing a listing of customers by city.

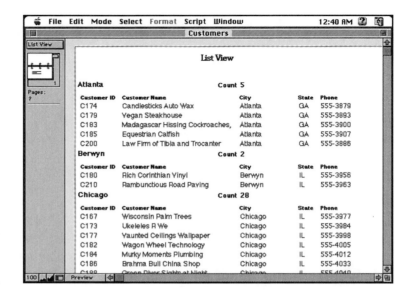

Just to make it a little more interesting, say you want to rank the cities by the number of customers in a city. In fact, all you really care about are your top five customer concentrations. You want a report that shows only your top five cities and also has a chart comparing all five cities, as shown in figure 20.2.

Fig. 20.2

Create a report showing the top five cities where you have customers, and display an embedded chart.

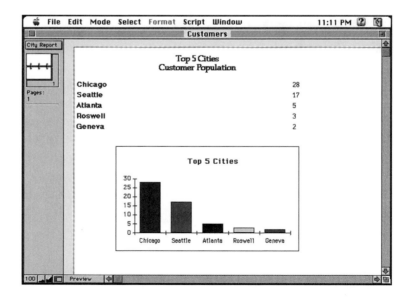

One of the skills you'll pick up along the way is how to create calculation fields that behave like summary fields in FileMaker. It's included in this chapter because it's typical of the kind of manipulation you'll need to have in your arsenal when you're preparing data for export to other programs.

Exporting Summarized Data to Excel

This is a long process, but the end result is worth it. You need to do a summarized export to get the data to Excel. A summarized export requires a summary field, so this process will start with the creation of the summary field. If you already have a summary field, skip that series of steps.

After you get a chart created in Excel, you need to copy it to the Clipboard, return to FileMaker Pro, paste it into a global picture field, and then preview the report. For the picture to show up properly, you need to have the container field on a trailing grand summary or footer part.

To create a top five subsummary report with an Excel chart, follow these steps:

1. In your report database, choose File, Define Fields to open the Define Fields dialog box.

2. Create a new summary field called Count. Click the Summary button to designate it as a summary field. In the Options for Summary Field dialog box, specify it as a count of the field you're using in your subsummary (see fig. 20.3). In this case, you're grouping by City.

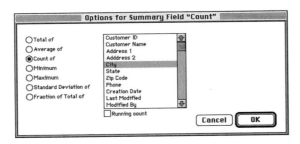

Fig. 20.3
When creating a summary field, you must decide what function to calculate and which detail field to summarize.

3. Click OK to close the Options for Summary Field dialog box.

4. Create a new calculation field called Count Calc. This field will contain the same values as Count, but you won't have to enter the Preview mode to get the values. Also, because it's a calculation field, you can perform finds on the field. In the Specify Calculation dialog box, choose Aggregate Functions from the Functions pop-up menu. You can see that these Aggregate Functions resemble the Summary functions shown in figure 20.3.

5. Double-click the Count function so it appears in the calculation area.

6. Choose Define Relationships from the pop-up above the field listing. The Define Relationships dialog box appears.

7. Click New to open the Open dialog.

8. Select the database you're currently working in and click Open. The Edit Relationship dialog box appears.

> **Tip**
>
> You're about to have the database create a relationship with itself. This might seem odd, but this "outside looking in" approach is critical to the trick of making a calculation field behave as if it were a summary field. Summary fields, after all, report on a grouping of records in their own database.

9. In both list boxes, select the field that triggers your subsummary report (see fig. 20.4).

10. Click OK to close the Edit Relationship dialog box and click Done to close the Define Relationships dialog box.

Fig. 20.4
Define a self-referencing relationship by setting the related file the same as the current file.

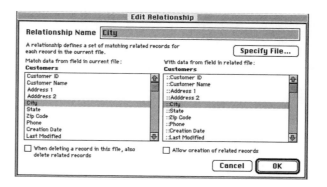

11. Select your new self-relationship and double-click the related field you just used to set up the relationship. The related field will have double colons in front of the field name, signifying that it's defined in a relationship to an external file. The field should now be in the argument of the Count function (see fig. 20.5).

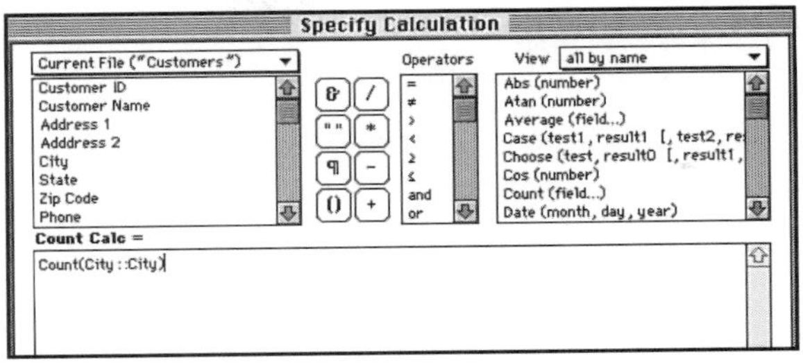

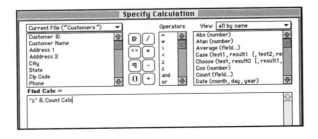

Fig. 20.5
The Count Calc calculation shows that you defined a relationship called City, through which you're counting records grouped by the City field.

12. Make sure the calculation result is Number and click OK to close the Specify Calculation dialog box.

In these steps, you created a calculation field that uses a self-referencing relationship to mimic the behavior of a summary field. Now you will use this field in another calculation and create a script to find only those customers who are in one of the top five cities.

1. Create another calculation called Find Calc. You will use this field to pre-format find criteria. In the Specify Calculation dialog box, click the quotation marks button. Now press Option-> to generate a greater-than or equal-to sign between the quotes.

> **Note**
>
> Another way of entering this symbol is to select the greater-than or equal-to sign from the Operators list. If you're going to do it this way, you must get rid of the unwanted space inserted before and after this symbol; otherwise the Find you will perform on this field won't work.

2. Click so the insertion point is after the second quotation mark and click the Concatenation button. Double-click the newly created Count Calc field from the list on the left (you might have to scroll down to find it) and it will appear in the calculation area. The final calculation should look similar to figure 20.6.

Fig. 20.6
Use the Find Calc calculation to find all customers in cities that have no fewer than a specified number of customers.

3. Make sure the calculation result is formatted as text and choose OK to close the Specify Calculation dialog box.

Here's the challenge: you want to know what customers are in the top five cities, but you don't know what cities those are and you don't even know how many customers a city needs to be ranked in the top five. That's where this next field comes in. Create a working variable called Counter with which a script will step down through counts of customers until it's visited five cities. You'll find that variables you use only in a script are best set up as global variables. Only one instance of that variable exists in the entire database, rather than occupying space in each record.

1. Create a global field called Counter and format it as a number data type (see fig. 20.7). Choose OK.

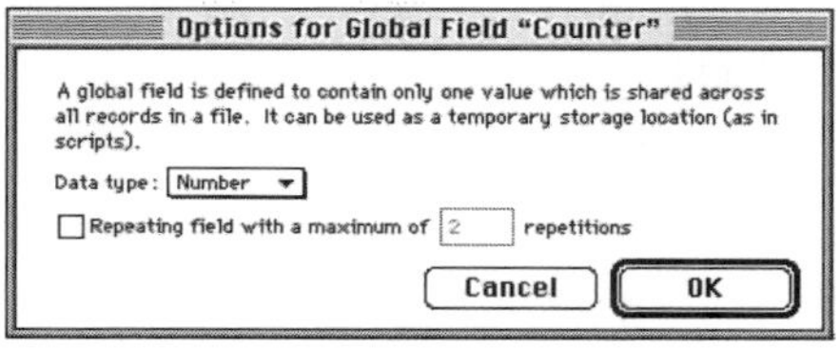

Fig. 20.7
When you create a global field, a single value is shared across all records in the database.

Options for Global Field "Counter"

A global field is defined to contain only one value which is shared across all records in a file. It can be used as a temporary storage location (as in scripts).

Data type: Number ▼

☐ Repeating field with a maximum of 2 repetitions

Cancel   OK

2. Create one more field, a global field called Chart. In the Options for Global Field dialog box, click Container from the Data Type pop-up menu. Choose OK.

3. Choose Done to close the Define Fields dialog box.

You need to create a layout called Data Entry that contains every field in your database, including the Count Calc, Find Calc, and Chart fields. Don't worry about how it's formatted, as long as each field is on the screen somewhere.

> **Tip**
>
> It's a good idea to create a layout that contains every field in the database. It can be invaluable when you're testing and debugging your creation if you want to look at an intermediate calculation field that doesn't appear on a layout. You can also reference this dummy layout in scripts when you need to copy and paste values from one field to another.
>
> You will never show this layout to anyone, so when your database is ready for others to use you should hide it from the Layouts menu. Press Command-L to enter Layout mode, then choose Mode, Layout Setup and deselect the Include in Layouts Menu check box.

Now you need to create a report layout called City Report that contains the City, Count Calc, and Chart fields. Place the City and Count Calc fields in a Sub-Summary by Count Calc (Leading) part, and place the Chart field in a Trailing Grand Summary part. Figure 20.8 shows how the City Report layout should look.

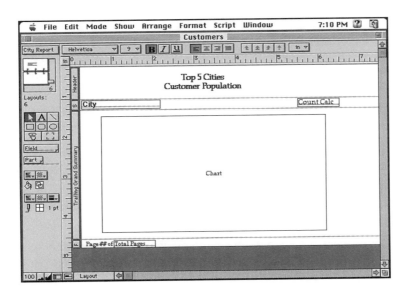

Fig. 20.8
The Chart field belongs in a Trailing Grand Summary part.

Up to this point, you have created and positioned all the fields you'll need for your calculations. Now prepare a Sort on the database to set the initial conditions for the script.

1. Make sure you're in Browse mode and choose Mode, Sort to open the Sort dialog box.

2. Click Clear All to remove any existing sort criteria and double-click the Count Calc field to move it into the sort order. Now choose the Count Calc field you just brought into the sort order and click descending order.

3. Click Sort or Done. This sets the sort that will be restored by the Sort script commands in your script.

Now, write the script that ties all the pieces together. It performs the calculations, makes the selection of records, and exports the selected records to be graphed in Excel. If you get lost as you're going through these steps, take a look ahead at figure 20.9 to help you get back on track.

1. Choose Script, ScriptMaker to open the Define Scripts dialog box.

2. Create a new script called Report with Chart and make sure the Include in Menu check box is selected. Choose Create to open the Script Definition dialog box.

3. Choose Clear All to remove the default script steps.

4. Double-click the Go to Layout script step to move it to the list on the right.

5. From the Specify pop-up list, select the Data Entry layout. You need to be on this layout because this script will be copying from the Find Calc field and pasting to the Count Calc field. For these operations to work properly, you need to be on a layout that contains these fields.

6. Double-click the Set Field script step to move it to the list on the right.

7. Choose Specify Field to open the Specify Field dialog box.

8. Select the Counter field and click OK to close the Specify Field dialog box.

9. Choose Specify to open the Specify Calculation dialog box.

10. Enter **0**, then click OK to close the Specify Calculation dialog box.

11. Double-click the Loop script step to move it to the list on the right. Notice that the End Loop script step automatically comes with it.

12. Double-click the Sort script step to append it to your script and drag it above the End Loop script step. Select the Restore Sort Order and Perform Without Dialog check boxes (these are the defaults).

13. Double-click the Go to Record/Request/Page script step to append it to your script, and drag it above the End Loop script step.

14. If it's not already selected, choose First from the Specify pop-up list.

15. Double-click the Copy script step to move it to the list on the right and drag it above the End Loop script step.

16. Choose Specify Field to open the Specify Field dialog box. Select the Find Calc field and click OK to close the Specify Field dialog box.

17. Double-click the Enter Find Mode script step to append it to your script, and drag it above the End Loop script step. Select the Restore Find Requests and the Pause check boxes (these are the defaults).

18. Double-click the Paste script step to move it to the list on the right and drag it above the End Loop script step.

19. Choose Specify Field to open the Specify Field dialog box. Select the Count Calc field and choose OK to close the Specify Field dialog box.

20. Double-click the Omit script step to move it to the list on the right. Drag it above the End Loop script step.

21. Double-click the Perform Find script step to append it to your script, and drag it above the End Loop script step. Deselect the Restore Find Requests check box.

22. Double-click the Set Field script to append it to your script, and drag it above the End Loop script step.

23. Choose Specify Field to open the Specify Field dialog box. Select the Counter field and choose OK to exit the Specify Field dialog box.

24. Choose Specify to open the Specify Calculation dialog box. Double-click the Counter field from the list of fields on the left to move it to the calculation area. Type + (a plus sign), and then type the number **1**. Choose OK to close the Specify Calculation dialog box.

25. Double-click the Exit Loop If script step to move it to the list on the right and drag it above the End Loop script step.

26. Choose Specify to open the Specify Calculation dialog box. Double-click the Counter field into the calculation area. Type = (an equals sign), then type the number **5**. Click OK to close the Specify Calculation dialog box.

Note

How's this loop going to work? You want the top five cities, so you set a Counter variable to zero, and the script passes through the loop and adds one to the Counter variable at the end of each pass. When the Counter hits five, you're done, so you exit the loop and continue with the rest of the script.

---

27. Double-click the Find Omitted script step to move it to the list on the right.

28. Double-click the Sort script step to append it to your script. Select the Restore Sort Order and the Perform Without Dialog check boxes (these are the defaults).

29. Double-click the Export script step to move it to the list on the right. Deselect the Restore Export Order and the Perform Without Dialog check boxes.

30. Choose Specify File to open the Save dialog box. Type **CHARTDATA.TAB** for the file name. You can accept Tab-Separated Text as the default type. Choose Save. Your script should look similar to figure 20.9.

Fig. 20.9

The Script Definition dialog box shows the Report with Chart script you entered in steps 1 to 30.

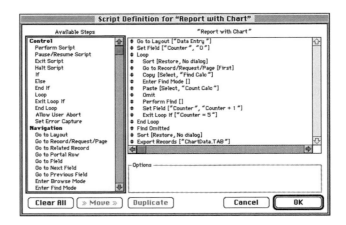

31. Click OK to close the Script Definition dialog box. Click Done to close the Define Scripts dialog box.

Your script isn't completed yet, but you need to do several things before you can finish it. First, you need to run the script once so it creates an exported CHARTDATA.TAB file.

1. Choose Script, Report with Chart to run your script. When it gets to the end it will open the Export Field Order dialog box. You only need to export three fields, so click Clear All to remove any fields in the field order.

2. Double-click the field you want to summarize in your report. In this example, it's the City field. This first field will be the label in your chart. Also double-click the Count Calc field to supply the values that get charted.

3. Because Count is a summary field, select it in the field order and choose Summarize By to open the Summarize By dialog box.

   The Summarize By dialog box will show any fields you've sorted the database on. If you haven't sorted the database, the Summarize By dialog box will be empty.

4. Select the Count Calc field to place a check mark in front of it (see fig. 20.10).

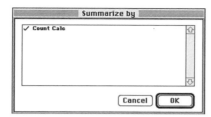

Fig. 20.10
You can select any field you've sorted on in the Summarize By dialog box.

5. Choose OK to close the Summarize By dialog box.

This creates a new entry in the field order called Count by Count Calc. By having this summary field in the field order, you get a summarized export instead of a detailed found set export. This is worth repeating. Even though you're not interested in the values in this field, you must incorporate the field into your list of exported fields to be able to group by City as you export the found set.

6. Select the Count field and click Clear. Figure 20.11 shows how the Export Field Order dialog box should now appear.

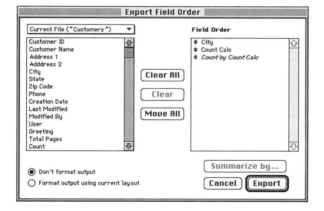

Fig. 20.11
The completed Export Field Order dialog box shows the three fields you will export from FileMaker to Excel.

7. Click Export to export the CHARTDATA.TAB file.

Creating the Chart from the FileMaker Data in Excel

There's one other thing you have to take care of before returning to complete your script. You need to open Excel and record a macro that creates a chart of your exported data. When you return to editing your script, you can insert a step to send an Apple Event that invokes the macro.

Because the Excel menus and commands (and the macro language) were extensively revised from version 4.0 to version 5.0 of the program, I provided step-by-step instructions to handle both versions.

To record a macro in Excel 4.0, follow these steps:

1. Go to the Finder and launch Microsoft Excel version 4.0.

2. Choose File, Open and select CHARTDATA.TAB. Choose Open.

3. Choose Macro, Record to open the Record Macro dialog box. Name the macro Chart and choose OK.

Caution

The macro is now recording your actions. If you make a mistake and correct for it, Excel will dutifully perform those steps when the macro plays back.

---

4. Highlight cells A1 to B5 and click the Chart Wizard button (see fig. 20.12).

5. Drag out an area for the chart that's a little less than the width of a page, then follow the instructions in the Chart Wizard and select the type of chart you want. When the finished chart appears, make any necessary formatting changes.

6. Choose Edit, Copy to copy the chart to the Clipboard.

7. Choose Macro, Stop Recorder to finish your macro. You can make mistakes now.

8. Choose Window, Macro1 to switch to your macro sheet.

9. Choose File, Save to open the Save dialog box. Name the macro Chart Top Five Cities Macro and choose Save.

10. Quit Excel and return to FileMaker. You don't need to save any changes to CHARTDATA.TAB.

To record a macro in Excel 5.0, follow these steps:

1. Go to the Finder and launch Microsoft Excel version 5.0.

2. Choose File, Open and select CHARTDATA.TAB. Choose Open.

3. The Text Import Wizard opens. Choose Finish to accept its choices and continue.

4. Choose Tools, Record Macro, Record New Macro to open the Record Macro dialog box. Name the macro Chart and choose the Options button.

5. Click the Store In New Workbook button and choose OK.

6. Highlight cells A1 to B5 and click the Chart Wizard button
(see fig. 20.12).

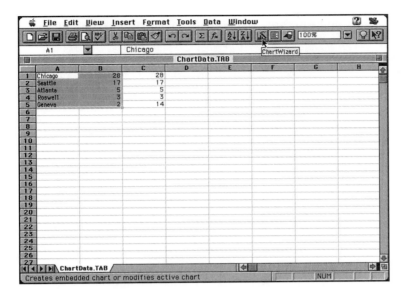

Fig. 20.12
The first step performed in the macro you're recording is to select a range of cells and click the Chart Wizard button.

7. Drag out an area for the chart that's a little less than the width of a page, then follow the instructions in the Chart Wizard and select the type of chart you want. When the finished chart appears, make any necessary formatting changes.

8. Choose Edit, Copy to copy the chart to the Clipboard.

9. Choose Tools, Record Macro, Stop Recording to finish your macro.

10. Choose Window, Workbook1 to switch to your macro sheet.

11. In the macro code that's been recorded for you, find both occurrences of Range ("A1:B5") and replace them with the term (A1:B5). These terms ought to be synonymous; indeed both work identically when the macro is run from within Excel. When called from FileMaker, however, only the latter variation works.

12. Choose File, Save to open the Save dialog box. Name the macro Chart Top Five Cities Macro and choose Save.

13. Enter any Summary Information you care to specify and choose OK.

14. Quit Excel and return to FileMaker. You don't need to save any changes to CHARTDATA.TAB.

Placing the Chart in the Report Layout

You've now completed the Excel macro, which has been instructed to create a chart derived from a range of cells in CHARTDATA.TAB and then copy that chart to the Clipboard. Now you need to launch FileMaker to finish your Report with Chart script. Your script already works up to the point where it exports summarized data to CHARTDATA.TAB; now it needs to be able to activate Excel and pass control to the macro. After the macro completes, control should return to your script, where you can then paste the chart from the Clipboard into a container field on your City Report layout.

1. Choose Script, ScriptMaker to open the Define Scripts dialog box.

2. Double-click the Report with Chart script to open the Script Definition dialog box.

3. Select the Export script step and select the Restore Export Order and the Perform Without Dialog check boxes.

   Now that the export has been set up, you can let it run automatically.

4. Double-click the Send Apple Event script step to move it to the list on the right.

5. Choose Specify to open the Specify Apple Event dialog box. From the Send the … Event pop-up menu, select Open Document.

6. Choose Specify File to open the Open dialog box.

7. Select your Top Five Cities Macro and choose Open. Select the Bring Target Application To Foreground check box.

8. Choose OK to close the Specify Apple Event dialog box.

9. Double-click another Send Apple Event script step to append it to your script.

10. Choose Specify to open the Specify Apple Event dialog box.

11. From the Send the … Event pop-up menu, select Open Document.

12. Choose Specify File to open the Open dialog box.

13. Select the CHARTDATA.TAB file and choose Open.

14. Choose the Specify Application button and locate your Excel program. Choose Open.

15. Choose OK to close the Specify Apple Event dialog box.

16. Double-click another Send Apple Event script step to move it to the list on the right.

17. Choose Specify to open the Specify Apple Event dialog box.

18. From the Send the … Event pop-up menu, select Do Script. Select the Script Text radio button. Click in the Script Text text box and type the following line:

RUN("'Top Five Cities Macro'!Chart",FALSE)

This line tells Excel to run your chart macro.

19. Again, choose the Specify Application button and locate your Excel program. Choose Open.

20. Choose OK to close the Specify Apple Event dialog box.

The previous steps provide for the transfer of control from FileMaker to Excel. First, the Top Five Cities Macro opens; then the CHARTDATA.TAB table that came from FileMaker opens; finally, the macro charts the data in a bar graph and copies it to the Clipboard. You can get the chart from the Clipboard and paste it into your layout, but there's a possibility that Excel hasn't completed its actions by the time your script regains control. As a precaution, tell the script to pause for a period of time (15 seconds, in this case), which should give Excel enough time to perform the macro.

1. Double-click the Pause/Resume Script script step to append it to your script.

2. Choose Specify to open the Pause/Resume Options dialog box.

3. Type a duration of 15 seconds, and choose OK to close the Pause/ Resume Options dialog box.

Now that you told your script to wait for Excel to catch up, the rest is straightforward. The script pastes the Clipboard contents into the Chart container field, then goes to City Report and views in Preview mode to display what's shown in figure 20.2. It pauses on this screen until the user clicks Continue. Then it returns the user to the layout they were on when they initially requested the report.

1. Double-click the Paste script step to move it to the list on the right.

2. Choose Specify Field to open the Specify Field dialog box. Click on the Chart field and choose OK to close the Specify Field dialog box.

3. Double-click the Go to Layout script step to move it to the list on the right. From the Specify pop-up menu, choose the City Report layout.

4. Double-click the Enter Preview Mode script step to move it to the list on the right. Select the Pause check box (this is the default).

5. Double-click the Enter Browse Mode script step to append it to your script. Deselect the Pause check box (this is the default).

6. Double-click the Go to Layout script step to move it to the list on the right. Select the Refresh Screen check box. From the Specify pop-up menu, select Original Layout.

The bottom of the completed script should look similar to figure 20.13. (The top should look the same as it appeared in figure 20.9.)

Fig. 20.13

The Report with Chart script requests Excel to perform certain actions, then waits for them to be carried out before proceeding.

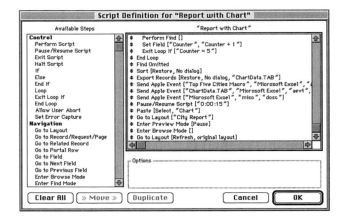

7. Choose OK to close the Script Definition dialog box. The FileMaker Pro dialog box appears (see fig. 20.14).

8. Select the Export Order Replace radio button and leave the other buttons set to Keep. Choose Done to close the FileMaker Pro dialog box.

Fig. 20.14

By replacing Export Order, you tell the script to remember the settings in effect the last time you performed an Export operation.

Your script is now ready to go. Refer to figure 20.2 to see how the result appears when you run your script.

Using BrioQuery to Run SQL Queries for FileMaker Pro

FileMaker Pro is an elegant, easy-to-use program. Working with mainframe databases is rarely easy or elegant. Often, though, you will need information that's stored on a mainframe. If you only need mainframe data once in a while, then you will probably just have a system administrator write the data to a text file and import it in FileMaker. If you need mainframe data on a regular basis, it's worth your while to automate the process.

FileMaker can't execute SQL queries directly, but it can use third-party query tools like Brio's BrioQuery to run queries on its behalf. The query results get written to a hard drive, and FileMaker imports the file. This is fine for batch processing several records a few times a day, but if you need real-time transaction processing where you're constantly moving information between FileMaker Pro and your mainframe database, you're better off working with an application that can perform SQL transactions directly. The trade-off is simplicity. Developing a similar application in a program other than FileMaker Pro always takes longer.

From Here...

In this chapter, you learned how to make FileMaker Pro work with third-party charting and query software. This capability to work with other applications adds functionality to FileMaker Pro.

From here, you might take a look at the following chapters:

- Chapter 15, "Scripting with ScriptMaker," focuses on practical examples of scripting in FileMaker Pro, such as using the Message (dialog box) command, creating scripts for error trapping, and finding and marking duplicate records.

- Chapter 21, "FileMaker Pro and the World Wide Web," describes how to create Web pages that display data from a FileMaker Pro database.

FileMaker Pro and the World Wide Web

It's old news that interest in the Internet has exploded, and this is largely due to the World Wide Web. What's not old news is that you can use FileMaker Pro on the Web. For example, you can use FileMaker to collect information from other people on the Internet, give world-wide access to any or all of your databases, and even update your published Web pages.

Say you maintain a database of your company's product line, complete with product photos. You also post this information to the Internet by routinely updating the Web files. After a while, you find that maintaining the database is easy—the real pain is keeping your Web pages up-to-date. Using AppleScript with FileMaker, you can automatically update your Web pages— even the HTML code and product photos. You also can let Internet users add data to the file, whether it be ordering information or product suggestions.

AppleScript lets FileMaker interact with the Web server software that's found on most Macs on the Internet. In this chapter, you learn how to use FileMaker as the "back end" of your Web page. The following topics are also covered:

- Where to get Web server software and how to set it up
- Where to get Web browsers and how to set them up
- How to configure Web browsers and servers to work with FileMaker Pro databases
- Where to find CGIs that work with FileMaker and how to use them
- How to write your own CGI

In short, this chapter is a crash course on working with the World Wide Web, and a pretty intensive course on how to make use of FileMaker data on the Web.

The Basic Ingredients

Before you get into making FileMaker dance with the World Wide Web, you need to get some background information on how the Web works. The essential ingredients for the Web are Web browsers, also called clients, and Web servers, the software that runs Web sites.

At the time of this writing, two surveys found Macintosh computers run anywhere from 17 to 20 percent of the Web servers on the Internet, a substantial percentage—second only to Sun machines at around 31 percent and far ahead of Windows machines at less than 10 percent. The server software found on most Macintosh Web servers is MacHTTP, now called WebStar in its commercial version.

Both WebStar and MacHTTP support AppleScript and can interact with add-on utilities called CGIs. *CGI* stands for Common Gateway Interface, and a CGI application can perform such tasks as handling e-mail, processing graphics maps, and interacting with FileMaker databases.

As you might imagine, this recipe has many ingredients, so you need to collect those before you can start. You can find most of these items on the Internet or on bulletin boards. While you don't have to have an Internet connection to do the exercises in this chapter, you might ultimately want to get signed up with an Internet service provider (an ISP) so you can check out various FileMaker sites, join FileMaker online discussion groups, or administer your own FileMaker Web site. A lot of ISPs provide most of these software components you'll need when you sign up.

If you don't have an Internet service provider yet, but still want to follow this chapter, see if you can find a friend who will get these various pieces of software down from the Net for you. The following is a list of items you need, as well as where you can find them on the Net:

- *MacHTTP 2.0 or later or WebStar from StarNine Systems.* MacHTTP is Web server software, as is WebStar. WebStar is the commercial successor to MacHTTP, and can take advantage of the Thread Manager, which allows for running multiple internal processes at once. The result is that WebStar is about three to four times faster than MacHTTP. At the time of this writing, WebStar costs $495 and MacHTTP costs $50. Regardless of which one you get, if you don't have MacTCP configured properly, your server software won't run. You can find both of these at **www.Starnine.com**.

> **Note**
>
> Because of the ever-changing nature of the World Wide Web, addresses and file locations change. You might find that some of the file locations listed in this chapter are no longer current. If that's the case, use your Web browser's search tools to locate the file.

■ *A Web browser that supports forms, such as Mosaic or Netscape.* The Web browser enables you to view the HTML documents that the server software makes available as Web pages.

You can find Mosaic 2.01 or later at **http://www.ncsa.uiuc.edu/ SDG/Software/MacMosaic/download.html** or **ftp.ncsa.uiuc.edu** (change to the /Mac/Mosaic directory).

You can find Netscape 1.12 or later at **http://www.netscape.com/ comprod/mirror/index.html**.

■ *MacTCP.* MacTCP is a control panel. TCP/IP is the network protocol of the Internet. MacTCP enables your Mac to "speak" TCP/IP. MacTCP can use either your LocalTalk port or a phone line using ConfigPPP's extension as its connection to the Internet. MacTCP is available from Apple Computer through anonymous FTP from **ftp.support.apple.com**, **ftp.info.apple.com**, and in Europe at **ftp.info.apple.com**. Additionally, Apple now ships MacTCP with System 7.5.

■ *ConfigPPP.* ConfigPPP is a control panel. PPP stands for point-to-point protocol. ConfigPPP along with the PPP extension are included in the MacPPP package. You can find it at **http://hyperarchive.lcs.mit. edu/HyperArchive/Archive/comm/tcp/conn/mac-ppp-201. hqx**

> **Note**
>
> MacPPP is just one of the PPPs available for the Macintosh. Others are available at **http://hyperarchive.lcs.mit.edu/HyperArchive/Archive/ comm/tcp/conn/**

■ *CGI programs.* These are AppleScript applets (see Chapter 16 for detailed information on AppleScript) that interact with FileMaker and the server software. The appropriate HTML reference on a Web page causes the server software to send an AppleEvent to the CGI, which then interacts with FileMaker Pro. The CGI then takes the results from FileMaker and creates what's called a *form*, a temporary HTML document in the form of a text message that's passed between the CGI and the server software. Because the form text is dependent on the query from the browser, it can be different from one query to the next.

ROFM.CGI is a CGI written by Russel Owen. You can find it at **http://rowen.astro.washington.edu/**. WEBFM.ACGI is another CGI written by the Web Broadcasting Company. It can be found at **http://macweb.com/webfm/**. Claris also maintains a list of current CGIs at **http://www2.claris.com/filemaker/cgi.html.**

- *Simple Text or Teach Text (or the word processor of your choice).* All you really need is something that can save files as text files. The language you use to create Web page documents is HTML, which stands for HyperText Markup Language. There's really nothing to it. You'll be able to write a Web page in HTML by the end of this chapter. Even though the pages are formatted in HTML, they're saved as text documents. HTML is more of a text layout scheme than it is an actual file format.

- *AppleScript 1.1.* This comes with System 7.5. See Chapter 16 for information on installing AppleScript.

- *Tokenize and Decoder Scripting Additions.* Put these in the Scripting Additions folder, which is inside the Extensions folder in your System Folder. They do some of the dirty work for your FileMaker CGI applications. You can find these scripting additions, as well as others that work with FileMaker CGIs at **http://www.comvista.com/net/www/lessons/CGIScripts.html** or at **http://www2.claris.com/filemaker/cgi.html.**

Yes, this is a lot of stuff. After you collect it all, though, you can do some pretty cool things with FileMaker Pro and the Web. When you run a Web browser on the Internet, the browser displays HTML documents as Web pages. For you to have a point of contact between your FileMaker database and users on the Web, you need to create a Web page. The main Web page that leads to your other Web pages is called a home page. To create a home page so people can interact with your FileMaker databases, you need to learn some HTML.

Creating a Home Page

You need to create a basic home page for your Web server. To do that, you need to learn a little HTML. The following is a sample home page:

```
<HTML>
<HEAD>
        <TITLE>Chris Moyer Home Page</TITLE>
</HEAD>
<BODY>
        <H1>Welcome!</H1>
        Greetings all. I think you're going to find that this Web
site is the cat's pajamas. I'm serving up a FileMaker Pro 3.0
numerology database for your psychic enjoyment.<P>
        <IMG SRC="http://www.equal_access.com/FMPro/FMLogo.gif"><P>
        <H3>Access in one of two ways:</H3>

            <LI>A <A
HREF="http://www.equal_access.com/FMPro/
Numerology.FMP3">Numerology</A> database that you can log onto if
you have a copy of FileMaker Pro 3.0. You'll need to designate
FileMaker as a helper application in your Web browser.
            <LI>A Web interface to the same <A HREF="http://
www.wyst.edu/">Numerology database</A>.
        </UL>
        <HR>
        <ADDRESS>Chris Moyer<BR>
            2305 North Campbell<BR>
            Chicago, IL 60647<BR>
            (312)252-5639<BR>
            <A HREF="http://www.equal_access/FMPro/mailme.html">
            jones@foobar.hsu.edu</A>
        </ADDRESS>
</BODY>
</HTML>
```

Take a look at this document. This might look a little intimidating, at first, but after you get the hang of it, you're going to marvel at how easy it is. If you remember the early days of the computer boom and the crude early word processors, you'll probably feel right at home with HTML. It's not much different from inserting formatting codes into documents with the old word processors. Figure 21.1 shows what this HTML document looks like when viewed in a Web browser.

Notice that the HTML document opens and closes with the tags <HTML> and </HTML>. The title element on the third line is bounded by <TITLE> and </TITLE>. The title element is part of the head element, denoted by the <HEAD> and </HEAD> tags above and below it. Are you beginning to notice a trend? The closing tag is the same as the opening tag except for the forward slash (/).

Elements delimited by tags at the beginning and end are called *container elements*. Container elements are sections of text, such as headers, body text, and so on.

Fig. 21.1
The HTML
document looks
quite a bit
different when
you view it with a
Web browser like
Netscape.

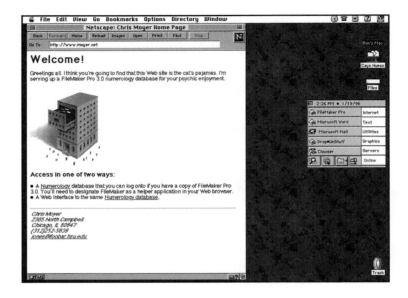

There's another type of element called an *empty element*. Empty elements only use one tag and they don't contain any text. Empty elements consist of such things as line breaks, new paragraph returns, and bullet points. Because tabs, extra spaces, and carriage returns are treated as a single space when displayed by a Web browser, all your layout formatting needs to be done with HTML tags. The following are some empty elements you can use for page layout purposes:

<P> creates a new paragraph.

 creates a line break. Text separated by line breaks is considered a single paragraph.

<HR> stands for horizontal rule and creates a line across the page.

<UL> creates an unnumbered list of items.

<LI> creates a list item on a new line within an unnumbered list. Typically, a browser will place a bullet in front of each list item.

<!*text*> the exclamation mark and accompanying text creates a comment inside the HTML document that is ignored by the Web browser. You can use this feature to describe the purpose of HTML code, much in the same way programmers include explanatory statements in their program code.

For formatting container elements, you need to use the following tags:

To bold enclosed text:

> <B>*text*</B>
>
> or
>
> <STRONG>*text*</STRONG>

To italicize the enclosed text:

> <I>*text*</I>
>
> or
>
> <EM>*text*</EM>
>
> or
>
> <CITE>*text*</CITE>
>
> or
>
> <VAR>*text*</VAR>

To display something in a fixed width font, such as courier:

> <TT>*text*</TT>
>
> or
>
> <CODE>*text*</CODE>
>
> or
>
> <KBD>*text*</KBD>

One of the most important elements is a *hypertext link*. Hypertext links contain a reference to an object outside the document. That object can be a graphic, another HTML document, a file such as a FileMaker database, or a reference to a CGI. These hypertext links are also called hypertext anchors because they anchor another object to your Web page.

To use a hypertext link, you simply click it. When you do, your Web browser discards the current Web page and requests the object referenced by the hypertext link—except in the case of a binary file, such as a FileMaker database or an Excel spreadsheet. Because Web browsers can't read binary files, they try to find a helper application to open the file while it retains the last Web page. You need to configure your Web browser to use specific programs as helper applications. While each Web browser is different, you set up helper applications in the preferences section of the Web browser software.

To create your own Web page, try opening your favorite word processing application or text editor and typing in the HTML document previously shown. Substitute your own name and snappy wit where appropriate. Don't worry about the hypertext anchors for now. You'll format them properly after you get your Web server running.

After you type the document in, save it as a text document with the name HOME.HTML. To create a Web page that will serve as your entry screen for people who don't have FileMaker Pro 3.0 but who still want to find information in your database, type the following document into your text editor:

```
<HTML>
<HEAD>
<TITLE>MacHTTP-FileMaker Pro / Find </TITLE>
</HEAD>

<hr>
<BODY>

<H1><center>MacHTTP-FileMaker Pro: Find</center></H1>

Please enter all <u>known</u> information below and click the
<b>Find</b> button to search for all matches.
For information that is unknown, please leave that selection blank.
Wild cards are allowed.<p>

<hr>
<FORM METHOD="POST" ACTION="fmpro.acgi$FIND">
<pre>
<B> ID: </B><INPUT TYPE="text" NAME="ID" SIZE=8 MAXLENGTH=8>
<B> Name: </B><INPUT TYPE="text" NAME="name" SIZE=40 MAXLENGTH=80>
<B> Phone: </B><INPUT TYPE="text" NAME="phone" SIZE=40 MAXLENGTH=80>
<B>Favorite Color: </b><SELECT NAME="color">
<option>*
<option>Red
<option>Green
<option>Blue
</SELECT>
</pre>
<INPUT value="Find" TYPE=submit>
<INPUT value="Start Over" TYPE=reset >
</FORM>
<hr>

</BODY>

</HTML>
```

To create a page where people can add information to your database, create another text document with the following information:

```
<HTML>
<hr>
<HEAD>
<TITLE>MacHTTP-FileMaker Demo / Add </TITLE>
</HEAD>

<BODY>

<H1><center>MacHTTP-FileMaker Pro: Add</center></H1>

Please enter all information below and click the <b>Add</b> button
to add a new record.<p>

<hr>
<FORM METHOD="POST" ACTION="fmpro.acgi$ADD">
<pre>
<B> First Name: </B><INPUT TYPE="text" NAME="name" SIZE=40
MAXLENGTH=80>
<B> Last Name: </B><INPUT TYPE="text" NAME="phone" SIZE=40
MAXLENGTH=80>
<B>Favorite Color: </b><SELECT NAME="color">
<option>*
<option>Red
<option>Green
<option>Blue
</SELECT>
</pre>
<INPUT value="Add" TYPE=submit>
<INPUT value="Start Over" TYPE=reset >
</FORM>
<hr>

</BODY>

</HTML>
```

Notice that these documents have container elements called *forms*. A form is similar to a virtual HTML document. It doesn't exist as an actual file on the hard drive. Instead, your CGI application generates it on the fly. In this case, the text is generated in response to a FileMaker query. The CGI takes the query, runs it against FileMaker, and formats the result as text. The CGI gives the form text to the server, which gives the text to the browser. Text is text as far as the browser is concerned. It doesn't care whether the information is on the hard drive.

Thus, forms differ from a regular HTML document in that they're dynamic. Depending on the data requested, the form can be different with each request. An HTML document, on the other hand, requires you to fire up a text editor and manually change it for it to be different. HTML documents are static, forms are dynamic.

Anyway, at this point you're probably thinking that CGIs are amazing things. They are pretty useful, but they're amazingly low-tech in what they actually do. It's time you learn how to build one.

Building Your Own CGI

It is a good idea to read Chapter 16, "Using AppleScript," before reading this section. If you haven't read it, you might want to make a quick peruse and make sure you have AppleScript installed correctly. To build your CGI, start the Script Editor and type the following text:

Note

The first line of the AppleScript tells the script the location of your database, in this case a database named foo.FM ("Macintosh HD:foo.FM"). When you try this script, make sure you change the path name in the script to the path name of your database. Otherwise, the script won't compile.

```
property database_name : alias "Macintosh HD:foo.fm"

property crlf : (ASCII character 13) & (ASCII character 10)

--standard HTTP/1.0 reply header
property http_10_header : "HTTP/1.0 200 OK" & crlf & "Server:
    MacHTTP/2.0" & crlf & ¬
        "MIME-Version: 1.0" & crlf & "Content-type: text/html"¬
            & crlf & crlf

--used to make self-referencing anchors for RETRIEVE and DELETE
--command URLs
--this hard coded hack is a Bad Thing.
property this_url : "204.95.21.213/"

--these properties map numbers to variables representing the 4
--fields in the FileMaker Pro
--database. Hard-coding the field numbers is only a good idea if
--you know your FMPro
--layout isn't subject to change.
property name_field : 1
property phone_field : 2
property color_field : 3
property id_field : 4
```

```
-------------------------------------------------------------
-- Main Event Handler for the MacHTTP Search Doc event
-------------------------------------------------------------

on «event WWWΩsdoc» path_args ¬
        given «class kfor»:http_search_args, «class
post»:post_args, «class meth»:method, «class addr»:client_address,
«class user»:username, «class pass»:¦password¦, «class
frmu»:from_user, «class svnm»:server_name, «class
svpt»:server_port, «class scnm»:script_name, «class
ctyp»:content_type

        try --wrap an error handler around everything.
            --Always a good idea!!!

                --build the URL of this script
                --set this_url to "http://" & server_name & ":" &
                    server_port & script_name
                --decode the %20 encoded space (if any) in the
                --path_args, so we have 2 words like
                --"DELETE 123" or "RETRIEVE 456" in path_args. Note that
                --ADD and FIND only have
                --one word in path_args
                --set path_args to Decode URL path_args

                --see what command we're being asked to perform
                if word 1 of path_args is "RETRIEVE" then --look up a
                --single record found with FIND
                        return http_10_header & DoLookup(path_args) & crlf
                else if word 1 of path_args is "ADD" then --add a new record
                        return http_10_header & DoAdd(post_args) & crlf record
                else if word 1 of path_args is "DELETE" then --delete
                        --the current record
                        return http_10_header & DoDelete(path_args)
                else if word 1 of path_args is "FIND" then --find allmatches
                        return http_10_header & DoFind(post_args)
                end if

                -- handle any errors that occur here
        on error msg number num
                return http_10_header & "Problem executing CGI, Main:"
                    & msg & " err: " & num
        end try

end «event WWWΩsdoc»


-------------------------------------------------------------
-- Perform the look-up function for a single record
-------------------------------------------------------------
on DoLookup(args)
    return MakeFullEntry(word 2 of args)
end DoLookup
```

```
---------------------------------------------------------------
-- Add a new record, using the data in the post_args to fill
-- in the fields
---------------------------------------------------------------


on DoAdd(post_args)
    try
        --divide the post_args up into the individual
        --name/value pairs
        set tlist to tokenize post_args with delimiters "&"
        set values to {}

        tell application "FileMaker Pro"
            activate --Make sure FileMaker Pro is running, in
                        --the foreground
            Open database_name --Make sure the proper document is
                                --open as well

            --for all the tokenized items in the list...
            repeat with titem in tlist
                set temp to tokenize titem with delimiters "="
                --divide each item into name and value
                if temp is not {} then
                    set arg to Decode URL (item 1 of temp)
                    if the (Count of temp) is 1 then --this was a
            --blank field
                        set value to "???"
                    else
                        --encoding of spaces.
                        set value to Decode URL (item 2 of temp)
                        --get rid of %xx encodings
                    end if
                    set values to values & {value}
                    --make a list of the values to shove in the new
                    --record
                end if
            end repeat
            Create New Record With Data values--tell FMPro to make a
                                        -- record with the new data
        end tell
        return "<title>Added</title><h2>Your record has been
        --added!" return some HTML to the user

    on error msg number num
        return "Problem executing CGI, DoAdd: " & msg & " err: " & num
    end try
end DoAdd


---------------------------------------------------------------
-- Delete a record with a specific ID field
---------------------------------------------------------------
```

```
on DoDelete(args)
    try
        tell application "FileMaker Pro"
            activate
            Open database_name
            Delete (every Record whose Cell id_field is (word 2 of args))
            --delete all records with this ID
        end tell

    on error msg number num
        return "Problem executing CGI, DoDelete: " & msg & " err: " & num & ¬
            "<br>Record wasn't deleted."
    end try

    return "<title>Deleted!</title><h2>The record has been deleted!"

end DoDelete

------------------------------------------------------------------
-- Search for all records that match the supplied form info
------------------------------------------------------------------

on DoFind(post_args)
    -- search for all the matches
    try
        -- divide the form args up into a list
        set tlist to tokenize post_args with delimiters "&"
        set form_args to {}
        set content to "Nothing."
        repeat with titem in tlist
            set temp to tokenize titem with delimiters "="
            --split each list item into name, value
            if temp is not {} then
                set arg to Decode URL (item 1 of temp)
                if the (count of temp) is 1 then
                    set value to "Ω" --if the field was empty, slap
                                    a FMPro wildcard in it, poof!
                else
                    set value to Decode URL (item 2 of temp)
                end if
                set form_args to form_args & {{arg, value}}
            --build the list for passing to SearchEm
            end if
        end repeat

        set content to "<title>Search Matches</title><h2>Search Matches</h2>"
```

```
        set all_recs to SearchEm(form_args) --do the actual search

        --generate a list of records that matched
        if (count of lists of all_recs) > 0 then
            set content to content & "<br><hr><br>"
            repeat with rec in all_recs
                set content to content & MakeEntry(rec)
            end repeat
            set content to content & "<br><hr>"
        else
            set content to content & MakeEntry(all_recs)
        end if

    on error msg number num
        set content to "Sorry, unable to find a match.¬
        (" & msg & " err: " & num & ")"
    end try

    return content & crlf
end DoFind


-------------------------------------------------------------------
--Perform the actual search with FileMaker Pro. Note that this
--is specific
--to the number of fields in your database. Searching numeric
--fields does
--not work! Not "MY" fault. Don't ask me why, I didn't do it!
-------------------------------------------------------------------


on SearchEm(tlist)
    tell application "FileMaker Pro"
        activate
        Open database_name
        return every Record whose Cell (item 1 of (item 1 of tlist))
        is (item 2 of (item 1 of tlist)) and ¬
            Cell (item 1 of (item 2 of tlist)) is (item 2 of (item 2
            of tlist)) and ¬
            Cell (item 1 of (item 3 of tlist)) is (item 2 of (item 3
            of tlist)) and ¬
            Cell (item 1 of (item 4 of tlist)) is (item 2 of (item 4
            of tlist))
    end tell
end SearchEm


-----------------------------------------------------------
-- build the title of an individual record
-----------------------------------------------------------


on MakeTitle(rec)
    return "<title>" & item name_field of rec & "</title><h2Record #"
        & item id_field of rec & "</h2>"
end MakeTitle


-----------------------------------------------------------
-- Make the name portion of an individual record display
-----------------------------------------------------------
```

```
on MakeName(rec)
    return "<b>" & (item name_field of rec) & "</b><br>"
end MakeName

on MakeMiniName(rec)
    return "<b>" & (item name_field of rec) & "</b> "
end MakeMiniName


------------------------------------------------------------
-- Make the phone number portion of an individual record display
------------------------------------------------------------

on MakePhone(rec)
    return "<b>" & (item phone_field of rec) & "</b><br>"
end MakePhone

on MakeMiniPhone(rec)
    return "<b>" & (item phone_field of rec) & "</b>"
end MakeMiniPhone
--
------------------------------------------------------------
-- Make the color portion of an individual record display
------------------------------------------------------------

on MakeColor(rec)
    return "Favorite color is: <b>" & (item color_field of rec) &
        "</b>.<br>"
end MakeColor


------------------------------------------------------------
-- construct a single line in the results list from the find
------------------------------------------------------------

on MakeEntry(rec)
    try
        -- set html to "#<a href=" & this_url & "$RETRIEVE%20" & ¬
        set html to "# <a href=" & "http://204.95.21.213/FMPro/¬
          fmpro.acgi" & "$RETRIEVE%20" & ¬
            (item id_field of rec) & ">" & (item id_field of rec) & ¬
              "</a> " --build a RETRIEVE command into the display
        set html to html & MakeMiniName(rec) & MakeMiniPhone(rec) & "<br>"
        return html
    on error msg number num
        return "MakeEntry: " & msg & " err: " & num
    end try
end MakeEntry


------------------------------------------------------------
-- construct a complete display for a single record look-up
-- (RETRIEVE)
------------------------------------------------------------
```

```
on MakeFullEntry(i_d)
    tell application "FileMaker Pro"
            activate
            Open database_name
            set rec to every Record whose Cell "ID" is i_d --find
            ➥the exact record (ID should be unique in FMPro)
    end tell
    return "<h2>Here's the record you requested:</h2>" & ¬
            MakeMiniName(rec) & MakePhone(rec) & MakeColor(rec) &¬
            "<br>" & MakeDeleteButton(i_d)
end MakeFullEntry

------------------------------------------------------------
-- Make the "Delete this record" button at the bottom of the single
-- record display
------------------------------------------------------------

on MakeDeleteButton(i_d)
    --return "<hr><a href=" & this_url & "$DELETE%20" & i_d &
    ">Delete this record."
    return "<hr><a href=" & "http://204.95.21.213/FMPro/fmpro.acgi"
    & "$DELETE%20" & i_d & ">Delete this record."
end MakeDeleteButton
```

> **Note**
>
> AppleScript uses a few characters you might be unfamiliar with. To create the line continuation character (¬), hold down the Option key as you press the Return key. To create the quillements (« and ») that surround the custom events, press Option-\ and Option-Shift-\. To create the Omega (Ω) on your Macintosh, press Option-Z.

Click the Check Syntax button to check for errors and correct any problems you find. If the Script Editor displays an error message, it will also point out the general location of the error. Usually, you'll find that the problem's simply a misspelled word or a missing quotation mark. After you locate and make changes to any errors in the script, or if you're lucky to not have made any errors, the Script Editor will reformat the script (see fig. 21.2). At this point, you're ready to save the script as an application.

To do so, choose File, Save As and format the result as an application. Select the Stay Open and Never Show Startup Screen check boxes. Name the file FM3.AGCI and click Save.

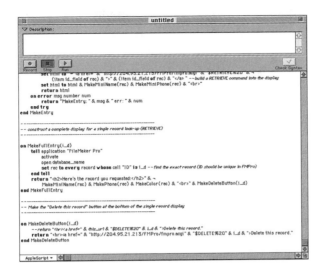

Fig. 22.2
Once the script's syntax is correct, the Script Editor will reformat the text you entered.

Setting Up the Server for Development

Ultimately, you'll want your Web page to be connected to the World Wide Web so people can access it. But because you're in development, you need to configure things so you can test your system without being live. To do this, you need to get your server software running without it being connected to the Internet. You need to trick the MacTCP so it thinks it's connected when it really isn't. To do this and install these other pieces, follow these steps:

1. Put MacTCP and ConfigPPP in your Control Panels folder in your System Folder. You don't need ConfigPPP for these steps, but you'll need it when you start working with the Internet.

2. Open your Network control panel and make sure it's set to LocalTalk Built In (see fig. 21.3). This ensures that your Web server and Web browser will look to your LocalTalk port, instead of dialing the Internet with PPP. Close the Network control panel.

3. Open the MacTCP control panel.

4. If MacTCP has already been set up properly, PPP is probably selected. Because you don't want it to work properly, select LocalTalk. Close and reopen MacTCP to make it reflect the network change.

Fig. 21.3
To make sure your
Web server and
Web browser don't
dial the Internet,
select the
LocalTalk option
in the Network
control panel.

> **Note**
>
> If your network is connected to the Internet, make sure you don't have a
> LocalTalk connector plugged into your printer port. If your network isn't
> connected to the Internet and you're not running TCP/IP on any part of your
> network, you can leave your LocalTalk connector in.

5. In the MacTCP control panel, click More (see fig. 21.4).

Fig. 21.4
You set your IP
address, domain
server informa-
tion, and routing
information in the
MacTCP control
panel.

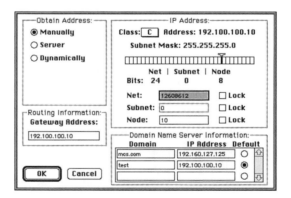

6. If you already have Internet service, you probably already have a gateway address and a domain name server set up. As long as you're running TCP/IP through the LocalTalk port and you're not connected to a
TCP/IP network anywhere on the line, you can leave these settings
alone. If you don't presently have Internet service, make up your own
gateway address and domain name server information. You can use the
numbers shown in figure 21.4.

7. Select the Manually radio button and click OK to close the MacTCP
settings.

8. Again, if you already have Internet service and you're not connected to the network, you can leave the IP address information alone. If not, you can use the IP address shown in figure 21.4. When you finish with your settings, close the MacTCP control panel.

9. Put the following items in the Extensions folder:

   - The AppleScript extension
   - The Finders Scripting extension
   - The Scripting Additions folder

10. Put the Tokenize and Decoder Scripting Additions into the Script Additions folder, or your CGI won't work right.

11. Launch MacHTTP or WebStar, whichever you have. On most Macintosh's, both of these are slow launching programs, but both of them will tell you right away if something is wrong. When MacHTTP starts, your screen should look similar to figure 21.5. When WebStar starts, your screen should look similar to figure 21.6. After about 30 seconds, the MacHTTP and WebStar screen look similar (see figures 21.7 and 21.8).

```
                        MacHTTP 2.0 Status

MacHTTP 2.0, Copyright ⊕1994 Chuck Shotton,
BIAP Systems, Inc. All rights reserved.

Loading MacHTTP.config...
680x0 (CW) Server is running on port 80.

|
```

Fig. 21.5
As MacHTTP starts up, it diagnoses any problems with the connection.

Fig. 21.6
WebStar shows only a splash screen when it starts up.

Fig. 21.7
After MacHTTP is running, it shows you the status of your current and past connections.

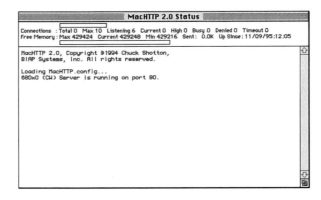

Fig. 21.8
When WebStar is running, it gives you the same connection information that MacHTTP does.

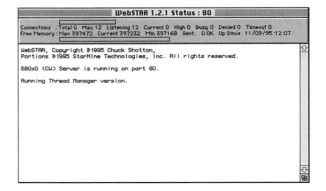

If you can get MacHTTP or WebStar to launch, then you're in business. As you connect to MacHTTP, it logs its interactions with your browser.

You need to create a folder in the WebStar or MacHTTP directory called FMPro. Put your CGI and your HTML documents in it, as well as the FileMaker databases you'll be putting on the Web.

If you want to see how this works in practice, there are several sites around the Internet with FileMaker links. One site I helped set up is Apple Computer's Apple Market Center Seminar Listing (at **http://www.apple.com/**).

If you want to get more information on the Status codes used by HTTP, go to **http://www.w3.org/pub/WWW/Protocols/**.

From Here...

This was a pretty long and technically demanding chapter. You should take time to practice writing HTML documents so you can get the results you're looking for. Surf the Web and view the source code of Web pages you like. For more information on writing HTML, see *Special Edition Using HTML* by Que.

You can spend days experimenting with different permutations of a basic AppleScript CGI. I just marvel at the fact that all these pieces can come together and even work at all.

From here, you might want to look at the following chapters:

- Chapter 15, "Scripting with ScriptMaker," describes how to create scripts for error trapping, automate page numbering, and find and mark duplicate records.
- Chapter 16, "Using AppleScript," teaches you what you can do with AppleScript, such as hot-wire processes in FileMaker Pro, and create integrated solutions involving FileMaker and other AppleScript-savvy applications like MacWrite Pro, Word, or Excel.

VII

Integrating FileMaker Pro

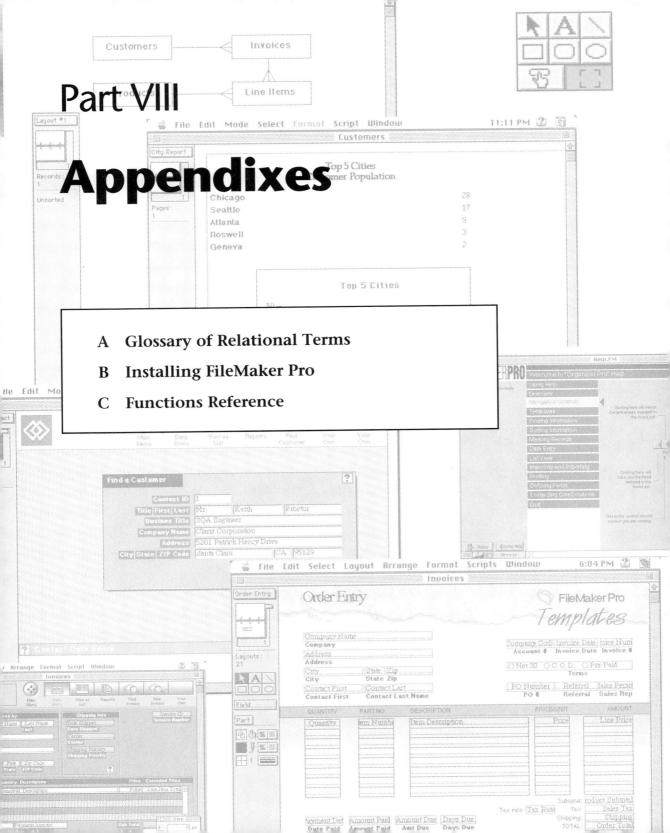

Part VIII

Appendixes

Glossary of Relational Terms

aggregate functions: Special functions that operate across multiple rows in a repeating field, or rows in a portal. The aggregate functions are Average Count, Max, Mean, Standard Deviation, and Sum.

attribute: A fancy name for fields.

break field: A field that the database is sorted on to trigger a sub-summary or a summary function.

cascading delete: A means of enforcing referential integrity that entails the deletion of all child records when a parent record is deleted. For example, if an invoice is deleted, all line items associated with that invoice need to be deleted as well.

cascading update: A means of enforcing referential integrity that entails the updating of all child records when a parent record is updated. For example, if an invoice is updated, all line items associated with that invoice need to be updated as well.

child table: A database whose records cannot exist without a parent record first existing in a parent database. For example, invoice line items cannot exist without belonging to an invoice.

column: A relational database term. A column is the same thing as a field in FileMaker 3.0. This is not the same as a column of fields on a report layout.

conditional scripting: A conditional script. A script that can identify certain conditions being met that can then branch, executing different portions of a script depending on what those conditions are.

database: In FileMaker Pro, the database consists of all the data, fields, layouts, and scripts in a single database file. In other database systems, a database can consist of several database files. These database files are called tables.

E-R diagram: Short for entity-relationship diagram. One of the steps in defining a relational file structure is to identify the entities (things) you keep track of and the relationships (actions) among them.

field: The smallest unit of information in a database. A database is composed of records, which in turn are composed of one or more fields. Fields are the containers for individual pieces of data.

file: In FileMaker Pro, a file is a database.

foreign key: A field used to identify a specific record in another database. For example, a customer ID number in an invoice database can be a foreign key to the customers database.

global field: A global field is defined to contain only one value that is shared across all records in a file. It can be used as a temporary storage location (as in scripts).

key field: Key fields are called match fields. They are used to match records between two different databases. See *match field, foreign key.*

lookup: The process of copying information from a foreign file into the current file. The current file must contain a field in which the information is placed. In FileMaker 3.0, the lookup function requires that the foreign file be related to the current file.

lookup field: A field in which information from a related file is copied.

lookup file: The source file for information that is copied into a lookup field.

looping: A scripted repetitive process that executes until a specific condition is met.

many-to-many: A many-to-many relationship cannot be directly created, because one of each two related files must contain unique key field entries. You relate a many file to another many file by creating a third file related one-to-many to each of the other files. See *one file, many file.*

many-to-one: A relationship where many records in one database match a single record in another database. An example might be many line items corresponding to one invoice.

match field: A field in the current file and a field in the related file that contain equal values, so that the two files can be related. Sometimes called key fields. The match field in the one file must contain only unique values. The match field in the many file can contain duplicate values.

merge field: A merge field displays information from a field in a text object, such as a form letter.

one-to-one relationships: A one-to-one relationship occurs when two files have one-to-one correspondence with each other. For example, a database of employees would have a one-to-one correspondence with a database of employee IDs. Typically, one-to-one relationships are merged into a single file.

paragraph formatting: Word processing features that allow the database designer to control formats for text elements on a layout and to establish default formats for text fields. The user can change the formatting in text fields from record to record.

parent table: Also known as parent file or parent database. It is a file that has data in other files dependent on its records. An example would be an invoice file that has a line item file dependent on it.

portal: A portal is a layout object used to display multiple related records.

record: All the information about one person or one thing in a database.

record locking: A database mechanism that prevents a record from being edited by two people at the same time.

referential integrity: A set of rules that ensure the data in one file that refer to data in another file are referring to information that exists. FileMaker Pro 3.0 can be made to enforce referential integrity.

related field: A field on a layout that displays data from a related file.

related file: When a relationship is established in a database, the file linked to the relationship is called a related file.

related record: A record in the related file whose match field contains a value equal to the value in the match field of the current file.

relationship: User-defined association between two files, characterized by equal values in a match field in each file. One record in the current file is associated with the one or more records (related records) in the related file that have the same value in the corresponding match fields.

report: A tabulated listing of information in a database.

restricted delete: A component of referential integrity, it requires that a record with a child record or records in another database cannot be deleted.

restricted update: A component of referential integrity, it requires that a record with a child record or records in another database cannot be updated.

VIII

Appendixes

row: A relational term that corresponds to a record in FileMaker Pro, as in a portal row.

table: A relational term that corresponds to a database file in FileMaker Pro.

unstored calculation: An unstored calculation is one that is not saved with other data but is recalculated when needed. A calculation that uses that information in a related file is automatically unstored, but any calculation can be set to be unstored.

value list: A list of values that can be used to automate data entry.

Installing FileMaker Pro

FileMaker Pro 3.0 is available on CD-ROM and on 3.5 inch disks. Install from the CD-ROM if possible—there are extra templates and support information available on the CD-ROM that are not on the 3.5 inch disks (because of space limitations). The following installation steps cover the Easy Installation for both types.

The Easy Installation installs all of the files you need to run FileMaker Pro 3.0. Included in an Easy Installation are all network modules, Help files, graphic translators, spelling dictionaries, templates, example files, and a tutorial. The Custom Installation is covered later in this appendix and is for doing partial installations.

Unlike earlier versions, all network modules are installed automatically and the network protocol required is chosen from Preferences in the application. Users no longer have to move networking files into the System Folder.

Requirements

You need the following hardware and software to install and run FileMaker Pro 3.0.

- A Macintosh, Power Macintosh, or any compatible computer system with a hard drive running System 7 or newer.
- At least 25M of free hard disk space available for full installation from CD-ROM or 10M for full installation from 3.5 inch disk.
- A CD-ROM drive or a high density (HD) floppy drive that reads 1.4M disks.
- At least 4M of RAM for a 680x0-based Macintosh and 8M of RAM for a Power Macintosh.

Before You Begin

Before you begin the installation you should do the following:

- Turn off any virus protection utilities in the System Folder—these can block the installation process.

- If you install from 3.5 inch disk, lock all of the disks by moving the small tab in the upper-right corner of the disk so you can no longer see through it. This protects your disks from being overwritten by accident.

Easy Installation

To take advantage of the Easy Installation, follow these steps:

1. Insert the disk.

   If you are installing from CD-ROM, insert the CD-ROM disk into the drive and wait for the disk to mount. Open the newly mounted disk icon by double-clicking it, if it is not already open.

   If you are installing from disks, insert Disk 1 into the floppy drive. Double-click the disk icon that appears on the desktop if it is not already open.

2. Double-click the Start Here for CD-ROM icon or the FileMaker Pro Installer for 3.5 Disk icon to launch the installation process (see fig. B.1).

Fig. B.1
Double-click the appropriate installation icon.

Start Here   FileMaker Pro Installer

3. Click OK in the startup screen.

4. Click Install in the FileMaker Pro Installer dialog box (see fig. B.2).

Fig. B.2
Click Install to start an Easy Installation of FileMaker Pro 3.

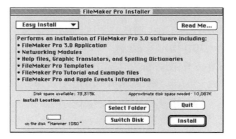

Tip

You can select a different hard drive to install onto by clicking the Switch Disk button.

The Installer will place application and associated files in the FileMaker Pro 3.0 folder. You can select a different folder by clicking the Select Folder button.

If the Install button is dimmed, you do not have enough disk space available on your selected hard drive. The disk space available and the approximate disk space needed are shown. Try switching disks or go back to the Finder to free up some space.

The Install button could also be dimmed if you are trying to install onto a read-only or locked disk such as a CD-ROM.

5. If you are installing from 3.5 disk, you will be asked for all of the disks in turn.

   The Installer will proceed, copying all of the files to your hard drive. You can click Stop at any time to halt the installation process.

   When the Installer has finished, it will tell you that the installation was successful.

6. Click Quit.

If you turned off any virus protection utilities, turn them back on now.

Custom Installation

Use a Custom Installation when you want to install only some of the files included with FileMaker Pro 3.0. This type of installation is useful if you are limited by disk space or you know there are some files you don't need, such as the templates and tutorial.

To perform a custom installation follow steps 1-3 of the easy installation and then follow these steps.

1. Choose Custom Install from the pop-up menu in the FileMaker Pro Installer dialog box (see fig. B.3).

Fig. B.3

Click Install to
start a Custom
Installation of
FileMaker Pro 3.

When you select this option, you can individually select each of file types for installation. Select each file type you want to install. If you are not sure what the file's purpose is, click the Info button for more information. The total amount of disk space required is shown.

2. Click Install in the FileMaker Pro Installer dialog box.

If the Install button is dimmed, you do not have enough disk space available on your selected hard drive. Try switching disks or go back to the Finder to free up some space. The Install button could also be dimmed if you are trying to install onto a read-only or locked disk such as a CD-ROM.

If you are installing from disk, you will be asked for all of the disks in turn.

The Installer will proceed, copying all of the files to your hard drive. You can click Stop at any time to halt the installation process.

When the Installer has finished, it will tell you that the installation was successful.

3. Click Quit.

If you turned off any virus protection utilities, turn them back on now.

Note

If you are installing FileMaker Pro 3.0 on a Macintosh Plus or SE and want to use the network capabilities of FileMaker Pro, be aware that AppleTalk is the only protocol supported on these machines.

Launching FileMaker Pro 3.0 for the First Time

You are now ready to launch FileMaker Pro 3.0. The first time you run the application, you can personalize your copy by entering your name, company name, and serial number. Before you click OK, make sure the information is correct—this is the only chance you have to enter this information. The serial number should be on the registration card included with your copy of FileMaker Pro 3.0, and is required if you need technical support.

VIII

Appendixes

Functions Reference

The following is a list of functions grouped by category. See Chapter 5, "Working with Calculation Fields," for more information on how to work with functions.

Date Functions

The Date functions allow you to perform calculations on date-formatted data. The Date functions are invaluable when working in conjunction with financial formulas or when using databases to schedule projects and events.

Date

Usage

Date (month, day, year)

Arguments

- *month*. A number representing the month of the year, from 1 to 12.
- *day*. A number representing the day of the month, from 1 to 31.
- *year*. A four digit number from 0001 to 3000.

Returns

The calendar date for the given values.

Details

The resulting date is formatted with respect to the date format of the field in the current layout. Date separators come from the current system settings.

Example

Date(02,06,1967) returns the date 2/6/67 or Monday, February 6, 1967, depending on the field date format.

DateToText

Usage

DateToText (date)

Argument

■ *date*. The date in question.

Returns

The given date formatted as text.

Details

The returned text will be displayed according to the date format used when the database file was created. This is usually in a MM/DD/YY format. Remember to format the calculation result as text or your results may vary.

Examples

"You were born on " & DateToText(BirthDate) returns: "You were born on 04/06/1967," if the field BirthDate contains April 6, 1967.

DateToText(Date(2,6,1967)) returns "02/06/67".

Day

Usage

Day (date)

Argument

■ *date*. The date in question.

Returns

A number from 1 to 31, which is the day of the month on which the passed date falls.

Example

Day (AndyMan) returns 3 if the field AndyMan contains "12/03/1967".

If(Day(Today) = 5, "The rent is due!","") returns "The rent is due!" if today is fifth of the month.

DayName

Usage

DayName (date)

Argument

■ *date*. The date in question.

Returns

A text string.

Details

Returns a text string that is the full name of the weekday for the supplied date.

Examples

DayName (Date(4,6,1967)) returns "Thursday."

DayOfWeek

Usage

DayOfWeek (date)

Argument

■ *date*. The date in question.

Returns

A number from 1 to 7, with 1 being Sunday, 2 Monday, and so on.

Examples

DayOfWeek(TextToDate("2/6/1967")) returns 2.

DayofWeek(BirthDay) returns 5 if BirthDay contains "4/6/1967".

DayOfYear

Usage

DayOfYear (date)

Argument

■ *date*. A date.

Returns

A number, the number of days from the start of the year to the date passed as a parameter.

Examples

DayofYear(Date(2,6,1995)) returns 37.

Depending on your stance on the "days until" issue, this formula will tell you how many days until Christmas:

    Abs(DayofYear(Date(12,25,Year(Today))) - DayofYear(Today))

The absolute value function is tossed in just in case you missed it. Of course, it would be an easy matter to modify this formula to count the number of days until next Christmas if you've already missed it this year.

Month

Usage
Month (date)

Argument
- *date*. A valid date.

Returns
A number from 1 to 12.

Details
The number returned corresponds to January = 1, February = 2, and so on for each month.

Example
Month(TextToDate("4/06/95")) returns 4.

MonthName

Usage
MonthName (date)

Argument
- *date*. A valid date.

Returns
A text string, the name of the month of the date in the passed argument.

Details
FileMaker Pro capitalizes the month name for you.

Examples
MonthName(TextToDate("4/6/1967")) returns April.

Today

Usage
Today

Argument
None.

Returns

A date, the current date at time of function evaluation.

Details

The Today function is perhaps one of the most loved and most hated of all FileMaker Pro functions. The great thing is that now you can toss this value into a global field if you want (depending on your needs) and it only has to be calculated once per database, rather than once for every record.

One point to watch out for: if you are hosting a file or using FileMaker Pro Server, you must close and reopen the file (by the host peer machine or Server) for the Today function to be properly re-evaluated.

Examples

If(DayofYear(Date(12,25,Year(Today))) - DayofYear(Today) < 30, "Time to start shopping", "Relax...")

WeekofYear

Usage

WeekOfYear (date)

Argument

■ *date*. A valid date.

Returns

A number from 1 to 54, the number of weeks because New Year's day of the year of the argument date.

Details

Why is it 1 to 54 weeks? Partial weeks at both ends of the year count as well, so you end up with 54 possible weeks.

Example

WeekOfYear(TextToDate("4/6/1967")) returns 14.

WeekofYearFiscal

Usage

WeekOfYearFiscal (date, starting day)

Arguments

■ *date*. A valid, if not very fiscal date.

■ *starting day*. A number from 1 to 7, with 1 representing Sunday, 2 Monday, and so on.

Returns

A number, between 1 and 53 inclusive, denoting the number of the week of the fiscal year.

Details

The date argument determines the point in time you are interested in. The starting day argument represents the day of the week you consider to be the first day of the week. This way, it's no problem if the accounting department wants weeks to start on a Wednesday.

A couple of fine points: for a week to qualify as the first week of the year, four or more days in that week (remember, you are setting the day to be considered the first day of the week) must be in the given year. In other words, if New Year's is on a Monday, Tuesday, Wednesday, or Thursday, you're okay. If New Year's was on a Sunday, such as 1/1/1967, then WeekofYearFiscal(TextToDate("1/2/1967"), 4) would return 53.

Example

WeekOfYearFiscal(Date(2,6,1967), 2) returns 6.

Year

Usage

Year (date)

Argument

- *date*. A valid date.

Returns

A number from 1 to 3000, the year component of the given date.

Details

Returns a number representing the year in which the given date occurs. For example, you can extract the year from the information in a field containing the date an item sold.

Examples

Year(BirthDate) returns the year in which someone was born.

Financial Functions

You can use these financial functions to perform all sorts of interesting calculations. All those future and net present value calculations that drove you crazy in finance class are a snap with FileMaker Pro. Now you can easily determine your payment on that next big PowerMac WorkGroup Server you are buying to run the FileMaker Pro 3.0 Server. Make sure to buy extra RAM and a good DAT backup drive!

FV (Future Value)

Usage
FV (payment, interest rate, periods)

Arguments
- *payment*. Amount of payment per period.
- *interest rate*. The interest rate per period.
- *periods*. Number of periods.

Returns
A number, the future value of the investment over time.

Details
Assumes constant intertest rate and payment value throughout the number of periods, with payments made at the end, not the beginning of the period.

Examples
Round(FV(10, .08/12, 72), 2) returns 920.25.

NPV (Net Present Value)

Usage
NPV (payment, interest rate)

Arguments
- *payment*. A repeating field containing payments of unequal values.
- *interest rate*. Interest rate.

Returns
A number, the net present value of the payments.

Details
Assumes that the interest rate is fixed and the periods are of the same length. The payments can be of unequal amounts.

Examples
Round(NPV(Pain, .07), 2) returns 1632.58 if Pain contains: (-10000, 1000, 2000, 3000, 4000, 5000). That is the amount of real world current dollars that my friend will make by loaning me money.

VIII

Appendixes

PMT (Payment)

Usage
PMT (principal, interest rate, term)

Arguments

- *principal*. The principal.
- *interest rate*. The monthly interest rate.
- *term*. The number of months.

Returns
A number, the monthly payment you need to make to satisfy the principal at a given rate over a set number of months.

Examples
Say you're buying a heavily loaded WorkGroup Server 9150, and it's four in the morning and you just can't do math anymore. Not a problem—FileMaker Pro 3.0 will come to your rescue. You are going to spend $13,000, pay an interest rate of 11 percent, and pay it off over 36 months.

Round(PMT(13000, .11/12, 36), 2) returns 425.60.

PV (Present Value)

Usage
PV (payment, interest rate, periods)

Arguments

- *payment*. Payment per period. If you are paying out, this value is negative; if someone else is paying you, it is positive.
- *interest rate*. Interest per period.
- *periods*. Number of periods (intervals between payments).

Returns
A number, the present value of a payment stream.

Details
Assumes a fixed interest rate, regular periods, and equal payments.

Example
Say your cousin borrowed $2,000 from you, offering to pay you back $500 a year for five years: a total of $2,500 at the end of five years. If inflation was five percent annually, with the following entry, you could find out what those payments are worth with the PV function.

PV(100, .02, 10) returns 898.258500624224.

Logical Functions

Logical functions evaluate a given test case and determine whether it is True or False. If it is True, the function returns a 1; if it is False, it returns a 0. Some logical functions also perform comparisons, make their True/False determination, and return other results besides True or False.

Case

Usage
Case (test1, result1 [, test2, result2, default result]...)

Arguments
- *test*. Any text or numeric expression.
- *result*. A result corresponding to each test, as well as an optional default result.

Returns
Text, number, date, time, or container.

Details
FileMaker Pro fans are quite happy with this function. The Case function can streamline the nested If functions and provide you with a clear set of tests and related results. Each test is evaluated in order, and as soon as a True test case is encountered, its corresponding result is returned.

Another great feature of the Case function is the default result. If no True case is found as the tests are evaluated, the default result will automatically be returned. If there is no default given, an empty result will be returned.

Examples
Case(Weather="Snow","Stay home", Weather="Rain", "Umbrella", Weather="Hot", "Shorts","Jeans") returns Umbrella if Weather contains Rain, and Jeans if none of the tests are True.

Choose

Usage
Choose (expression, result0 [, result1, result2]...)

Arguments
- *expression*. A calculation or function that can have values from 0 to n–1, where n is the number of results in the Choose function.
- *result*. One or more results. All but the first (zero valued) results are optional.

Returns

Text, number, date, time, or container.

Details

The result of the expression is used as an index value, corresponding to the list of results. If the expression evaluates to 0, the first (or zero value) expression is returned, if it is 1, the next result is returned, and so on. If the value of the expression is not an integer value, the result is first truncated, and then used to find the proper index value. For example, an expression result of 1.99999 would yield an index value of 1, and return result1.

Example

If you wanted to report to the user which calendar quarter the date fell, the following Choose function would do nicely:

> Choose(((Month(TheDate) + 2)/3), "Illegal date", "We're in Q1", "We're in Q2", "We're in Q3", "We're in Q4")

If you are more fiscally minded, the following version would properly report the fiscal quarters for a company that starts its fiscal year on October 1:

> Choose(((Month(TheDate) + 2)/3), "Illegal date", "We're in Q4", "We're in Q3", "We're in Q2", "We're in Q1")

If

Usage

If (test, resultIfTrue, resultIfFalse)

Arguments

- *test.* Logical expression or numeric value.
- *resultIfTrue.* Text or numeric expression.
- *resultIfFalse.* Text or numeric expression.

Returns

Text, number, date, time, or container.

Details

First test is evaluated. If it evaluates as True (any value other than 0), the resultIfTrue expression is evaluated and returned. If test evaluates to False (a 0 value), the resultIfFalse expression is evaluated and returned.

FileMaker Pro's default condition is to skip an If function and return an empty result if the field it refers to does not contain a value. Making sure the Do Not Evalute if All Referenced Fields Are Empty check box is deselected will keep FileMaker Pro from behaving this way. There are certainly cases in which you may or may not want this extra functionality.

Both the ResultIfTrue and ResultIfFalse components of this function can be If functions. Nesting multiple If functions can be a very powerful tool, but the Case function might prove to be easier to read and even easier to debug in your calculations.

Examples

If(Weight > 100, "Too Heavy, must pay extra shipping fee", "Package may ship at the normal rate") reports the surplus if the package is too heavy.

IsEmpty

Usage

IsEmpty (value)

Argument

■ *value*. Any text or numeric expression.

Returns

A number.

Details

If the value passed to the function is empty, IsEmpty will return a 1 (it is True that the field is empty); otherwise, it will return 0.

Examples

IsEmpty(AccountBalance) returns 1 if the field "AccountBalance" is empty.

IsEmpty("Lum Lum") returns 0.

IsValid

Usage

IsValid (field)

Argument

■ *field*. Any field name.

Returns

A number.

Details

Returns False(0) if the named related field is missing from the file or if the related field contains an invalid value; otherwise returns True(1).

VIII

Appendixes

A field reference can be invalid for two reasons: the referenced related field cannot be found, or the field contains invalid data. The field's type defines what type of data the field can contain. A field contains invalid data when, for example, a user has typed text in a date field.

IsValid is intended to check for the following conditions:

A field contains an invalid value due to a data type mismatch.

A related file cannot be located (temporarily or permanently).

A field has been deleted from a related file, and therefore the references to that field in the master file are invalid.

Numeric Functions

Numeric functions are used to manipulate numerical data. For example, you can truncate a number to display only the number of digits you need, or round off a number to the nearest acceptable value.

Abs (Absolute Value)

Usage

Abs (number)

Argument

■ *number*. Numeric expression or field containing one.

Returns

A number.

Details

This function returns the absolute value of a number, defined as Abs(number) = number if number >= 0, or –number if number < 0.

Examples

Abs(–770) returns 770.

Abs(391) returns 391

The absoulte value of a number can be useful when you want to track the magnitude of a change, but aren't too concerned with whether or not it is positive or negative.

Abs(yesterdayTemp - todayTemp) provide a positive number representing the amount of change in temperature between two days, but no information as to whether it went up or down.

Exp (Exponent)

Usage

Exp (number)

Argument

■ *number.* Numeric expression or field containing one.

Returns

A number.

Details

Returns the value of the constant "e" (the base of the natural logarithm, equal to 2.7182818) raised to the power (number). The Exp function is the inverse of the Ln function.

Examples

Exp(1) returns 2.71828182845905.

Exp(Ln(28)) returns 28.

Exp(0) returns 1.

Int (Integer)

Usage

Int (number)

Argument

■ *number.* Numeric expression or field containing one.

Returns

A number.

Details

Returns only the whole number (integer) part of the value passed.

Examples

Int(3.1415927) returns 3.

Int(98.7654321) returns 98.

Mod (Modulo)

Usage

Mod (number, divisor)

Arguments

- *number*. Numeric expression or field containing one.
- *divisor*. Numeric expression or field containing one.

Returns

A number.

Details

Returns the remainder portion of the result of dividing number by divisor.

Examples

Mod(28, 2) returns 0. (we know the number is even).

Mod(19,5) returns 4.

NumToText

Usage

NumToText (number)

Argument

- *number*. Numeric expression or field containing one.

Returns

A text string containing the text representation of the passed numerical value.

Examples

NumToText(770391) returns 770391 (as text).

Random

Usage

Random

Arguments

None

Returns

A number, random value between 0 and 1.

Details

This random number will be recalculated whenever a formula using this function is re-evaluated.

Example

If (Random < .5, "Heads", "Tails").

Round

Usage

Round (number, precision).

Arguments

■ *number*. Numeric expression or field containing one.

■ *precision*. Numeric expression or field containing one.

Returns

A number.

Details

Rounds the given number to the specified number of digits, rounding to a negative precision drops digits and then rounds, always rounds .5 up.

Examples

Round(64.5, 0) returns 65.

Round(69241.99, -3) returns 69000.

Round(821.345, -1) returns 820.

Sign

Usage

Sign (number)

Argument

■ *number*. Numeric expression or field containing one.

Returns

A number.

Details

Returns 1 when the value passed is positive, 0 when it's zero, and –1 when the value is negative.

Example

Sign(770) returns 1.

Sign(–32) returns –1.

Sign(AccountBalance) returns –1 if you are in trouble with the bank.

VIII

Appendixes

Sqrt (Square Root)

Usage

Sqrt (number)

Argument

- ■ *number.* Numeric expression or field containing one.

Returns

A number.

Details

Calculates the square root number for positive values of number.

Example

Sqrt(16) returns 4.

Truncate

Usage

Truncate (number, precision).

Arguments

- ■ *number.* Numeric expression or field containing one.
- ■ *precision.* Numeric expression or field containing one.

Returns

A number.

Details

Returns the passed value truncated to the number of decimal places given by precision.

Examples

Truncate(9.123, 2) returns 9.12.

Truncate(99231.99, –3) returns 99000.

Aggregate Functions

Aggregate functions let you perform calculations on sets of data, in both repeating and regular fields; they even operate on related records.

Average

Usage

Average (field...)

Argument

- *field.* Repeating or nonrepeating field.

Returns

A number.

Details

Returns the average of all the values in the given field, disregarding empty values. If the calculation result is defined as a repeating field, the Average function then returns the average for all values in corresponding field repetitions.

Count

Usage

Count (field...)

Argument

- *field.* Any repeating or nonrepeating field.

Returns

A number.

Details

If the calculation is defined with a regular field as the resulting field type, Count returns the number of non-blank, valid fields. A defined return type of repeating field will cause the function to count the associated repeating field repetitions.

Max

Usage

Max (field...)

Argument

- *field.* Any repeating or nonrepeating field.

Returns

A number.

Details

Returns the greatest value in the specified field. Max returns the highest value for all values in the corresponding repetitions for arguments that are repeating fields.

Example

Max(sales) returns 12 when sales contains three repetitions with values 2,6,12.

Min

Usage

Min (field...)

Argument

■ *field.* Any repeating or nonrepeating field.

Returns

A number.

Details

Returns the smallest value in a specified field. In a repeating field, Min returns the smallest value for all values in the corresponding repetitions.

Example

Min(sales) returns 2 when sales contains three repetitions with values 2,6,12.

StDev (Standard Deviation)

Usage

StDev (field...)

Argument

■ *field.* Any repeating or nonrepeating field.

Returns

A number.

Details

Returns the standard deviation of a specified field. In a repeating field, StDev returns the standard deviation for all values in the corresponding repetitions.

Example

StDev(sales) returns 5.033 when sales contains three repetitions with values 2,6,12.

StDevP (Standard Deviation of Population)

Usage

StDevP (field...)

Argument

■ *field.* Any repeating or nonrepeating field.

Returns

A number.

Details

Returns the standard deviation of population of a specified field. In a repeating field, StDevP returns the standard deviation of population of all values in the corresponding repetitions.

Example

StDevP(name) returns 4,109 when name contains three repetitions with values 2,6,12.

Sum

Usage

Sum (field...)

Argument

■ *field.* Any repeating or nonrepeating field.

Returns

A number.

Details

Returns the total of a specified field. In a repeating field, Sum returns the total of all values in the corresponding repetitions.

Example

Sum(sales) returns 20 when sales contains three repetitions with values 2,6,12.

Status Functions

The Status functions allow you to query the current FileMaker Pro environment. Variables such as the current script's name, the current file's size, the number of guests, and more are available to your calculations.

With Status functions, you can customize your databases and allow them to behave more intelligently by trapping errors, analyzing them, and acting upon them accordingly.

Status (CurrentAppVersion)

Usage
Status (CurrentAppVersion)

Arguments
None

Returns
A text string containing the version of the current running FileMaker Pro application such as "Pro 3.0."

Status (CurrentDate)

Usage
Status (CurrentDate)

Arguments
None

Returns
The current date formatted according to the display format of the field.

Status (CurrentError)

Usage
Status (CurrentError)

Arguments
None

Returns
A number.

Details
After completing execution, each step of a script may report a numerical error code. Status(CurrentError) will let you query this error code and have your script execute accordingly.

Examples
Status(CurrentError) returns 0 when the most recent script step executed without error.

Status (CurrentError) returns 401 if the found set is empty after the Find Records step has completed.

The Set Error Capture [On] script step will disable alerts and some dialog boxes. You can then trap errors and bring to them to the user's attention in a manner you choose using the Show Message script step. Errors generated by an AppleScript script will be returned to you as the AppleScript error codes.

Errors	Description
−1	Unknown error
0	No error
1	User canceled action
2	Memory error
3	Command is unavailable (for example, wrong operating system, wrong mode, and so on)
4	Command is unknown
5	Command is invalid (for example, a Set Field script step does not have a calculation specified)
100	File is missing
101	Record is missing
102	Field is missing
103	Relation is missing
104	Script is missing
105	Layout is missing
200	Record access is denied
201	Field cannot be modified
202	Field access is denied
203	No records in file to print or password doesn't allow print access
204	No access to field(s) in sort order
205	Cannot create new records; import will overwrite existing data
300	The file is locked or in use
301	Record is in use by another user
302	Script definitions are in use by another user
303	Paper size is in use by another user
304	Password definitions are in use by another user
305	Relationship or value list definitions are locked by another user
400	Find criteria is empty

(continues)

VIII

Appendixes

(continued)

Errors	Description
401	No records match the request
402	Not a match field for a lookup
403	Exceeding maximum record limit for demo
404	Sort order is invalid
405	Number of records specified exceeds number of records that can be omitted
406	Replace/Reserialize criteria is invalid
407	One or both key fields are missing (invalid relation)
408	Specified field has inappropriate data type for this operation
409	Import order is invalid
410	Export order is invalid
411	Cannot perform delete because related records cannot be deleted
412	Wrong version of FileMaker used to recover file
500	Date value does not meet validation entry options
501	Time value does not meet validation entry options
502	Number value does not meet validation entry options
503	Value in field does not meet range validation entry options
504	Value in field does not meet unique value validation entry options
505	Value in field failed existing value validation test
506	Value in field is not a member value of the validation entry option value list
507	Value in field failed calculation test of validation entry option
508	Value in field failed query value test of validation entry option
509	Field requires a valid value
510	Related value is empty or unavailable
600	Print error has occurred
601	Combined header and footer exceed one page
602	Body doesn't fit on a page for current column setup
603	Print connection lost
700	File is of the wrong file type for import
701	Data Access Manager can't find database extension file
702	The Data Access Manager was unable to open the session
703	The Data Access Manager was unable to open the session; try later
704	Data Access Manager failed when sending a query

Errors	Description
705	Data Access Manager failed when executing a query
706	EPSF file has no preview image
707	Graphic translator can not be found
708	Can't import the file or need color machine to import file
709	QuickTime movie import failed
710	Unable to update QuickTime file reference because the database is read-only
711	Import translator cannot be found
712	XTND version is incompatible
713	Couldn't initialize the XTND system
714	Insufficient password privileges do not allow the operation
800	Unable to create file on disk
801	Unable to create temporary file on System disk
802	Unable to open file
803	File is single user or host cannot be found
804	File cannot be opened as read-only in its current state
805	File is damaged; use Recover command
806	File cannot be opened with this version of FileMaker
807	File is not a FileMaker file or is severely damaged
808	Cannot open file because of damaged access privileges
809	Disk/volume is full
810	Disk/volume is locked
811	Temporary file cannot be opened as FileMaker file
812	Cannot open the file because it exceeds host capacity
813	Record Synchronization error on network
814	File(s) cannot be opened because maximum number is open
815	Couldn't open lookup file
816	Unable to convert file
900	General spelling engine error
901	Main spelling dictionary not installed
902	Could not launch the Help system
903	Command cannot be used in a shared file

VIII

Appendixes

Status (CurrentFieldName)

Usage
Status (CurrentFieldName)

Arguments
None

Returns
Text.

Details
Returns text for the name of the current field.

Example
Status(CurrentFieldName) returns Salary when the current field is Salary.

Status (CurrentFileName)

Usage
Status (CurrentFileName)

Arguments
None

Returns
Text.

Details
Returns the name of the current database file.

Status (CurrentFileSize)

Usage
Status (CurrentFileSize)

Arguments
None

Returns
Numbers.

Details
Returns the size (in bytes) of the current file.

Example

Status(CurrentFileSize) returns 670000, when the current file size is 670,000
bytes.

Status (CurrentFoundCount)

Usage

Status (CurrentFoundCount)

Arguments

None

Returns

Numbers.

Details

Returns a number equal to the number of records in the current found set.

Status (CurrentHostName)

Usage

Status (CurrentHostName)

Arguments

None

Returns

A text string.

Details

Returns the system name of the machine that is hosting the database file that
is executing the current script.

Example

Status(CurrentHostName) returns The Tick when The Tick is registered as the
host name for that machine.

Status (CurrentLayoutCount)

Usage

Status (CurrentLayoutCount)

Arguments

None

Returns
Numbers.

Details
Returns the number of layouts in the database.

Status (CurrentLayoutName)

Usage
Status (CurrentLayoutName)

Arguments
None

Returns
Text.

Details
Returns the name of the current layout in the database file.

Status (CurrentLayoutNumber)

Usage
Status (CurrentLayoutNumber)

Arguments
None

Returns
Numbers.

Details
Returns the number of the current layout.

Example
Status(CurrentLayoutNumber) returns 3, when the current layout is the third layout in the database.

Status (CurrentLanguage)

Usage
Status (CurrentLanguage)

Arguments
None

Returns
Text.

Details
Returns the current language set on the current system.

Example
Status(CurrentLanguage) returns "English," when English is the current language set on the system.

Status (CurrentMode)

Usage
Status (CurrentMode)

Arguments
None

Returns
Numbers.

Details
Returns a number denoting the FileMaker Pro mode at the time of the calculation: 0 for Browse mode, 1 for Find mode, and 2 for Preview mode.

Status (CurrentMultiUserStatus)

Usage
Status (CurrentMultiUserStatus)

Arguments
None

Returns
Numbers.

Details
Returns 0 for a single user file, 1 for a multi-user file on the host computer, or 2 for a multi-user file on a guest computer.

Status (CurrentPageNumber)

Usage
Status (CurrentPageNumber)

VIII

Appendixes

Arguments

None

Returns

Numbers.

Details

Returns a number which is the current page being printed or previewed. It returns 0 if nothing is being printed or previewed.

Status (CurrentPlatform)

Usage

Status (CurrentPlatform)

Arguments

None

Returns

Numbers.

Details

Returns 1 if the current platform is Macintosh or 2 if the platform is Windows.

Example

Status(CurrentPlatform) returns 2, when the current platform is Windows.

Status (CurrentPortalRow)

Usage

Status (CurrentPortalRow)

Arguments

None

Returns

Numbers.

Details

Returns the number of the current row in a selected portal. If no portal is selected the return value is 0.

Status (CurrentPrinterName)

Usage

Status (CurrentPrinterName)

Arguments
None

Returns
Text.

Details
Returns a text string identifying the selected printer name.

Status (CurrentRecordCount)

Usage
Status (CurrentRecordCount)

Arguments
None

Returns
Numbers.

Details
Returns the total number of records in a file.

Status (CurrentRecordNumber)

Usage
Status (CurrentRecordNumber)

Arguments
None

Returns
Numbers.

Details
Returns the number of the current record in the current found set.

Example
Status(CurrentRecordNumber) returns 28 when the current record is the 28th record in the current found set.

Status (CurrentRepetitionNumber)

Usage
Status (CurrentRepetitionNumber)

Arguments

None

Returns

Numbers.

Details

Returns a number representing the current (active) value of a repeating field. The first value is 1. If the current field is not a normal (non-repeating) field, the function returns 1.

Example

Status(CurrentRepetitionNumber) returns 5 when a repeating field contains ten values and the current iteration is the fifth value.

Status (CurrentRequestCount)

Usage

Status(CurrentRequestCount)

Arguments

None

Returns

Numbers.

Details

Returns the total number of find requests defined in the database file.

Status (CurrentScreenDepth)

Usage

Status (CurrentScreenDepth)

Arguments

None

Returns

Numbers.

Details

Returns the number of bits needed to represent the color or shade of grey of a pixel on the main screen. A value of 8 allows for 256 colors or shades of grey, 4 bits enables 16 colors/shades of grey, 2 permits 4 colors/shades of grey, and 1 means only black and white.

Examples

Status(CurrentScreenDepth) returns 1 on a black-and-white display.

Status(CurrentScreenDepth) returns 4 on a VGA display.

Status (CurrentScreenHeight)

Usage

Status (CurrentScreenHeight)

Arguments

None

Returns

A number, the height of the screen (that contains the currrent file) in pixels.

Details

On a Macintosh with multiple monitors if the window spans more than one monitor, FileMaker Pro determines which screen owns the greatest percentage of the files display area and reports the height of that screen.

Example

Status(CurrentScreenHeight) returns 480, on a 640 × 480 monitor setting.

Status (CurrentScreenWidth)

Usage

Status (CurrentScreenWidth)

Arguments

None

Returns

A number, the width of the screen (that contains the current file) in pixels.

Details

On a Macintosh with multiple monitors if the window spans more than one monitor, FileMaker Pro determines which screen owns the greatest percentage of the files display area and reports the width of that screen.

Example

Status(CurrentScreenWidth) returns 640, when FileMaker is running on a PowerBook 5300c at 640 × 480 resolution.

Status (CurrentScriptName)

Usage

Status (CurrentScriptName)

Arguments

None

Returns

A text string containing a script name.

Details

Returns the name of the script that is currently running or paused.

Examples

Status(CurrentScriptName) returns Taking a Vacation when the Taking a Vacation script is executing.

Status (CurrentSortStatus)

Usage

Status (CurrentSortStatus)

Arguments

None

Returns

A number denoting the sort state of the records.

Details

Returns 0 if the records in the current file are unsorted, 1 if they are sorted, and 2 if they are only partially sorted.

Example

Status(CurrentSortStatus) returns 1 when the records in the file are sorted.

Status (CurrentSystemVersion)

Usage

Status (CurrentSystemVersion)

Arguments

None

Returns

A text string with the system version of the machine the application is running on.

Examples

Status(CurrentSystemVersion) returns 7.5 for the Macintosh version of FileMaker Pro.

Status (CurrentTime)

Usage

Status (CurrentTime)

Arguments

None

Returns

Time

Details

Returns the current time.

Example

Status (CurrentTime) returns 03:30:00 when the clock shows a bleary-eyed user 03:30:00.

Status (CurrentUserCount)

Usage

Status (CurrentUserCount)

Arguments

None

Returns

A number, the number of users logged into the file.

Details

Returns 1 for a single user file. The return value for a multi-user file would be the number of guests plus the host.

Example

Status(CurrentUserCount) returns 11, when a file has 10 guests.

Status (CurrentUserName)

Usage

Status (CurrentUserName)

Arguments

None

Returns

Text

Details

Returns the FileMaker Pro user's name, entered in the General area of the Preferences dialog.

Example

Status(CurrentUserName) returns Simon Jester when Simon Jester is the current user.

Summary Functions

There is only one function in this catagory, GetSummary, which replaces the function Summary in earlier versions of FileMaker. Its purpose is to obtain the summary of a summary field.

GetSummary

Usage

GetSummary(summary field, break field)

Arguments

- *summary field*. A summary calculation for a found set of records.
- *break field*. A field that the database must be sorted by to group values together to obtain the summary value.

Returns

Numbers

Details

The GetSummary function returns the value of the specified summary field for the current found set of records when the database is sorted by the break field. The value will remain blank until the database is sorted and usually only appears when the datebase is printed or previewed.

Examples

GetSummary(monthlysales, salesperson) returns a summary of monthly sales for all records in the found set for each salesperson.

Text Functions

You can use Text functions to analyze, rearrange, extract, and build text strings. For example, you could use the MiddleWord function to extract specific words from supplied text.

Exact

Usages

Exact(original text, comparison text)

Exact(original container, comparison container)

Arguments

- *original text.* Text, text expression, or field that evaluates to text.
- *comparison text.* Text, text expression, or field that evaluates to text.

Returns

A number; 1 if there is an exact match, 0 otherwise.

Details

The two strings must exactly match in case usage, length, and so on.

Examples

Exact("Smith", "Smith") returns 1 (True).

Exact("SMITH", "SmItH") returns 0 (False).

Left

Usage

Left(text, number)

Arguments

- *text.* Text, text expression, or field that evaluates to text.
- *number.* Text, text expression, or field that evaluates to text.

Returns

A text string.

Details

Returns (number) characters from the source text starting from the left.

Examples

Left("Manufacturing", 4) returns Manu.

Left(Name, Position(Name, " ",1)) returns William, when the text field Name contains William Blackwell.

Left(ZipCode, 3) & Upper(Left(LastName, 4)) returns 481JOHN when the text field ZipCode contains 48187 and LastName contains Johnson.

Length

Usage
Length(text)

Argument
- *text.* Any text expression or field containing text.

Returns
Numbers

Details
Returns the number or characters in the input string including all spaces, numbers, and special characters.

Examples
Length("She sells sea shells!") returns 21.

Lower

Usage
Lower(text)

Argument
- *text.* Any text expression or field containing text.

Returns
Text

Details
Forces all characters in the given text to lowercase.

Examples
Lower("Apple Pie") returns apple pie.

Middle

Usage
Middle(text, start, size)

Arguments

■ *text.* Any text expression or field containing text.

■ *start.* Any numeric expression or field containing a number.

■ *size.* Any numeric expression or field containing a number.

Returns

Text

Details

Returns characters from the input text, starting at the position given by start and containing the number of characters set by size.

Examples

Middle("(770)391-0117",2,3) returns "408".

MiddleWords

Usage

MiddleWords(text, starting word, number)

Arguments

■ *text.* Any text expression or field containing text.

■ *starting word.* Any numeric expression or field containing a number.

■ *number.* Any numeric expression or field containing a number.

Returns

Text

Details

Returns the specified number of words from the given text, beginning with the starting word.

Examples

MiddleWords("One Bright Day We Shall", 2, 2) returns Bright day.

PatternCount

Usage

PatternCount(text, pattern)

Arguments

■ *text.* Any text expression.

■ *pattern.* Any text expression.

Returns
Numbers

Details
Returns the number of occurrences of the source pattern in the sample text.

Examples
PatternCount("DoBeDoBeDo", "Do") returns 3.

Position

Usage
Position(text, search string, start, occurrence)

Arguments
- *text*. The text to search in.
- *search string*. The text you are searching for.
- *start*. The position in the string.
- *occurrence*. A non-zero value, the number of the occurrence of the search string you are hunting for, a negative value forces search in opposite direction.

Returns
Numbers

Details
Position parses through the text string looking for the instance (occurence) of the search string, starting at the start character. A number is returned denoting where in the string the occurrence was found. If the search string is not located, or the proper numbered occurrence is not found, the function returns 0.

Examples
Position("The Cellar Door", "oo",1,1) returns 12.

Position("The Cellar Door", "r",1,2) returns 15.

Position("he Cellar Door", "r",3,6) returns 0.

Proper

Usage
Proper(text)

Argument
- *text*. Any text expression or field containing text.

Returns

Text

Details

Converts the first letter of each word to uppercase and all other letters to low-ercase.

Examples

Proper(Behavior) returns Don't Chew With Your Mouth Full, when the text field Behavior contains Don't CHEW with yOUR mouth Full.

Proper("We're from the government, we're here to help.") returns We're From The Government, We're Here To Help.

Replace

Usage

Replace(text, start, size, replacement text)

Arguments

- *text*. Text string, expression that evaluates to a text string, or text field.
- *start*. A number specifying the start postion within the text.
- *size*. A number representing the number of characters to replace starting from the given start position.
- *replacement text*. The text to replace with.

Returns

Text, the modified text string.

Details

If the input text (the text being modified) is coming from a field, the size limit is 64k; if it is typed directly into the formula, the limit is 250 characters.

Examples

Replace("ABCDEFGHIJKL",3,2,"*Happy*") returns AB*Happy*EFGHIJKL.

Replace("1234567890",2,6,"$") returns 1$890.

Right

Usage

Right(text, number)

Arguments

- *text*. Text string, expression that evaluates to a text string, or text field.
- *number*. Number of characters to grab from the input string, starting from the right.

Returns

A text string made up of the (number) of characters from the original string, starting from the right.

Examples

Right("Bluejay",3) returns jay.

Upper(Right(LName, 5)) & Right(Zip,4) returns FIELD7503 when the text field Zip is 17503 and LName contains Warefield. These types of calculations are great for cooking up your own unique key field values.

RightWords

Usage

RightWords(text, number of words)

Arguments

- *text*. Text string, expression that evaluates to a text string, or text field.
- *number of words*. The number of words to extract.

Returns

Text containing the specified number of words from the given text, with counting starting from the right.

Example

RightWords("Cut the blue wire but first cut the green wire", 4) returns cut the green wire.

Substitute

Usage

Substitute(text, search string, replace string)

Argument

- *text, search string, replace string*. Text string, expression that evaluates to a text string, or text field.

Returns

The modified text string.

Details

Searches through the text string looking for all occurrences of the search string. When it finds matches, it replaces the search string with the replace string. The modified version of the original string is returned. This function is case sensitive in its matching effort.

Examples

Substitute("Who knows if Dr. Who knows that Mrs. Who sang back up for the Who", "Who", "Fred") returns "Fred knows if Dr. Fred knows that Mrs. Fred sang back up for the Fred."

TextToDate

Usage

TextToDate(text)

Argument

- *text*. Text string, expression that evaluates to a text string or text field.

Returns

A date, the date represented by the given text string.

Details

Much like the TextToTime and Time functions, TextToDate and Date are the functions used for directly placing dates in calculations. The input text string must have the same date format as the initial date format in place when the file was originally created.

Example

TextToDate("03/21/1996") returns 3/21/96.

TextToNum

Usage

TextToNum(text)

Argument

- *text*. Text string, expression that evaluates to a text string or text field.

Returns

Numbers

Details

TextToNum looks at the given text string and systematically removes all non-numeric data, creating a number as it moves from left to right. This is useful when dealing with part numbers, serial numbers, and shipping codes.

Examples

TextToNum("$357.91") returns 357.91.

TextToNum("Warefield, AFS2667") returns 2667.

TextToNum("And a 1 and a 2") returns 12.

TextToTime

Usage
TextToTime(text)

Argument
- ■ *text*. Text string, expression that evaluates to a text string or text field.

Returns
Time equivalent to the time expressed in the text string.

Examples
TextToTime("04:06:28") returns 4:406:28.

Trim

Usage
Trim(text)

Argument
- ■ *text*. Text string, expression that evaluates to a text string or text field.

Returns
A text string.

Details
The returned text string has had all trailing and leading spaces removed.

Examples
Trim(" Lorin ") returns Lorin.

Upper

Usage
Upper(text)

Argument
- ■ *text*. Text string, expression that evaluates to a text string or text field.

Returns
The orginal text just converted to all uppercase.

Details

This is especially useful in multi-user databases where consistent data entry is hard to achieve. Let the user enter data in the way he prefers, then convert it yourself with one easy function.

Examples

Upper("thx1138") returns THX1138.

Upper("Segenthaler Warefield") returns SEGENTHALER WAREFIELD.

WordCount

Usage

WordCount(text)

Argument

- *text*. Any expression evaluating to a text string, a text string, or a field containing text.

Returns

A number, the count of words in the given text string, expression, or field.

Examples

WordCount(Article) returns the number of words in field Article.

WordCount("A full time consideration of another endeavor might be in order") returns 11.

Time Functions

Use the Time functions to perform calculations that deal with time. You can break a time into its constituents to easily compare two values or add and subtract times.

Hour

Usage

Hour (time)

Argument

- *time*. Any valid time value.

Returns

A number, the hour portion of the given time.

Examples

Hour(TextToTime("4:03:02")) returns 4.

Minute

Usage

Minute(time)

Argument

■ *time*. Any valid time value.

Returns

A number, the minute portion of a time value.

Example

Minute(TextToTime("1:02:03")) returns 2.

Seconds

Usage

Seconds(time)

Arguments

■ *time*. Any valid time value.

Returns

A number, the seconds portion of a time value.

Example

Seconds(TextToTime("2:06:28")) returns 28.

Time

Usage

Time(hours, minutes, seconds)

Arguments

■ *hours*. The hour.

■ *minutes*. The minutes.

■ *seconds*. The seconds.

Returns

Time

Details

The time format of the layout field determines the appearance of the result. Use the Time function (or TextToTime) to directly supply a time in a calculation.

Example

Time(4, 6, 28) returns 4:06:28.

TimeToText

Usage

TimeToText(time)

Argument

■ *time*. Any valid time value.

Returns

A string containing the text version of the given time value.

Details

This is useful for when you need to manipulate the time as text. The resulting text string receives its format from the format set when the database was created. The layout field format options of the time field have no influence on appearance of the text string.

Examples

TimeToText(quitingTime) returns 17:30:00 when quitting time contains 5:30 pm.

Trigonometric Functions

All of FileMaker Pro's trigonometric functions use radians as the unit of measure. Most likely, you'll become handy with the Degrees and Radians functions, which let you convert values back and forth.

Atan (Arc Tangent)

Usage

Atan(number)

Argument

■ *number*. A tangent value of an angle.

Returns

A number, the angle in radians whose tangent is equal to the number given as an argument.

Examples

Atan(.7575) returns .64828385430992.

Cos (Cosine)

Usage
Atan(number)

Argument
- *number*. The angle in radians.

Returns
A number, the cosine of the given angle (in radians).

Example
Cos(1.21) returns .35301940121933.

Degrees

Usage
Degrees(number)

Argument
- *number*. A number or expression that evaluates to a number (radians).

Returns
A number that is the equivalent number of degrees to the given radians.

Details
Converts the supplied number from radians to degrees. This conversion is required when you want results in degrees from FileMaker Pro trigonometric functions, which use radians. A radian is equal to 180/P degrees.

Examples
Degrees(Radians(66)) returns 66.

Degrees(1.75) returns 100.267614147919.

Ln (Natural Log)

Usage
Ln(number)

Argument
- *number*. A number or expression that evaluates to a number.

Returns
A number, the base-e (natural) logarithm of the given value.

Details
Ln is the inverse of Exp.

Examples

Ln(Exp(100)) returns 100, as does Exp(Ln(100)).

Ln(16) returns 2.77258872223978.

Log

Usage

Log(number)

Argument

- *number*. A number (positive) or expression that evaluates to a positive number.

Returns

Numbers

Details

Calculates the common logarithm (base 10) of a positive number.

Examples

Log(1000) returns 3.

Pi

Usage

Pi

Arguments

None

Returns

A number.

Details

Calculates the value of the constant Pi.

Example

Pi × 3 returns 9.424777960767.

Radians

Usage

Radians(number)

Argument

- *number*. An angle in degrees.

Returns

A number, the radians equivalent of the given number of degrees.

Details

Because all of FileMaker Pro's trigonometric functions require that their arguments be in radians, this function becomes extremely handy. Use this to first convert values in degrees to radians.

Examples

Radians(76) returns 1.32645023151536.

Cos(Radians(60)) returns .50000000000022.

Sin (Sine)

Usage

Sin(number)

Argument

- *number.* Numeric expression or field containing a numeric expression, which represents an angle in radians.

Returns

A number, the Sine of the given angle.

Example

Sin(Radians(31)) returns .51503807490993.

Tan

Usage

Tan(number)

Argument

- *number.* An angle in radians.

Returns

A number, the tangent of the given angle.

Examples

Tan(.67) returns .79225417472825.

Tan(Radians(44)) returns .9656887748067.

Index

Symbols

3D layouts, designing
3D boxes, 271-274
3D fields, 266-270
3D text, 274-275
backgrounds, 261-266
cross-platform
environments, 275
guidelines, 259-261

A

**About This Macintosh
command (Apple menu),
415**
**Abs (Absolute Value)
function, 516**
access privileges
groups, defining, 278-283
layouts, 283-288
networks, 404
guest access
limitations, 406-407
passwords, 277-283
alternate password
system, 288
binding solutions,
436-438
creating, 280-283
restricted deletes, 323
setup, 277-283
templates, time-bombing,
288-295
testing, 282-283

**Access Privileges command
(File menu), 278, 322, 437**
**Access Privileges dialog
box, 281**
**activate command
(AppleScript), 385**
**Add Files command (SDK
menu), 443**
additions (scripting)
AppleScript
Display Dialog,
379-383
John's Commands,
390-391
Decoder, 474
installing, 378-379
software Web site, 379
Tokenize, 474
**Administer command (File
menu), 420**
aggregate functions
defined, 122, 495
fields, multiple repeating
fields, 127
finding averages, 124-125
list of, 520-523
relationships, creating,
124-127
single databases, 127
subtotaling portals,
122-123
**Aggregate Functions
command (View menu),
123**

alignment
fields, reports, 59-60
mailing labels, 40
**Alignment command
(Arrange menu), 59**
**Allow User Abort
command (ScriptMaker),
214**
anchors, *see* **hypertext
links**
Apple Events, defined, 378
Apple Installer, 450
**Apple menu commands,
About This Macintosh,
415**
AppleScript, 474
additions
Display Dialog,
379-383
installing, 378-379
John's Commands,
390-391
software Web site, 379
administrative functions,
schedules, 423
commands, activate, 385
conversations with other
applications
activating
applications, 385
closing, 385
end tell command,
385

T

A V I A C O M S E R V I C E - E

The Information SuperLibrary™

 Bookstore

 Search

 What's New

 Reference

 Software

 Newsletter

 Company Overviews

 Yellow Pages

 Internet Starter Kit

 HTML Workshop

 Win a Free T-Shirt!

 Macmillan Computer Publishing

 Site Map

 Talk to Us

CHECK OUT THE BOOKS IN THIS LIBRARY.

You'll find thousands of shareware files and over 1600 computer books designed for both technowizards and technophobes. You can browse through 700 sample chapters, get the latest news on the Net, and find just about anything using our massive search directories.

All Macmillan Computer Publishing books are available at your local bookstore.

We're open 24-hours a day, 365 days a year.

You don't need a card.

We don't charge fines.

And you can be as **LOUD** as you want.

The Information SuperLibrary
http://www.mcp.com/mcp/ ftp.mcp.com

Complete and Return this Card
for a *FREE* Computer Book Catalog

Thank you for purchasing this book! You have purchased a superior computer book written expressly for your needs. To continue to provide the kind of up-to-date, pertinent coverage you've come to expect from us, we need to hear from you. Please take a minute to complete and return this self-addressed, postage-paid form. In return, we'll send you a free catalog of all our computer books on topics ranging from word processing to programming and the internet.

☐   Mrs. ☐   Ms. ☐   Dr. ☐

Name (first) [_____] (M.I.) [_] (last) [_____]

Address [_____]
[_____]

City [_____] State [__] Zip [_____] [____]

Phone [__][____][____] Fax [___][___][_____]

Company Name [_____]

Email address [_____]

Please check at least (3) influencing factors for purchasing this book.

Front or back cover information on book	☐
Special approach to the content	☐
Completeness of content	☐
Author's reputation	☐
Publisher's reputation	☐
Book cover design or layout	☐
Index or table of contents of book	☐
Price of book	☐
Special effects, graphics, illustrations	☐
Other (Please specify): _____	☐

How did you first learn about this book?

Saw in Macmillan Computer Publishing catalog	☐
Recommended by store personnel	☐
Saw the book on bookshelf at store	☐
Recommended by a friend	☐
Received advertisement in the mail	☐
Saw an advertisement in: _____	☐
Read book review in: _____	☐
Other (Please specify): _____	☐

How many computer books have you purchased in the last six months?

This book only ☐	3 to 5 books ☐
Books ☐	More than 5 ☐

4. Where did you purchase this book?

Bookstore	☐
Computer Store	☐
Consumer Electronics Store	☐
Department Store	☐
Office Club	☐
Warehouse Club	☐
Mail Order	☐
Direct from Publisher	☐
Internet site	☐
Other (Please specify): _____	☐

5. How long have you been using a computer?

☐ Less than 6 months   ☐ 6 months to a year
☐ 1 to 3 years   ☐ More than 3 years

6. What is your level of experience with personal computers and with the subject of this book?

	With PCs	With subject of book
New	☐	☐
Casual	☐	☐
Accomplished	☐	☐
Expert	☐	☐

Source Code ISBN: 0-7897-0662-8

7. Which of the following best describes your job title?

Administrative Assistant .... ☐
Coordinator .... ☐
Manager/Supervisor .... ☐
Director .... ☐
Vice President .... ☐
President/CEO/COO .... ☐
Lawyer/Doctor/Medical Professional .... ☐
Teacher/Educator/Trainer .... ☐
Engineer/Technician .... ☐
Consultant .... ☐
Not employed/Student/Retired .... ☐
Other (Please specify): _____ ☐

8. Which of the following best describes the area of the company your job title falls under?

Accounting .... ☐
Engineering .... ☐
Manufacturing .... ☐
Operations .... ☐
Marketing .... ☐
Sales .... ☐
Other (Please specify): _____ ☐

9. What is your age?

Under 20 ....
21-29 ....
30-39 ....
40-49 ....
50-59 ....
60-over ....

10. Are you:

Male ....
Female ....

11. Which computer publications do you read regularly? (Please list)

_____
_____
_____
_____
_____
_____
_____
_____
_____
_____

Comments: _____
_____
_____

Fold here and scotch-tape to m